WHY THE M___ LAGGED BEHIND

The Case of Iran

Kazem Alamdari

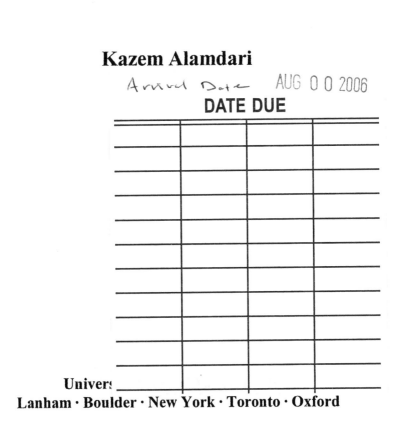

Univers___
Lanham · Boulder · New York · Toronto · Oxford

Copyright © 2005 by
University Press of America,® Inc.
4501 Forbes Boulevard
Suite 200
Lanham, Maryland 20706
UPA Acquisitions Department (301) 459-3366

PO Box 317
Oxford
OX2 9RU, UK

Library of Congress Control Number: 2004105763
ISBN 0-7618-2868-0 (paperback : alk. ppr.)

Contents

Part II

Preface

The book is organized in two parts. The first part explains the historical status of the land tenure system in Iran, which underwent no major change up to the mid-20th century. The second part examines the land reform programs in pre-and post-revolutionary Iran. The main objective is to discover the socioeconomic and political structure that impeded capitalism in the Middle East. Part one consists of four chapters. The first chapter is a theoretical review of development in the 20th century as well as an examination of ten different views on why and how Iran did not develop like the West. Chapter one also deals with clarification of some pertinent concepts such as the impact of the geographical situation on human actions and societal development, the role of the state in the East, and the relationship between development of the West and underdevelopment in the Middle East.

Chapter Two is a review of the land tenure system in the history of Iran. It covers the period from the time of the first Iranian dynasty to the 20th century. Reviewing the entire history provides an opportunity to learn about the ups and downs of the land tenure system in Iran, because some believe that Iran has, at least in some periods of time, experienced feudalism as in the West. My study shows that the land tenure system in Iran experienced some changes in the Middle Ages but never achieved European feudalism. Greek culture influenced Iran in a short period after Alexander the Great invaded Iran, Islamic laws influenced the Iranian land system after the Muslim conquest, and the Turks of Central Asia modified land system during their rules. Tribal characteristics, however, were the dominant form at all times. Chapter Three explores why, unlike the West, feudalism did not grow in Iran, and Chapter Four examines why capitalism did not develop. This chapter concludes the first part of the book.

The second part consists of six chapters. These chapters cover the socioeconomic effects of the land reform in Iran (1962–1981). The United States, under the "modernization" project, pushed capitalist relations from the top in Iran. This was seen by American experts as a cure to remove the old land tenure system, to make Iranian economic structure more compatible with capitalism, and to neutralize peasants' motivation for possible revolt over land.

This part of the book also attempts to answer the question of why Iran—a country that used to be one of the largest civilizations in the world, a country that occupies 628,000 square miles of land; a country as large as England, France, Germany, Italy, Belgium, Netherlands, and Denmark combined; a country that has a population of 65 million, compared with the aggregate population of the above countries, which is nearly 300 million—is unable to produce enough food to meet its own needs.

Geographical obstacles, which cannot be easily removed, are often offered to explain such a shortage. Vast areas of Iran consist of barren plain and salt deserts (the Kavir and Lut deserts) that are the most arid in the world and are almost entirely devoid of any sign of life. Iran has also has several high mountain ranges that cross the country and surround the vast central plateau, functioning as natural barriers to sea moisture. The highlands extend throughout the Afghanistan border region from north to south. The extreme cold weather (temperatures below zero Celsius) in some areas is another natural barrier to economic growth. Finally, the issue of water shortage is among the most serious factors that give rise to the current problems in Iranian society, since land without water is practically worthless. The problem was not only the shortage of water, but also the control and allocation of water resources that resulted in despotic states in the East. These geographical and climatic restrictions have, in short, been responsible for much of the historical fate of Iran. Climatic change or human abuse of natural resources changed the direction of development in some societies. However, ecological factors, which caused slow development in some societies, are not permanent. In other situations, other factors like religion, culture, or political power can play a prohibitive or supportive role in the development of a society. In Iran, however, the very geology and climate have, historically, been significant barriers to development. The question, conversely, is how these natural disadvantages were converted into human socioeconomic, political and cultural obstruction. This book intends to answer this question.

If, at some juncture in the history of Iran, the role of climate was considered significant, it does not mean that this factor has played an unchanging role throughout the history of this society. Today the climatic factor in Iran plays a minor role in the status of the country as less developed. Other factors, such as the unification of religion and the state, have turned into more serious obstacles. In fact, the integration of religion and the state, as discussed in this book, has played a prominent role at many historical junctures in Iran. These barriers cannot be identified properly unless the economic status and structure of the society is taken into account.

As stated before, Iran has experienced pre- and post-revolution land reform programs. However, it still faces many agrarian questions. While the implementation of a land reform program includes consideration of both environmental and socioeconomic factors of the society as a whole, in this work I felt it would be more fruitful to deal with the legal and socioeconomic factors of land reform in order to learn whether the old land tenure system could be replaced with a modern, integrated property system compatible with capitalism. Development of the Middle Eastern societies, like development in all developing societies, is dependent upon the creation of a true industrial capitalist system.

In brief, the second part of the book deals with implementation of the land reform program and its consequences. This part is organized in several chapters as follows. Chapter Five reviews theories of land reforms and discusses the concepts and definitions necessary for an understanding of the land reform program in Iran. Chapter Six examines the land tenure system before the land reform program. This chapter looks at the recent history of the struggle between landlords and peasants and provides a brief review of the period beginning with the Constitutional Revolution of 1905 and ending with the land reform program in 1961. Within this section a number of regional peasant movements against the central and local governments of the landlords are investigated. This period is marked with several achievements such as termination of tribal rules, extinction of *tuyul* system and formation of the nation-state. For the first time, Iranians would learn about modernity in the West. Finally, this chapter provides an assessment of the socioeconomic and political conditions preceding the land reform. Chapter Seven reviews the land reform laws, while the execution of these laws is examined in Chapter Eight. Chapter Nine analyzes the social, economic, political, and cultural consequences of the reform. In this chapter, the relationship between the land reform and the 1979 revolution is evaluated. Chapter Ten covers the agrarian question under the Islamic republic rule. The final part concludes the study with a summary of the results and more specifically addresses the questions raised in this introduction.

    * An important note about the dates being used in this book: Dates for Persian sources in this book are based on the Islamic calendar, *Hijra*, or the migration of the Prophet Mohammad in 622 ACE.

Introduction

The fact is that today the Middle East lags behind the West economically and in many other ways. The total gross national products (GNP) of the Middle Eastern countries is the lowest in world, except for sub-Saharan Africa. This fact amazes anyone who realizes that the Middle East was one of the centers of world civilization and ahead of the West before the 16th century. What has kept these nations behind? What made the West move forward? Are developments in the West and the underdevelopment in the Middle East two sides of the same coin? In other words, has the West been responsible for the underdeveloped status of the Middle East, as some argue? Isn't it true that human beings as members of a single species, regardless of their ethnic or regional status, have common roots? Thus, what caused them to end up with different socioeconomic, political, and legal systems in different parts of the world? Finally, how can the gap between the East and the West be bridged? These are some of the questions that this book attempts to address.

If we are to summarize the historical causes of backwardness in the Middle East, two factors emerge prominently: (1) a lack of immunity for the private property, and (2) lawlessness, or arbitrary decisions, by the rulers. Although these distinctive characteristics of dominant systems by themselves have impeded development in the Middle East, they are rooted in the land tenure system, by which they became entrenched because of natural or geographical conditions. The claim of the king as "the owner of all land," and his word as "unquestionable law" were two major aspects of this land tenure system and of the "oriental despotism" that was its political consequence in the East. As

Francois Bernier in *Travels in the Mongul Empire* wrote in 1670 "in *Hindoustan* every acre of land is considered the property of the King, and the spoliation of a peasant would be a robbery committed upon the King's domain."[i] We need to know how law and the prevailing legal system were initially established. Marc Bloch, the author of *Feudal Society*, in regard to the basis of law writes: "Jurisprudence, in short, was the expression of needs rather than of knowledge". [ii] What needs existed in the Eastern societies by which the king's word was considered law? In general, the basis for written law is tradition, and the basis for tradition is, on the one hand, the most appropriate means and of operating a society, and, on the other, an unwritten contract for the circulation of life at a particular time in history. A society, old or new, cannot exist without developing shrewd, learned ways of dealing with the demands of life.

But once traditions are established, regardless of their basis or the needs they addressed, those whose interests justified the existence of ongoing traditions perceive them as law and even divine, and thus eternal. Both state-men and religious institutions attribute the traditions to divine authority and therefore presume them to be unchangeable. For example, the Quran and *hadith*, (sayings attributed to Prophet Muhammad or the science of tradition) provide the foundations of Islamic laws *(fiqh)*. This not only applies to Muslim societies but also to the entire East, so that Max Weber was amazed at how the entire history of the East was the history of religion. While Roman law, the foundation of law in the West, was secular, law in the Middle East has been related to religion and therefore, again, presumed to be unchangeable. This difference, interestingly, has had its basis in the land tenure system, and thus invisible religious law has run even the secular states in the Middle East.

Also, two factors prevented the formation of an aristocracy as a social class and backbone of capitalism in these societies: (1) confiscations of land by the king, including even land owned by the members of the court and the grand vazir, and (2) dominant tribal relations which were usually accustomed to insecurity and looting of properties. Marx described these as characteristics of "Asiatic despotism," and Weber saw them as "oriental partrimonialism." Such factors, though they were not crucial with regard to development in an agrarian era, have had severe adverse effects on the development of the East in modern times when capitalism revolutionized the productive system in the West. Capitalism could not establish itself without a solid legal system and a predictable economic system. The despotic system and tribal mentality stubbornly survived in the East until the late 20th century. The cause of these characteristics, which the author believes to be the most important and wishes to investigate, is first and foremost the system of land tenure, or the property system—a static socioeconomic and political structure of the past, which impeded these societies' development of capitalism.

In a pre-capitalist and agrarian economy, life depends upon the land as the main source of production to meet human needs. If ownership of land is not immune from arbitrary confiscation, then living conditions are not secure either. Sometimes, confiscation of land went along with accusations of wrongdoing; therefore, the victim's life was endangered, too. When the king's word was unquestionable law, then there was always the possibility that an arbitrary decision would be made. In these societies, the king was equal to the state, and thus the confiscation of property was done in the name of the state. Historical evidence indicates that confiscation of individuals' property has been a common mode of ruling and a norm in the entire history of the East. The productivity of an economy depends heavily upon the accumulation and circulation of capital, but under the threat of confiscation of property, asset holders prefer to hide their wealth— to avoid the risk of plundering—rather than invest it. In the history of the East, wealthy individuals would even bury their treasure to keep their belongings from the "evil eye" and possible confiscation. Nonetheless, they were not immune. Under such circumstances, the direct result was to keep the surplus money out of circulation and make it useless for promoting production through investment. The short-term consequence of this was low growth rates, and its end result was socioeconomic backwardness.

Development, underdevelopment, and backwardness are relative concepts. In the modern era, the East is considered underdeveloped relative to the West. No one is taller or shorter than others unless people are compared. If this gap is to be overcome, the causes of development in the West and the obstacles to development in the East need to be known.

Pre-capitalist societies had agricultural economies. An agrarian economy developed into an industrial economy in the West but this failed to happen in the East. What are we to make of this? First, agriculture is dependent upon land. Therefore, in order to understand this difference, the land tenure systems in the East and West need to be comparatively examined. This is the focus of this study, which follows from my previous book published in 2001 in Persian language under the title *Why Iran Lagged Behind and the West Moved Forward.* Recently, I have read two books with views parallel to the thesis in my

first book. The first, in English, is *The Mystery of Capital: Why
Capitalism Triumphs in the West and Fails Everywhere Else*, by
Hernandez De Soto, published in 2000.The second, in Persian, is
*Despotism, the Question of Property, and Capital Accumulation in
Iran*, by Ahmad Seyf, published in 2002. I discovered similar views in
these books. In my first book, I considered capitalism as the engine of
development in the West, with feudalism as its seed, and a non-feudal
land tenure system as an obstacle to capitalism in Iran that was
primarily responsible for the nation's backwardness in modern times.
De Soto has put emphasis on a unique legal system or "system of
property" in the West that was responsible for capitalist development.[iii]
Ahmad Seyf has found the lack of immunity for private property and
life as the main obstacle to development in Iran.[iv] All of these parallel
studies independently have reached almost a common conclusive
answer to the question of development in the West and backwardness
in the East. While De Soto primarily analyzed the development of the
West and Seyf concentrated on the backwardness of Iran, I did a
comparative study to find answers for both situations.

In addition to natural disadvantages, there are social, economic,
political, legal, and cultural factors that have adversely affected
development in Iran. However, the phenomenon of slow development
is not purely economic and does not mainly originate from the
incapacity of society to fulfill its material needs. The less-developed
status or "underdevelopment" in the present era embodies all aspects of
social and human relations, including politics, culture, laws, women's
rights, and the rights of ethnic and religious minorities. Thus, when we
refer to "underdevelopment," we are alluding to slow development in
all of these areas. When the issue of achieving growth and development
is raised, one cannot and must not confine it to economic or political
arenas. Instead, one must look for the secret behind the lasting
suppressive measures in the Middle East in the region's politics,
culture, social relations, and religion.

In the present work, I have intensely focused on the history of the
land tenure system in Iran. The objective was to discover the roots of
the current land tenure system in the Middle East. I presumed that the
land tenure system had roots in nature and the prevailing natural forces
that constrained human decision-making. In order words, I began with
the belief that land tenure systems in the East were not rationally made
to be different than those in the West by human beings. Instead, they
were caused primarily by natural conditions that existed prior to the
formation of any social laws. Thus, I have devoted the main part of my
study to learning why such a difference between the West and the East

had developed in the first place. Needless to say, almost all civilizations in both ancient and modern times have been built adjacent to water resources. In the ancient period, agrarian civilizations were mainly built alongside the rivers that irrigated the agriculture, and in modern times ports were built on edges of the major rivers and seas to facilitate transportation of industrial goods. Against this background, the natural settings of both the East and the West should be comparatively studied.

In this book, I have chosen Iran as a case study for two reasons. First, Iran, like the West, had developed a great ancient civilization, which remained developed and even much ahead of the West during the Middle Ages. Second, unlike China and India, two other major civilizations in the East during the agrarian period, Iran was under Islam, which many observers have assumed is responsible for the current backwardness in the Middle East. I have argued that not Islam, but rather a common factor in the East—the land tenure system—kept Eastern societies, including Muslims, underdeveloped when capitalism led the West in a continuous growth in modern times. Development in the West and underdevelopment in the East occurred when capitalism emerged in the West. In other words, the gap between the East and the West did not exist in the pre-modern era. The East was not behind as long as agrarian economies remained dominant in both the East and the West. The land tenure system in the East was not compatible with European feudalism, under which private land ownership gave birth to capitalism. This book attempts not only to explain the difference but also to explore the reasons for the dissimilarity.

The old traditional land tenure system in the Middle East received a major crack by the beginning of the 20th century. Several social revolutions shook Eastern societies and their despotic regimes. These revolutions were manly influenced by Western penetration, both economically and culturally, as the result of a new wave of communications between the East and the West. Eastern intellectuals educated in the West were particularly the agents of cultural and political change in their own native countries. However, none of these revolutions led these societies into industrial capitalism like the West. The societies lacked the infrastructure required for such development. Therefore, the old land system continued to exist until World War II.

After World War II and the success of the socialist revolutions in some countries in Europe and Asia, the United States concluded that continuation of the traditional land tenure system in the Third World countries was neither beneficial to the political stability of its allies nor to the economic interests of the West. Therefore, American economists

and politicians proposed land reform programs in the developing
societies, including Iran. These reforms from the top, however, did not
remove the main obstacle to development in these countries. To learn
about the implementation and consequences of these projects, the
Iranian land reform program has been studied in the second part of this
book. Land reform programs aimed to reduce economic tension and to
change the old land tenure system into modern capitalist relations in
these societies. The U.S. initiated such a plan, known as the
"modernization" project. In the case of Iran, "modernization" created a
cultural vacuum and a cultural backlash that eventually drove the
society into a revolutionary situation. Despite both pre- and post-
revolution land reform programs, the legal basis of property still has
not been fully resolved in Iran. The reasons for this are discussed in
detail in several chapters.

---

[i] Francis Bernier. *Travels in the Mongul Empire A.D. 1656–1668.* Westminster,
UK: Archibald Constable and Company, 1670.

[ii] Marc Bloch. *Feudal Society* (Chicago: University of Chicago, 1961), p. 11.

[iii] Hernando De Soto, The Mystery of Capital: Why Capitalism Triumphs in the
West and Fails Everywhere Else, (New York: Basic Books, 2000), p. 69.

[iv] Ahmad Seyf. Despotism, the Question of Property, and Capital Accumulation
in Iran, (Tehran: Resaanesh, 1380 (2001)), p. 178.

Chapter 1
Theoretical Perspectives

Clarification of Definitions

We often hear the comment that the Middle East is a backward or underdeveloped region. Yet, we do not know exactly what is meant by these terms, because first, in most cases, the terms "backward" and "underdeveloped" are used interchangeably, and second, these terms have been defined in different ways. In this chapter, these concepts are explained, and the terms "backward," "delay in development," and "lesser development" are used for low technological growth and the term "underdevelopment" is for low economic growth. To clarify my reason for doing so, I will present a few brief definitions out of hundreds found in the thousands of books written on this topic.[1]

In brief, backwardness refers to the subsistence mode of a society in a comparative assessment with other societies in this regard. Without such a comparison, the term backwardness is meaningless. Paul Baran considers a society in which the livelihood of the majority of the population still depends upon agriculture, which accounts for a larger share of the total output a backward society.[2]

Dividing societies into either agricultural or industrial, or into traditional or modern, as a way of explaining backwardness is an approach that has been criticized and challenged by many sociologists in the past two decades. These critics believe, instead, in classifying societies as feudalist or capitalist societies, a classification that is applied to societies starting with the beginning of the sixteenth century.

Immanuel Wallerstein, Charles Tilly, and Eric Wolf are among supporters of this view.[3] Wallerstein believes that the dominant form of capitalist relations in its early stages was still an agricultural economy, which gradually evolved into an industrial economy. He adds that the transformation of feudalism into capitalism was the cause of the emergence of the industrial economy of the West.[4] Although Wallerstein has Marxist tendencies, he believes that Marx and Marxists have committed a fundamental error in their analysis of capitalism, in that they have analyzed capitalism within the confines of a society and nation-state. However, capitalism was an international phenomenon from its inception and grew on the basis of a social division of labor at the global level. That is, capitalism was a world economic system with many cultures and states. Wallerstein considers the Third World countries backward industrially, and underdeveloped economically.[5] Thus, backwardness is the outcome of a gap that exists between core countries (developed) and peripheral countries (underdeveloped). Therefore, the movement toward industrial capitalism determines the center of development and the backwardness of some societies, including Iran. The emergence of capitalism was the point at which the development of the West began.

Underdevelopment is a phenomenon that emerged in marginal societies after the globalization of industrial capitalism in the West. Rodolfo Stavenhagen sums up the varying definitions of the term underdevelopment—which is not a concise term when applied to Iran—as follows: "Underdevelopment as a structure and as an ongoing process can only be understood as the implantation or imposition of a capitalist economy on pre-capitalist and non-industrialized societies."[6] Franz Schuurman, in a review of the impasse of development theories, illustrates underdevelopment as an inherent consequence of the international capitalist system's performance, not a condition necessarily intrinsic to the Third World.[7] This performance drains marginal societies of natural resources in a way that "leads to development of the core and underdevelopment of periphery."[8] According to Andre Gunder Frank, one of the prominent theorists in this field, in such conditions, "development in some societies leads to underdevelopment in others." He calls this phenomenon "the development of underdevelopment."[9] Fernando Cardozo, who was optimistic about the relations between the core and peripheral countries, called it "dependent development."[10] The above-mentioned definitions do not explain why societies, including the West, developed at a slow rate before the emergence of capitalism and modern civilization. Instead of analyzing the phenomenon of backwardness and underdevelopment in the East independently, these theories consider it the consequence of the West's development.

The Modernization Theory was developed as a response to the above theory that considers the structure of the capitalist world economy the cause of underdevelopment in the East. Modernization Theory considers development a natural and historical trend in all societies in which the direction of the movement is from static traditional conditions to dynamic modern conditions. This theory emphasizes the role of individuals, not the structure, in determining the speed of movement in this course.[11]

Unlike the previous theory, the Modernization Theory indicates the need to explain the progress and development that took place in Western industrial societies, not the East's underdevelopment because Western societies were also traditional and poor like the East, but the emergence of innovators and pioneers, merchants, inventors, and new technologies pushed the West from the traditional to the modern stage. This theory also stresses that the West has not been the cause of the East's underdevelopment, and it adds that if the same factors become available in the East, the East can also reach development. Of the prominent theories that belong to the spectrum of the Modernization Theory, the theories of Walt Rostow, Marion Levy, and Samuel Huntington are the most popular.[12] According to the Modernization Theory, Eastern societies should follow the pattern and culture of the West in order to attain development. Hence, the political elite, as leaders of development projects, play an important role at the top.[13]

Neither the Dependency Theory nor the Modernization Theory succeed in explaining the phenomenon of underdevelopment in Iran, since the causes of Iran's underdevelopment are historical, internal, and structural, and not contemporary, external, or motivational.[14] The traditional, poor, and static nature of this society is not the cause of underdevelopment, but the effect of other conditions. The growth of this society would entail ending poverty and rejecting its traditional and static norms. The starting point is to identify the factors that facilitated the emergence of growth in the West and the persistence of its conditions. Unless the phenomenon of development in the West are examined thoroughly, the causes of Iran's underdevelopment cannot be discovered. Therefore, both the phenomena of development in the West and underdevelopment in the East need to be studied—not just one or the other.

The terms "delay in development," "the slow rate of development," "lesser development," and "the underdevelopment or backwardness of a society" will only be meaningful if they are compared with the development and progress in other societies; these terms do not carry an independent meaning. Therefore, one has to ask what this development or progress is that the Middle East has not been able to attain. To answer this question, we define progress as the conditions that the West has succeeded in attaining, since the term modern advanced society[15] is equated with Western civilization.[16] Modern societies enjoy features that are not accessible to less-developed societies such as Iran.[17] Here, two more questions can be raised. First, what are the features that characterize the modern Western civilization and why have the Eastern societies, including Iran, not been able to attain them? Second, what are the factors that have contributed to the contemporary development of the West? To answer these questions, one needs to consider both the causes of backwardness in the East and the factors that facilitated the growth of the West. Moreover, one has to find out whether there is a relationship between development and backwardness/underdevelopment or not.

Studies suggest that there is no relationship between the emergence of contemporary Western civilization and backwardness/under-development of the East in general, and Iran in particular. As the gap between the East and the West grew wider, these two phenomena, however, gradually became related. In other words, in the era in which societies grew closer as the result of the growth of the world economy, progress and growth in the West and underdevelopment in the East became related. This connection is most obvious today, but this connection does not justify looking for the causes of the East's backwardness/underdevelopment in the West.

What is Development?

What is known as contemporary Western civilization is a combination of elements, such as capitalist relations, the growth of sciences and rational philosophy, the Industrial Revolution, nationalism and nation-state building, urbanization, political democracy, the modern elected and legal government, individualism, secularism, civil society, observance of the human rights and civil rights of citizens, economic growth, the growth of social welfare, and, in short, more comfortable living, both mentally and physically, under the laws of a democratic order.[18] Or "development is at least as much a process of cultural, social, and political changes as it is of economic growth."[19] Many people evaluate development and underdevelopment by the index of per capita income, and many others consider development the result of the growth in social establishments.[20] Norman Jacobs defines an economically developed society as follows: a "(1) rational, (2) self-generating economic system."[21] What is meant by underdevelopment is the lack of the factor of self-sufficiency. No doubt, self-sufficiency is a relative concept. Norman Jacobs adds: "An underdeveloped (or, less romantically, an undeveloped) economic system, in contrast, is a system that does not treat rational profit as the primary goal of the economic system."[22]

Modern development is a phenomenon that has its roots in the sixteenth century or perhaps in the beginning of the Renaissance at the end of the thirteenth century.[23] Thus, the analysis of the historical causes of the demise of the ancient civilizations in Eastern societies, including Iran, and the discussion of factors that decelerated growth or even backwardness in some eras due to the presence of external factors such as the Arab or Mongol invasions, cannot justify lack of development in these societies in the present era. Therefore, the Arabs or the arrival of Islam cannot link the causes of the underdevelopment of Iran in the contemporary era to the defeat of the Sasanian government in ancient times. Similarly, the growth of sciences at some junctures in Iran's history (between the eighth and the twelfth centuries) and their decline at other times cannot have any connection to Iran's underdevelopment in the contemporary era. The nature of growth in modern times is essentially different from the nature of growth in previous eras.

The phenomena that have occurred in Western territories within the past three centuries are generally new and go back to the emergence of capitalism. Historically, the main cause of development in a society is production in excess of consumption, which Adam Smith called the "wealth of nations." Therefore, the most salient feature of contemporary Western civilization is the growth of the capitalist mode of production, which made the excess a possibility. The other features of Western civilization emerged gradually and in relation to one another, and each in turn reinforced the factor that facilitated its own emergence—i.e., the capitalist mode of production.

The demise of serfdom (European feudalism) occurred in the fourteenth century, and the emergence of capitalism is believed to have occurred in England in the sixteenth century (1575). The Industrial Revolution (1770) occurred two centuries later, rational philosophy emerged in the seventeenth century,[24] political democracy emerged in the nineteenth century, civil society in the eighteenth century, parliamentary government in the eighteenth century, and secularism in the seventeenth and eighteenth centuries. Why did capitalist relations emerge in England, and what were the factors that facilitated this phenomenon? Why were capitalist relations pushed forward in the direction of Western countries and Northern Europe, instead of the East? These questions are thoroughly discussed in the sixth chapter.

Another point that merits an explanation here is whether the causes of growth or lack thereof in a society are internal or external. The main cause of Iranian society's underdevelopment lies inside Iranian society. External factors cannot have a long-lasting and decisive influence over the overall growth of a society if they do not become internalized. Phenomena such as the emergence of Islam in Iran and the neighboring tribes' invasions cannot be simply considered external factors that inhibited the growth of the Iranian society. Iran is composed of various ethnic groups like Persians, Turks, Kurds, Balouch, and Arabs and a few ethnic-religious groups such as Zoroastrians, Armenians, Assyrians and Jews. None of these ethnic and ethno-religious groups can be considered alien. Islam has also been integrated into this society and must be considered an internal force. Neither in pre-Islamic nor in post-Islamic historical eras is a thorough study of Iranian society possible without the consideration of the role of the religious establishment as an internal factor.

Any perspective that considers the development of the West a result of the underdevelopment of the East, or vice versa, without attributing an independent role to this duality, is not based on historical realities.

The Sociological View of This Study

We should not speak about historical findings as if we were present at the scene of the events, or presume that our answers final. We are solely the narrators and analysts of historical stories chosen rationally based on objective evidence. For instance, no one has presented any hard evidence to prove the existence of advanced ancient civilizations among nomadic Arabs or Mongolian tribes equal with that of the Persians or Greeks. By the same token, no one can present evidence of the development of rational philosophy in ancient Iran.

To sociologists, historical events are concrete, not abstract, and occur in historical relations to other social phenomena that occur within the core of society, not in nature. In other words, human beings are the creators of their own history in concrete circumstances. The nature of historical events emanates from the bonds and relations that exist among human beings at each historical juncture. Human beings actively, not passively, mold the events of history. The roles played by individuals and social groups in shaping historical events are also concrete. Therefore, historical events are the products of their own times.

Historical and social events do not always move along a straight line or in the same direction. Historical ups and downs are the products of heterogeneous relations human beings create. For example, it is true that the glory of the Sasanian civilization ended with the Arab invasion and the emergence of Islam in Iran, but one must keep in mind that neither nomad Arabs nor Islam were responsible for the decline of Sasanian, just as neither Christianity nor nomad Germans were directly responsible for the decline of the Roman Empire. The causes of these downfalls must be sought within their own socioeconomic and political systems. Despite domination of tribal Arabs after the emergence of Islam, particularly between the eighth and the twelfth centuries (C.E.), Iran witnessed growth of another kind, an Islamic civilization. Neither the Sasanian civilization nor the civilization of the first few centuries of Islam survived. The Arabs were not Iranians, but Islam became internalized in Iran. Could we then come to the conclusion that the emergence of Islam in Iran caused the growth or the decline of the Iranian civilization? To answer this question one needs to engage in an objective and comparative analysis of the history of the Iranian and Islamic civilization. This question has been examined elsewhere in this book.

Prominent Theories about the Causes of Underdevelopment in Iran[25]

The obstacles to Iran's development and the causes of backwardness/underdevelopment in Iran have been discussed in various theories. Let us briefly consider some of the existing theoretical classifications and then offer a detailed discussion of some of these theories within the context of this book. These theories can be classified under three main groups, each with three subcategories, and a single theory that links two other theories. **The first group of theories considers external factors as the most salient reasons that caused underdevelopment in Iran. The second group of theories deems mental, cultural, and personality factors responsible for Iran's underdevelopment. The third group of theories stresses economic factors, or more precisely, the mode of production in a society.**

Another important theory, which deserves consideration, is the Institutional Sociological Analysis Theory in relation to development. This theory makes a connection between the value system and the economic system of a society and finds the root of Asian backwardness in the patrimonial system. Due to the unique approach of this theory, which does not fall within the above-stated categories, it will be discussed independently as the tenth theory in this section.

The First Main Group includes the following three subgroups: (1) theories that consider the invasion of the Arabs and the arrival of Islam a decisive factor; (2) theories that deem the invasions by the Turks of Central Asia and the Mongols the most important cause of Iran's underdevelopment; and (3) the group that regards colonization as responsible for the phenomenon of underdevelopment in Iran. All of these theories consider the main cause of underdevelopment to be outside the Iranian society.

The first theory in this group points out that Islamic development and Iran's defeat by the Arabs coincided with the demise of the Sasanian dynasty, the highest point of ancient Iranian civilization. These events were followed by a long interruption (over a century) in the newly born intellectual and scientific development of the Iranian civilization. Some scholars claim that when Muslims conquered Iran they destroyed the books by water and fire and that therefore the sciences of the Persians were lost.[26] Zabihollah Safa describes the event of burning the libraries using other sources such as Ibn al-Asier. He says that once Islam became dominant in Iran it turned into an instrument for repressing scientists and philosophers.[27] He adds in a different source, "Burning books written by philosophers and harassing the owners of these books were considered an ordinary affair in the fifth and the sixth centuries and we run across tragic events of this nature in historical texts."[28] On burning books by Arabs, Mohammad Ghaferi referring to several sources argues that the report is baseless.[29] I found the assessment by Ghaferi is logical and acceptable.

From this point on, scientific development was derailed. This theory deems the emergence of Islam, a religious-ideological establishment, a determining factor in the evolution of social organizations, and suggests that this development was responsible for the deviation of the Iranian society from progress to its subsequent stagnation. Ebrahim Pourdavood, Ahmad Kasravi,[30] Sadeq Hedayat,[31] Mirza Aqa Khan Kermani,[32] Fatali Akhund Zadeh,[33] and to some degree Ali Mir Fetrus[34] are among the theorists who in varying degrees consider the religious factor to be the cause of underdevelopment in Iran. Mirza Aqa Khan Kermani writes, "Each branch of Iran's forbidding tree of ethics has its roots in the activities of the Arabs and is planted by them. All the evil behaviors and habits of the Iranian people are either what the Arab nation left in Iran as a deposit, or the fruit of the invasions Iran had to endure."[35]

These theories also consider the subjective factor more important than the objective and structural factors. Another version of this theory is put forth by Fatali Akhund Zadeh who considers Islam "both the cause of misfortune for the Arabs and the only cause of destitution for the Iranians..."[36] He believes the solution to the society's problems should be "Islamic Protestantism" to facilitate the separation of politics from religion.[37]

The second theory in this group considers the invasion by the Mongols destructive and devastating for Iranian civilization. Among proponents of this theory are Muslim scholars who view Arab invasion and the arrival of Islam constructive for Iranian civilization. In addition to the ruins these nomadic Mongol tribes left behind, they made the backward feudal system dominant in Iranian society. As an example, one can refer to Mohammad Reza Feshahi's theory postulated in his book entitled *Intellectual and Social Developments in Iranian Feudalistic Society.*[38] Ibn Khaldun and other theorists consider both the Arabs and the Mongols to be the carriers of the nomadic mode of production, blood relations, and the people who stood against the city-dwelling population, thus causing the destruction and decline of the Iranian civilization.[39] Ibn Khaldun considers the domination of desert-dwelling tribes over the more advanced city-dwelling population a function of the political power or group feeling that justified tribal relations.[40] "This is because aggressive and defensive strength is obtained only through group feeling, which means affection and willingness to fight and die for each other."[41] I will discuss Ibn Khaldun's theory in the forthcoming chapters.

The third subgroup of theories considers the emergence of colonization and the prevalence of imperialism responsible for Iran's underdevelopment. The proponents of this theory believe that the appearance of the Western capitalist system, the development of a modern military industry in the West, and the development of global politics and economies, created enormous obstacles to the growth of underdeveloped societies. "During the different historical eras when the world developed and changed, the East encountered a powerful and wise competitor—i.e., the West—that was ready to attack. Thus, the East fell victim to the colonizing West."[42] The proponents of this theory use the term "kept underdeveloped" instead of "underdeveloped," since they consider powerful external forces the cause of the gap between the West and the East.[43] This theory, which was predominantly supported by socialist countries, practically equated Western civilization with the dominant imperialist system and considered underdeveloped countries such as Iran victims of the conspiracies of world powers and power-mongers. The theory suggests that objective factors in development, especially the economic factors, are more important than the subjective factors. Similar theories are abundant in the literature of leftist and socialist movements of the world, including those in Iran. Lenin's "Theory of Imperialism,"[44] "the Dependency Theory,"[45] and "the Global Economic System Theory" [41]are among the Marxist, Neo-Marxist and critical Marxist theories in this area.[46] These theories, in particular Lenin's Theory of Imperialism, have undoubtedly gained an irrefutable and unchallengeable status in Iran's leftist movements. The main axis of these theories is class differences and the exploitation of the deprived classes of society on the one hand, and the unjust relations of the global capitalist economy on the other. The latest development in this regard is the emergence of the Cultural Imperialism Theory that is linked to the Globalization Theory,[47] and "The Structural Adjustment Programs." (ASPs)[48] Other aspects of this theory are present in the considerations of cultural contacts, cultural contradictions, and cultural confrontations.[49]

The consideration of culture includes two opposing interpretations. One is that the cultural domination of Western countries in underdeveloped societies through commercialization of culture and its sale to consumers in the Third World promotes development. The second interpretation is that of cultural imperialism, through which native cultures in underdeveloped societies are destroyed and replaced by Western culture. The positive interpretation of this influence is held by the promoters of the Modernization Theory and is considered an attempt to help the growth of developing societies. In both cases, in the age of globalization the result is more cultural uniformity and harmonization across the world through the mass media, especially television. Cultural uniformity and harmonization are, no doubt, one-sided in underdeveloped societies due to the influence and power of Western capitalism. This causes a cultural identity crisis in poor countries. The cultural influence of poor societies over affluent societies is almost non-existent, or at best very diminutive. Such imbalanced power relations cause more conflict and tension between developed and underdeveloped societies and divide the domestic culture into two hostile cultures of traditionalism and modernity.

The second main group of theories considers cultural aspects, intellectual factors, and human values the cause of underdevelopment in Iran. Three theories are discussed in this category.

The first theory in this group places enormous emphasis on cultural factors and suggests that the cultural and social relations governing Iranian society inhibit the emergence of new, rational, innovative, and creative ideas. In short, this culture is either barren or destructive. For example, Aramesh Doostdar's theory, presented in his book entitled *Derakhsheshhay-e Tiereh (The Tarnished Glows)*,[50] refers to the barren nature of Iranian culture, a culture smeared in Islamic philosophy and the religion of Islam, a culture that inhibits logical and scientific thinking. Therefore, the prohibitive factor that deters growth in Iran is a subjective factor. Other proponents of this theory, who refer to the cultural factor less emphatically, believe that creative and constructive thinking in Iran's eroded, impotent, and unproductive culture hardly exists. Since a destructive culture seems to be dominant in Iran, any constructive effort on the part of informed, creative intellectuals ends up being defeated. One outstanding example based on this theory is *Jame'eh Shenasi-e Nokhbeh Koshi (The Sociology of Elite Killing)* by Ali Reza Qoli.[51] Cultural and social relations are introduced as the cause of underdevelopment in Iran. On the one hand Qoli blames Iranian culture, and on the other he considers the political elite responsible for the backwardness of Iranian society (the elitist history). At the end, he states that people who allow the corrupted elite to govern their society are to blame (the populist history). However, the author fails to distinguish between "culture" and "society" (p. 160). Within the pattern of development, these terms carry specific meanings that should not be misunderstood. In a sociological study of society, three key components—social structure, culture, and personality—should be included.[52] A similar mistake seems to occur when the author considers development in the West. He believes that the culture and the spirit of capitalism are the basis of industrial growth in Europe and tries to explain Iran's underdevelopment based on this assumption, thus overlooking the difference between the objective aspects of the culture and the temperament of people in the West versus that of people in Iran. The work under consideration here is influenced by Max Weber's theory, but unlike Weber's views it fails to take into account "the unique occurrence of a number of important structural phenomena,"[53] including the different roles of the religious establishment and its agents in shaping the social and cultural norms of a society.[54]

The remarkable point about culture and its role in the development of a society is that culture is part of a society's identity. That is to say that there can be no society without a culture. Culture, as a way of life that transfers and changes from one generation to the next, cannot be considered the sole factor that facilitates or inhibits development in a society. Some attribute the cultural identity of individuals in a society to nature. It is misleading to separate culture from the historical, social, and other relations of a society. Some may attribute this difference to race. However, to be part of a certain civilization or to have certain cultural accomplishments has nothing to do with physical attributes because differences among societies do not originate in natural differences among humans but are a function of their mutual relations under certain circumstances. Culture is learned, not inherited. Often, differences in behavior and moral values of different nations are discerned as originating from their cultures, while cultural norms have their origin in environmental factors. The substance of human beings in the West and the East is the same. Natural, historical, and social factors, some of which are controlled by human beings and some the outcome of human relations, have resulted in differences that exist in the Western and Eastern worlds. The culture of a particular civilization cannot be considered entirely independent of other civilizations. Sometimes, a given culture has the elements of several civilizations. For example, the culture of ancient Greece is the outcome of a combination of different regional cultures such as the Sumerians, Acads, Babylonians, Egyptians, Assyrians, Aramaic, and Phoenicians, whom the Greeks had encountered through trade.[55] Therefore, one cannot attribute this culture to one nation. This is true of other civilizations as well. For example, early Islamic civilization was a combination of Byzantine, Egyptian, Iranian, and Indian cultures.[56]

In the present era, due to the fact that progress has been made in the field of technology, the role of natural (climatic) factors has diminished considerably. Advanced technology has enhanced human domination over nature and placed humans in a new relation with environment.

Mutual relations of human beings in a social unit govern societies today. Iranian culture is not inherently barren or corrupt. A poor society, both economically and intellectually, gives rise to a culture that resists the sciences. The more illiterate a society is, the less access its members have to literature, information and thought-provoking resources. In such a society, the power of judgment is placed in the hands of those who are capable of reading, thinking, deceiving, deviating from healthy thoughts, avoiding productive thoughts, and thinking spitefully and selfishly.

The second theory in this group considers the development of a society a function of the development of the sciences. For example, in *Ma Chegoneh, Ma Shodiem* (*How We Became We*)[57] by Sadeq Zibakalam, the main reason for Iran's underdevelopment is argued to be lack of growth, or more precisely the decline of the sciences. This theory both implicitly and explicitly deems the growth of contemporary Western civilization and its superiority over Eastern civilization a result of the emergence and growth of the sciences in Western societies. Culture as a factor hindering development was the focal issue among many intellectual reformists in early twentieth century in Iran. Leading intellectual reformists like Fatali Akhund Zadeh and Mirza Malkom Khan would argue that development was conditioned to achievement of a modern legal system in Iran.[58] For this end, sciences had to be developed first, because people have to be able to read and understand laws.[59] However, they retreated to a simplistically solution as they argued that the stated goal could not be achieved unless the Persian alphabet were modified.[60]

The third theory in this group emphasizes human values and the role of personality and social psychology. According to this theory, one of the prerequisites for the development of a society is the existence of new and creative human values and individual and social innovations.[61] This theory suggests that in advanced societies people believe in values that contribute to the relations of growth. Such individuals, who value progress, creativity, and innovation, are scarce in underdeveloped societies.[62] The reason(s) for this difference lies in political repression or the dominance of traditional values that repress any alternative forms of innovation or new experiences. This situation results in the underdevelopment of a society. This theory, which aims at explaining the differences between the East and the West, is based on the views of Weber and the theories dealing with modernization, including David McClelland's *The Achievement Motivation*,[63] and Everett Hagen's *The Innovative Personality*,[64] and it is reflected in *The Sociology of Elite Killing* by Ali Reza Qoli.[65] Of course, the view in the last book is apparently not compatible with such theories since it criticizes (page 148) the Modernization Theory, with which the above-mentioned theorists are identified. Nevertheless, emphasizing the differences between individual characteristics of the Iranians as lazy and the British as hardworking people cannot yield a result different than what Modernization theorists imply. Qoli stresses the point that the reactionary culture of the Iranian society characterized by submission to political power forced such reformist individuals as Prime Ministers Mirza Abolqasem Farahani (1814-1847), Mirza Taqi Khan Amir Kabier (1800-1852), and Mohammad Mossadeq (1882-1967), who were the initiators of structural reforms in Iran, out of the political scene.[66]

The Modern Man's Role Theory, put forth by Alex Inkeles,[67] the Cultural Values Theory, put forth by Robert Bellah,[68] and Abraham Maslow's theory[69] about the ideal form of "self-realization" fit in this category. Robert Bellah believes that development depends upon the ability of "learning to learn." Based on this view, as Ronald Robertson also agrees, "East Asia and South-East Asian societies have learned from Japan how to *learn how to learn*."[70] To Maslow, some of the personality traits such as a deep, clear understanding of reality, willingness to accept new experiences, creativity, objectivity, and resistance to one-sided perspectives are the ideal characteristics of human personality, which facilitate growth.[71]

The third main group includes theories which emphasize various socioeconomic formations in society, including (1) feudalism, (2) tribal relations, and (3) the Asiatic mode of production. Each of these economic structures has been considered as the main cause of underdevelopment in Iran.

The first theory in this group emphasizes the persistence of the feudalistic mode of production in Iran after the arrival of Islam, in particular after the Seljuq era (1038–1153), and the pronounced role that Nizam-al Mulk,[72] the renowned Prime Minister (Grand Vazir) in the Seljuq Dynasty, played in it. This theory considers this influence the main obstacle to the emergence of capitalist relations in Iran.

The main theory in this subgroup has been adopted from the combined works of well-known Russian historians such as Diakonov, Pigolo Sekaya, I. P. Petrooshefski, M. R. Aroonova, K. Z. Ashrafian and others whose political views influenced many Iranian thinkers in certain periods about socioeconomic formations, including the form and content of the feudalistic mode of production in Iran. We will refer to examples of these works in the text of this book. Believing in a linear and universal evolution of history in four stages (slavery, feudalism, capitalism and socialism), this theory equates pre-Islamic Iran with the slave system and considers the post-Islamic era, the era of feudalism in Iran, but the international capitalist system worked as the main obstacle to the growth of capitalism in Iran.

Since this theory is an ideological theory, it places all societies, including Iranian society, in a five-stage, unilinear historical evolutionary process, thus undermining its scientific value. In their theoretical description of Iran's historical evolution, these theorists offer a stereotypical explanation of the first three phases—i.e., the early commune, the slave, and the feudalist phases—and they stop short at the fourth stage—i.e., capitalism—because in their view colonization and Western imperialism inhibited the emergence of capitalism and growth in these societies. By throwing a pre-tailored theoretical garment on the body of Iranian society, they undermine the credibility of their research.

The second theory in this group emphasizes the tribal relations in Iran and suggests that because the Iranian tribes were not settled in a certain region the social and political development in Iran was severely impeded. In the Eastern territories, including Iran, the reason that tribes had to move constantly was that a shortage of water forced them to migrate to more moderate climates. This way of life gave rise to certain political and cultural relations, reinforced tribal relations, and inhibited the growth of agriculture as well as city dwelling. The water shortage persisted until the Reza Shah Pahlavi era (1921–1942). Therefore, the factor that prohibited the emergence of capitalism in Iran can be viewed predominantly as being the product of such tribal relations. Among the works that deal with the relationship between migration and underdevelopment in ancient Iran, one can refer to Habibollah Paymaan's article "About Iranian Despotism."[73] Ahmad Ashram's "The Historical Obstacles to the Growth of Capitalism in Iran in the Qajar Era" also describes the relationship between tribal life and the failure of capitalism to appear in contemporary Iran.[74] Both perspectives are discussed in this book.

The third theory in this group considers the domination of the Asian mode of production in Iran the main factor that inhibited the emergence of capitalist relations and kept the country underdeveloped. Emphasizing the water shortage for agricultural purposes, this theory arrives at the conclusion that this factor (i.e., the shortage of water) has not only defined the form and the content of agriculture that make it distinct from that of the West but has also had an affect on the political and social relations of Iranian society. The "oriental despotism" form of government has also been the consequence of the Asian mode of production. The theory, which explains the Asian mode of production and oriental despotism, is discussed in one of the chapters of this book.

In the classification of the theories in this ten-fold category, and in keeping each theory distinct from the rest, the mention of two points is necessary. The first is the contribution of each theory to the explanation of the phenomenon of underdevelopment in Iran, and the second is their interrelations. In other words, an attempt is made to avoid a deterministic view, which ultimately results in neglecting different factors that have caused backwardness and underdevelopment in Iran.

Historical events and realities cannot be considered a function of a single factor. Each of the elements that create a society, such as the economic structure, war, religion, politics, ideology, leadership, or all of them combined, can, in certain historical conditions, act as a factor that contributes to the progress or stagnation of a society. However, these factors may not always remain stable and cannot always determine the historical fate of human beings. Just as the economy of a society in a certain era can be a function of other unpredictable factors, and just as a war can change the course of development of a society, religion can also be a decisive factor in a certain historical era or lose its status as the dominant force or ideological format and turn into a secondary factor affecting development or underdevelopment in another era. Determining the relations among these factors in certain eras requires a scientific approach to them. Therefore, deterministic views and stereotyping cannot explain the concrete and evolving events in history.

The tenth theory, "The Institutional Sociological Analysis of Development," is an accurate perspective in the analysis of Iran's underdevelopment as a case of patrimonial society. This theory concretely links social (non-economic) and economic (profit) values. Norman Jacobs notes that in the analysis of growth, development, and behavior, emphasis on social, cultural, structural, and institutional issues is essential. Analyzing the issue of Iran's underdevelopment from an "institutional perspective," he states: "The economic action in the Iranian society, *a priori*, is subordinated to the primacy of certain non-economic considerations, which are non-rational from the economic standpoint, and, hence, tend to positively impede the development of rational economic action in Iranian society."[75] Using the perspective of this analysis, Iran's non-economic considerations are mostly political. It is better to view these considerations with respect to the fundamental values, or goals, of the seven principal institutions of Iranian society rather than the active values within the political power structure or merely economic institutions.

According to Jacobs, these seven institutions are political power, economy, labor relations, social classes, blood relations (generation, religion, and an undisturbed and stable social order—i.e., traditions), and justified development (social values).[76]

Based on this theory, if we accept that Iranian culture lacks the needed rationality for economic prosperity and that this shortage inhibits growth in Iranian society, one has to ask what factors have given rise to similar problems in other Eastern societies. Despite the presence of rationality in Chinese thought, whether in orthodox Confucianism,[77] Taoism, or innovative religions such as Buddhism, China was afflicted with retardation like other Eastern societies.[78] Therefore, one needs to find other common factors that have caused underdevelopment in all Eastern societies.[79] According to Jacobs this factor is partrimonialism. Partrimonialism is "a form of traditional domination occurring in larger social structures that require an

administrative apparatus to execute edits."[80] Of course, Jacobs does not
believe that all Asian societies have identical development problems,
but these societies do share certain similar characteristics rooted in the
patrimonial system.[81] This system, which is different from feudalism
and has some common characteristics with the Asian mode of
production, will be explained in Chapter Five of this book.

The Approach and the Main Thesis of this Study

The goal of the present book as a sociological study is to find the
causes of Iran's underdevelopment as a social phenomenon. This book
adopts a critical view toward the historical developments of Iran.

The approach of this study is to analyze events as social realities in
the process of history and to find the causes of these events (historical
sociology or sociology with historical backgrounds). Wallerstein
believes that history and social sciences belong to a single paradigm.
He states that history is entirely based on social sciences; hence, there
is no non-historical phenomenon.[82] This approach, known as the
diachronic approach, stands against the synchronic approach, which
considers history outside of its time frame. Using the diachronic
approach, many historical suppositions can be studied in a dynamic
rather than static social process and within the framework of historical
realities.[83] Therefore, national, ethnic, linguistic, religious (and anti-
religious), and ideological biases are eliminated from the framework.
This approach studies historical realities as they are, not as they should
be.

In other words, this approach analyzes a society in a social process
throughout its history as it progresses and changes. Thus, society is
viewed not as an inflexible, closed system but as a system of existing
and prevalent relations among human beings in a social fabric,
including relations of production, the ruling system, beliefs, interest
groups, norms and regulations, etc., all interacting with one another.
This approach interrelates individuals' actions with the social structure.
Thus, "society must be understood as a process constructed historically
by individuals who are constructed historically by society"[84] Societies
do not have fixed and lasting organizations, for new organizations or
movements occur in it to bring harmony to life in its existing potentials
and conditions. The causes and consequences of these changes must be
studied. Therefore, this approach is immune to ideological frameworks.

The author believes that the root of underdevelopment or
development in a society should be located in the economic
organization and the subsistence mode of that society, which is

influenced by ecological factors. However, as Norman Jacobs indicates, no matter how underdevelopment is conceived, underdeveloped societies like Iran need changing before economic development.[85] Politics or religion can play the dominant role in development or underdevelopment in different eras. For Iran to develop today, the integration of religion and state (theocracy) must first end. But as Marx pointed out, one has to note which socioeconomic conditions come into existence in each phase to give politics or religion a dominant role.[86] As an institution in which mutual social relations among individuals and groups mold events, a society is the product of relations between social, cultural, and personality structures. One has to find out what type of society these relations create. For the role of personality is also a sociological concept, not a psychological one.

To this end, the economic history or the land tenure system of Iran has been analyzed from the ancient era to the present using a comparative approach in which the features of Iran's history are compared with the features of the economic history of Western developed civilization so that the causes of Iran's backwardness and underdevelopment and the West's development can be clarified. The development and growth of the West and the underdevelopment of Iran are not the two ends of a phenomenon, and the study of one end does not necessarily shed light on the other. With the exception of certain eras, the causes of development and the obstacles to growth in the East should be found within eastern societies.

The following four concepts—development, underdevelopment, the factors that give rise to development, and the obstacles that inhibit development—are relative concepts, and underdevelopment in a society has to be evaluated in relation to progress within other societies. The factors that lead to development in all societies are not identical or absolute, in the same way that the obstacles to development in all underdeveloped societies are not the same or absolute. However, the factors that caused the development of modern civilization—i.e., the civilization that first came into existence in the West—emanate from the same source. In short, and from a general point of view, the backwardness of Iran and the development of the West are based on two crucial factors: (1) the emergence of capitalism and separation of state and church in the West, and (2) the absence of capitalist relations and the integration of state and religion in Iran.

The characteristics of the economic history of Iran are examined in the pre-Islamic era, the era of the Islamic caliphate, and thereafter. The features of the economic history of the West are also examined in three eras: the ancient era, the medieval era, and the era after the emergence of contemporary civilization. The goal of this historical-comparative study is to understand the trends of growth in Eastern and Western civilizations, for they have resulted in different outcomes.

Emphasis on the economic organization of a society does not negate the role of factors that affect the structure of society. When the cultural identity of a society is lost or disintegrates for any reason, social unity will also be lost. To regain cultural unity, social unity is necessary. Social unity depends upon a unified attitude toward national history, common interests, and the values of society. The social and political identity of Iran has been entwined with religion throughout history, to the point that Iranian nationality is identified with religion. Therefore, to study factors of and obstacles to development, the role of religion has to be determined. The relationships between religion and society, religion and state, and differing and opposing attitudes toward religion play an important role in the development and underdevelopment of society, and they have been examined in different chapters of this book.

The Relationship Between Man and Nature, or the Role of the Geographic Factors in Development

Human beings establish a relationship with nature through their labor, for labor is the mediator between nature and value. In Adam Smith's view, labor is the unit of measurement for value.[87] In Marx's view, labor is both a unit of measurement and a source of value.[88] Throughout history, in human life, wealth has been primarily the outcome of the combination of labor and nature.[89] The relationship between man and nature gradually shapes the relationship between human beings. This relationship is in turn another source of value. George Lucas states that labor does not necessarily have to be directly related to nature; it can influence others through education, organization, and leadership.[90] For example, the emergence of the power institution (i.e., the government) can be considered the outcome of labor, production, and the accumulation of products. By controlling the surplus products, the ruling class influences the entire society. As C. S. Lewis pointed out, "Man's power over Nature often turns out to be a power exerted by some men over other men with Nature as its instrument."[91] Nikki Keddie also indicates that geographical, ecological, and technological factors and their interrelationship with human beings explain the difference of civilizations in the world. These factors are especially important to justify the backwardness of Middle Eastern societies, the first center of world-advanced civilization, when compared with Europe in modern times.[92] Misused nature and environmental change in the Middle East caused the decline of its ancient civilization. Ecological advantage caused higher development in the West in modern times. Max Weber also mentions geographical conditions as a favorable factor in the growth of capitalism in the West in modern times. Capitalism was not born in pre-modern civilization of the Middle East because it was "predominately coastal, whereas early modern capitalism in Europe was born in the cities of the interior."[93] In addition to these factors, the interrelationship between material culture (technology) and non-material culture (norms, values, ideas, religion, philosophy, polity, etc.) must be considered in the formation of civilizations.[94]

Marvin Harris's anthropological perspective leads him to think that the initial wealth was accumulated through hard and intense work and that this affected the power relations among the people. He writes: "the rise of pristine states would appear to be best understood as a consequence of the intensification of agricultural production."[95] Under certain ecological conditions, some people manage to become the ruling class of the first states by playing the role of hard-working, ambitious, and public-spirited individuals. They could have gradually set themselves above others.[96] This is a good example of the effects of labor/nature relations on human relations. One fact must be concluded here: that the influence of the geographical environment cannot directly affect human relations such as type of politics or religion but can affect human beings through the medium of the relations of production. A desert land is not responsible for despotism, nor is a green land responsible for freedom. However, the outcomes of human relations with these two geographical environments (production) may reach two different power relations.

Jared Diamond has referred to the relationship between the quality of nature and the living environment with the level of food production on the one hand and the relationship between producing in excess of consumption and the growth of technology on the other, in different societies and different eras.[97] No doubt, if the quality of labor is better and nature is richer, the fruit they will yield will be greater. The quantity and the quality of these two elements are different in human beings in their environments and in their social interactions. For example, when technology was at an early stage of development, even rich natural resources such as seas and mountains were obstacles to development. It was only advanced technology that enabled man to dominate natural obstacles and turn them into productive resources.

In Hegel's book *The Philosophy of History*, he writes about the geographical foundation of the history of the world: "Seas and rivers bring men closer together, whereas mountains keep them apart."[98] This is part of the relationship between man and nature. Plekhanov, the Russian philosopher, agrees with Hegel's statement and adds that seas bring human beings closer only when productive forces—i.e., technology and human knowledge—have reached a relatively high level.[99] At the lower levels, and when the growth of technology is limited, as Fredrick Ratzel, a German geographer, notes, "the sea is a great hindrance to intercourse between the tribes which it separates."[100] It means that a third factor such as technology could reverse the entire nature of relations between the geographical environment and human beings and, consequently, change the relations among people themselves. Thus, the geographic factor is important in considering the degree of produced values. Race and physical characteristics, culture, customs and rites, traditions, food, and clothing all take their final form in a process through which human beings learn to cope with nature.

Examples are the native Indian tribes living on the continent of America and the Mayans (after the disintegration of the Mayan civilization), or the natives of Australia living isolated from the more advanced worlds in Europe and Asia for centuries. Seas, forests, and mountains were the biggest obstacles to their communication with the outside world. The growth of the navigation industry resulted in the discovery of these new territories. Marx believed that the richness of the land has not been the only feature that distinguished different nations, but that the differences in the nature of nations and people have resulted in differences as well.[101] The complexity of the relationship between human beings and the climate, the growth of this relationship and the domination of man over nature, the reproduction of new human needs following the fulfillment of man's basic needs, the utilization of modern tools, and the discovery of greater and quicker modes of access to natural resources have all played a role in creating these differences.[102] The culture of each society is the generator or the result of economic or subsistence relations. As the components of culture, these relations lead to a specific order. Therefore, one can arrive at the conclusion that the basis and foundation of value—i.e., labor, the mode and tools of production, human needs and capabilities, and the culture of a society—all come into existence as a product of nature and lay the foundation for specific social relations, although they do not grow at the same rate. Daniel Chirot writes

Changes occurred because of ecological pressures—that is, the interaction between geographic change and the ways in which humans themselves altered their environment by reproducing themselves, migrating, and adapting products available to them. Growing crops changed the environment as cultivated fields replaced wild grasslands, forests, and swamps; humans learned to further adapt geography by such techniques as irrigation; population size changed and put new and greater pressures on resources; and humans altered their behavior to adapt.[103]

In short, in the historical process, the main factor in promoting or preventing development is initial geographic conditions, which affect the amount of production and consequently human relations. Natural factors such as fertile lands or shortages of water are out of human control, but they affect economic and social life. At a more advanced level of production, human-made situations such as technological, economic, political, and religious factors and wars influence the outcome of development in a society.

Value, at the ultimate level, is the product of the combination of labor and nature. The quantitative and qualitative differences in these factors are the starting point of differences in human life in other domains. For instance, the differences in the natural domain, which are accidental, can be the origin of many other social differences such as the existence of oil resources in the Arab counties of the Persian Gulf in the present era. The tools used in production are a very important factor in determining how natural resources are utilized today. The more advanced the tools (technological or intellectual), the greater will be the human domination over nature. Conversely, the more backward a society is, the less sophisticated its tools will be, and as a result the greater will be nature's domination over human beings (e.g., natural disasters such as earthquakes and the construction industry). The social, economic, and political relations among human beings are a function of the level of progress people have made in the natural domain. Informed people who have more access to knowledge and technology have a better chance of establishing closer human relations. Power in the political form (i.e., the government) can be a determining factor in preserving traditional and natural resources, or it can cause a change in them. This is the starting point for the preservation or the removal of differences.

The relationship between government and the economy, which is the main topic in political economy as far as experts are concerned, leads to a specific type of social relations among people. The role of the civil society, which has resulted from the economic relations of a particular period in history, is to separate these two realms (i.e., the realms of the individual and the public interest). Civil society, in general, provides for individual freedom, social order, and economic growth in a modern nation.

The role played by the geographical domain in defining human relations and allowing a society to grow is discussed in the next chapter. The historical differences among ancient civilizations, which have given rise to the differences between the East and the West, will also be discussed in the following chapters.

Is Development in the West Rooted in the Eastern Civilization?

The fact that Muslim societies were more developed than the West during the Middle Ages caused some people to conclude that the West achieved its development from Muslim nations. This is not true. These people do not consider the nature of development in the East and the West. Development in modern times in the West was the result of the invention of capitalism and has nothing to do with the level of development in the East during its agrarian economy. Capitalism was a product of the dissolution of feudalism. As I will argue in other chapters, this system was absent in the East, including the Muslim nations. At this point, I wish to challenge the view that the development of the West and the backwardness of the East are two sides of one coin.

Some theorists argue for the existence of a direct relationship between development in the West and underdevelopment in Iran. They believe, on the one hand, that the roots of development in the West lie in the ancient Eastern civilization, as though foreigners took it to the West during the Crusades. On the other hand, they consider the underdevelopment of Iran in the contemporary era the product of the restrictions imposed on Iranians by Western colonists. For instance, criticizing the Asian mode of production, Parviz Piran writes:

> If the traditional system in the Eastern societies, including Iran, was a static system, how could we explain the outstanding developments that took place in Eastern countries and were transferred to Western Europe later on, during the Crusades? Were these developments not the same developments that paved the way for the emergence of global capitalism?[104]

First of all, this argument does not reflect the true reality. Considering the transportation possibilities in the 12th and 13th centuries, what kind of developments could have practically been taken from the East to the West? Does Piran mean that an advanced form of technology was developed by the people in the East and was then taken to Europe? Or, does he mean that the scientific knowledge and rational philosophy that had initially been brought to the East by the Westerners were later on translated back to Latin? If he is referring to the intellectual treasure of the Eastern civilization, we have to admit that this treasure belonged to the West in the first place. Second, if the outstanding development Piran is referring to have an objective base, why were the Easterners not able to use them to bring about capitalism and modern civilization as in the West? Third, if it was possible to set the stage for capitalism by transferring these developments from one area to another, then why did the Easterners not undertake that transfer after capitalism developed in the West?

The second group of theorists, who consider colonization the factor that caused underdevelopment in Iran, probably argue in response to the last question posed above that Western colonizers did not permit the Easterners to bring capitalism to their societies. But some countries such as Iran and Turkey were never colonies. Until World War I, Turkey was itself an empire that controlled large territories from Africa to the Southwest of Europe.

Until modern times, the underdevelopment of the East was not considered to have been caused by a conspiracy of the West; rather, it was believed to be a situation that had resulted from the development of global capitalism. According to this argument, the developments in the West not only did not help the growth of generative forces in underdeveloped regions of the world, but they also caused the disintegration of these forces following the decrease in the costs of production. Subsequently, a new division of labor at the global level came into existence and turned part of the less-developed world into the source of raw materials for advanced Western industries.[105] However, if foreigners involved in the Crusades stole the developments that had occurred in Eastern countries, why are some remote areas the Crusaders were not able to reach, such as China, India, and Iran, considered underdeveloped as well? Even four centuries after the Crusades, the East was not technologically less developed than the West. The gap between the West and the East began in the 16th century. The political advancement of the West, comprising such things as the parliamentary system, which began in the 12th century in Europe, had no roots in the East. The Eastern societies entered into aborted parliamentary systems in the late 19th or the 20th centuries, modeled after Western governments. It is true that the Westerners took gunpowder from the Easterners, but the crucial question is why the military machine and the technology that was based on gunpowder grew in the West and not in the East. Using this example, one should concentrate on how this military machine was developed and not on how gunpowder was discovered.

In my view, these perspectives emanate from two factors: the ethnocentric mentality that prevails in Iran and a sense of victimhood (i.e., victim psychology).[106] Ethnocentrism emerged among Iranians after the nomadic and tribal Arabs conquered Iran and defeated the Sasanian Empire in 7th century. Psychologically, ethnocentrism was a defense mechanism to give defeated Iranians a better feeling about themselves. Dominant Arabs called non-Arab Muslims *Mawali,*[107] which meant "below the Muslim Arabians."[108] According to Zarrinkub, "Arabs treated *Mawali* with contempt and oppression."[109] They did not walk or eat with Mawali.[110] Victim psychology is also a defense mechanism that blames others for the backwardness of Iranian society. In other words, Iranians consider themselves victims and seek external factors responsible for their failure because they want to justify their weakness in order to feel better. People who engage in victim psychology believe that if they do not succeed in getting what they want it is because other people did not allow them to succeed. Victim psychology and a self-centered perspective have led some people to claim that if Islam had not arrived in Iran and if the glory and the power of the Achaemenian and Sasanian dynasties (which were the largest empires of their era) had lasted, Iran today would be the only superpower in the world, instead of the United States.[111]

The actual truth of the events of the Crusades and the emergence of capitalism in the West, not the East, should be sought in the West, not in the East. One may find a relationship between the emergence of contemporary Western civilization and the Crusades, but not of the kind some Iranians, like Piran, suggest—i.e., that the Western aggressors took Islamic civilization to the West. The truth is that when Western kings and feudal lords set out to conquer the Muslim countries in the East they had to free the serfs they controlled. Some of these leaders were killed during the Crusades and never returned to their homes. Therefore, hundreds of families from the class of aristocrats were destroyed, and the serfs they controlled gained their freedom.[112] One of the prerequisites for the emergence of capitalism in the West was the freedom of the serfs from the yoke of the feudal lords. In addition, the serfs were now free from any sort of ownership of land

and were forced to sell the only commodity they controlled (their labor) to make a living. The newly established bourgeois class made use of this fact and engaged in the accumulation of capital. Can we consider this development the East's contribution to the development in the West?

Granting that the Eastern and Western civilizations were different, we can follow the effects of this duality in the trend of development in these societies, including the emergence of capitalism. So far, different aspects of the divergence between the East and the West have been discussed. Among the important factors were the discovery of precious metal mines and the outstanding growth of the population in Europe. But the most important factor that accounts for the difference between the East and the West is the growth of the monetary economy. This economy was in a position to take advantage of the above-mentioned developments in shaping the capitalist system. For example, in a society like the Chinese society, the growth in the population paralleled the growth of population in the West, but the rational monetary economy did not grow; traditionalism grew instead.[113]

One can claim that the emergence of capitalism was a response to the growth of population and the increase in the demand for commodities that the self-sufficient feudal system in the West could not meet. Capitalism was the solution to this problem under certain circumstances because it increased production as much as its available capacity allowed. When serfdom had disappeared, capitalism freed the peasants who had been dependent upon the self-sufficient land, and it sent them on their way to urban production centers. The profit that ensued from this development was the incentive that promoted capitalism to an international level and enabled it to gain raw materials, a cheap labor force, and the market it needed for its products. Thus, as Weber wrote, "With almost lightning speed everything that stands in the way of capitalistic culture is being crushed."[114]

Because the bourgeois class and proletariat did not appear in the East, the capitalist culture had no reason to emerge. Traditional norms governed society and reproduced the existing forces within it. No particular incentive for self-profiting resulted from the centralized political power of the state and common ownership of the land. Indeed, the tribes and the economy based on raising cattle and migration threatened monetary relations. The central state, which had a tribal structure, had the power to confront unorganized commercial and industrial groups like its own servants. Accordingly, even in the 20th century, when Reza Shah gained power in the last stage of the traditional agrarian system, he seized much of the land that belonged to landlords and local governors and registered it in his own name.[115]

The growth of capitalism in Europe followed the demise of the serf system. The landowning system in Iran, including the kind of ownership that was prevalent there, was the foundation of a centralized state that strongly supported pre-capitalist relations. In the West, the new monarch was the representative of the newly established bourgeois class. In the East, the landowning state continued to remain a supporter of the old landowning relations in which it had a big share. The traditional landowning system in Iran lasted until the imperialistic design known as "The White Revolution" broke its back in 1961. In other words, a bourgeois class strong enough to confront the power of the landowners was never created in Iran. The interests of global capitalism were in conflict with the old landowning relations in Iran, and so, using pressure and threats, global capitalism destroyed the old system. After World War II, in order to expedite capitalistic relations, the U.S. dictated a land reform program in many developing societies, including Iran. This program was designed to neutralize any socialist-oriented agrarian revolutions and open the markets for world capitalism. The details and implementation process of this program will be discussed in the second part of this book.

In the West, when the system of serfdom broke down, the labor force of the peasants was released. The free peasants formed an army of workers to help capitalism grow. In Iran, the peasants remained completely dependent upon the land, and this dependence strengthened the landowners in their struggle against the capitalist elements. The Iranian bourgeoisie remained within the confines of internal trade, and therefore it did not need the labor force of the peasants, either. These were the key factors that inhibited the growth of capitalism in Iran. In this process, the colonial West had no direct role in the backwardness of Iran, and Eastern civilization was not the root of the modern civilization of the West.

A Common Mistake

Despite the common belief, Bernard Lewis, among many others, revealed a solid fact about the status of Muslim and Christian societies before the fifteen century. He writes: "under the medieval caliphate, and again under the Persian and Turkish dynasties, the empire of Islam was the richest, most powerful, most creative, and most enlightened region in the world, and for most of the Middle Ages Christendom was on the defensive. In the fifteen century, the Christian counterattack expanded."[116] Then, during the sixteenth century and after, the situation changed dramatically in favor of the West, so that a few small Western countries succeeded in building vast empires in the East and establishing a dominant role in trade as well as military affairs.[117] However, some scholars who rely on these facts come to the wrong conclusions. While some of these scholars, such as Abbas Milani, argue that modernity existed in the East before the West achieved it, others, such as Parviz Piran, go much beyond this point, claiming that the West seized its modern civilization from Muslims.[118] Some scholars have embarked upon similar endeavors to locate the sources of Western civilization or solutions to modern problems in the East.[119] We must ask: What is the reality?

In determining the differences between the East and the West and the causes of development in the West and underdevelopment in the East, a crucial factor has remained unnoticed. Overlooking this factor can produce misleading explanations and false analyses. This factor is simply that contemporary Western civilization or modern societies should not be considered the same as the civilizations that existed in previous eras, whether in the West or the East. Economic relations, political and class conflicts, government alternatives, and essentially all other relations within the realm of the social rights of individuals changed in modern civilization. This change began in the West and precipitated change throughout the world, a process that still continues today. Modernity with its positive and negative characteristics was born in the West. The development of the West and the underdevelopment of the East in the modern era cannot be understood unless we distinguish contemporary Western civilization from the civilizations that existed before the emergence of capitalism and the bourgeois class. Marx and Engels, in *The Communist Manifesto*, wrote:

> The bourgeoisie, during its rule of scarce one hundred years, has created more massive and more colossal productive forces than have all preceding generations together. Subjection of Nature's forces to man, machinery, the application of chemistry to industry and agriculture, steam-navigation, railways, electric telegraphs, the clearing of whole continents for cultivation, canalization of rivers, whole populations conjured out of the ground—what earlier century had even a presentiment that such productive forces slumbered in the lap of social labour?[120]

Many scholars have not distinguished the uniquely different era of modern civilization from the civilizations of the past, and thus they have mistakenly searched for the same characteristics in pre-modernity civilizations in the East.

Abbas Milani wrote in his book, *Modernity and Opposition to Modernity in Iran*,[121] "The first buds of modernity[122] in Iran" appeared in the eleventh century (A.D.) before the West.[123] He argues "the background of modernity was available in Iran as much as in Europe because, precisely in eleventh and twelfth centuries, a type of modernity existed in Iran."[124] Searching through classic texts in literature and history, Milani hoped to find the "harbingers of modernity" in Iran. Referring to three movements—religion, Sufism, and individualism—in a section of his book, Milani introduces *Chahar Maqaleh Aruzi (Four Essays of Aruzi)*[125] as an example of the last movement—i.e., a form of rational intellectual modernism that appeared in Iran before the West but that could not grow and develop.[126] If we locate the background factors that led to the emergence of rationalism in Iran and the world of Islam, we will realize that what Milani calls a form of Iranian modernity or rationalism did not originate in Iran but instead came from the influence of Greek philosophy on Iranian intellectuals. This point has been further elaborated upon in other sections of this book. In the same way that the existence of such philosophies (i.e., rationalism and individualism in the West) could not by itself result in the emergence of modernity, these influences also could not have yielded such results in Iran.

Essentially, it is not appropriate to use the term modernity (which speaks of an era with features that are different from those found in previous eras) when referring to Iran, which was in the grip of the most centralized form of agricultural economy (i.e., Asian), and in which political power depended upon the unity of religion and the state. The roots of modernism in the West were not based on subjective factors but rather on factors that essentially have objective grounds. For instance, ancient Greece could not be called modern simply because of the existence of rational philosophy. Milani's definition of modernity is ambiguous because he finds this concept in literature. The word "modernity," on the other hand, refers to a specific period of time that produced a new industrial and colonial world that could be described as "modernization"—"a term denoting those processes of individual-ization, secularization, industrialization, cultural differentiation, co-modification, urbanization, bureaucratization, and rationalization [which] together have constituted the modern world."[127] As Lawrence Cahoone wrote, modernity refers to the new civilization—unique in human history— that developed in Europe and North America over the last several centuries and became fully evident by the early twentieth

century.[128] This modern Western civilization generally consists of
capitalism practiced within a secular culture, liberal democracy,
individualism, rationalism, and humanism. Milani refers to some of
these characteristics elsewhere in his book[129] but disregards them when
he analyzes Iranian classical literature.

Iran, as will be discussed in the upcoming chapters, was not able to
develop these characteristics in any of the periods of its history.[130]
Resorting to the language and the metaphors used in literature, and
pointing to signs of rationalism in the works of Iranian thinkers, leaves
us with the bewildering question with which Milani has concluded his
book: "Why was that modernity aborted?"[131] Milani intends to find in
the literary and historical texts of Iran in the past a form of local and
native modernity free of Western influence. Despite his attempts, the
basic foundations of modernity are all products of the West.
Phenomena such as native capitalism, rationalism, pluralism, and
secularism do not exist in reality. Those phenomena were first Western
and then global. Contrary to Milani's view, Iranian society, not only in
eleventh century but even in the twentieth century, did not achieve
rationalism and individualism and still continues to oppose these
philosophies. We are impelled to ask: Why is this so?

Contemporary development of the West was realized through the
capitalist system. The order of the capitalist economy originated in the
termination of the feudalist economy. During the era of feudalism, the
West was underdeveloped, like the East. In other words, until the
beginning of the sixteenth century there was not much difference
between the East and the West. Many researchers have attempted to
find evidence of factors in pre-capitalist Iran—such as the arrival of
Islam; the invasions by Arabs, the Mogul Turks, or the Turks of Central
Asia; or the decline of the sciences—to prove that Iran could have
reached the advanced civilization similar to the present era before the
West if these factors had not existed. This mistake emanates from the
fact that these researchers overlook the fundamental differences
between capitalist and feudalist (agricultural) relations. Two facts
should not be disregarded. First, before Islam arrived in Iran, the
Sasanian Empire had been demoralized and was declining; even before
the Mogols' attack on Iran, Islamic civilization was falling down.
Second, had capitalism not emerged in the West, there was a great
possibility that the Islamic Ottoman Empire would have conquered
most of Europe. Capitalism is a particular stage in human history. What
capitalism has produced in modern times could never have been
achieved in pre-modern societies.

In Iran's system, which was based on the Asiatic mode of production, there were no grounds for the emergence of industrial capitalism. The contemporary emergence of capitalism in Iran has been limited to commercial capitalism, which has no fundamental conflict with religious institutions, the absolute monarchy, or the agrarian economy.

The truth is that if capitalism had not appeared in the West, or if the empire of Spain (during the Hapsburg era) had been able (as it intended) to bring the entire continent of Europe under its centralized domination in the fifteenth century, the emergence of capitalism would probably not have occurred at that time. This attempt at domination, seriously pursued by Charles V, was beyond the military and economic capabilities of Spain. Therefore, the Hapsburg's military aspirations destroyed the growing trade in Spain, and its ambitions were resisted.[132] Wallerstein has written, "Spain could afford neither the bureaucracy nor the army that was necessary for the enterprise, and the event went bankrupt, as did the French monarchs' making a similar albeit even less plausible attempt."[133] As a result, the severe control of the official Catholic religion, which Charles V supported, lost its power as human thinking flourished. Daniel Chirot has commented about the role played by the repression of thought by religious authorities: "Had Newton been living in Italy at that time, his work would have been banned, and like Galileo he would have been arrested, or worse."[134] The difference between England, Isaac Newton's homeland, and Italy, where the Pope was established, was that the bourgeois class was able to attain political power in England. The rest were all peripheral factors.

The thing that made contemporary Western civilization a reality was the capitalist mode of production, and the capitalist mode of production was a result of the feudalist relations in Europe. Feudalism, in turn, became a reality due to the private ownership of land. All three fundamentals were absent in Iran.[135]

The penetration of the Western capitalist system into Iran in the nineteenth and twentieth centuries could not provide the above-mentioned prerequisites. Quite to the contrary, the domination of the norms of the traditional and religious culture in Iran, and the resistance to the emergence of industrial capitalism and the West's influence, formed the framework of the intellectual and political movements of this era. Due to these circumstances and the interest in protecting national resources, the mission of Iranian culture and its intellectual guardians was to confront the external elements, not to disseminate Western civilization and help the growth of industrial capitalism in

Iran. A common belief was based on the assumption that the West was unsurprisingly focused upon its own interests in Iran, not Iran's development. Nevertheless, these external elements succeeded in establishing new economic, political, and cultural foundations and supporting the landowning khans and kings in preventing industrial capitalism from growing. The influence of the West intensified the conflicts among the different ideological groups, and the national, cultural, and political gap between the two cultures turned into the main issue of Iranian society. These conflicts and their consequences are treated in the last chapter of this book.

Is State Ownership of the Means of Production in the Modern Era the Legacy of the Asian Mode of Production?

The study of the relationship between the state and the means of production in the modern era owes its significance to two facts: (1) this relationship is indicative of relations that—in contrast to European feudalism—governed the Asian mode of production, and (2) in many of the developing countries, including Iran (to a lesser degree) and the socialist countries such as China and Russia (to a greater degree), this feature has existed. At the end of the section dealing with the special features of the Asian mode of production, partrimonialism, and Oriental despotism, the discussion of the relationship between state ownership of the means of production and the degree of growth on the one hand, and the dictatorship and anti-democratic policies of the state on the other, is presented, because this discussion will help in the understanding of the events in these societies.

The main reason for including this part is that a state economy is still one of the main aspects of Eastern societies. For instance, currently 80% of the Iranian economy is controlled by the state. Thus, it is not the state that is dependent upon the people's tax payments but the people who are dependent upon the state as the main source of their income. In this situation, the state can easily manipulate the society for its objectives. As in a patrimonial system as described by Weber, an absolute authority controls the economy through the government bureaucracy. Finally, it is important to ask whether privatization can remove the present economic backwardness and dictatorship in these societies.

In this section, these relations will be discussed briefly. An in-depth study of this topic is a relatively difficult task that would require further independent work. Therefore, we will here only refer to the findings of research done specifically on the Soviet and Chinese societies. While this research is predominantly a theoretical analysis of "the Asian society," it is an attempt to enhance the understanding of the nature of the dominant policies in these societies and to offer an explanation for why socialism in these societies deviated from the right track. The main objective in presenting this theory at this point is to raise some questions the reader can begin to think about.

From a Marxist point of view, the state is the means that the dominant class uses to gain political domination. With this principle in mind with respect to the background of the Asian mode of production in Russia and China, we may ask what effects the principle has had in the modern era. Who is the dominant class in a society in which the state owns the means of production? Under such circumstances, how are the boundaries between the classes determined?

The special feature of the Asian mode of production is the state ownership or the group ownership of the means of production (i.e., the land and the water). The special feature of a socialist government is state ownership of the means of production or the collective ownership of these means. In a modern society, the means of production have of course extended far beyond the agricultural land and natural resources.

In the Asian mode of production, due to state ownership of the means of production, state despotism appeared. The relationship between state ownership of the means of production and state despotism was direct and straightforward. Excess value was paid to the owner (primarily the shah) in the form of ownership interest. The political aspect of this relationship manifested itself as despotism. In previous pages, the relationship between the two phenomena (political and economic) and their relevant details were described. The question this section addresses is the following: if monopolistic state ownership of the means of production resulted in political despotism in the agricultural era, will this type of ownership also result in a monopoly of political power and dictatorship in the modern industrial era?

Objective studies and observations of the former Soviet Union and China have shown that the dictatorship of the new class[136]—i.e., the "class of bureaucrats"[137]—has been a requirement for the preservation of the state's monopolistic ownership of the means of production. This class gains possession of part of the excess value produced through the monopolization of party and state officials.[138] Although the dominant party justifies this policy under the name of the proletariat dictatorship, the policy has been in contradiction with the known principles of socialism based on equal rights for all citizens.

Marxists have considered the relationship between the ownership of the means of production and the political power of the dominant class in capitalist societies the cause of exploitation and the class democracy. Socialism advocates the negation of these relations. This duality resulted in skepticism about the nature of these societies. Karl Wittfogel[139]—a theoretician of the "Comintern"[140]—undertook an examination of the Asian mode of production and the prevailing situation in Russia and China in 1930. Wittfogel, who later became one of the critics of socialism in the era of Stalin, believed that there was a connection between the Asian mode of production dominant in Russia and China and the existing kind of socialism.[141] In his informative book entitled *Oriental Despotism: A Comparative Study of Absolute Power*, which was the product of thirty years of study, he has attempted to show that there was a relationship between the bureaucracy of the Soviet Union during Stalin and the state ownership of the means of production (the special feature of the Asian mode of production). His goal in this work was to describe the Asian mode of production, the anti-democratic products of these relations in Russia, and the effects of cultural factors on the underdevelopment of the Eastern societies as compared with the West. Many Marxist and non-Marxist experts have criticized his views. As we shall see in the forthcoming pages, Wittfogel was not the only or even the first person to emphasize the cultural effects in Eastern societies as the factor responsible for the difference between the East and the West. He was not even the only person who presented and undertook the critique of party policies with respect to hiding the presence of the Asian mode of production. This material was evaluated at the Leningrad Conference in 1931, and, despite the dominant opinion, experts such as G. Papayan, L. Medyar, and S.Y. Govalev started defending the thesis of the Asian mode of production in the East.[142]

Wittfogel led one of the most essential research projects in this respect, and he became convinced that Eastern societies should be distinguished from the Western societies because water has been a key issue in the Eastern societies. He considered special features of this civilization to be agricultural management and despotic governments whose main responsibility was securing water.

Wittfogel examined the theory of Oriental despotism with respect to the central irrigation system in China.[143] Expanding the views of Marx and Engels on this issue, he stated that as far as the Asian mode of production is concerned two basis factors are identifiable. The first is the relationship between human beings and their natural environment, because different situations of collective ownership of the water resources and irrigation networks can affect the process of productive work in a society. The second factor is the question of whether or not the dominant class can control the means of production, the state machinery, and the economy of the society as a bureaucrat class, without private ownership of the means of production.[144]

Wittfogel believed that political dictatorship in Stalin's era in the former Soviet Union was the result of the relationship that existed between the state and the control of the means of production. This is the same as the Asian mode of production, or at least its extension.

The relationship between the dominant class and the ownership of the means of production is a direct relationship. Control of the means of production, from the Marxist point of view, guarantees political domination by a class. The opposite could be very difficult for those who have turned Marxism into a framework for measuring social realities. Addressing this issue in fact functioned as a polemical device used by the Communist Party of the former Soviet Union. Wittfogel's goal in raising this issue was to prove that the leaders of the Communist Party were capable of controlling the political establishment (the state) as a class of bureaucrats without having the ownership of the means of production—as in the Asian mode of production, in which the private ownership of the means of production was meaningless, as well. What existed was the state and collective ownership, which in the case of Russia continued to exist in the form of Mir communes until 1868. Wittfogel argued that after the 1917 revolution in the Caesar-type Russia, a new class of bureaucrats that was the extension of the previous system came to power.[145] This view is consistent with Max Weber's perspective as he stratifies society based on the means of administration rather than on Marx's definition of the means of production.

Wittfogel revealed the fact that Stalin prevented the study and analysis of the Asian mode of production in order to conceal the reality of the existence of this mode in the Soviet Union.[146] After Stalin died, research on Oriental despotism became part of the Marxist teachings, and thus the domination of the previous one-dimensional perspective on the evolution of history came to an end.[147]

If the relationship between the dominant class and the ownership of the means of production is the foundation of the domination by that class, it is fair to ask which class rules when there is state ownership of the means of production. Will it be a specific social class or group that gains access to the economic resources and the privileges resulting from them by relying on state power? During the pre-modern era in Asian societies, water was the main means of production, and the state continued its despotism through the control of this natural resource. In the modern era, however, other natural resources such a soil can play the same role. The state in these societies uses the financial resources it controls, and its independent power, to make the society dependent. Putting and end to the state's dictatorship means preventing it from stealing the independent income resources. Unless the relationship between politics and the economy is reversed, and unless these two entities are independent from one another and the rentier economy ends, state absolutism continues.

[1] See Radolfo Stavenhagen, *Social Classes in Agrarian Societies*, trans. Judy Adler Hellman (New York: Anchor Books, 1975). Stavenhagen writes, "thousands of books have been published on the underdeveloped countries, and hundreds of definitions have been advanced of underdeveloped or backward economies." (p. 3). Since that time (i.e., 1975), numerous additional books and articles have been published to continue this trend.

[2] A. Paul Baran, "A Morphology of Backwardness," in *Introduction to the "Developing Societies,"* eds. Hamza Alavi and Teodor Shanin (New York: MR, 1982), 195–204. To be sure, this situation does not apply to present Iran. This was a feature that all societies shared in past centuries. The terms "developing societies" or "underdeveloped societies" refer to societies such as Iranian society in the present era, which have gone beyond the agricultural economy but are not considered developed since they still have not attained the features that are associated with development.

Underdevelopment is a term used in political economy by theorists who use the arguments put forth in the Dependency Theory in order to reject Modernization Theory. If we consider backwardness an internal phenomenon, the term underdevelopment cannot express such conditions because it does not have a sufficient degree of accuracy. For example, Iran and Turkey are presently considered underdeveloped or developing, while they have never been colonized by the West. In fact, Turkey was an empire until the beginning of the twentieth century. Therefore, its present backwardness has its roots in economic and political history and has not been imposed by external powers. Unlike many of the previous colonies in Africa and Latin America, Iran and Turkey should not be considered "underdeveloped," but "backward." If historical and structural roots are not linked with the backwardness of these societies, then an underdeveloped country can use external factors such as advanced technology and sciences in reaching economic growth—i.e., the first phase of development. Middle-range developed countries such as Taiwan, South Korea, and Brazil were able to attain relative development due to the political considerations of the cold war that made available to them technical and economic assistance and other special privileges from the United States. These societies, however, as Norman Jacobs has stated, have attained modernization without development. (See Norman Jacobs, *Modernization Without Development: Thailand As An Asian Case Study* (New York: Praeger Publications, 1971), and Norman Jacobs, *The Korean Road to Modernization and Development* (Chicago: University of Illinois Press, 1986). Immanuel Wallerstein calls this type of progress "development by invitation," and the neo-dependency school calls it "export-led growth," and "import substitution" based on "infant industry" as a strategy of development—or simply "dependent development." (See Bruce Cumings, "The Origins and Development of the Northeast Asian Political Economy: Industrial Sectors, Products Cycles, and Political Consequences," *International Organization* 38, no. 1: 1–4, 0–14, 22–29, 33–35, and 38–40. Reprinted in Stephen Sanderson, *Sociological Worlds:*

Comparative and Historical Readings on Society. (Los Angeles: Roxbury Publishing Company, 1995), 155–166, and Franz J. Schuurman, (ed.), *Beyond the Impasse: New Directions in Development Theory* (London: Zed Books, 1993.) To review the theory of development in the world system, see Peter Evans, *Dependent Development: The Alliance of Multinational, State, and Local Capitalism in Brazil* (Princeton, NJ: Princeton University Press, 1979). Also, see Saeed Hajjarian, "The Development Planning and the Three-Dimensional Alliance Perspective," in Ettela'at-e Siasi va Eqtesadi, *Political and Economic Journal*: 10, nos. 103–104 (April–May 1996) (Tehran: Ordibehesht, 1974).

[3] To study the views of these three sociologists, see the following sources: Immanuel Wallerstein, "The Rise and Future Demise of the World Capitalist System: Concepts for Comparative Analysis, Comparative Studies," *Society and History* 16: 387–394 and 397–415; Eric Wolf, "Europe and the People Without History," Regents of the University of California (1983): 267–278 and 290–302; and Chares Tilly, "Flows of Capital and Forms of Industry in Europe, 1500–1900," *Theory and Society* 12 (1983): 102–113.

[4] Terry Kandal discusses the contemporary theoretical and political debate about the workings of a world-system rooted in classical Marxism. (See Michael T. Martin and Terry Kandal, eds., *Studies of Development and Change in the Modern World* (New York: Oxford University Press, 1989).

[5] Wallerstein, Immanuel, op. cit. His World System Theory contains three fundamental segments: a core, (technologically advanced and economically developed), a periphery, (relatively technologically backward and economically underdeveloped), and semi-periphery (with an intermediate level of techno-economic development).

[6] Rodolfo Stavenhagen, ibid, 6.

[7] Franz J. Schuurman, *Beyond the Impasse: New Direction in Development Theory* (London: Zed Books, 1993).
Ibid, 5.

[9] Gunder Andre Frank. "The Development of Underdevelopment," *Monthly Review* 18, no. 4 (year?): 17–31. Reprinted in Stephen K. Sanderson, ibid, 135.

[10] Fernando Cardoso, "Associated Dependent Development: Theoretical and Practical Implications," in *Authoritarian Brazil: Origins, Policies and Futures*, ed. Alfred Stepan (New Haven, CT: Yale University Press, 1973), (pages…).

[11] For theoretical and historical weaknesses of modernization theory, see Anthony D. Smith, *The Concept of Social Change: A Critique of the Functionalist Theory of Social Change* (Boston: Routledge and Kegan Paul, 1973).

[12] See Walt W. Rostow, The *Stages of Economic Growth: A Non-Communist Manifesto* (London: Cambridge University Press, 1960). Rostow's "non-communist manifesto," as an anti-Marxist theory, is a perspective that suggests a unilinear path in the development of history. See also *Marion J. Levy, Modernization, and the Structure of Societies* (Princeton, NJ: Princeton University Press, 1966); and Samuel P. Huntington, "The Change to Change:

Modernization, Development, and Politics," in Cyril E. Black, *Comparative Modernization* (New York: Free Press, 1976).

[13] See Sidney Hook, *The Hero in History* (Boston: Beacon Press, 1955). Hook argues that great individuals play historical roles and that men and women make history. See also Everett Hagen, *On the Theory of Social Change* (Homewood, IL: Dorsey Press, 1962). Hagen considers innovative personality as the prerequisite for economic development.

[14] For a review of intellectual trends and diverse policies with regard to Iran's development in recent decades, see Jamsheed Behnam, "Social Sciences, Intellectual Trends, and the Issue of Iran's Development Between 1337 and 1357, *Iran Nameh*, Year 15, no. 2 (Spring 1376), 175–198.

[15] It is true that modernism in turn created new problems for human societies and met great resistance, but the fact that all societies try to obtain more technologies, new sciences, and better material conditions indicates the fact that a more accepted and balanced alternative does not exist and that human societies have chosen to follow a path in which going back is not possible. Sociologists predicted this situation in the 19th and early 20th centuries. For example, we can refer to Marx's theory about "alienation;" Durkheim's theory about "anomie;" Ferdinand Tonnies's theory about the "mass society;" Max Weber's theories about the "iron cage" of bureaucracy, rationalism, and the side effects of the speed at which the environment is being damaged; and, finally, Lenin's theory about the drastic gap between the social classes in the world as a result of the differential in the rate of the growth in technology and the emergence of global imperialism. For more information about the views of these sociologists, see Piotr Sztompka, *The Sociology of Social Change* (Oxford, UK: Blackwell, 1994), 78-80.

[16] Differing views have been offered on whether there exists a source or center other than the West for contemporary Western civilization. In his treatment of this issue, Seyyed Mohammad Khatami has correctly stated, "...today the dominant civilization is the Western civilization, and it would not be an exaggeration if we made a connection between the events that occur in various regions of the world and the Western civilization." See *Fear of the Wave: Selected Articles* (Tehran: Ministry of Culture and Islamic Guidance, 1372), 171).

[17] S. Huntington argues that it is false to equate Western civilization with Modern civilization. (*The Clash of Civilizations and the Remaking of World Order*, New York: the Touchstone Book, 1997).

18 Modernity can be defined historically or by its content as a different mode of social life. The above definition refers to its contents or the characteristics of modernity. Historically, Anthony Giddens writes that this mode of life emerged in Europe from about the 7th century onward and subsequently and gradually expanded in the world. (Anthony Giddens, *The Consequences of Modernity* (Cambridge: Polity Press, 1990). There are two images of modernity: rational capitalism, and socialism. Marx and Marxist theorists consider capitalism as the first stage of modernity; Jurgen Habermas calls it the "unfinished project"

because to him capitalism is simply an irrational way to run the world. See Anthony Giddens, "Post-Modernity or Radical Modernity? A Phenomenology of Modernity," in *Social Theory: The Multicultural and Classic Readings,* Charles Lemert, ed. (Boulder, CO: Westview Press, 1993), 531–537.

[19] H. Wiarda. Political Development in Emerging Nations: Is There Still a Third World? USA: Wadsworth, 2003, 160.

[20] Gunnar Myrdal, *Asian Drama: An Inquiry into Poverty of Nations,* 3 vols. (New York: Twentieth Century Fund/Random House, Penguin, 1968). Myrdal, who takes a position against the Modernization Theory and the Dependency Theory, deems the roles of education, awareness, policy making, and the evolution of a social establishment—not just the role of the political elite—as being important in the course of development. In his view, development cannot be judged merely by taking per capita income into account

[21] Norman Jacobs, *The Sociology of Development: Iran as an Asian Case Study,* Praeger Special Studies in International Economics and Development (New York: Fredrick A. Praeger, 1966, 10.

[22] Ibid, 10.

[23] There is no consensus about the beginning of the modern era. Arnold Toynbee considers 1475 the beginning of the modern era and divides Western history after ancient times into four stages, as follows: the Dark Ages (675–1075), the Middle Ages (1075–1475), the Modern (1475–1875), and the Postmodern (1875-present). (See Arnold Toynbee, A *Study of History,* D.C. Somervell, ed. (New York: Oxford University Press, 1974). Bertrand Russell believed that Modern Times began in the 17th century, which coincides with modern intellectual developments and the emergence of Newtonian physics. Immanuel Wallerstein considers the 13th century to be the beginning of the modern era. See Immanuel Wallerstein, *The Capitalist World-Economy* (London: Cambridge University Press, 1979).

[24] Bertrand Russell divided the history of philosophy into three main eras. The first era began with the Greek philosophy six centuries before the birth of the Christ. The second era covered the period between the 11th and the 14th centuries, and the third era covered the period between the 17th century and the present era, a period marked by the emergence of the Enlightenment pioneered by Issac Newton (1642–1727) and Rene Descartes (1596–1650). See *The History of Western Philosophy* (New York: Simon and Schuster, 1945–1972), and David Ashley and David Michael Orenstein, *Sociological Theory: Classical Statements* (Boston: Allyn and Bacon, 1995).

[25] After the Constitutional Revolution in Iran (1905–1911) Heya't Mihan Parastan Iran dar Berlin (the Iranian Patriotic Group in Berlin), also known as the Komite-y Melliun-e Iran (Iranian National Committee), a group of migrant Iranian intellectuals with the support of the German government, published several periodical journals in Germany to research and analyze the question of backwardness and the path to development (modernity) in Iran. This group, which included several well-known writers and politicians such as Seyyed Hasan Taqizadeh, Jamal Zadeh, Kazemzadeh, Ebrahim Pourdavood, Moshfeq

Hamedani, Allameh Mohammad Qazvini, Haydar Amo Oqli, and Zeka al Mulk Foruqi, published five periodicals from 1916 to 1931. These journals included *Kaveh* (1916–1922), *Iranshahr* (1922–1927), *Farangestan* (1922–1927), *Elm va Honar* (1927–1928), and *Paykar* (1930–1931). The main message of the journals could be seen in the following solution given by Taqizadeh, the leading figure of the group. In order to achieve modernity, Taqizadeh suggested, "Iran must be westernized physically, mentally, and by its apparent and nature." Although this view was not shared by all members, Kazemzadeh, another key figure of the group, also advocated an "Iranian modernity" (1922). Four years later, Taqizadeh, after being harshly criticized by many, modified his view to a more moderate position. For a review of the contents or these journals and the mission of the group, see Berlaniha Jamsheed Behnam, *Berlinians: Iranian Intellectuals in Berlin* (Tehran: Farzan, 1379 (2000)), and Abbas Milani, *Tajadod VA Tajadod Setizi dar Iran (Modernity and Opposition to Modernity in Iran)* (Tehran, Atiyah, 1378 (1999)), 173–193.

[26] Ibn Khaldun, *The Muqaddimah: An Introduction to History*, trans. Franz Rosenthal, edited and abridged N. J. Dawood (Princeton, NJ: Princeton University Press, 1970), and Zabihala Safa, *The History of Rational Sciences in Iran until Early Mid-Fifth Century*, vol. 1, 4th ed. (Tehran: Amir Kabier Press, 2536 (Monarch Calendar)).

[27] Zabihala Safa, *The History of Rational Sciences in Iran until Early Mid-Fifth Century*, vol. 1, 4th ed. (Tehran: Amir Kabier Press, 2536 (Monarch Calendar)).

[28] Ibid, 140.

[29] Ghaferi refers to two sources: first, Ketab al-Fadeh va al-A'tebar by Abulatif Baghdadi (557–628 A. H.), and second, Ketab Mokhtasar al-Doval by Abul al-Faraj Ibn Abri (662-684 A. H.). These books are one century older than Ibn Khaldun's book, Al-Muqaddimah. (See "Burning Books by Arabs—Myth or Reality?" Rahavard, No. 53, Year 1379/2001, pp. 92–99).

[30] It should be noted here that Kasravi did not oppose religions in general; he was opposed to reactionary religions and religious superstitions as obstacles to rational thinking. See Ahmad Kasravi, *Thoughts, Attempted by Alizadeh* (Tehran: Toos, 1378). Also see *Some Articles, Germany, 1374, Shiism, Sufism and Bahaism* (Place of public: Tooka, 1992). To get a better understanding of Kasravi's views, also see Arvand Ebrahimian's comprehensive article entitled "Ahmad Kasravi: A Nationalist Defending a Unified Iran," trans. Asgar Azari, *Kankash*, nos. 2 and 3, 1367, pp. 177–217; and Arman Nehchiri, "Ahmad Kasravi: Aasy, ya Mosleh?" ("Kasravi: Rebel or Reformer?") *Negah-e Nou*, no. 26, Aabaan 1374 (1976), pp. 52–79.

[31] Sadeq Hedayat did not write any books about the role religion played in development, but his views and critiques of religious superstitions and the mental backwardness they cause are reflected in some of his works. For an analytical and comprehensive study of Hedayat's thought and works, see Navid Sadeq, "In Search of Cultural Renaissance," *Nazm-e Novin*, no. 8, 1987, pp. 133–177. Also see Abbas Milani, "Hedayat va Jahan Bieni Tragic" in ibid., pp. 220–232.

[32] Fereydoon Adamiyat, *The Thoughts of Mirza Aqa Khan, Navid*, 1992. To get a clearer picture of Aqa Khan Kermani's views, see the letters he sent to Mirza Malkom Khan Nazem-al-Doleh, found in Mirza Aqa Khan Kermani, *Letters From Exile*, contribution of Homa Nateq and Mohammad Firuz, Germany, Hafiz, 1365.

[33] Fereydoon Adamiyat, *The Thoughts of Mirza Fatali Akhund Zadeh* (Tehran Kharazmi, 1349). Mirza Aqa Khan Kermani and Mirza Fatali Akhund Zadeh believed Islam to be the obstacle to the modern development in societies. The traditional clergy considered modernity opposed to Islam and created serious obstacles against its influence in Iran. Unlike this group, freethinkers such as Zeinalabedin Maraqei and Abdul Rahim Talibov Tabrizi did not consider modernity to be in contradiction with Islam. See Ali Ashtiani, "The Sociology of Three Eras in the History of Intellectualism in Contemporary Iran," *Kankash*, nos. 2 and 3 (1367): 87–137. For more information about the life and views of Talibov, see Ehsan Tabari, op. cit. Talibov was so influenced by Rousseau that he wrote a Persian version of Emil (named Ahamd), Rousseau's discussion of education. For more information on the intellectual debates of Iranian intellectuals about Western civilization and the East's opposition to it, see M. Tiva, "The Confrontations of the East and the West and the Views of Iranian Intellectuals," *Kankash*, ibid: 11–47.

[34] Ali Mir Fetrus, "Some Considerations About the History of Iran, Islam, and "the True Islam," Canada/France: Farhang (First Edition, Germany) (1998); and Behruz Raffia, *Perspectives, An Interview With Ali Mir Fetrus*, 2nd ed., (Germany: Nashr-e Nima, 1997. Mir Fetrus also heavily emphasized the productive relations of a society, and thus created a contradictory view.

[35] Mirza Aqa Khan Kermani. "Three Letters," quoted from Fereydoon Adamiyat, *The Thoughts of Mirza Aqa Khan Kermani*, reprinted in Germany, December 1992, p. 193.

[36] Aramesh Doostdar, "Derakhsheshha-ye Tiereh" ("The Tarnished Glows"), 2nd ed., *Khavaran*, (Winter 1377) (1999) 120. Also the journal *Kaveh* (noted above) advocated a type of Protestantism in Islam. (See *Kaveh*, new period, no. 10 (Oct. 1921), 5–9).

[37] Mirza Fatali Akhund Zadeh, "Kamal al-Dole's Letters," in Fereydoon Adamiyat, *The Thoughts of Mirza Fatali Akhund Zadeh* (Tehran: Kharazmi, 1349) 109–110.

[38] Mohammad Reza Feshahi, *A Short Report on the Intellectual and Social Developments in the Iranian Feudalistic Society*, Tehran: Gutenberg, 1354.

[39] Abdul Rahmaan Ibn Khaldun, *The Muqaddimah: An Introduction to History*, trans. Franz Rosenthal, edited and abridged N.J. Dawood, Princeton, NJ: Princeton University Press, 1970.

[40] To read about the concept of group feeling, see Baqer Parham's short and concise article entitled "Ibn Khaldun and the Power Theory" *Borj*, no. 5 (1360), or Baqer Parham, *Thinking Together and Uniformly, Selected Articles* (Tehran: Aagaah, 1378) 217–231.

[41] Ibn Khaldun, op cit., 123.

[42] *The Historical Roots and the Development of the Tobacco Movement* (collection of historical research in the recent era), unknown author, no. 1, Tehran: no date, p. 12. Also see Norman Jacobs, ibid, Chapter 3.

[43] Works in the political literature of the leftist movement either accepted the views of the Communist parties of the Eastern block or the Dependency Theory postulated by the Marxists and Neo-Marxists of Latin America on the issue of the emergence of a dependent capitalist system in Iran. To examine the analytical study of the dependent capitalist system in Iran, see Bijan Jazani, *Capitalism and Revolution in Iran (1358), the History of the Past Three Decades in Iran,* and the selected articles of Bijan Jazani in "The 19th Bahman Theoretic Notes," 1353.

[44] V.I. Lenin, *Imperialism as the Latest Phase of Capitalism* (Peking: Foreign Languages, 1371). Also see Harry Magdoff, *Imperialism: From the Colonial Age to the Present* (New York: Monthly Review Press, 1978).

[45] Robert I. Rodes, ed.), *Imperialism, and Underdevelopment: A Reader* (New York: Monthly Review Press, 1970).

[46] To examine the revisions of different views of the Dependency and Neo-Dependency schools and the alternatives that have been offered in the 1980s, see Franz Schuurman, ibid.

[47] To become familiar with the notion of Globalization, see Samir Amin, *Capitalism in the Age of Globalization: The Management of Contemporary Society* (London: Zed Books, 1997/1998). Also see Kazem Alamdari, "Globalization: Development in the Global Community, From the Perspective of Post-Developmentalism, *Farhang-e Towse'a,* nos. 37 and 38 (1377), 62–67.

[48] To become familiar with the structural adjustment of the economy and the privatization of the economy and its results, see *Beyond Economic Liberalization in Africa: Structural Adjustment and Alternatives,* eds. Kidane Mengisteab and Ikubolajeh Logan (London: Zed Books, 1995). Also see Kazem Alamdari, "Ta'adiel-e Eqtesadi and Masa'le-y Towse'a" ("Structural Adjustment Program and the Question of Development"), *Iran-e Farda,* no. 26 (1374).

[49] Works published by leftist organizations in Iran in recent decades reflect this view. The remnants of these views either still divide the world into two camps—the imperialists and the oppressed classes (as in the works by the Tudeh Party)—or explain world developments by the Globalization Theory, which is a much more complex and involved system than dividing the world into two camps.

Unlike the traditional Marxists' views, globalization does not exclusively entail the globalization of economies. It also involves the globalization of cultures and, unlike the 19th-century model, the possibility of national development within the global system. (See Immanuel Wallerstein, op. cit., 1974). According to the views of traditional Marxists, globalization is not a new phenomenon and has existed since the 19th century, and even before that Marx repeatedly referred to it. Contrary to this claim, globalization is seen as a new phenomenon that belongs to the era of "information technology."

According to a common definition, globalization means globalizing the unique and particular qualities of cultures, not the sharing of universal values by different cultures. Examples would be the arrival of the Chinese culture and values in the United States, Iran, Saudi Arabia, and vice versa, or the Westernization of non-Western cultures. In the past, other societies adopted some of the values of the Western societies and made them universal, like the parliamentary system. See Robertson, *Globalization: Social Theory and Global Cultures* (London: Roland Sage Publications, 1996), 130).

Furthermore, globalization includes global management. Samir Amin believes that globalization needs a global management system to deal with crises. The International Monetary Fund and the World Bank are leading this management. No other political, social, ideological, or cultural framework worldwide, except the regulations of the free market, governs these relations. See Samir Amin, *Capitalism in the Age of Globalization: The Management of Contemporary Society* (London: Zed Books, 1997). Also see Immanuel Wallerstein, *Culture as the Ideological Battleground of the Modern World-System, in Global Culture: Nationalism, Globalization, and Modernity*, ed. Mike Featherstone (London: Sage, 1990), 31–55.

[50] Aramesh Doostdar, op. cit.

[51] Ali Reza Qoli, *Jamea' Shenasi-e Noukhbeh Koshi (The Sociology of Elite Killing): Qaem Maqam, Amir Kabier, and Mossadeq, Ney*, 8th ed. (Iran: 1377).

[52] This is based on the Weberian model of the most general components of social organization. See Jonathan H. Turner et al., *The Emergence of Sociological Theory*, 4th ed. (New York: Wadsworth Publishing Company, 1998).

[53] Turner et al., op. cit., 170.

[54] For Max Weber's view of the role of religion in modern civilization in the West, see M. Weber, *The Protestant Ethic and the Spirit of Capitalism* (Los Angels: Roxbury Publishing Company, 1995).

[55] Fereydoon Adamiyat, *The History of Thought From the Sumerians to the Greeks and Romans* (Tehran: Roshangaran, 1374).

[56] Phillip Hitti states that some of the Arab civilizations before Islam, such as the civilizations of Palmer and Nabataean—the highest point of the desert-dwelling Arabs' civilization—were an interesting combination of the civilizations of the Sumerians, the Greeks, and the Iranians. For more information, see Phillip Hitti, *The History of the Arabs*, op. cit., 1970, Chapter 6. These Arab nations were able to benefit from the advantages of more advanced civilizations of their era because they were engaged in trade with them and had the opportunity to gain wealth and access to scientific and literary accomplishments. Later, translators who were well-known in the Arab world, such as Ibn Wahshiyah (who had some publications of his own, as well), emerged from the Nabataean nation. See Zabihollah Safa, *The History of Rational Sciences in the Islamic Civilization* (Tehran: Amir Kabier, 2536), 86-

87. Also see Ibn Wahshiya's book on agriculture entitled *al-Fallahih al-Nabataean* (need publication data), and Philip K. Hitti, op. cit., 1970.
[57] Sadeq Zibakalam, *How We Became We: Finding the Roots of Underdevelopment in Iran*, 4th ed., (Tehran: Rozaneh, 1377).
[58] The reform movement in the Ottoman Empire in late 19th century led by young officers heavily influenced these reformist intellectuals.
[59] Abdulrahim Talibov Tabrizi, *Ketab Ahmad: Constitutional Literature* (Tehran: Shabgir, 2536 (1977)).
[60] Hamid Algar, *Mirza Malkom Khan* (Berkeley, CA: University of California Press, 1973).
[61] To examine this point more comprehensively, see Jalil Dehqani, "Behavior: The Main Factor in Development," *The Social Sciences Magazine*, 2, no. 3 (Winter 1376): 40–51.
[62] It is necessary to note that these theories at best show the difference between advanced and underdeveloped societies in the present era, while Iran's underdevelopment is rooted in the past history of the country. Furthermore, the structural differences between the East and the West cannot be explained based on individual differences. These differences are the product of factors that are outside human control.
[63] David C. McClelland, *The Achieving Society* (New York: Free Press, 1961).
[64] Everett Hagen. *On the Theory of Social Change* (Homewood, IL: Dorsey Press, 1962).
[65] Of course the theorists who have expressed their views in this regard are not all mentioned here. For a more comprehensive description of modernization, see the works of other researchers such as T. Parsons, Daniel Lerner, and Clark Kerr, and to analyze a practical example of these works, view the "White Revolution" project in the period between 1341–1350 in Iran. Also, with regard to the White Revolution in Iran see Kazem Alamdari, *The Socioeconomic Effects of the Land Reform Program in Iran*, Ph. D. Dissertation, University of Illinois, Champaign-Urbana, 1982.
[66] Ali Reza Qoli, op. cit.
[67] A. Inkeles and D.H. Smith, *Becoming Modern* (Cambridge, MA: Harvard University Press, 1976). Also see Alex Inkeles, "A Model of the Modern, Theoretical and Methodological Issues," in *Comparative Modernization*, Cyril E. Black, ed. (New York: Free Press, (need date)), 320–348.
[68] Robert Bellah, *Habits of Heart* (Berkeley, CA: University of California Press, 1968). Also see R. Bella, *Religion and Progress in Modern Asia* (New York: Free Press, 1965).
[69] Abraham Maslow, "Psychological Data and Value Theory," in *New Knowledge in Human Values*, Abraham Maslow, ed. (New York: Harper & Row, 1959) 119–136.
[70] Ronald Robertson, op. cit., 85.
[71] Maslow, op cit.
[72] Nizam al-Mulk (D. 1092) was the Prime Minister of Malik Shah and Sultan Sanjar of the Seljuq dynasty. He wrote the *Siyasatnameh*, the book of

government and politics, the legal system and court procedures, and the restriction of arbitrary rule.

[73] Habibollah Paymaan, *About Iranian Despotism, Towse'a*, contribution of Javad Mousavi Khuzestani, no. 10, 1374.

[74] Ahmad Ashraf, *The Historical Obstacles to the Growth of Capitalism in Iran in the Qajar Era*, (Tehran: Payam (Zamineh Publications), 1359).

[75] Norman Jacobs, op. cit., 416.

[76] Ibid, 15–16.

[77] J. Turner et al. have written: "According to Weber, Confucianism was a rational religion concerned with events in this world but with a peculiarly individualistic emphasis." (*The Emergence of Sociological Theory*, 4th ed. (New York: Wadsworth Publishing Company, 1998), 169). Weber wrote: "None of three mass religions of Asia, however, provided the motives or orientations for a rationalized ethical patterning of the creaturely world in accordance with divine commandments." (*The Sociology of Religion*, trans. Ephraim Fischoff (Boston: Bacon Press, 1964), 269).

[78] J.E. Goldthorpe, *The Sociology of Post-Colonial Societies: Economic Disparity, Cultural Diversity, and Development* (New York: Cambridge University Press, 1996), 179.

[79] Weber believed that these religions evolved no "capitalist spirit" similar to ascetic Protestantism. op. cit., 269.

[80] J. Turner et al., op. cit., 174.

[81] Norman Jacobs, op. cit., 1966 & 1971.

[82] Immanuel Wallerstein, *The Capitalist World Economy* (New York: Cambridge University Press, 1979).

[83] Piotr Sztompka states: "the idea of process helps to bridge both the traditional oppositions, of static and dynamic, as well as of structure and action." (*The Sociology of Social Change* (Oxford, UK: Blackwell, 1993) 208).

[84] Philip Abrams, *Historical Sociology* (Ithaca, NY: Cornell University Press, 1982), cited in Piotr Sztompka, ibid., 208.

[85] Norman Jacobs, op. cit., 1966.

[86] Karl Marx, *The Capital*, vol. 1, in Bryan S. Turner, *Religion and Social Theory*, 2nd ed., (London: Sage Publications, 1997).

[87] Adam Smith, *An Inquiry into the Nature and the Cause of the Wealth of Nations*, abridged, with commentary and notes by Laurence Dickey (Cambridge: 1993).

[88] Karl Marx, *The Capital*, vol. 1, chapters, 5, 10, 14, and 16 (New York: International Publishers, 1967).

[89] Quoting Sir William Petty (1623-1687), English economist and statistician, about the role of nature and labor in the production of value, Marx stated that "labor is its father and the earth its mother." (See *The Capital*, vol. 1, 1867, 42). Marx called Petty the founder of the New Economic Science, (p. 42f).

[90] George Lucas, *Introduction to the Ontology of the Social Object* (Warsaw: PWN (Polish Scientific Publisher), 1982-4) in Piotr Sztompka, op. cit.

[91] Cited in Joel Mokyr in *The Lever of Riches: Technological Creativity and Economic Progress* (New York: Oxford University Press, 1990) 155.

[92] Nikki Keddie, "Material Culture, Technology, and Geography: Toward a Holistic Comparative Study of Middle East," in *Comparative Muslim Societies and State in a World Civilization*, Juan Cole, ed. (Ann Arbor, MI: University of Michigan Press, 1992) 31–62.

[93] See Randall Collins, op. cit., f.p. 930.

[94] Ibid.

[95] Marvin Harris, op. cit., 1970, 70.

[96] Ibid.

[97] Jared Diamond, *Guns, Germs, and Steel: The Facts of Human Societies* (New York: W.W. Norton and Company, 1997/1999). Diamond refers to four sets of factors, which objectively constitute environmental differences. These factors include wild plant and animal species, factors affecting the rates of diffusion and migration, factors that affect diffusion within and between continents, and the size of the populations in different areas. Areas with larger populations have more potential for innovations (pp. 405–409).

[98] See G. Plekhanov, *Fundamental Problems of Marxism* (New York: New World, 1975), 50.

[99] G. Plekhanov, *The Evolution of the Monistic Theory of History*, trans. Jalal Alavinia and Saa'dollah Alizadeh, no publisher, no publication date.

[100] Fredrick Ratzel, *Anthrogeographic* (Stuttgart, 1882) 92. Cited in George V. Plekhanov, *Fundamental Problems of Marxism*, ibid, 50.

[101] Plekhanov, G. Op cit., 1975 (English text), and Karl Marx, Capital, vol. 1, Ibid.

[102] Ibid., 1975 (English Text).

[103] Daniel Chirot, op. cit., 11-12.

[104] Parviz Piran, "The Three Levels of Analyzing an Event," in *New Choice: Sociological Analysis of the Events of the Khordad the Second, Abdolali Rezaie/Abbas Abdi* (Tehran: Tarh-e-no, 1377), 41–42.

[105] Some people, such as Andre Gunder Frank and Immanuel Wallerstein, believe that the phenomenon of underdevelopment in the last four centuries in the Third World countries is an irrefutable consequence of development in Western societies. Wallerstein believes that there is but one international economic system with an international division of labor in the world market. He calls this system the international division of economy. Underdeveloped or marginal countries are producers of the raw materials needed by this system, in the same way that semi-marginal countries that enjoy partial growth are agents that mediate between the central and the marginal countries. Here, I refrain from the explanation of these views and the numerous criticisms they have faced. For more information, see Immanuel Wallerstein, *The Modern World System: Capitalism, Agriculture, and the Origins of the European World-Economy in the Sixteenth Century* (New York: Academic Press, 1994), and Andre Gunder Frank, *The Myth of Feudalism in Capitalism and Underdevelopment in Latin America* (New York: Monthly Review Press,

1967), and *Sociology of Development and Underdevelopment of Sociology, or Underdevelopment or Revolution* (New York: MRP, 1969).

[106] I referred to some aspects of the ethno-centric mentality of Iranians in this Chapter.

[107] "Mawali, sing. Mawla, a non-Arab embracing Islam and affiliating himself with an Arabian tribe. His ill-defined rank placed him below the Muslim Arabians." (Philip Hitti, *The History of the Arabs*, 10th ed. (New York: St. Martin's Press, 1970), 172).

[108] A.H. Zarrinkub, *History of Persia in the Islamic Period (Early Islamic Centuries)* (Tehran: Kharazmi, 1990).

[109] Ibid., 379.

[110] Ibid.

[111] This is a dominant view among fanatic monarchists. For a specific source, see Shoja'adin Shafa, Tavalodi Digar, Nashre Farzad. 1999.

[112] Friedrich Engels, "The Peasant War in Germany" cited in Zeitlin, op. cit.

[113] Max Weber, *Religion in India*, op. cit.

[114] David Ashley and David M. Orenstein, *The Sociological Theory: Classical Statements* (Boston: Allyn and Bacon, 1995) 266.

[115] Jami, (The National Liberation Movement of Iran), no author, *The Past is the Leading Light for the Future*, 1354. For a detailed history of the confiscation of properties in Iran by the rulers, see *Vaqay'a al Etefaqiyeh*, Saeedi Sirjani, ed. (Tehran: 1361 (1983)).

[116] [115] Bernard Lewis, "The Revolt of Islam: When the Conflict With the West Began, and How It Could End," *The New Yorker*, 5 January 2002, 4.

[117] Ibid.

[118] For instance, see Parviz Piran, "Se Sat-h-e Tahlil-e Vaqa 'ah" in *Abdolali Rezaie/Abbas Abdi, Intekhab-e Nou (New Choice: Sociological Analysis of the Event of Khordad the Second)* (Tehran: Tarh-e-no, 1998), 17–48. Also see David Hall, American comparative philosopher (David Hall, "Modern China and the Postmodern West" in *Culture and Modernity: East-West Philosophic Perspectives*, Eliot Deutsch, ed. (Honolulu, HI: University of Hawaii, 1991); reprinted in Lawrence Cahoone, ibid., 698–710. Hall attempts in this essay to show that pre-modern Chinese philosophy (both Taoism and Confucianism) contain resources that answer some of the problems represented by the debates over modernity and post-modernism.

[119] For example, see Mohammad Lahori Iqbal, *The Reconstruction of Religious Thought in Islam* (Lahore, by Muhammad Ashraf, 1965).

[120] Karl Marx and Friedrich Engels, *The Communist Manifesto* (London: ElecBook, 1998), 15.

[121] Among many other issues, Milani examines several Iranian classic histo-literature books, including *Tahrikh-e Bayhaqi, Tazkarat al Olia, Rostam al Tavarikh* and *Chahar Maqaleh Arozi* in search of signs of modernity in Iran during the Middle Ages. Here, I have no intention of reviewing the entire book but merely wish to point out a typical misunderstanding of the concept of modernity and the recent attempts of intellectuals who wish not only to invent

Iranian or Islamic modernity but also to change its origin as an Eastern phenomenon. Modernity is a universal and Western occurrence. There is no clear base for Iranian or Islamic modernity, democracy, or capitalism. Gema Martin Munoz writes about particular democracy in Muslim societies. He states: "As Khoury claims, 'democracy is a process that can be used to translate cultural values into political structures, systems, and goals. The Western debate about Arab democratization has largely failed to admit this. Instead, it has designated democracy as a criterion, measure, and goal of Arab political culture, on the simplistic and presumptuous assumption that democracy should be a defining Arab value because it is the Western defining value." (*Islam, Modernization, and the West* (New York: I.B. Tauris Publishers, 1999), 20). If democracy can be reduced to voting, then there is only one democracy that is universal.

[122] Modernity can be distinct from modernism and modernization. For this study, I disregard the differences and, like Milani, use "modernity" as a general concept representing both subjective and objective characteristics of modern times.

[123] Abbas Milani, op. cit., 1378, 14.

[124] Ibid., 350.

Chahar Maqaleh Aruzi (*Four Essays of Aruzi*) was published in 1156/57 A.D., This book is available in English, translated by Edward Brown.

[126] Ibid. See the last chapter in *Modernism and Political Thought in Chahar Maqaleh Aruzi*, pp. 350–370.

[127] Steven Best and Douglas Kellner, *Postmodern Theory: Critical Interrogations* (New York: The Guilford Press, 1991), 3.

[128] Lawrence Cahoone, ed., *From Modernism to Postmodernism: An Anthology* (Cambridge, UK: Blackwell, 1996).

[129] We who are the products of contemporary Western civilization, under modernity and post-modernity, learn to analyze and criticize Euro-centrism. This knowledge tells us that modern phenomena, which developing societies eagerly wish to achieve, were born and developed in the West. Thus, the search for the seeds of modernity in the East is neither necessary nor helpful in resolving the current underdevelopment question in developing societies. We should avoid ethnocentrism and embrace universalism.

[130] Cahoone adds, "Many historical societies have had relatively free markets, have respected individuality, engaged in rational planning and rational inquiry, regarded at least part of social life as largely secular or profane, and so on. As a package, the modern Western combination of science, technology, industry, free market, liberal democracy, etc., certainly is unique in human history, but whether each of the elements separately considered is unique is less clear." (Ibid., p. 11).

[131] Ibid., 370.

[132] The Ottoman and the French governments in Italy and the Eastern European and Mediterranean countries confronted the Hapsburgs' military forces and stopped their expansionist attempts (see Ira Lapidus, ibid.)

[133] Immanuel Wallerstein, op. cit., 58.

[134] Daniel Chirot, ibid., 66.

[135] In a way, one can claim that it was Marx who discovered that capitalism was a special phase of human history and that, unlike the previous phases, its main force was production in excess of consumption. Yet, many contemporary economists consider Marx's theory as well as the theories of classical economists such as Adam Smith and David Ricardo irrelevant to the complexity of the present era's economic problems. For example, see J.A. Shumpeter, *Imperialism and Social Classes* (New York: Kelly, 1951). There are those, such as Schumpeter, who acknowledge Marx's contribution as a sociologist-historian-philosopher but who contend that his economic theories are wrong." (Howard Selsam et al, eds., *Dynamics of Social Change: A Reader in Marxist Social Science* (New York: International Publishers, 1975), 260.

[136] Milovan Djilas, *The New Class: An Analysis of the Communist System* (New York: Fredrich A. Praeger, 1957).

[137] Pierre Bourdieu, *In Other Words: Essays Towards a Reflective Sociology* (Cambridge: Polity Press, 1990).

[138] Robert Michels, *Political Parties* (New York: Dover Publications, 1959).

[139] K. A. Wittfogel, *Oriental Despotism: A Comparative Study of Power,* New Haven, CT: Yale University Press, 1957.

[140] For details about the Comintern and the international communist activities after the Russian Revolution of 1917, see R.A. Ulyanovsky (ed.), *The Comintern and the East* (Moscow: Progress Publishers, 1979).

[141] Karl Wittfogel, op. cit.

[142] Stephen P. Donn, *The Collapse and the Emergence of the Asian Mode of Production*

[143] Karl Wittfogel, op. cit.

[144] Ibid.

[145] Ibid.

[146] Ibid.

[147] Wittfogel also worked in the Research Institute of Frankfurt, known as the Frankfurt School, which advocates critical perspectives. He later emigrated to the United States.

Chapter 2
The Land Tenure System in Iran
A Historical Review

The Main Features of Feudalism

Here, the intention is not to present a detailed description of feudalism. Such a description is not needed. We are only concerned with the unique features of feudalism, because these features contribute to the understanding of the differences between feudalism and land ownership in Iran.

By feudalism we mean the special system of land ownership, legal relations, and political establishments that were dominant in Western countries from the Middle Ages to the fourteenth century. This system protected the landowning aristocrats' privileges in Europe, including their headstrong political power, which they used against peasants.

The classic form of feudalism existed in the West and in the territories that the migrating tribes were able to seize from the Roman Empire. In the territories dominated by the Byzantine Empire and the Eastern Roman Empire, where the centralized power of the empire lasted, feudalism did not emerge in its classic European form. The difference between development in Western and Eastern Europe has been the result of this duality, among other factors. As Max Weber wrote, "Not every kind of 'feudalism' involves the fief in the Western sense."[1] Generally, we can refer to two types of feudalism—one based on fiefs and the other based on benefices. All other types have a patrimonial character.[2] The fief is Western and the others are Eastern.

The differences among these types mainly lie in the powers and rights of exercising authority. A fief (land) is granted for specific services, primarily military, and it is personal for the lifetime of the lord and the recipient of the fief, his vassal. Vassals form a class of "knights." This contract is important because it provides personal solidarity and a system of royalty, which form the basis for a political system. The hierarchy of social rank (not political) corresponds to the hierarchy of the fief. Those who do not hold fiefs, such as serfs and slaves, remain under the direct authority of the lords.[3]

A benefice, unlike a fief, is granted according to the income the holders provide, not on a personal basis and a system of royalty. It is a type of tax farming or leasing of taxes. "It is rather a matter of fiscal considerations in the context of a system of financing which is otherwise patrimonial, often sultanistic."[4] This type of arrangement led to the development of landlordism rather than feudalism. If there is any military service involved in such a system, it is to supply the patrimonial army. This is the type of system that was typical of the Middle East, Turkey, India, and the Mongols.

The main features of European feudalism between the tenth and the thirteenth centuries, and the differences between it and the feudalism in Iran, can be summarized as follows.

First, in Europe the feudal lords lacked a centralized, powerful government establishment. The government power of big landowners was eliminated following the collapse of the Roman Empire, and the ruling barbaric governments and the Roman Empire's successors were unable to reconstruct the centralized power effectively. In other words, a power that was able to enact general laws for tax collection, social affairs, and the formation of a unified army to secure order and peace and suppress rebellion never came into existence. Instead of such official political and military power, the Christian Church establishment became powerful. But the power of the church was more internal than external, and the church could, at best, control smaller groups in different regions. The church, the feudal lords, and the kings were separate establishments that sometimes cooperated with each other but that were also in competition and were often in conflict with each other. Small, local governments formed under the dominance of feudal landowners became the most prevalent system. The feudal lords ruled their regions, kept order, solved problems, and decreed and executed laws.[5] In sum, the general power was the personal possessions of these feudal lords.

Second, the European feudal landowners and their subordinates were related to military leaders and professional fighters. These military elites laid the foundation for the national aristocracy of European countries and later employed military groups to defend their domains of power. Fief or feud means land that is a source of income. The feudal lord, in return for military support, donated this land to his functionary.[6] The exchange of a source of income and other privileges such as the donation of a palace as a feud could be transferred by inheritance from one generation to another or bought and sold between the owners of the fief. Naturally, owners of larger territories were in a better position to employ the services of the military servicemen, which meant that smaller feudal lords were forced to share the military services of a functionary among themselves. The relationship between a feudal lord and the owner of a fief was voluntary, deliberate, and impersonal. Unlike in the East, kinship, family, and tribal relations did not govern this relationship. In other words, the European feudal system was a relatively stable form of relations that involved the exchange of service for a source of income. Contrary to the system of land ownership in Iran, for example, people were generally not considered the king's farmers and were not forced to participate in wars. The relationship between the feudal lords and their functionaries was very well-defined and could be terminated if one of the parties violated the terms of their agreement.[7]

Third, the economic system in European feudalism was decentralized, like its political system. The central government of the era of the Roman Empire lost power following the demise of the empire. In its place, local relations came into existence. The economy of this system was based on the principles of self-sufficiency and production for consumption. Relations with the outside and remote areas were only formed to facilitate buying luxury goods. This is why developed monetary relations did not come into existence in these regions. The main source of income for the feudal lords was agricultural land and the farmers. Thus, political power also emanated from the amount of agricultural land owned by feudal lords, and it determined the amount of military power that could be made available to them. The feudal lords had to donate sources of income, such as land, in return for support by the military provided through the functionaries. Sometimes, a few feudal lords shared the military services of a single functionary. So, land determined power, and land was vastly distributed among the feudal lords. The distribution of military, political, and social power among the functionaries and the feudal lords somehow ensured the balance of power. Perhaps the main reason that the functionaries, or the professional fighters, could not dominate the landowners and gain the control of the land was the existence of this balance of power on the one hand, and the multiplicity of land and military functionaries on the other. Therefore, as Peter Duss stated, it would be a mistake to equate feudalism with the system of land ownership.[8]

In the system of landlordism in Iran, military benefice was only one form of exchange among the legal, personal, endowed, and donated exchanges. In the land ownership system of Iran, the king and his associates officially owned the major part of the land. These lands were called *Khaleseh*. Thus, the king could donate a piece of land or an entire region to whomever he wished in exchange for tax returns. Land was considered the king's gift. Of course, a feudal lord in the West could also donate part of his land, but there was significant difference between the land donated by a landowner and a gift from a king who considered himself the owner of all the land and the people who worked on them.

It should be noted that European feudalism was not the same everywhere, and different relations between a feudal lord and his functionary existed in different regions.[9] It seems that such a situation, in which a centralized political and military power did not exist and land ownership determined the economic system, provided suitable ground for the emergence of a new merchant class whose interests were not compatible with the interests of the feudal lords unlike the merchants in Iran. In Iran, trade was also managed by city-dwelling landowners.

It is clear then that feudalism in Europe was the result of a prolonged period of development, from the collapse of the Roman Empire to the French Revolution. However, my goal here is to show the differences between feudalism and the system of land ownership in Iran, not to present the characteristics of this prolonged process. Some of the special features of feudalism are listed below.

1. In the feudal system, the power of the king depended upon the power of the feudal lords. "The king had to share his power with the feudal aristocracy..."[10]

2. Politically, the dictatorship of feudal lords was very distinct from the dictatorship found in the East. In the dictatorship of the feudal lords, only one class existed, and the centralized government establishment was not despotic.

3. The relationship between the king and his farmers was different in the feudal system. Peasants were mainly subordinates of their feudal lords, not the king, and they "obeyed" the king through the relationship of their masters with the king. In other words, if a feudal lord did not support the king—unlike the Asian mode of

production in which the king considered all people his farmers—
the king had no control over him.

4. The warriors, who were subordinates of the feudal lord, provided
   the military power of the king. The army, unlike in the East, did
   not belong to the king but was a possession of the feudal lords.
5. In Europe, unlike Iran, specific legal relations existed between
   feudalists and the central government on one hand, and feudalists
   and peasants on the other.
6. Also, the Catholic Church was a parallel power to and a competitor
   of feudalism and the central government of the monarch. The
   existence of multiple powers prevented the growth of a centralized,
   absolute power, as in the East. "All the armed force was on the
   side of the kings, and yet the Church was victorious. The Church
   won, partly because it had almost the monopoly of education,
   partly because the kings were perpetually at war with each other,
   but mainly because, with very few exceptions, rulers and people
   alike profoundly believed that the Church possessed the power of
   the keys."[11]
7. Unlike Iranian landowners who lived in cities, feudalists in Europe
   would reside in their own territories.
8. In the West, the bourgeoisie, relying on the conflict between the
   king and the feudal lords, and enjoying the direct support of the
   king against the feudal lords, brought about the disintegration of
   the feudal regime. Of course, initially this made the power of the
   king absolute. But as the bourgeois class gained more power and
   the feudal lords became weaker, the king's power gradually fell
   under the control of this new capitalist class. The king resorted to
   feudal lords again, for example in England, France, and Spain in
   the fifteenth century. But in the end, the bourgeois class became
   strong enough to eliminate both the dictator king and the feudal
   lords.[12]

Three Views

The current differences between the Middle East and the West are
based on the land tenure systems in the past. As stated in the first
chapter, what made contemporary Western civilization a possibility
was the capitalist mode of production, which came about as the result
of feudalist relations in Europe. What made feudalism a possibility was
the private ownership of land. All of these elements were absent in
Iran.

The land tenure system in Iran has been viewed as (1) feudalism, (2) semi-feudalism (Eastern feudalism) or a system based on benefice, and (3) an Asiatic mode of production that is patrimonial in character. This chapter demonstrates the characteristics of the centralized Iranian land tenure system, which differs from European feudalism. Despite the shift of power among Persian, Arab, and Turk rulers, the Iranian land tenure system remained almost unchanged throughout history until the twentieth century. Only in the period of Seljuk dynasty did a system of benefice become dominant. This chapter discusses how and why Iranian land tenure, unlike feudalism in Europe, contained no seeds of capitalism. It also examines the sources of the persistency of the land tenure system in Iran. The following chapter (Chapter 3) will focus on the Asiatic mode of production and partrimonialism, which resembles the Iranian political and economic structure.

In the analysis of the unique features of the land tenure system in Iran, the differences between the systems of landowning in Iran and in the West should be taken into consideration. In the Iranian case, several factors are important. The first is the shortage of water, the second is the role of the village, and the third is the role of tribal groups. All of these factors contributed to preventing a bourgeois class from developing in Iran, and they are discussed in later chapters.

The Importance of Starting with the Land System

In determining the causes of development in the West and how Europe surpassed the East after the seventeenth and the eighteenth centuries, it is hard to avoid the conclusion that what constituted the moving force behind contemporary Western civilization was capitalist relations. These relations emerged in the West but not in the East. To understand why this happened, we have to first understand the legal and economic system and the subsistence mode that existed in the West and the East, respectively, before the emergence of capitalism, and we need to find the roots of the transformation of the European system. This will lead us to the feudal mode of production as a factor that instigated the transformation to capitalism. In the East, capitalism has either not existed at all or it has only partially existed in the form of Eastern commercial relations. Assuming that capitalism was the origin of contemporary Western civilization and that feudalism, as a mode of production, was the basis for capitalist relations, we can claim that the failure of capitalism to develop in the East was the result of obstacles to such a production system that were related to the way Eastern societies were legally, economically and politically governed. This government system, the obstacles to capitalism contained in it, and the reasons for the existence of these obstacles should all be clearly understood. Because Iran is the focus of the present study, our scope will be limited to Iran. When necessary, differences from and similarities to other Eastern societies will be discussed.

Land Relations in Iran: Feudalism or the Asian Mode of Production?

The importance of this issue is that it relates to the reason capitalism did not appear in Iran. Many, perhaps half, of the major theories about this consider the underdevelopment of Iran to be a consequence of the special characteristics of landowning and the relationship between landowners and peasants. Therefore, two issues have to be clarified. One is the relationship between development and land relations, and the other is the nature of landowner-peasant relations in Iran.

The assumption here is that there is a direct relationship between contemporary development in the West and feudalism. The birth of capitalism in Europe was the result of feudalism, a decentralized relationship between feudal and his vassals. In Iran, on the other hand, such a relationship did not exist; instead, the central government controlled the land system, which was a more patriarchal and Asiatic mode of production. This system will be explained in detail in a later chapter.

The Unique Features of the Land Tenure System in Iran

The land tenure system in Iran, although persistent, has not been a uniform phenomenon. During the course of history, forms of ownership fluctuated with changes in circumstances and governments.[13] Before the land reform of 1962, five land ownership modes were found in Iran: private landed estates (*melk-e arbabi*), state lands and public domain (*Khaleseh*), crown lands (*amlak-e saltanati*), endowment lands (*vaqf*, pl., *ouqaf*), and peasant proprietorships (*khurdeh maliki*). With the exception of peasant proprietorships, these forms of land ownership were largely dominated by two types of socioeconomic relations— *muzara'eh*[14] (a share-cropping contract between two parties) and tenancy. At the beginning of Iran's history and during the Achaemenian (550-334 B. C.E.), Parthian (247 B. C. E. -224 C. E.), and Sasanian dynasties (224 C. E. –642 C. E.), possession by the king was the predominant form of land ownership, and during the most recent era, possession by private landed estates has been the main form of land ownership. Unlike feudalism, all forms of land ownership in Iran except peasant proprietorships involved absentee landowners, or khans. Ownership by absentee landowners was the most prevalent form of land ownership (56 percent) for agricultural land.[15] This was one of the most important differences between Western feudalism and the mode of landowning in Iran. The evolutionary process of landowning in Iran, from land owned by the kings (crown lands) to land possessed by private landed estates (melk-e arbabi), took place through mechanisms employed by the state. The government transferred the state-owned land or the king's donated land to individuals. This turning point took place during the era of the domination of the Seljuq dynasty over Iran in the twelfth century. The latest dominant form of ownership in Iran more closely resembles European feudalism and the first dominant form, Crown lands (amlak-e saltanati), was closer to the Asian mode of production. However, in none of these forms did feudal-vassal relations exist.

Owners of the largest plots of land in Iran often lived in the cities, away from rural areas.[16] The absentee landlords held the most power in Iran, except for the tribes. This constituted another difference between Western feudalism, in which the feudal lords lived in their own forts, and Iran. Until the land reform in 1962, only two groups owned 69 percent of the agricultural land: the tribes (owning 13 percent) and the khans (owning 56 percent). In the ancient era, the major form of ownership was that of kings. Before the era of Reza Shah Pahlavi's reign (1921–41), there was no difference between the state-owned land and the land owned by the kings. In fact, the king or the caliph could have control over the land in its entirety. Local rulers were usually given lands in exchange for a fixed amount of tax. These lands were rented out to peasants or assigned to peasants as shareholders. To clarify the features of the landowning system in Iran, its development, and its difference from the European feudalism, a historical review of land relations seems necessary. First, let's review the environmental difference.

Shortage of Water—The Main Obstacle

The quality and quantity of production, the rate of population growth in a region, the methods of irrigation, the types of plantations, and the organization of the peasant population (buneh) all depend on the amount of water available in any particular area.[17] Ehsan Tabari writes on the issue of the shortage of water and its inevitable consequences in Iran:

> The crucial issue in Iran is the issue of water. Iran is located in a vast area that faces the water shortage problem. This area extends from the African Sahara to the deserts in China. To maintain agriculture, artificial irrigation networks have to be constructed, a task that poor peasants or even the feudal lords or merchants cannot manage on their own. A large group of disciplined workers is needed to build dams, vesicas, and subterranean canals and dig canals and gutters. The reason why the ancient irrigation techniques have been so advanced in Iran is the existence of this pressing need. Evidence of numerous incidents of direct interference by the Achaemenian, Parthian, and Sasanian governments in constructing artificial irrigation systems, has been found. The tradition of dam construction was pursued by Iranian kings during the period after the arrival of Islam.[18]

The emergence and the development of innovative irrigation systems such as the subterranean canals in ancient Iran and the holiness of water in the Iranian culture, in Zoroastrianism, and in Islam are in themselves indications of the shortage of water in this country. Charles Issawi writes that before the domination of the Arabs, the techniques of construction of the subterranean canals reached other regions ruled by Iranians. During the Islamic era, these techniques were exported to Africa as well and were called "Fugaras."[19] This reality confirms the problem of water shortage in the region, the Iranian civilization's advanced status, and the fact that Islam transferred these advanced techniques to other regions.

The control of water resources and its allocation by the government establishment was the main obstacle to the emergence of private ownership in Iran. As Heredot indicates, the shah owned the rivers and would assign an officer to monitor the allocated water used by peasants. Peasants were heavily taxed for the usage of the water.[20] This is one of the main differences that existed between the civilizations of Greece and Rome and that of Iran. Private ownership of the land in Greece was a decisive factor in determining the form of government. Due to the shortage of water and the low level of production (compared with the needed level), the monopolistic control that the government establishment exerted over products, and the consumption of products by the ruling class and the king, independent trade and urban trade centers were not formed.

The Period Before Islam: Undivided Land

Before the arrival of Islam, four Iranian dynasties ruled in Iran: the Medes, the Achaemenians, the Parthians, and finally the Sasanian. For a short period, Iran was ruled by a non-Iranian government, that of the Seleucids (323- 141 B.C. E.), which was established by Alexander's generals. After the arrival of Islam, with a few exceptions (such as the Mongols 1220–1501) either the caliphates (642–820), Iranian Turk and non-Turk sultans under the caliphates (820–1258), or independent tribal Iranian Turks (1501–1920) ruled Iran for a period of fourteen centuries. The land tenure system during this period, from ancient to present times, will be examined.

Before the migration of the Medes to the Iranian plateau in the first millennium, native tribes lived in this area. Accurate information on the ethnic and family origins of these indigenous tribes is not available.[21] However, some sources refer to "the frontier districts inhabited by the hill-people with whom the Sumero-Semitic population of the plain was continually in contact." [22] These native tribes were the *Elam, the Kassitess, the Lullubi,* and the *Guti.*[23] However, the details about, and differences between the dynasties that ruled in Iran for thirteen centuries (624 B.C.–624 A.D.) have little bearing on the objectives of this book. What needs to be emphasized here is the nature of the relations with regard to production, or the land tenure system. Comparing these relations with those found in Greece and Rome reveals the fact that land relations have yielded different outcomes in the civilizations of the East and the West.

The Medes and Persians. These two Aryan tribal groups migrated to the Iranian plateau from central Asian between 1500–800 B.C. They were among the first Aryan people to succeed in forming a unified and centralized government in the region. According to Herodotus, the Aryan nations consisted of six tribes,[24] led a simple life as shepherds, and arrived on the Iranian plain as migrating tribes. In the third millennium B.C., taming wild animals, especially horses, was considered a major development in the lives of these people. This development guaranteed their dominance over the native inhabitants of the Iranian plateau as well as the Parsians and Assyrians.[25]

Once the Aryan tribes of this period were settled in Iran, the pastoral mode of production extended to agriculture. Before engaging in agriculture, the Medes trained other animals such as cows, sheep, goats, and shepherd dogs, in addition to horses.[26] Raising horses and domesticating dogs kept these groups in a pastoral society that remained nomadic, while raising cattle directed them toward horticultural society and agricultural life. Because "they no longer had to abandon an area as the food supply gave out, these groups developed permanent settlements."[27] It was these people who founded the first civilization and empire territories on one of the most fertile land of its time in the world, Mesopotamia.

Change in climate and the consequent shortage of water became one of the most serious problems in the agriculture of the vast territory of Iran. Aside from creating problems for agriculture and production, this reality had self-evident effects on social relations, which will be discussed later. Both the form of land ownership (undivided land) and the centralization of power during the period of the Mede dynasty were natural results of the shortage of water.

Achaemenian Dynasty (550–334 B.C.). After the collapse of the Medes dynasty, the Achaemenians ruled in Iran. In this period, which lasted about three centuries, agriculture constituted the dominant mode of production. Making use of the production opportunities, including the digging of subterranean canals (*qanat*), the Achaemenians were able to find a solution for the problem of water shortage. They connected the water resources in rocky and hilly areas to the flat land where water was rare. Using this technique they increased the volume of agricultural products on one hand and empowered the government establishment on the other. The continuation of this trend strengthened the power of the government in controlling the water resources and fertile land. Control of water resources caused state ownership of land and the absence of private property. Thus, the growth of agriculture became the influencing factor in the emergence of the great Achaemenian civilization. This same factor was responsible for giving the monarch absolute power, which eventually led to despotism. Ehsan Tabari explains:

> The domination of the Achaemenians over the irrigation system and vast pieces of land pushed despotism (which Marx calls the "Eastern despotism") to the limit. This extreme form of despotism took a deep theocratic form, especially during the Sasanian dynasty, turning the king into a supernatural being.[28]

Tabari adds:

> The documents relating to the Achaemenian period speak of villages called *"Dida"* (wall), *"Vardaneh,"* which is *"Varzaneh"* in Avesta and *"Vajenam"* in Indian (sometimes translated "the common village"), and *"Avehna"* (having the same root as the Armenian word Avan, meaning village). The difference between these words is not

very clear. Nevertheless, they refer to a village where farmers lived in a natural economy, crafts and agriculture were not separate, ownership was joint, and the principles and values of patriarchy and tribal life ruled. The inhabitants of these villages formed the king's "troops," especially his foot soldiers (known as *Kara* in the ancient Parsi language). In the subsequent periods—i.e., the era of the Parthians and the Sasanian—these joint agricultural units were where Iranians were concentrated. Cooperation and joint responsibility, which were probably the objective basis of the rural communalism of the Mazdak movement, ruled in these units.[29]

During the rule of the Achaemenians, the landowning system gave all land to the king. The custom was to donate land to cover wages.[30] In this period, some methods of the feudal systems were also used. Mohammad Ali Khonji has written a critique of the views of the Russian historians who study the Medes, including Diakov, saying that they have ignored the difference between feudalism and the Asian mode of production. He sums up his view as follows:

> In the Achaemenian society, the system governing their social foundations, the conditions governing the production relations, and, at the political level, the system governing their institutions and political, judicial, and administrative establishments, have no equivalent in the Greek system.[31]

Mohammad Ali Khonji argues that politically this system functioned in a way that was different from all that had occurred in Europe, where the society was first divided into classes and then the state was formed in response to the conflicting interests of the classes. But in the East, a powerful government emerged first, and then society was divided into two classes: the ruling class and the oppressed class (or the exploiting class and the exploited class).[32] Although class relations in the East did not emerge in the same way as they occurred in the West, class conflict and the structure of state, as the instrument of sustaining the privileges of the ruling class, has been a universal phenomenon. Many historians mistakenly consider the beginning of civilization on the Iranian plateau to be agrarian while, in fact, the migrant tribes were initially engaged in pastoral activities. The main sources of the emergence of state in the East were similar to those in the West. Throughout the history of Iran, both before the emergence of Islam and after its arrival, evidence points to the tyranny of the landowners and the oppression of the peasants. That is, the ruling class (i.e., the rulers and their associates) enjoyed the unconditional possession of the wealth of society, which was the outcome of ordinary people's work. There is no doubt that these resources were used to build palaces and temples and to cover the heavy expenses of military expeditions and destructive wars and that they were secured by increasing taxes and recruiting the youth to the army. The ancient civilization of Iran was the result of such relations. Protests, rebellions, and revolutions were instigated by economic pressure and functioned as a mechanism to reduce the level of exploitation, but we cannot necessarily consider these revolts as anti-feudalist or as anti-slavery resistance by the peasants or slaves. [33]

Seleucid Dynasty (323–141 B.C. E.). After the collapse of the Achaemenians and the influence of Greek civilization in Iran, some minor changes took place in landowning system. During the eighty-year period of the Seleucid dynasty, in which a feudal system existed, trade grew alongside agriculture. The Seleucids developed new government policies that regulated the distribution of land among the governors. They also constructed new cities and roads.[34] Despite the effect of the Hellenic civilization on Iran, a fundamental change did not occur, and land relations in Iran remained different from those in the West.

Parthian Dynasty (247 B.C. E. –224 C. E.). The conflicts among Alexander's successors on the one hand, and the attempt by the Iranians, including the tribal groups from northeastern Iran (the Parthians) to establish an Iranian government on the other put an end to the Seleucid government after eighty years. The Parthians then succeeded the Seleucids. This was the end of the direct influence that Greek culture and civilization had in Iran. But the indirect influence of Greek civilization—both before and after the Seleucid government—continued.

During the rule of the Parthian dynasty, Iran's unification was re-established, but the effects of Greek civilization during the Parthian era, including the land tenure system, remained more or less intact. Parthians were initially a tribal kingdom in northeastern Iran. A type of feudal system also survived in different tribes up until the Sasanian era.[35] In the political domain, the existence of two consultative parliaments known as "Moghestan" or "Mahestan," a mixture of the Magi and the aristocratic tribes, also influenced the decisions to nominate or depose the Shah. But the Parthian ruling system had tribal establishments, as opposed to the establishments found in the eras of the Medes and the Achaemenians. Arsaces, the founder of Parthian rule, was a tribesman. However, the production relations were more advanced than in previous eras. Industries and trade grew alongside agriculture, and later city and road construction transformed the society to some extent. The closer relationship between the Parthians and the West was probably the main factor causing this development. As far as culture was concerned, the influence of the Hellenic culture still continued to exist. Despite all these changes, the production relations of agriculture still remained generally in the form in which the share going to the producers was based on only one factor—work. In the agriculture system, there was not much of a difference between a peasant and a slave. According to Khosrow, "Agricultural land belonged to powerful landowners and the king stood at the top of the hierarchy and functioned as the state."[36] Agricultural production was based on a share-holding system. The peasants' share was also based on work as opposed to other factors, and it was so meager that it secured only a hand-to-mouth subsistence. Therefore, production in excess of consumption—the origin of the emergence and development of city dwelling, industries, and trade—remained in the possession of landowners, and mainly the king. Landowners leading an aristocratic lifestyle spent what was produced.

Sasanian Dynasty (224–642 C. E.). With the beginning of the Sasanian dynasty, the concentration of land in the hands of the central ruler reemerged. As mentioned earlier, after the dominance of the Macedonians over the territory of Iran, the opportunity to expand the feudal government was there, but Ardeshir Balkan—Sassan's son and the founder of the Sasanian dynasty—was able to preserve the control of the land under the centralized power of the Shah. This situation prevailed from that point on in Iran. According to Abolhassan Ali Masoudi, this unique situation was carried over to the Islamic era and lasted until the Islamic caliphates disintegrated.[37]

Unquestionably, common factors will be found in the collapses of the Sasanian and Roman empires, although as empires they were somewhat different in nature. More important than the fact of the collapse of the Sasanian Empire is the manner in which this empire collapsed and the system that replaced it. Specifically, the fall of the Roman Empire facilitated the growth of feudalism in the West, whereas after the fall of the Sasanian Empire no drastic change was witnessed in the economic system of Iran or in the concentration of the country's political and administrative system.

Despite the fact that some people see the Sasanian Empire as a period of slavery, the agricultural mode of production in this era was really the basis of Iran's economy. Also, as Khosravi says, "trade and industry did not enjoy prominence in this era."[38] The landowning system continued to exist based on the principle that "the land and the peasants all belong to the king" And in this period, no one but the king had any right to the land. The foundation of the agricultural society was not touched. The king transferred the agricultural land based on contract as benefice to others. This was a system that survived for centuries, and the political and governmental developments, including the demise of the Sasanian dynasty and the emergence of Islamic caliphates, did not eliminate it.

Although sufficient information is not available, some historians state that during the Sasanian era the same relations that existed during the Parthian era prevailed.[39] Historians Pigolo Sekaya et al.[40] have only speculated on this subject. They conclude that the feudal relations in Iran had developed during the reign of the Sasanian. In these periods, in addition to collective ownership, features of the feudal system were also found and the society was divided between two sections or two classes. The powerful class of landowners and owners of smaller amounts of land gradually formed a rustic, semi-slave system or caste system in Iran.[41] But in the course of these relations, leaders rose among the people whose power originated from two sources: the tribes they belonged to and the land they owned. These leaders played an important role in their countries during the reign of the Achaemenians.[42] This group, which might be called the village head masters (*dihqan*), was the origin of a new class or caste in ancient Iran. These people, who owned land and lived in the village, were representing the central government in the villages. Their main responsibilities were to collect taxes and draft young men to serve in the king's army. In addition, villagers were used as an unpaid labor force for by the village head master. If we with to make a comparison with early Iranian society, it should be with the slave systems of Greece and Rome and not with European feudalism.

This point is addressed here because the perspective that divides Iranian history based on a universal and unilinear path of development attempts to consider all protests during the era of the agriculture economy as anti-feudal protests. Anti-feudal resistance has a very specific meaning, in that it requires an alternative. The peasant movements in the era of the agriculture economy are only responses to strained circumstances and economic pressures, not protests against the feudal mode of production. The alternative in the peasant movements was the practice of old, self-perpetuating production relations under other tribal or sectarian leaders. An anti-feudal movement can only be found in the West in the era of the emergence of capitalism, which provided an alternative to feudalism. In Iran, mass protests had existed since the ancient era, but despite the fact that power was transferred from one tribe to another or even to social groups from lower classes, such as the *ayyaraan* movement of Yaqub Leyth Saffaar[43] after the arrival of Islam, such Robin Hood-style movements did not give rise to changes in the production system. These protest movements were concerned with bringing the rulers back to what they were supposed to be according to tradition, not more.

In different eras, local rulers under the rule of the Shah (or the Caliph during the Islamist rule) were engaged not only in a suppression of the people but also in fighting against rivals and even occasionally against the Moslem caliphs, the Turkish kings, and the Mongol tribes. Aside from these conflicts, tribal and sectarian fighting was another part of the continuing struggle in the history of Iran. Yet, these cannot be considered resistance against feudalism either. To conclude that feudalism has been dominant in Iran we need resist this perspective.

Social Stratification During the Sasanian Empire: The Semi-Caste System

The author believes that Iran was not truly a slavery system at any time in its history. Some scholars influenced by the Russian historians have attempted to locate a slavery system during the Sasanian era to match the linear path of historical development. I would like to challenge that view.

The nature of the agricultural economy in Iran prevented the formation of conditions that were necessary for the emergence of a slave system. Instead, a tribal system, or a kind of semi-cast system, was dominant. Semi-cast relations, especially in the Sasanian era, became very solid because they found strong religious support, as in India. The society was divided into four castes,[44] or four estates[45]: the religious class (*azerbanan*); the warriors (*artashtaran*); the bureaucracy, including the men of the pen (*dabiran*); and the peasants, shepherds, merchants, and artisans (*pieshevaran* and *keshavarzan*).[46] Like the caste system in India,[47] but to a lesser degree, individuals were assigned their fixed status, and no one could step outside the limits of his or her own caste. Accordingly, as Lambton says, the castes were social classes "each of which was to be kept in its appropriate place and within which each person was to be employed in that occupation to which he was best fitted."[48] The basis of a caste system is kinship and blood. Factors such as hard work as opposed to idleness, or talent and efficiency as opposed to lack of efficiency, did not affect people's positions in their castes. The semi-caste system in Iran disintegrated after the Sasanian dynasty, and its supportive religious establishment collapsed. Such caste relations had no place in Islam, but the class order remained, with some modification.[49] In a slave system, positions were not based on kinship and blood but on other factors such as possession of land and military superiority. Prisoners of war were often taken as slaves because they had lost their power and dominance over their land and possessions. In Greece, people who experienced bankruptcy, people who were not able to pay back their debts, and some convicted people were taken as slaves. As Arthur Christensen puts it, in the Sasanian era "each person had a fixed position and had no right to engage in any profession, except for professions assigned to them by God."[50] The basis for the cast system is religion, which is why it has survived in India. Abdulhosein Zarrinkub writes in relation to the above- mentioned classes: "These four classes were quite distinct from each other in the Sasanian era, and except for rare occasions, people from a low class did not make their way up in the society."[51] The government and the religion in the Sassanid society protected these relations. The government reflected the unique climatic situation in the society. Khosrow Khosravi states that cultivating land was affected by two important social factors in the Sasanian era: the caste system and the king's absolute ownership of the agricultural land. This trend has clearly existed in subsequent eras as well.[52]

Thus, despite the view of some historians, Iranian society in the Sasanian era and the period after that cannot be considered a slavery system. At the time Iran was conquered by the Arabs, no report indicated that the slaves were set free or joined the Islamic forces. This does not mean that slaves did not exist in Iran. It only means that a comprehensive slavery system did not exist in Iran. In a slavery system, slaves are bought and sold as commodities. In addition to taking prisoners of war as slaves, slave hunting is prevalent and debtors can easily end up as slaves. Such a system, which was the originator of economic trade relations in Rome and Greece, should not be equated with the Iranian system, in which some people owned slaves. In Iran, neither a slave system nor any rebellion by slaves against the government establishment occurred. No valid historical resource has referred to the existence of a slave system in Iran based on objective data.[53] The resources that refer to the existence of a slavery system in Iran (predominantly Russian sources or those influenced by them) have used the global patterns of fixed phases in the evolution of history. In a tribal environment such as the one that existed in early Iran, the system of joint ownership of land, the collective, and government work and ownership relations were different from those in a slave system.

A slave system, in essence, has not been seen among the immigrating tribes.[54] Throughout Iranian history, the nomadic economy—which was based on raising cattle—has existed alongside the government (king) and the collective ownerships, two prominent forms of ownership that were dominant among the settled inhabitants. The main elements of the production mode in a slave system were private ownership (not governmental or collective), trade, and the elimination of tribal relations. Governmental or collective ownership is a mode of production in landowning that makes the ultimate level of land cultivation under unsuitable natural conditions a possibility.[55] In tribal relations and among immigrating tribes, tribal ownership (instead of private ownership) existed, in which the chief of the tribe or the khan controlled the land. Tribal life and the Asian mode of production are both results of the shortage of water. Engels wrote about the eastern states, in which the shortage of water determined their structure. Many despotic governments rose and fell in Iran and India. Everyone knew that these governments were, more than anything else, agents that supervised the irrigation of the plains located near the adjacent rivers, rivers without which agriculture would not have been possible in those regions.[56]

In this system, the state-owned property becomes the dominant form, and instead of private property collective land ownership develops. Collective land ownership has historically been incompatible with a slavery system.

The Landowning System After the Arrival of Islam (642–1258 AD): Beginning of the Benefice

Following the demise of the centralized government of the Sasanian dynasty, another centralized government replaced it. Instead of the formation of a non-centralized feudal government, the Sasanian Empire fell into the hands of the relatively centralized power of the Islamic caliphates and the subsequent new governments, and it continued in the same form except for some minor changes in the government form and the governmental land ownership. Khosrow Khosravi, in referring to this situation, writes:

> Apparently the fact that the invasion of Iran by the Arabs disrupted the political system of the Sasanian and shook the religious beliefs of the Iranians did not hurt the agriculture production system in Iran. Although the civil wars of the first century of arrival of Arabs in Iran created fundamental difficulties in the rural societies, these wars did not transform the production system. Following the domination of the Umayyad regime, the agricultural system of production in the villages was strengthened.[57]

The Abbasid Caliphate, the pinnacle of the Islamic world at the time, copied the Persian offices of ministers and bureaucracy, including even court ceremonial procedures. Some of Persian elites, such as Barmakid family, became key architects of the political structure of the new government. Several members of the Barmakid family served as grand viziers during the Abbasid Caliphate.

Nevertheless, the arrival of Islam affected the semi-cast relations of the Sasanian era to some extent. The new situation favored the ordinary people in production. These relations were the result of a relative increase in agricultural products, an increase in the volume of land under cultivation, increased access to newer modes of irrigation, and peasant rebellions.[58] Peasant society was also based on the joint cultivation system. In this system, the five factors of production (land, water, seeds, oxen, and labor) were specified more clearly and found a special place in the Islamic religious jurisprudence.[59] One could argue that the benefice mode in the Sasanian era, which ranked second highest after the king's ownership, turned into the joint ownership system in the Islamic Period;[60] but in both systems peasants constituted the work factor. Relations based on a poll tax, prevalent in the Islamic period, were used to secure the government's income during the Sasanian era, as well. Taxes were in the form of land taxes that did not have very clear-cut regulations.[61] Therefore, the tax system during the Islamic period, according to Khosravi, "was the extension of the tax system during the Sasanian era, although some minor differences existed between them."[62]

The point worth noting here is that the relations of the old agricultural economy continued despite the fact that the centralized political regime of the monarchs changed to the religious regime of the Islamic caliphs, who shared some power with several regional rulers who recognized the divine rule of the caliphs. As far as the form of government was concerned, the Umayyads and the Abbasids returned to the modes used by the Sasanian. This point reflects the fact that when the relations of production do not change, the political and the cultural values do not change independently. Harmony between the social structure, the political system, and cultural values is a function of the society's holistic organization. The reason this structure continued to exist has to do with the quality of the climatic situation in Iran. Growth is not possible unless there is a production in excess of consumption, and the latter depends on such factors as the amount of water and the practical conditions in agriculture. The fact that the Iranian society did not go much beyond production for the sole purpose of consumption reflects the relative poverty of this land. The wealth of society was accumulated in the hand of ruling groups in Iran—the king and the members of his court.

The Baghdad caliphs, like the monarchs of the Sasanian era, prevented the division of power between the large private landholders, as in the West. If anyone rose above the caliph's predetermined status, his forces would repress him. This trend continued during the domination of caliphate until late nineteenth century, despite political, economic, and cultural changes that Iranian society went through. In the West, the monarch, the feudals, and the church were in a rivalry for power, challenging each other but also maintaining a balance of power in society. Therefore, no major change occurred in the class system and the laws concerning the relationship between landowners and peasants in Iran. Zarrinkub states: "As in the Sasanian era, the villagers were forced to work on the land and pay the major part of their wages to the Arab government in the form of taxes".[63]

During the first period after the arrival of Islam in Iran, the Arabs were still heavily involved in military expeditions and did not have much time to get involved in the land relations directly. Therefore, they gave the task of attending to agriculture to the inhabitants and the landowners of the regions and collected taxes from them. If this situation had continued in Iran—i.e., the military and agricultural affairs being treated separately—and if, instead of the centralized power of the Muslim caliphates, a system had developed in which power was distributed, then we would expect to see a situation similar to that following the demise of the Roman Empire and the emergence of feudalism in Europe. However, the Arabs' lack of interest in interfering in agricultural affairs was only temporary, and they soon formed the most centralized empire of the era in that vast territory.

After the consolidation of the Islamic caliphate, and especially during the reign of the Abbasids, benefice turned into some form of profitable enterprise. Other taxes were charged for leasing of the agricultural land and sometimes there were poll taxes. Gradually, alms became prevalent among the Muslims. Due to the distinction between the Arabs and non-Arabs and the fact that the non-Muslims paid tribute to the Muslims and the fighters, the laws concerning agricultural affairs became more complicated. The major part of the conquered land became the property of the public treasury.

The government lands were gradually transferred in the form of benefices (*iqta*) to the regional rulers and other associates as assignees (*muqta' s*) for agricultural purposes and for administrative and personal use. This approach to transferring land, which was sometimes followed for agricultural purposes and sometimes for the purpose of giving a reward, at the same time, resulted in the oppression and exploitation of most of the peasants. The centralized power of the government was in a position to take back the land it had given away at any time it desired. For, in essence, the king was the owner of all the land, and even the owners of the benefices, and the governors were the king's or the caliph's agents to force the peasants to work and to collect taxes from them. This was something the Shah himself did directly on his crown land, unless the land was transferred in the form of *soyurghal'* (administrative *iqta*) or inherited feud.[64] Inherited feuds functioned much like land in the European feudal system and this weakened the central government's power. In *soyurghal*—unlike simple feud—the owner of the feud enjoyed more rights and privileges.[65] However, the second type of assignment—i.e., *tuyul* (the personal *iqta*), was given for a temporary benefit of collecting government taxes.

During the era of the Islamic government other forms of ownership, including crown land and endowed land, came into existence. After the victory of Islam and the conquest of new territories, crown land was essentially the land under the control of the kings. During the first period of the Islamic caliphates, joint forms of ownership, prevalent in Iran, continued, and after the Arabs' domination over Iran, land became the possession of religious leaders. The volume of crown land increased due to the fact that one fifth of all the spoils was allocated to the prophet and his successors.[66] The land seized from the conquered territories was predominantly considered part of the special land owned by the royal families, or it turned into crown land or endowed land. As mentioned earlier, the volume of this land was great. For example, Spuler says, "the governmental land or the installment given to the king comprised two-thirds of the land in the province of Fars (in 390 A.H. or 1000 A.D.)."[67] Later on, the land belonging to individuals was registered as endowed land to protect it against the aggression of the rulers and to make land non-transferable indefinitely so it could remain in the name of its original owners.

The Era in Which the Landowning Mode and Feudalism Almost Overlapped in Iran

From the beginning of the ninth century, the Abbasid caliphate began to disintegrate. The Baghdad caliphate lost the centralization of its politics, and the regional power in the vast territory of Iran became evident.[68] But the great wealth the Abbasid caliphate had accumulated was amazing. The Sasanian era's love for splendor was revived among

Arab aristocrats. Yet despite the accumulation of wealth, no signs of constructing luxurious palaces, carving epigraphs in the heart of mountains, or creating engravings on rocks—witnessed during the ancient Iranian civilization—were evident. Compared with the previous period, the society had been transformed, and part of the production in excess of consumption was allocated to the construction of cities and the expansion of industries and mines. This economic development affected the political arena as well, and for the first time after the emergence of Islam, independent Persian dynasties such as the **Tahirids** (821–873), the **Saffarid** (867–903), the **Samanids** (873–999), the **Ziyarids** (928–1077), and the **Buyids** (945–1055) came into existence.[69] The Buyids defeated the Arab armies and captured Baghdad, the capital of the Caliphate. However, they allowed the Caliph to retain his position as a religious figurehead. The new governments considered themselves the custodians of Islam. During this period, two types of benefices (*Iqta*)[70] were adapted to replace the dominant forms of public (undivided) land and *khaleseh* (shah's land). This caused some changes in the dominant land tenure, but it did not come close to feudalism. The internal conflicts between the rulers, the mass rebellions, the instability of the governments, and the domination of the Turkish tribes over other Iranian people prevented the production forces from following their natural course, and the major part of the production resources was devoted to destruction rather than construction. Every battle between rival groups could easily damage or destroy the water resources upon which the agricultural production was dependent. This trend continued until the domination of the Mongols in the thirteen-century.

During the rule of the Saffarids and the Buyids and at the beginning of the Samanids' rule in Iran, some attempt was made to pay the military staff's salaries in the form of agricultural products. However, Spuler writes, "this trend did not continue for a long time. The salaries were still generally covered by general taxes on land."[71]

Iran Under the Nomadic Turks

Following the Persian regional dynasties, few major Iranian Turks ruled Iran under the Islamic figurehead of caliph. These dynasties were The **Ghaznavids** (962–1186), the **Seljuqs** (1038–1153), and the **Khwarazmis** (1153–1220).[72]

The Seljuqs were tribal people with a nomadic lifestyle who were based on the Central Asian steppe. When they dominated the entire Iranian territory, they adapted the autocratic sovereign of the Persians into their tribal land relations, so that the land was considered *yurt* or tribal grazing land, and the leader (*khan*) was the guardian of the people. The adapted system persisted in Iran in one form or another down to the Constitutional Revolution.[73] Lambton states,

> Nizam ul-Mulk [the grand vazir of the Seljuqs] appears to have regarded the sultan as the sole owner of the soil. In so doing it is possible that he is extending the theory of the ruling khan as the representative of the tribe to cover the position of the sultan as the ruler of a territorial empire over which he held proprietary rights. Or perhaps he was attempting to invest the theory of the steppe with the content of the theory of absolute ownership, which derived from Sasanian tradition.[74]

Since the eleventh century (during the reign of the Seljuk rulers), some changes had been witnessed in the mode of landowning in Iran. The benefice mode (*iqta*) became more widespread. *Iqta '* was a form of landowning relation that had existed before the Seljuqs. In *iqta '*, land was transferred to the military staff or government employees to cover their salaries. At the beginning, *iqta '* had a governmental form, and later on a military *iqta '* was introduced. The military benefice was transferred to the military staff and was considered another example of relations found in feudalism in its Western form. But a comparison between the *iqta '* and the fief or feudal tenure in the West immediately shows that despite some similarities these two modes were quite different in nature. As Lambton indicates, in the Iranian system, "the element of mutual obligation inherent in the nexus of feudal tenure in Western Europe is notably absent."[75] Spuler comments on this issue: "Land (unlike, for example, the endowed land) could be allocated as desired. Later on, the Seljuks did so by turning government land into military benefice on a large scale. But we must also note that even after land ownership underwent changes, the peasants still remained *ra'iyat* (peasants) of the government."[76] The major change in this period was that the administrative *iqta* changed into a military system to meet the needs of the absolute power of the sultan.

The governmental basis of benefice in Iran always ensured the domination of the central government. The presence of a centralized government power supported by great wealth and financial clout kept the local powers from acting against the wishes of the central government. This preserved the centralized power and maintained absolute submission to the king and the caliph. Yet, this development paved the way for the growth of various powers and the disintegration of the monumentally expensive establishment of the central governments.

Backwardness in the Mongol Era

The domination of the **Mongols** (1220–1501) over Iran coincided with the domination of tribal modes of living and prevented the formation of a feudal system, as it existed in the West. One of the main reasons that European-style land relations did not develop in Iran was the fact that the migrating tribes, who were engaged in raising cattle, attacked the settled tribes, who were engaged in agriculture. The contradictory nature of these two lifestyles was itself a result of the climatic situation in Iran. The shortage of water and provisions for the cattle necessitated immigration, and a lifestyle based on raising cattle was the outcome of continued mobility and immigration. The migrating tribes looking for green pastures invaded the agricultural land of the settled people. Because the migrating tribes were quite agile, had fighting and organizing skills, and were experienced in military affairs, they often defeated the settled tribes. The invasion of the Mongols was one example. Regardless of the mode of agriculture, tribal relations enjoyed less historical growth. Tribal life does not have the complexities of city life such as industries and progress in thinking. The production relations are very simple and primitive and do not pose a serious challenge to the relations between man and nature. The invasion of the Mongols turned agricultural land into pastures for their cattle and further inhibited the growth of agriculture. Ann Lambton writes:

> The conquered lands were looked upon as the *yurt* of the Mongol ruling family, in which their flocks and those of their followers grazed: the conquered population was not regarded as having any rights *vis-à-vis* the Mongols. It does not appear, however, that in the early period the Mongols regarded themselves as the proprietary owners of the soil although as conquerors they no doubt considered the produce of the land as their rights. In due course, however, as the Mongol leaders began to acquire land under propriety title, by hereditary grant, occupation, and usurpation, land began to fall into the following classes: *yurt, divani, inju, ouqaf,* and *milki.* The first-named was nothing but a continuation of the practice of the steppe and did not originally imply proprietary rights over the soil.[77]

Inju consisted of crown land distributed among the members of the royal family. The income produced by this land was set aside to pay the expenses of the Shah's establishments and the members of the royal family, and was probably also used for the maintenance of the army. Yet, this kind of land was not exempt from government taxes. The state land consisted of the land that belonged to the government. Since the difference between the government and the royal family was not always clear, the difference between the government and the crown lands was not always clear, either.[78]

The title "benefice" gradually changed to "feud" during the Mongol era. This title and the relations surrounding it continued to exist even after the collapse of the Mongol tribes and the victory of the **Safavid** dynasty (1501–1722). But the tribal and migrating modes and the political and land systems were not eliminated in Iran and remained more or less the same until the twentieth century.

The benefice, which during the period of the Mongol tribes' domination was a tuyul system, did not resemble European feudalism. As Schirazi notes, "In the tuyul system, the shah grants the income from certain estates as a salary to individuals who are in his service or as a reward to those who have rendered him particular services."[79] No doubt, the unique features of a feudal society, and feudalism as a coherent system, could not take form in Iran for the fate of local rulers was still determined by the Shah, part of the outcome of the peasants' work was still confiscated in the interest of the government, and the government's agents were still in charge of the harvest of the products.

Mohammad Ali Khonji considers the benefice mode a semi-feudal system that resulted from the decline of the Asian mode of production.[80] He believed that this new system had special qualities that were no longer compatible with the Asian mode of production. He referred to the development of agricultural land and the existence of internal and external trade. Khonji considered these developments to be in contradiction with the centralization of power and believed they would gradually eliminate the national centralized ownership and the Asian system. Yet, he believed that the phenomenon of agricultural communities would survive. He considered the military leaders, to whom land was transferred, the originators of the big landowner dynasty.[81]

The benefice, considering the fact that it continued to survive into the twentieth century, was not a solution to the deadlock the centralized power of the government faced. The system as a whole preserved its Eastern characteristics. These characteristics were not optional and selected but were born out of the climatic conditions of the East and the old economic, political, and social relations that required a fundamental change before development occurred. Lambton writes on the *iqta*:

The *iqta* system is sometimes spoken of as feudalism, but the circumstances in which the *iqta* system became established and the causes which gave rise to it were different from those which prevailed in Western Europe when feudalism developed. The results were dissimilar, and it is misleading to talk of feudalism in the lands of the Eastern Caliphate, including Persian, unless it is first made clear that Islamic feudalism does not correspond to any of the various types of feudalism in Western Europe. The element of mutual obligation inherent in the nexus of feudal tenure in Western Europe is notably absent.[82]

Lambton confirms this point and the existence of differences in the Iranian *iqta* system, including the military benefice in which a person received land in return for service for the Shah. Quoting C. H. Becker,[83] Lambton adds:

The *muqta'* had originally no military duties, and it was only with the militarization of the state that the military, by abuse, penetrated into the already existing system of assignees. In [Becker's] view the *iqta '* system grew up as an administrative and bureaucratic system and changed into a military system as the result of an attempt to meet a military problem when the gold economy had broken down. It differed thus from Western European feudalism both in origin and in the fact that the *muqta '* had originally no duties.[84]

Other research done on Islamic feudalism led Lambton to believe that the differences in the benefice mode in Islamic countries and feudalism in the West emanated from the fact that the Moslem feudal lords, unlike the feudal lords in the West, lived in cities.[85] Furthermore, feudal relations in Iran simply did not exist between the landowners and the peasants. A governor in a certain area transferred feuds to people in return for a certain amount of taxes.[86] And when the local governors failed to submit the collected taxes to the caliph, the caliph seized back the transferred land. This, of course, often led to conflicts and disputes between the caliph and the disobedient governor, and "sometimes the rebellious governor won."[87]

During the reigns of the Seljuks, the Mongols, and the early Safavids, the forms of government, military, and personal benefices were prevalent. "The Safavids, like the Seljuq, came to power through tribal support."[88] However, they returned to a more centralized system as they revived the notion that "all lands belong to the king and all people are his subjects" (*ra'iyat*). The dominant form of landowning was, however, endowment land (*vaqf*). With endowment land, the shah created a religious protection for his control over the land, which could prevent aggressors from regaining the land. Under this system, the shah could secure his control over the land without losing the benefits.

These relations continued without a major change until the era of **Nader Shah** (1729–1747) and the **Zand** dynasty (1747–1779). Nader Shah ordered the return of all endowment lands and made them crown lands again.[89] Karim Khan Zand modified this system in favor of the peasants by setting new tax laws.[90]

During the **Qajar** period (1795–1925), land tenure did not change in any major way from previous eras. Lambton in her book on Qajar Persia writes: "The Qajar land system was inherited form the Safavids and goes back through the Ilkhanids and Saljuqs to the early centuries of Islam, and, in the case of some strands to pre-Islamic times."[91] Some tribal regions, however, underwent change. "Under the Qajar, who were also, by origin, tribal leaders, attempts were made by the government of the day to control the tribes by nominating the tribal leaders. Tribalism as an obstacle to development of feudalism and capitalism in Iran was another difference with the West. Regardless of the change on tribal relations during Qajar, the despotic position of the Shah, as "asylums of the Universe" with "divine origins" and "celestial rights of conquest" remained the same as in the past. He still continued to claim ownership of all land among other privileges. In this respect, Ervand Abrahamian writes the following.

> The shahs, also as Shadows of God, Divine conquerors, and Guardians of the Flock, exercised extensive authority over life, honor, and property. The[y] claimed ownership of all land they had not previously granted. Thy possessed sole right to give concessions, privileges, and monopolies. They intervened in the economy, occasionally regulating production and prices, frequently buying, selling, and stockpiling food. They considered their word as law as long as it did not openly contradict the fundamentals of Islam. As one chronicler stressed, 'wise men realize that when you have an opinion contrary to that of the Shah, you must make a sacrifice of your blood.' They moreover made and unmade all high officials: the famous Hajji Ibrahim was boiled in oil, another minister was strangled, yet another had his veins cut open, some were blinded, and many had their property confiscated. Fallen ministers so often lost their property that when one such minister did not, the court chronicler wrote in surprise, 'I have never before known or heard of a shah dismissing a minister yet not confiscating his wealth'.[92]

This neither was a feudal system nor had it developed out of a feudal system.[93] The Qajars succeeded in reuniting Iran but lost the Caucasus and central Asia to the Russians. The local affairs were managed traditionally, and the feuds slowly turned into personal lands of the shah and members of his court. Once again, the endowment lands reverted to becoming crown lands. The financial and the judicial establishments of the country still remained under the leadership of one man. During the reign of Naser al-Din Shah, unlike the relations between the functionaries and the feudal lords in the West, Iran experienced struggles over the payment of taxes between the rulers and their subordinates on the one hand and the peasants and the officers of the rulers on the other.

Analysis of the Landowning System in Iran

Lambton mentions a few features of the specific situation of agriculture and landowning in Iran. The first feature is the issue of water shortage. She believed that the issue of irrigation was in fact what inhibited the growth of agriculture in Iran. This problem existed in regions where natural irrigation was prevalent. Access to water was an important factor in determining the place of residence, and it was a big obstacle to the building of individual and secluded farms.[94] This feature was responsible for the creation of joint ownership in Iran. The second feature is the nature of the distribution of population in Iran, which played a key role in the political developments in this society in ancient times. This feature is responsible for the formation of the organization of villages. Lambton writes that from ancient times villages have been one of the fundamental establishments that determined the nature of the social life in Iran.[95] Villages were the necessary economic and political organizations that brought about progress in production in the somewhat adverse geographic environment of Iran. But villages were, at the same time, obstacles to the formation of individual ownership, which was the basis of the emergence of the capitalistic relations. The third feature is the tribal nature of the Iranian society. The tribal relations are considered inhibiting factors that thwart progress toward a developed civilization economically, politically, and socially. These relations prevent the formation of individual interests, political rights, and the emergence of individualism. Individual identity is a prerequisite to the growth of capitalist relations and civil society. The fourth feature Lambton mentions is the lack of security of the farms. This feature keeps the farmers dependent on the land and the feudal lord. The fifth feature is the existence of the share-owning system in farming, which is different from the wage-earning system in capitalism. The sixth feature is the tradition of forcing the farmers to work for free and engage in giving free services to the landlord. And the seventh feature is the absence of the owner from the village. The constant traveling between the village and the city and his involvement in city affairs such as trade, created a division in his status as a businessman and as a landowner.

Lack of a distinction between trade and agriculture did not mean lack of development in city and urban life in Iran. Before Europe could reach the stage of forming an urban civilization, after the middle-ages, progress toward urbanization was witnessed in all the Islamic countries, including Iran. This point has been stressed in many sources. The development of the urban civilization in this region motivated the European kings to mobilize the masses and provoke their religious sentiments in an attempt to start the Crusades and occupy these more advanced regions. Before the emergence of city and trade centers in the West in modern times, large trade and city centers had been developed in Iran. The centers in Harat, Toos, Balkh, Kabul, Neyshabur, Isfahan, Rey, Amol, Hamedan, Qom, Estakhr, Fasa, Ahvaz, etc., were among these centers. Therefore, the roots of underdevelopment in Iran cannot be found in the lack of growth in urban and trade regions. The presence of these roots can be attributed to the fact that these centers did not grow in the same way capitalism grew in the West, because the mode of living in the cities was not different that of existed in the villages. As mentioned earlier, the reason for this drawback was the domination of the merchant landowners over the economy of these centers. The European feudal lords lived in their own forts, and newly established craftsmen and businessmen ran the urban economy. This difference resulted from the nature of the European feudalism and the presence of the conditions for the separation of trades and agriculture. In Iran feudal lords were involved both in agriculture and trade.[96] In other words, merchants devoted part of their capital investments to agriculture. Land was one of the most profitable investments and brought prestige to the owners.[97]

In Europe, the feudal lords and the merchants were two distinct classes. The former looked to the past and the latter, to the future. The economic competition and conflicts that existed among the members of these two classes extended to the political arena as well. In Europe, the class of the merchants did everything in its power to gain access to the cheap labor of the peasants and to eliminate the domination of the feudal lords and thwart the attempts made to free the peasants from the limitations imposed on them by the land. In Iran, these two classes were not distinct. In fact, these two interests—i.e., the interests that lay in the agriculture relations and those that had their roots in trade activities—were realized in one class: the landowners. The merchants, whose economic interests necessitated the growth of the villages, agriculture, and the dependence of the peasants on the land, had no sympathy for industrial work. When industries grew in Europe, tradesmen and landlords in Iran were engaged in trading industrial goods manufactured by others instead of promoting the production of agricultural goods. In other words, this class of people not only did not take any steps toward the industrialization of their society but also actually inhibited the growth of national industry.

Peasant Organization

The following chart reflects the reality that the landowning relations in Iran have been very unvarying and always centralized. Although in different eras these relations changed a little, the changes were not sufficient to bring the landowning system in Iran close to Western feudalism. In the forthcoming pages, features of these forms and their evolutionary changes will be discussed. The purpose of this study is to show that the possibility of the emergence and development of capitalist relations as the initial core of the development of contemporary civilization did not exist in Iran due to the nature of its landowning system. This system was a function of the geographic situation and the economic and political systems that governed the nation. Specifically, the form of social organization of production in Iranian villages, which has a long history, came into existence because of the features of Iran's climate—i.e., the problem of water shortage. This form of joint agriculture, or peasant organization, existed under the names of "*buneh*," "*sahra*," and "*haraseh*" (peasant organization) in different areas of Iran (south, center, and east) and provided the grounds for production at the subsistence level for the villagers.[98] Javad Safi-Nejad, who has devoted fourteen years to the study of "*buneh*" in Iran, speaks of "ancient cooperatives" that came into being because of the specific climate in Iran. In relation to the conditions that led to the formation of ancient cooperatives, he writes:

> Boneh (or sahra or haraseh), formed and organized in the eastern half of the country during the ancient history of agriculture in Iran, was the product of the shortage of rain in this region. It was the product of a continued effort on the part of the villages to gain domination over nature. Due to their agricultural needs, they created traditional joint-production systems in similar forms throughout the region.[99]

The Transformation of Production Relations in Iran's Rural Society

Phase	Producer	Mode of labor	Distribution of income from production	Amount of excess of production	Beneficiary		Central establishment	Type of relation with beneficiary	Comments
					Group	Type of benefit			
1	Rural society	Joint labor	Distribution of product among all	No excess production	Rural society	—	—	—	—
2	Farmer	Working for wages	Earning shares regardless of the five elements	Little excess of production	King as the government, Maqta—land owner	Tax on property income	The caliphate establishment/ "the state"	Tax	From Anushiravan
3	Peasant	Farming	Earning shares considering the five elements	Considerable excess of production	Government (caliphate), Maqta-land owner	Tax on property income	The government establishment	Tax	The Islamic period
4	Farmer "peasant"	Farming	Earning shares considering the five elements	Considerable excess of production	Feudal lord—owner	Property income "central"	State "government"	Tax	The constitutional revolution after 1310 (A.H.)
5	Peasant	Family	For the family	Considerable excess of production	—	—	—	—	—

Conclusion

The Iranian society enjoyed features that in general brought it closer to the models found in Asian countries. Due to the shortage of water, ownership has historically been collective in Iran. The creation of agricultural production in the villages in the form of *buneh* is an example of joint activity to secure water for agricultural purposes. Aside from this, the feudal system and government ownership gave the government the freedom to control the land and transfer it to its dependents. Even big landowners did not enjoy legal security in protecting their land. This situation lasted until the time of the Reza Shah (1921–41). Reza Shah confiscated a large amount of land from different landowners and turned himself into the largest landowner of his era.[100] Petty ownership, another form of landowning in Iran, was considered a weaker form of ownership.

The power institution, which was very centralized, was considered patriarchal. The king was considered the father of the nation, and the people were considered the farmers of the shah. The unity of religion and state in different forms existed from the period before the arrival of Islam, and it was the result of the need for more efficiency in the centralized system with only one leader. The absence of the landlord in the village delayed the recognition of distinctions between the city and the village or the trades and agriculture on the one hand and the accumulation of capital on the other. These features are the basis of the Asian mode of production.[101] Therefore, Iran has been closer to the Asian system than to European feudalism, which was based on private ownership of the land, the autonomy of feudal lords, the presence of ownership laws to protect the landlords against the monarchs' interference, the presence of the feudal lord in the vicinity of his land, feudal/vassal loyal relations, the observance of laws by all parties, and finally the presence of the power of the Catholic Church as the rival of both monarch and feudal lords. These relations were very different from the relations found in Iran, where religion and the state were allies. The land tenure system in Iran from the very beginning, including the ancient dynasties, the Islamic caliphate, the local Iranian kings, the Turks, the Mongols, and all of the rulers after them was not a close match for European feudalism.

In the Asian mode of production and in a patrimonial system, voluntary cooperation does not make sense. Here, only government force, collective work, and the wrath of nature exist. In such a system, the government plays the role of the father, employer, and governor. These modes and relations have been a serious obstacle to the development of a civil society, which must be based on voluntary cooperation rather than government force.

In the next chapter, the features of the Asian mode of production are discussed in detail. The comparison between these features and what we have presented in this chapter on the landowning system in Iran will clarify the nature of the obstacles that prevented the emergence of industrial development in Iran.

The Land Tenure System in Iran: A Historical Review

[1] Max Weber, *The Theory of Social and Economic Organization*, ed. Talcott Parsons (New York: Free Press, 1947), 378.

[2] Ibid.

[3] Ibid.

[4] Ibid., 379.

[5] Peter Duss, *Feudalism in Japan*, 2nd ed. (New York: Alfred A. Knopf, 1933).

[6] Fiefs or feuds were the developed form of benefices. Benefices were temporary and not transferable by inheritance, but fief could be inherited. A benefice usually referred to land seized by the king or taken back from the church and donated to the functionaries in exchange for their support of the military.

[7] Peter Duss, op. cit.

[8] Ibid.

[9] Ibid. Also, for further study about feudalism see Mark Bloch, *Feudal Society* (Chicago: University of Chicago, 1961), and Carl Stephenson, *Mediaeval Feudalism* (New York: Great Seal Books, 1942).

[10] Bertrand Russell, *A History of Western Philosophy* (New York: Simon and Schuster, 1945), xvii.

[11] Ibid., xvii-xviii.

[12] To study the details, see Keyvaan Dadjoo, Abbaas Schirazi, Ali Asqar Schirazi, Ebrahim Malik Esmaili, Bahman Mofid, and Emanuel Yousefi, *The Scientific Socialism and the Class Struggle*, no. 1, (Tehran, no publisher indicated, Farvardin 1358 (1980)).

[13] For a brief review of the forms of land tenure in Iran, see Hossein Mirhaydar, Az Tuyul ta Enqelab-e Arzi, *Tuyul System to Agrarian Revolution*, Chapter 1 (Tehran: Amir Kabier, 2535 (1975)).

[14] *Muzara'eh* is a sharecropping contract between two parties—i.e., peasant and landlord—based on the agricultural elements of land, water, seed, plow animals, and labor.

[15] Farhad Nomani, "Origin and Development of Feudalism in Iran: 300–1600 A.D." (Ph.D. Dissertation, University of Illinois, 1972). Also, see Ann Lambton, *Landlord and Peasant in Persia: A Study of Land Tenure and Land Revenue Administration* (London: Oxford University Press, 1953).

[16] The groups that owned the largest plots of land were the following. The first group consisted of members of the ruling family, both military and civil high-ranking officials. This group obtained their lands by conquest, inheritance, gift, and purchase. The second groups were the tribal leaders, who acquired their land in various ways. Some of them were absent from their estates and lived in larger towns, while others lived among their own people in tribes, ruling as the regional rulers. They had special military manpower to defend their properties and to force the people to pay them. Third were the village merchants, whose landed properties near the villages were acquired in two ways—first, from the transfer of land from peasants who had borrowed money from the merchants

and were unable to pay their debts when they came due, and second, from direct purchase. These landowners also were absentees. The fourth group consisted of clergymen, a remarkable group whose land was derived from grants and pensions from the state, inheritance, or purchase.

[17] Hossein Mirhaydar, "Az Tuyul ta Enqelab-e Arzi" (from *Tuyul System to Agrarian Revolution*), op. cit.

[18] Ehsan Tabari, *Some Analyses on Worldviews and Social Movements in Iran*, from the publications of the Tudeh Party of Iran, 1358 (1980), p. 19. He writes: "In Iran and its neighboring countries, including the Arabian peninsula, Turkistan in China and Russia, and Afghanistan, the tribal system—in varying degrees—persisted, perhaps due to the geographic situation." See also *The Disintegration of the Traditional System and the Birth of Capitalism in Iran*, from the publications of the Tudeh Party of Iran, 1354 (1976), p. 23. (translated from Persian).

[19] Charles Issawi, ed., *The Economic History of Iran, (1800–1914)* (Chicago: University of Chicago Press, 1971).

[20] Cited in Abouzar Vardaasbi, *Iran Dar Pouyeh Tariekh (Iran in the Dynamics of History)* (Tehran: Qalam, 1357 (1979)).

[21] Calman Havar, *Iran and the Iranian Civilization*, trans. Hasan Anoosheh (Tehran: Amir Kabier, 1375 (1996)). See also Shahla Lahiji and Mehrangiz Kar, *Discovering Iranian Women's Identity in the Prehistoric Era and the Historical Era* (Tehran: Roshangaran, 1371 (1992)).

[22] Roman Ghirshman, *Iran: From the Earliest Times to the Islamic Conquest* (New York: Penguin Books, 1954), 50.

[23] Ibid.

[24] Colman Hovar, ibid. These tribes included the Medes, Parses, Parths, Bakhtars, Soghds, and Sokaids.

[25] The English historian Arnold Toynbee writes in *The History of Civilization*: "Horses were great vehicles for transportation and traveling when distances were long. The logistics of 'immigration' in a society of shepherds resemble military expeditions and require severe discipline and absolute submission to the 'leader.' This requirement turned the migrating tribes into a formidable military force. Using war vehicles and horses, motivated by an urgent need to find a suitable place to live, and knowing that the possibility to return did not exist, these 'fighters' obtained considerable skill in the fields of military and political domination. (See Shahla Lahiji and Mehrangiz Kar, op. cit., 243) As far as the fame of the Medes in taming horses is concerned, we may as well add that the city of Nisabeh near Gerrus and Hamedan was famous for having fine horses known as "the horses of the Medes." Hamedan was one of the cities the Medes had made their home. (See Badri Atabai, *A Review of Iranian History*, ed. Mahmood Goodarzi (Tehran: Dounya-y Ketab, 1377 (1998)).

[26] Colman Hovar, op. cit.

[27] M. James Henslin, *Essentials of Sociology: A Down-to-Earth Approach*, 3rd ed. (Boston: Allyn and Bacon, 2000), 87.

[28] Ehsan Tabari, op. cit., 20. (translated from Persian)

[29] Ibid, 22. (translated from Persian)

[30] A.K.S. Lambton, *Landlord and Peasant in Persia: A Study of Land Tenure and Land Revenue Administration* (Oxford, UK: Oxford University Press, 1953).

[31] Mohammad Ali Khonji, *An Essay on the Analysis of the History of the Medes and the Origin of D'iakonov's Theory* (Tehran: Tahoori Library, 1358 (1980)), 56. (translated from Persian)

[32] Ibid.

[33] There is no unified definition of the concept of "peasant." Words such as *dihqan*, which meant landowner in ancient Iran and peasant proprietors in later times, and *barzigar* (peasants as landless agriculture laborers) are being used to describe the same concept in Iran. (See Ann Lambton, op. cit. and Teodor Shanin, "Defining Peasants: Conceptualization and De-conceptualization Old and New in a Marxist Debate," *Peasant Studies*, 8, no. 4, 1979). For the Persian translation of this article see Syrus Parham, in *The Question of Land and Peasants, Aagaah Book: A Collection of Articles* (Tehran: Aagaah, 1361, (1983)), 340–361.

[34] The "feudal government" of the Seleucids and Western feudalism should not be considered the same. In the Iranian agrarian system, governors were the agents of the central government, while the European feudal lords were independent. Some sources argue that Iran witnessed a slavery system after the invasion by the Greeks. This could have happened due to the dominant system in Greece and the high numbers of war prisoners. (Abouzar Vardaasbi, op. cit.)

[35] A.K.S. Lambton, ibid., and Khosrow Khosravi, *The Land Cultivating Systems in Iran (From the Sasanian Era to the Seljuk Period)* (Tehran: Payam, 1352 (1973)).

[36] Khosrow Khosravi, *The Peasant Society in Iran* (Tehran: Payam, 1357 (1979)), 41.

[37] Seyyed Javad Tabatabaie, *The Decline of Political Thinking in Iran* (Tehran: Kavir, 1373 (1995)).

[38] Khosrow Khosravi, *The Land Cultivating Systems in Iran*, op. cit., 1352 (1974)), 62.

[39] N.V. Pigolo Sekaya et al., *The History of Iran from the Ancient Era to the End of the Eighteenth Century*, 5th ed., trans. Karim Keshavarz, (Tehran: Payam, 1363), and. A.K.S. Lambton, ibid.

[40] Ibid.

[41] Ibid.

[42] A.K.S. Lambton, op. cit., 50.

[43] Yaqub Leys Safari (879 C.E.), the leader of a popular Robin Hood-style movement, was the first Persian regional ruler to openly revolt against the Arabs. He succeeded in bringing large a portion of Iranian land under his control, and he promoted the Persian culture.

[44] Abdolhossein Zarrinkub, *The History of Iran After Islam* (Tehran: Amir Kabier, 1368 (1990)).
[45] A.K.S. Lambton, *Islamic Society in Persia* (London: University of London, 1954).
[46] Abdul Hossein Zarrinkub, op. cit.
[47] In India, the caste system was based on the Hindu religion and had deep roots that lasted until the independence of India in 1949. The caste system was pronounced illegal after the independence, but it was not eliminated entirely. The roots of the Indian caste system are so deep that groups such as the Harijons and the Shudrais are still called filthy groups. This belief is so strong among the prejudiced Hindus that some in fact believe that even the shadow of these people can contaminate others. For this reason, the members of the Harijons group were not permitted to enter certain areas frequented by members of higher castes. (See Richard Lannoy, *The Speaking Tree: A Study of Indian Culture and Society* (Oxford, UK: Oxford University Press, 1975).

In this culture, women were repressed and men were regarded as the core of the society. Women were forced to die by being burned alive with the body of their deceased husbands. The Indian caste system, which has penetrated the deepest corners of Indian society, rose from the Hindu religion, and the religion turned into a government power. More recently, the government approved a quota system that allowed the members of the so-called filthy castes to work for the government. Each year, a few men burn themselves to death in public as a protest against this law. Of course, this protest is intended to convey the message that youth are angry because this law has decreased job opportunities for them. Yet, however we interpret the causes of this phenomenon, the result is the same. (See John Macionis, *Society: The Basis,* 3rd ed. (New York: Prentice Hall, 1991).

This phenomenon has been one of the causes of underdevelopment in India. See Barrington Moore, Jr., *Social Origins of Dictatorship and Democracy: Lord and Peasant in the Making of the Modern World* (Boston: Beacon Press, 1966). On the issue of the slow rate of growth in India, Joel Mokyr believes that the caste system that was first created by the victorious Aryans and was gradually integrated into Indian Brahmanism, which was the main obstacle to the development of the Indian society. Brahmanism and its caste organization strengthened the dominance of the invading group over the other tribes. Therefore, between development and the strengthening of the system, they chose the latter. In the caste system, individual progress is essentially nonexistent, and people are born with relatively fixed positions. Mokyr adds the caste system as another factor that caused underdevelopment in India. He also considers the Mongol invasion in 1520 C.E. and colonization by the British as factors that blocked India's development, one after the other. Religiously, the caste system considers poverty a God-given situation that is somehow holy. Therefore, not much effort is invested in removing it. See Joel

Mokyr, *The Lever of Riches: Technological Creativity and Economic Progress* (Oxford, UK: Oxford University Press, 1990))

[48] A.K.S. Lambton, op. cit., 1954, 3.

[49] These orders were (1) men of the pen; (2) men of the sword; (3) men of affairs, such as merchants, craftsmen, artisans, and tax-collectors; and (4) husbandmen (A.K.S. Lambton, op. cit.).

[50] Arthur Christensen, *Iran in the Sasanian Era*, 8th ed., trans. Rashid Yasemi (Tehran: Dounya-ye Ketab, 1375 (1997)), 427. (translated from Persian)

[51] Abdolhossein Zarrinkub, *The History of Iran,* op. cit., 162–163.

[52] Khosrow Khosravi, *The Land Cultivating Systems in Iran*, op. cit., 1352 (1974).

[53] M. A. Khonji has written about a great slave rebellion in a salt mine near Basra (currently a city in Iraq) during the rule of Abbasian, an Islamic khalifa (op. cit.). This event does not confirm the existence of a slavery system in Iran because the proponents of this idea refer to a slavery system in the pre-Islamic era, whereas the salt rebellion occurred two centuries after the emergence of Islam, a period that is called a "feudal stage" of development.

[54] Gunnar Landtman, *The Origin of the Inequality of Social Classes* (New York: Greenwood Press, 1968).

[55] Javad Safi-Nejad, *Boneh: Nezaam ha-y Twolid Zeraei Jamei Qabl va Ba'ad az Aslahaat Arzi, The Collective Agrarian Productive Systems Before and After the Land Reform*, 3rd ed. (Tehran: Tous, 2535 (1975)).

[56] Friedrich Engels, "The Force Theory," in *Guerrilla Warfare & Marxism*, ed. William J. Pomeroy (New York: International Publishers, 1968), 63–72.

[57] Khosrow Khosravi, "The Peasant Society in Iran," op. cit., 49. (translated from Persian)

[58] Khosrow Khosravi, *The Land Cultivating Systems in Iran*, op. cit. 1352 (1974).

[59] See Minu Alvandi, "On the Distribution of the Harvest Based on the Five Factors of Production," in *The Question of Land and Peasants* (Tehran: Aagaah, Aagaah Book Collection, 1361), 401–417.

[60] Khosrow Khosravi, *The Land Cultivating Systems in Iran,* op. cit., 1352, 61.

[61] For more information on the taxes and their types, see Khosrow Khosravi, *The Land Cultivating Systems*, ibid.

[62] Khosrow Khosravi, ibid., 1352 (1974), 23.

[63] Abdolhossein Zarrinkub, *The History of the Iranian People (2) From the End of the Sasanian Era to the End of the Buyid Era* (Tehran: Amir Kabier, 1368 (1990)), 49. (translated from Persian)

[64] Parts of these lands were assigned to others, such as the king's relatives and his servants, in the form of *iqta* (benefice). Two forms of *iqta'—soyurghal* and *tuyul*—were used during the Seljuq era.

[65] N. V. Pigolo Sekaya, Pigolo et al., op. cit., 527.

[66] A.K.S. Lambton, op. cit.

[67] Bertold Spuler, *The History of Iran During the First Centuries of Islam*, vol. 2, trans. Maryam Mir Ahmadi, (Tehran: The Scientific and Cultural Publications, Inc., 1369 (1991)), 299. (translated from Persian)

[68] See Abdolhossein Zarrinkub, *Two Centuries of Silence: The Description of Events and Historical Situations of Iran During the First Two Centuries of Islam From the Arab Attack to the Emergence of Taherid's State* (Tehran: No publisher, 1330 (1952)).

[69] These governments ruled various parts of Iran for a period of 185 years.

[70] These two *iqta'* were *iqta' al tamliek* and *iqta' al esteqlal*. See Hossein Mirhaydar, *From Tuyul to Agrarian Revolution* (Tehran: Amir Kabier, 2035 (1975)).

[71] Bertold Spuler, op. cit., 298–299.

[72] These Iranian Turks totally ruled Iran for a period of 280 years while keeping the caliph as the figurehead.

[73] A.K.S. Lambton, op. cit.

[74] Ibid., 61.

[75] A.K.S. Lambton, 54.

[76] Bertold Spuler, op. cit., 289-299. (translated from Persian)

[77] A.K.S. Lambton, 77-78.

[78] A.K.S. Lambton, op. cit.

[79] Asghar Schirazi, *Islamic Development Policy: The Agrarian Question in Iran*, trans. P.J. Ziess-Lawrence (Boulder, CO and London: Lynne Rienner Publishers, 1993), 63

[80] Mohammad Ali Khonji, op. cit.

[81] Ibid.

[82] A.K.S. Lambton, op. cit, 1954, 53–54.

[83] Max Weber writes: "C.H. Becker was the first to understand the difference of the Near East from the European fief." (*The Theory of Social and Economic Organization*, 1947, p. 380).

[84] Ibid., 54.

[85] Ibid.

[86] Bertold Spuler, *The History of Iran in the First Centuries of Islam*, trans. Javad Falatoori (Tehran: The Scientific and Cultural Publications, Inc., 1349 (1971)).

[87] Ibid., 150.

[88] A.K.S. Lambton, *Islamic Society in Persia* (London: University of London, 1954), 7.

[89] For the first time, these lands were officially recorded under the shah's name, Roqabat-e Naderi. (See Hossein Mirhaydar, op. cit.).

[90] Ibid.

[91] A.K.S. Lambton, *Qajar Persia: Eleven Studies* (Austin, TX: University of Texas Press, 1987, 33.

[92] Ervand Abrahamian, *Iran Between Two Revolutions* (Princeton, NJ: Princeton University Pres, 1982), 48.

[93] A.K.S. Lambton, *Qajar Persia* (Austin: University of Texas Press, 1987).

[94] A.K.S. Lambton, *Landlord and Peasant in Persia* (London: Oxford University Press, 1953).

[95] Ibid.

[96] Ahmad Ashraf, *The Obstacles to the Development of Capitalism in Iran During the Qajar Period* (Tehran: Zamineh, 1359 (1981)).

[97] A.K.S. Lambton, 1953.

[98] A *buneh* as an organization for peasant teamwork usually had four to six members, with membership depending upon several factors, including farming ability. For details see Javad Safi-Nejad, pp. 238–261.

[99] Javad Safi-Nejad, op. cit., 21. (translated from Persian)

[100] Jami (no editor) *The Past is the Leading Light for the Future.* Jami (the Iranian People's Liberation Front), (Tehran: Farvardin, 1355 (1977)).

[101] For more information, see Mohammad Ali (Homayoon) Katuzian, *The Political Economy of Iran from the Constitutional Revolution to the End of the Pahlavi Dynasty*, trans. Mohammad Reza Nafisi and Kambiz Azizi (Tehran: Nashre Markaz, 1372 (1994)).

Chapter 3
Why Did Feudalism Not Grow in Iran?

The key to the question of underdevelopment in Iran and the reason why the country has not been able to reach the development level witnessed in Western civilization lie in the fact that feudalism did not appear in Iran. As I have emphasized throughout this book, contemporary Western civilization is the product of capitalist relations, and the feudal system gave rise to these relations. In the Middle East, "The dominance of the Oriental despot precluded genuine, private ownership of land, the precondition of feudalism".[1] This system was a direct result of the shortage of water. Ann Lambton writes: "where water has to be shared for irrigation, this fact has influenced the shape and distribution of the holdings."[2] Therefore, capitalism (the moving engine of contemporary Western society) did not develop in Iran, either. None of the mental, industrial, and political dimensions of modern civilization were feasible without the growth of the bourgeoisie as a class and capital relations as the pre-established economic basis for relations among the classes, groups, and members of the society, with individual incentives. The initial conditions for the emergence of these features did not exist in Iran, which was a natural coincidence that was outside the control of human beings.

Separating Western Europe from the East and stressing the existence of the seed for the emergence of capitalism in the West (unlike the East), Marx wrote that the development that extended to capitalism in the West was the transformation of one form of private ownership (feudal) to another (capitalist). In contrast, it was the transformation of public ownership to private ownership that was required in the East.[3] Therefore, Marx stressed the evolution to capitalism in Western Europe and distinguished between this area and the rest of the world.

The view that is adopted in this book is that the indexes for development and underdevelopment exist in the core of social institutions. Among the determining factors in development, we can refer to the nature of major social institutions (economy, politics, religion, family, laws, the army, and so on) and the mode of subsistence. In each period in history, the subsistence mode has affected the social relations among the members of a society as a whole and has represented the core of the established institutions. This mode has not been optional, and it has been selected—if not imposed—on human beings based on possibilities that existed in nature, along with man-made accomplishments, by trial and error. Therefore, the causes of underdevelopment in Iran or other Eastern societies do not lie primarily in a social establishment such as religion but in the climatic and environmental circumstances of that society. The emergence of the ancient civilization in Greece was spawned by these factors. For example, the issue is not whether it was the shortage of water or the existence of migrating tribes that gave rise to despotism in Iran, since both factors were the products of the climatic situation in this country. Living near the sea teaches one fishing skills. Living beside the desert and in dry areas teaches one the skills of securing, storing, and saving water.

The factor responsible for the shortage of water in Iran was the origin of special relations that fit into the framework of the "Asian mode of production." Thus, becoming familiar with the special features of these production relations and the mode of subsistence is necessary. This chapter deals with the analysis of the Asian mode of production and its patrimonial characteristics. For a comparison, it also presents two other views: (1) the fact that the Iranian system was despotic was due not to the shortage of water, as contended in the Asiatic mode of production outlook, but rather to external tribal threats; and (2) the Iranian land tenure system was similar to European feudalism.

The Differences Between the Modes of Production in the East and the West: The Asian Mode of Production

> "In *Hindoustan* every acre of land is considered the property of the King, and the spoliation of a peasant would be a robbery committed upon the King's domain."[4]

Before Marx, the social thinkers of the Age of Enlightenment had paid attention to the differences between the East and the West. This interest can be traced back to C. H. Becker, Hegel, Montesqueiu, Hobbes, and Francois Bernier, and even back to the Greek philosophers. For instance, Montesqueiu referred to Asian despotism, a system that makes resistance against the centralized power of the government impossible because of the weakness of the organized groups of civil society versus the political institutions. In this system, some degree of equality existed between the dominated people: equality in opportunities to serve the dominators. "Bernier rightly considered the basis of all phenomena in the East—he refers to Turkey, Persia, Hindustan—to be the absence of private property in land."[5] According Marx, "this is the real key even to the Oriental heaven."[6] However, according to Max Weber, it was C. H. Becker who clearly showed the difference between Eastern landlordism from the European fief.[7]

The classical economists in England also stressed the differences between the East and the West in their analysis of production relations. Adam Smith considered the similarities among Eastern governments the result of their complicated irrigation systems and the laws that governed these systems.[8] To him, the centralized power of the governors in Egypt, China, and India was determined by its role in the management and control of these irrigation networks and the regulations governing them. James Mill distinguished between the "government based on the Asian model" and European feudalism.[9] Richard Jones depicted a distinct picture of the Eastern system or the "Asian societies."[10] And in his book *The Principles of Political Economy*, John Stuart Mill placed the Eastern societies and the European societies in different frameworks.[11]

There were two outstanding features in early Eastern societies. The first was the public water resources controlled by the centralized government, and the second involved the division of the land in the empires into villages, each having an independent organization and creating a small world within its boundaries. Each village was a self-sufficient unit. The chief of the village was appointed by the central government as a representative with absolute authority, and he was expected to resolve conflicts among the villagers, keep order in the region, and collect taxes through his supervision over the local sheriff.

In addition, the economic organization of the village included a bookkeeper, an inspector who was responsible for overseeing the harvest and fairly distributing the water to the farms, and finally a fortune-teller, who predicted the suitable time for planting and harvesting the agricultural products. In addition to farmers, there existed craftsmen such as blacksmiths, carpenters, potters, laundry men, barbers, artisans who produced copper and silver objects, and a clergyman to oversee religious ceremonies. This was a relatively stable arrangement, and the productive and the economic status in the village underwent little change over long periods of time. The relations between the villagers and the rulers were based on the understanding that the relations that had been so closely tied with their fates should be preserved and guarded heavily. Marx, one of the major analysts of the emergence and development of capitalism and the Asiatic mode of production, believed that one cannot imagine a more stable foundation for continued stagnation under Oriental despotism. The secret of the continuity of this despotism lay in the lack of unity between the isolated and disjoined villages, which posed no threat as a unified force of resistance against the central government. The government was responsible for securing water and building irrigation networks, and it used the villagers (farmers) to perform the construction tasks. When such production relations exist and last for centuries in a society, they gradually create traditions of their own that last even after the initial background of production has changed, and they govern the relations in society as social regulations that motivate and guide behavior. For example, in India, after colonization by the English, the Asian mode of production was challenged,[12] although the immediate result of this influence was the disintegration of the agriculture system in India. The colonizer eliminated the Oriental despotism that had survived for thousands of years in that country, and following the demise of the central government the irrigation networks that had been run by the government also disintegrated, along with agriculture, itself. The reason for this development was that the colonizers created a vacuum in the society due to the fact that they did not understand the relationship between the centralized power of the government and the agricultural products and failed to find an alternative for these relations.[13] Marx writes in this regard, forced dissolution of common ownership in India was a British savage action that not only did not develop India but also forced them into regression.[14]

As mentioned, Marx and Engels distinguished between the Asian mode of production and European feudalism. They believed that lack of private ownership of the land (a prerequisite for feudalism) is responsible for the existence of this difference. Marx and Engels were primarily interested in China and India and rarely referred to Iran. But the historical analysis of Iran's economic and political systems suggests that the system was closer to the systems in the East than to the European feudal system. This claim is the basis of the present argument.

With respect to the differences between the modes of production before capitalism in the East and European feudalism, Marx writes, "The broad basis of the mode of production here is formed by the unity of small-scale agriculture and home industry, to which in India we should add the form of village communities built upon the common ownership of land, which, incidentally, was the original form in China as well." [15]

Karl Marx first explained the Asian mode of production in 1853, through letters he wrote to his colleague Engels. Subsequently, Engels responded to Marx's views favorably, in his own letter to Marx. Marx later explained the Asian mode of production in more detail in his book *The Grundrisee*.[16] The Asian mode of production is an issue about which Marxists are not in complete agreement.[17] Engels omitted this argument from one of his last works, *The Origins of Family, Private Ownership, and the State*.[18] Lenin first referred to it as "Asiaticism" or "the government system," [19] but later he referred to it as a socio-economic formation. Lenin argued that in this patriarchal system the production of goods and class differences were hardly molded.[20] Following Marx and Engels, he saw Russia as a semi-Asian society and called the regime of the ancient Roman emperors Oriental despotism.[21] Plekhanov—a Russian Marxist—eventually rejected the existence of the Asian mode of production, first in Russia and then in history altogether.[22] He wrote that not only Russia, but also Egypt, Chaldia, Assyria, Iran, Japan,[23] China, and almost all oriental civilizations and countries have experienced feudalism in its Western form.[24] Leon Trotsky referred to the existence of the Asian mode of production in Russia in the form of the domination of the rural economy over the urban economy and the country's consumption orientation on the one hand and the unity between trade and agriculture on the other.[25] Stalin, however, insisted that all societies during the course of history have passed through the four stages of primitive communes, slavery, feudalism, and capitalism.[26] Ernest Mandel justifiably rejects Stalin's views and argues that migrating tribes and clans, such as the Mongols and the Turks, cannot be placed in this four-phase framework of history. The migrating mode, due to the specific climatic conditions that necessitated it, was very different from the other modes.[27] Marx believed that this mode was very rigid and inflexible and survived only until the emergence of capitalism.

Marx and Engels base their analysis on the special features of the subsistence mode in these societies—i.e., the Asian economy, from which governmental despotism quite naturally follows. Marx believed that "One of the reasons for the emergence and the development of Oriental despotism should be sought in the special form of ownership in these societies."[28] Engels, in a letter he wrote to Marx on June 6, 1850, explained this form of ownership as follows:

> ...The absence of property in land is indeed the key to the whole of the East. Herein lies its political and religious history. But how does it come about that the Orientals did not arrive at landed property, even in its feudal form? I think it is mainly due to the climate, taken in connection with the nature of the soil, especially with the great stretches of desert, which extend from the Sahara straight across Arabia, Persia, India, and Tartary up to the highest Asiatic plateau. Artificial irrigation is here the first condition of agriculture, and this is a matter either for the communes, the provinces, or the central government. An Oriental government never had more than three departments: finance (plunder at home), war (plunder at home and abroad), and public works (provision for reproduction).[29]

Marx and Engels believed that the problem of irrigation in the East made land ownership a government monopoly from the very beginning. Petty landowners and the isolated people were not able to solve the problem of water shortage (water is considered the most essential element in life). Routing water from mountainous areas to dry plains required unity among the rural people. The collective irrigation endeavor brought along collective ownership. Governments played and important role in organizing this collective task. Monopoly in land ownership (with water at its core) resulted in monopoly in politics. According to Marx, The monopoly of charitable efforts and public duties such as irrigation and communication belonged to the government and gave rise to Oriental despotism.[30] Marx considered tribal and collective ownership and lack of private ownership the main basis for Oriental despotism.[31] Engels agreed with this view and argued that among the Russian and Indian rural populations in which private ownership did not exist, the power of government inevitably appeared despotic.[32]

Group Affiliation a Base for Absolute Authority

The relations of the Asian mode of production and Oriental despotism have directly affected the nature of individual identity. According to Dadfar et al., "Lack of private ownership, in other words, is the same as lack of development in individual identity."[33] Individual identity, as distinct from group or collective identity, is the prerequisite for the recognition of individual rights. In Eastern societies individual interests are mixed with the interests of the groups. This causes the negation of individual identity and the emphasis on collective identity, including tribal and family identities that have led to the strong patriarchal structure found in those societies. As Max Weber writes: " 'Patriarchalism' is the situation where, within a group, which is usually organized on both an economic and a kinship basis, as a household, authority is exercised by a particular individual who is designated by a definite rule of inheritance."[34] He adds: "...traditional authority tends to develop into 'partrimonialism'".[35] Therefore, another aspect of these relations is their patriarchal nature. The roots of this cultural tradition lie in the form of collective production, lack of private ownership of the land, and lack of independence of individuals from the groups.

The power of people who identified themselves with the members of a group was manifested through the power of the head of the family, the tribe, and the nation. Lack of economic independence prevents individuals from freely establishing a relationship with their living environments. Under such circumstances, the central government recognizes the rural population as a whole, not as individuals. The government, as the absolute power in society, views individuals as its objects, its farmers, or its servants. This attitude is easily accepted because people are influenced by the norms of the traditional culture. Weber writes: "Primary Patriarchalism is related to it in that the authority of the patriarch carries strict obligations to obedience only within his own household."[36] Marx considered these relations the solid basis for Oriental despotism, because in his view these relations confine the human mind within the closed circle of the present reality.

Collective Ownership of Land

The initial form of land ownership in Europe was also collective ownership. But after the occupation of the Roman Empire by German tribes, collective ownership gradually turned into private ownership. Private ownership in Rome had developed to the stage of centralized ownership.[37] The distribution of the occupied territories among the German tribes and the continuation of their wars over these territories eventually led to private ownership.[38] The material basis for this development was formed because of Europe's climatic situation that allowed individuals and families to remove natural obstacles in agriculture individually. The concentration of these ownerships provided the suitable ground for the feudal system.

According to Engels, the disintegration of the collective ownership of land and the emergence of private ownership occurred first in Rome and then in Greece during antiquity.[39] Engels analyzes the three large Greek, Roman, and Germanic systems with respect to this development. The cause of these developments is known to be the climatic situation in these territories, which allowed people to eliminate or surmount natural obstacles in agricultural production without the assistance of a group or collective. These conditions brought about an increase in production on the one hand and helped in the development of trade on the other. Trade, which is considered an important factor in the disintegration of the early collective organizations, can take place if there is production in excess of consumption. In a natural economy, production remains at the level of self-sufficiency. The process of production in excess of consumption in the West led to landowning by large tribes first and then the emergence of the slave system and petty landowners. In this system, unlike the Asian system of production, in which the production market was owned and controlled by the powerful government, petty landowners were able to keep the excess products for themselves. Therefore, collective ownership was reproduced in the East and prevented the emergence of private ownership in the form that existed in the West.

Irrigation Systems, Tradition, and Law

Weber was amazed by the fact that the history of the East manifested itself as the history of religion. This reality is the result of integration of religion and the legal systems in these societies, which restrained the relations both inside and outside all social institutions. The origin of law, as Marc Bloch explains, is "the system of territorial custom" or more accurately "group custom."[40] Bloch adds: "each human group, great or small, whether or not it occupied a clearly defined area, tended to develop its own legal tradition."[41] Roman law prior to its secularization was initially based on tribal traditions, the word of the king and diviner.[42] As I wrote in the introduction, in the East, religious institutions have enforced the existing community traditions not only as law but also as the truth and the word of God; hence the traditions have been assumed to be unchangeable, consequently applicable to the entire human society. For example, "The Koran and tradition provided the foundation upon which theology and *fiqh* (law), the obverse and reverse of sacred law, were raised. Law in

Islam is more intimately related to religion than to jurisprudence as modern lawyers understand it."[43] In such circumstances, the king declares himself as divine and his word as law. Francois Bernier writes that in Hindoustan "[t]he custom is regarded as a matter of law and duty, and the observance of it is rarely neglected."[44] As far as economics was concerned, Weber, like Marx, referred to the complicated system of artificial irrigation. In his opinion, this system of irrigation formed the basis of the economy of the Mediterranean and the Egyptian societies—the oldest centers of world civilization.[45] Ann Lambton also indicates that "Irrigation, indeed, is the great limiting factor to agricultural development in Persia, and in the irrigated farming areas has largely determined the type of husbandry which is practiced."[46]

The irrigation networks had existed since the Sumerians in these regions,[47] and the maintenance of these canals required a vast work force that could be managed only by a centralized, bureaucratic state. In Weber's opinion, the Sumerians and the Babylonians basically went to war to conquer the facilities needed for the construction of new canals in new cities. These facilities were nothing but human forces. He compares this system with the ancient Egyptian economy or "an enormously large royal oikos."[48] In this system people are basically considered the state's servants and enjoy no independence.

In the ancient Egyptian civilization, aside from the utilization of the work force to extract water from the Nile and to construct canals, the people were used in construction work by the state. Therefore, the entire human work force in the society was devoted to the construction and the maintenance of irrigation systems and all other facilities controlled by the monarch. The management of this system required a political and bureaucratic structure. Weber called it a liturgy-state, which is a state in which people are committed to the duties the social system has assigned them. In other words, the people in this system are considered the tools of the monarchical power.[49]

In such a system, the peasants who owned little pieces of land had to pay heavy taxes. Weber says that when the tax officials suddenly appeared at the peasants' doorsteps, the women started to cry and the men were subjected to beatings. Therefore, Weber considers this a tradition based on repression and the monarch's centralized bureaucracy to be the basis of Oriental despotism that subsequently led to the increase in wealth and the military power of the heads of the tribes and their associates. In Eastern countries, political power only belonged to the king and the prince who succeeded him. The king, who was also the leader of the military, had successfully managed to minimize the role the government officials played in controlling key resources and to keep them dependent. Weber contrasts this feature with Western feudalism, in which the king transferred pieces of land to associates who had to pay for the production expenses in return for considerable autonomy. He concludes that the decentralization of power and the autonomy of the landowners in the West gave rise to economic growth and political independence, while the relationship between the king and his associates in the East only made the associates more dependent.

With respect to these two different types of state, Weber writes:

The political and social constitution of the state would be entirely different. *Economic considerations largely determined which form would win out.* The East and the West show in this respect the usual contrast. For oriental economies—China, Asia Minor, Egypt—irrigation husbandry became dominant, while in the West, where settlements resulted from the clearing of land, forestry set the type.[50] This could be done once and for all. Irving Zeitlin adds that to understand the difference between the basic structures of the East and the West, the economic process of production and its products have to be taken into consideration.[51] This difference extends itself to all of the institutions existing in a society.

In short, farmers in the West won the ownership of uncultivated land when they could develop it. Once woods were cleared, individuals could cultivate the land for good. In the end, they could do the farming alone, because unlike in the East agriculture was not dependent upon artificial irrigation. In the East, clearing barren land was only the beginning of development. Peasants had to provide water resources if the cultivation was to continue. Providing water in a dry natural environment was not an easy task, and peasants could not do it alone. Thus, they were dependent either upon the state for assistance or on some form of teamwork for irrigation, because irrigation required a major work effort that individual peasants were unable to provide. Land without water had no value in this region, as elsewhere. Therefore, the ownership of the cultivated land was often split between the peasants and the authorities who managed to control the water resources and the other factors of agriculture. Alternatively, due to the requirement for teamwork, collective ownership of undividable land (*mosha'a*) gradually developed instead of individual ownership. Westerners did not experience such difficulties.

In the United States, the federal government under the Homestead Act of 1862 welcomed the settlers to the West by giving land to those who promised to farm it. Each of these people became the owner of

160 acres of land. Family members were able to do farming because like Europe, and unlike the East, in the U.S. farmers had enough rainfall for the cultivation. It was this natural difference between the East and the West that created different political and social consequences.

Development of Cities

The emergence and the development of cities also had a direct relationship with the nature of land ownership. Weber states that the kingdom—an establishment that was older than the city—was always an obstacle to the development of the cities in Eastern societies.[52] The unity of trade and agriculture, along with the residence of the feudal lords in cities and their involvement in urban activities, prevented the independent formation of the cities.[53] Engels named three specific periods with regard to the role of cities and production relations: (1) the ancient era, during which cities enjoyed economic superiority over rural areas; (2) the Middle Ages, during which villages were dominant formations; and (3) the modern era, during which a new class came into existence in the city and engaged exclusively in the exchange of goods.[54] This class laid the foundation of the European industrial bourgeoisie. In the Asian mode of production, the superiority of the villages over the cities was preserved all along. The governments prevented the growth of the city as a way of controlling the society. To understand the nature of these relations and how Eastern cities were built, one may refer to François Bernier's invaluable work,[55] a work Marx praised highly. In a letter to Engels, Marx wrote:

As far as the construction of oriental cities is concerned, no one has been able to produce a more outstanding and effective work than François Bernier's *Description of the Journeys to the Kingdom of the Great Mongul.* Bernier was Aurng-Zebe's[56] private doctor for nine years. His description of the military system and the eating habits of these great armies is also very lucid. On these two issues (the military system and the eating habits), he writes:

> The cavalry constitutes the major part of the army. The foot soldiers, contrary to the common belief, were not a large body in the army, unless the servants, the tradesmen, and the merchants who marched behind the cavalries were mistaken for foot soldiers. In that case, I can easily accept the estimates of 200,000 to 300,000 and sometimes even more men accompanying the King when he planned to be absent from the capital for a while. This would not be very amazing for those who are aware of the strange problems with the tents, the

kitchen, the clothes, the provisions, the women, the elephants, the camels, the oxen, the horses, the porters, the men that oversaw the provender, the hosts, the merchants, and the servants that these armies brought along. This would also not be surprising for those who understand the special circumstances and the governments of that country, a country in which the shah alone was considered the owner of all the land. Therefore, sometimes the army fed an entire capital such as Delhi or Agra. In such a situation the people were obliged to leave the city and accompany the shah on his war expeditions. These cities did not and could not resemble Paris, since they were in fact just military camps, only slightly more equipped than the camps set up in an open desert.[57]

Marx adds that Bernier had extensively described the advancement of one of the Mogul kings with an army of 400,000 men in Kashmir. The interesting question here is how such a huge army, comprising people and animals, could live in one place. We can only assume that the Indians were content with little food and one in ten or one in twenty cavalries ate meat during their expeditions. Bernier wrote:

> You are no doubt at a loss to conceive how so vast a number both of men and animals can be maintained in the field. The best solution of the difficulty will be found in the temperament of the Indians and the simple nature of their diet. Of the five-score thousand troops, not a tenth, no not a twentieth part, eat animal food; they are satisfied with their *kichery*, a mess of rice and other vegetables, over which, when cooked, they pour boiled butter. It should be considered too that camels endure fatigue, hunger, and third in a surprising degree, live upon little, and eat any kind of food. At the end of every march, they are left to browse in the fields, where everything serves for fodder. It is important likewise to observe that the same tradesmen who supply the bazaars in *Dehli* are compelled to furnish them in the camp; the shops of which they are composed being kept by the same persons whether in the capital or in the field.

> These poor people are at great pains to procure forage: they rove about from village to village, and what they succeed in purchasing, they endeavor to sell in the army at an advanced price. It is a common practice with them to clear, with a sort of trowel, whole fields of a peculiar kind of grass, which having beaten and washed, they dispose of in the camp at a price sometimes very high and sometimes inadequately low.[58]

Marx continues, saying that Bernier had acknowledged the fact that in the East private ownership of the land was not the basis of all phenomena. He uses the examples of Turkey, Iran, and India. This is the key even to the Promised Land in the East.[59]

Besides describing the military system and the eating habits of the Moguls, Bernier presented a concise picture of the meaning of the city in the East (and its difference with the West), the role of the merchants as people whose identities depended upon the kings' objectives, and the relationship between cities and villages. The information contained in this objective report attracted the attention of Marx and Engels. In spite of the rigid and one-dimensional understanding some Marxists had of the development of history, they agreed on the special features of the modes of production in the East. They seemed to agree that these features were responsible for the fact that feudalism (in its Western form) did not appear in these societies and that, consequently, the bourgeoisie was absent in these societies. These features can be summarized as follows:

1. The climatic situation, nature's poverty, the shortage of water, the mode of subsistence
2. The closed natural economy, the collective ownership of the land as a solution to the shortage of water
3. The absence of private ownership of the land
4. The domination of the rural economy over the urban economy
5. The unity between trade and agriculture
6. Oriental despotism
7. Existence of landlordism ("the possession of extensive government power in the political organization"[60]) versus landownership in the West
8. The lack of growth of independent cities and trade centers
9. The absence of individual identity.

Unity of Politics and Economy

One of the structural features of the Asian mode of production is the unity of politics and economics. (The unity of these two establishments points to the backwardness of the society and the separation of this establishment indicates the growth of modernism and bourgeois relations). In the Asian system, both historically and structurally, these establishments have been the same. In the present era, the control of the economy by the state continues as before. However, the growth of a society is not possible without the separation of these establishments. Marx and Engels, with respect to these relations in the East, concluded that the evolution of the Asian societies and the disintegration of government monopoly in economics would only be possible through external forces such as the influence of the West. Marx considered the caste system in India a kind of enduring, rigid division of labor that the British colonialism debased.

What we say about the destructive attempts of Britain in India should not divert our attention from the reality we referred to earlier—the reality that at this point (i.e., during the colonial period) the rural population of India, which had been the basis for the stagnation of this country for thousands of years, disintegrated.[61] Marx said, "England has to fulfill a double mission in India: one destructive, the other regenerating—the annihilation of old Asiatic society, and the laying of the material foundations of Western society in Asia."[62]

But the influence of the West in these societies, whether in the colonized form, the semi-colonized form, or the neo-colonized form, led to other problems, including dual exploitation, the exit of capital, political dependency, contradictions and conflicts, crisis in cultural identity, and the increase in extremist national, religious, and ideological trends. These societies—contrary to Marx and Engels' expectations—could not make use of the opportunities modernism and the West's industrial economy offered. Therefore, underdevelopment continued and in some cases was intensified. In the twentieth century, escape from economic underdevelopment and political dictatorship in these societies became the function of numerous other factors that will be described later.

Citizenry

The form of collective ownership of the land also prevented the growth of the phenomenon of citizenry with independent rights, which is the necessary condition for the development of capitalism and democratic relations. Citizenship in Europe was, from the beginning, based on individual private land ownership.[63] Collective land ownership in the East was an obstacle to the phenomenon of citizenry. Although the collective form of ownership has disintegrated in these societies, due to the persistence of the culture of collective identity and dependence of individuals on groups and the lack of economic independence the state power as the legacy of the old relations is still the main obstacle to the development of individual identity and individuals' rights as citizens. For democratic relations to develop, the growth in the phenomenon of citizenry (i.e., the recognition of individual rights by the government and the society) is needed. The continued existence of the dependency culture and patriarchy compels individuals in present societies to look for a savior to solve their problems and underestimates the role of individuals in the social development.

In his analysis of Marx's views on the Asian mode of production, Ernest Mandel referred to five principles, as follows:

1. The first, and most important, is the lack of private ownership of land.

2. As the result of the above-mentioned situation, rural communes turned into a very coherent force in the organization of the village.

3. The internal consistency of these organizations grew even more because of the presence of unity among people, the unity of trade and agriculture, and the available handicraft.

4. Because of the climatic and geographic conditions, the agricultural land in these regions required a lot of work in irrigation. Artificial irrigation was the first prerequisite to agriculture in these regions. This system of irrigation required, almost everywhere, a central power to regulate it and to mobilize a vast work force.

5. For this reason, the governments succeeded in bringing the major part of the "production in excess of consumption" under their control. As the result, a certain class in the society turned into the absolute ruling class. This force has been called Oriental despotism. The "internal logic" of this society has been based on the justification of stability to produce and preserve the production relations.[64]

Mandel adds that the government or its "Satraps," as second-class regions, controlled the cities. This meant that production remained basically at the level of production for consumption. The increase in the exchange value in the cities provided the ground for the initial accumulation of capital and production for the market. Therefore, the monetary growth and its domination in underdeveloped societies led to the domination of villages over the cities. As far as the production and the financial domains were concerned, the domination of villages over the cities and the domination of the central power over the citizens inhibited the growth of capitalism, and this situation in turn led to inhibition of the growth in productive forces under the Asian mode of production.[65] Such a society, which does not produce beyond its domestic needs, remains underdeveloped.

It should be mentioned that the Asian mode of production in general and its existence in Iran in particular has not been and still is not an uncontested point. Views range from complete negation to the acceptance of some of its aspects in Iran. The opponents of the Asian mode of production believe that the land system in Iran has been either identical to feudalism as it existed in Europe or very close to it. The acceptance of these views can lead us to an array of different conclusions about the reasons for underdevelopment in Iran. Therefore, solving this puzzle seems a necessity.

Military Organization

The organization of military establishments was also different in the East and the West. According to Weber, "The king also expressed his power in the form of a military monopoly, which is the basis of the distinction between the military organization of Asia and that of the West."[66] In the East, the military organization was based on the self-sufficiency of the soldiers. In the West, professional fighters supported the military establishment, and the soldiers were not expected to supply their own military equipment. This situation resembled the independence of workers from the production tools and the land in the West in the modern era, whereas in the East farmers remained dependent upon the land. In the East, the king's power lay in the monopolistic form of military force, while in the West military force was composed of professional fighters. All these differences emanated from the distinct economic mode in the East based on the irrigation system Marx and Engels had analyzed. Therefore, Weber also underscores the importance of the economic factor in the Asian mode of production. As Zeitlin says, "It is therefore undeniable that Weber's analyses of the East largely coincide with Marx's conception of the Asiatic mode of production."[67] However, Weber emphasizes more the political, military, and religious factors. He believed that in the East (specifically, in China and India) certain ruling religious norms made the automatic growth of capitalism in its Western form impossible. In particular, Weber considered Islam to be devoid of the rationalism necessary for the growth of capitalism. He argued that Islam is a religion of "worriers" and that its economic principles are consistent with feudalism, not capitalism.[68]

In conclusion, it should be noted that Iranian political and religious structure, before and after Islam, would no doubt have had common characteristics with partrimonialism. This structure arose from the dominant mode of subsistence, which was based on the geographical conditions. This mode of production does not fit within the European feudal model.

Views on the Land Tenure System in Iran

In the previous chapter, an attempt was made to describe the land system in Iran throughout history from the ancient to the modern eras.

This was done with the objective of showing the rational and natural continuity of the slow growth of this society based on land relations that were born of Iran's climatic conditions. It was shown that during the two thousand five hundred years of this country's history, the land system in Iran has undergone little change, making the investigation of the factors that resulted in this situation relatively easy. In this chapter, the close relation between these features in production and the Asian mode of production has been examined.

Scholars have also analyzed the land tenure system in Iran as the Asian mode of production, or Oriental despotism, as described above. However, it should be mentioned that these views cover a wide spectrum and that while they share common arguments in some respects they suggest the existence of differences as well. Still, the basis for all the explanations offered is the shortage of water. Some of these experts are: Mohammad Ali Khonji,[69] Mohammad Ali (Homayoon) Katuzian,[70] Ann Lambton,[71] Ahmad Ashraf,[72] Khosrow Khosravi,[73] Parviz Pooriya,[74] Sadeq Ziba Kalam,[75] and Habibollah Paymaan.[76] For example, Paymaan criticizes the view of Katuzian that "Iran's political economy has never been feudalistic,"[77] while explaining another aspect of the difference between the subsistence relations and the resulting political economies in Iran and the West. He concludes:

> Although feudalism, as it existed in the West, was not realized in Iran in general, but like slavery, some of its essential elements such as private ownership, the emergence of a class of aristocrats and affluent landowners with administrative, religious, and military power, and the conditional dependence on benefice and fief, and the different forms of benefice, fief and "Soyurghal" are common in both societies and reflect the common tendencies and positions in social development and evolution in each society.[78]

In his critique of Katuzian's view, Paymaan adds, "In my view the form of management used in irrigation and farming is not the main factor that gives rise to the central despotic government."[79] He adds in his description that "The most important factors that initially challenged the security and the stability in these societies and then endangered their existence were the migrating and husbandry tribes that stood in opposition to the agricultural societies from the very beginning, when they had to separate themselves from the early communities."[80] But in response to Paymaan's view it could be said that migration was itself the product of the poverty in nature and then the cause of backwardness. Migrating tribes moved around in search of natural resources and were deprived of a settled civilization. Individual freedom was the product of moving from the tribal mode to the agricultural mode, and that eventually led to the right of land ownership. Despite his differing view on how Oriental despotism came into existence, Paymaan considers climatic factors the origin of the difference between the East and the West. Yet, Paymaan does not consider the form of the management employed in irrigation networks and agriculture and the lack of private ownership of land to be what instigated the emergence of despotism in Iran. In his view, the existence of two kinds of societies (migrating tribes engaged in raising cattle and agricultural societies) and the conflicts between them were the cause of the emergence of Oriental despotism. While emphasizing the factor of water, Paymaan suggests that "The mobile mode of raising cattle is more vulnerable to draught than the agricultural mode."[81] Agricultural societies dealt with the problem of the shortage of water by inventing tools and creating artificial irrigation mechanisms such as constructing subterranean canals and creeks to reach self-sufficiency. However, societies that engaged in raising cattle and those that migrated reacted to the shortage of water by attacking villages and plundering agricultural products. Eventually, the fighting that resulted from these conflicts forced agricultural societies to form armies and organize a defense system to protect their land. The migrating tribes responded mutually. All of the social establishments of that era were affected by these conflicts and the two sides' military organizations. Centralized monarchy and despotism as the best leverage against the migrating tribes took shape in settled societies.[82] Therefore, Paymaan considers the cause of Oriental despotism to be not internal but external.

In my view, the above-mentioned factors constitute the main impetus that led to the invention of the state establishment, not to the emergence of state despotism. It was essentially the conflict of interest between the two parts (one internal and one external) among the tribes—both the settled and the migrating—that led to the invention or the emergence of the government. This has been true on an overall scale and in all societies. What distinguishes the kind and the nature of despotic states from the governments of non-despotic states, in the first stage, is the character of people's relationship with nature and their mode of subsistence, not the nature of their relationship with other human beings. (This reality does not negate the other function of the government, which is bringing together the nation as a central unit.). Throughout the world, the migrating tribes invaded the settled agricultural societies because they had a different mode of subsistence.

Two factors motivated these invasions. One was the exotic appearance of the settled agricultural societies, and the other was drought and nature's hostility, which forced the migrating tribes to undertake the invasions in hope of gaining access to the rich resources. But when powerful governments and empires invaded other territories, their objective was to expand their territories and governments. These invasions were not motivated by the need to unify people.[83] In other words, despotism was not necessarily a defense mechanism against invasions; it was a mechanism for preserving and developing financial, political, and social privileges. In Eastern societies, events such as internal coups and the assassination of ministers and intellectuals took place not as a reaction to attacks by the invading tribes but as a way to gain and preserve wealth and power.

Government despotism in the East was not a phenomenon unique to the East, but throughout the history of the East this was a dominant feature. Moreover, despotism aimed its attack at the internal forces not the external ones—i.e., the lower classes, the elite as a rival, or an obtrusive class. Sometimes centralized governments used the forces of the migrating tribes and united with them against their powerful enemies. For example, the Hyksos, who lived in the Palestine area as a settled population and engaged in agriculture, united with the Jewish population that was a migrating nation and attacked and conquered Egypt in the sixteenth century before the first millennium. The Jewish nation at first enjoyed a status equal to that of the Hyksos population, but in the sixteenth century before the first millennium a number of Egyptian kings succeeded in defeating them and gaining power. As a result of this development, the Jewish nation lost its status, became an inferior nation, and subsequently left Egypt and returned to its original homeland. The story of the journey to Egypt and back is cited in the Old Testament. In Iran and China, the migrating tribes were also able to dominate the settled tribes (farmers and city dwellers). In Iran, the Arabs, the Turks, and the Mongols, and in China the Turks and the Mongols were the invaders that created their own governments in the conquered territories. These invading tribes did not have a class state of their own prior to their victory over these territories.

The interesting point in this regard is the continuous state despotism in these societies. In other words, despotism was the nature of these states as the result of the shortage of water and state ownership or undivided collective land, not because of the attack of migrating tribes. The state in Iran, before and after the domination of Islam or the attacks of other tribal groups, was despotic.

The fact is that the cycle of evolution that resulted from the duality in the mode of subsistence of the migrating tribes and the settled ones extended from Africa to China throughout the history of the East. Ibn Khaldun has described this cycle from a sociological perspective. The main reason for this duality, which has resulted in successive attacks, destruction of civilizations, and their revival, lies in the climatic situation of these regions and the different social orders that were the consequence of it. The cultural contradiction between the settled or the urbanites who engaged in agriculture and the migrating tribes is the outcome of the difference in their relations with their environment, or the degree of their climate's potentials. When one of the two factors dominated—i.e., when the internal contradiction in the settled population heightened and alienated the people, or when absolute poverty afflicted the migrating tribes due to successive droughts or freezing weather—the migrating tribes that were surrounded by a less generous nature attacked the settled tribes. Such developments interrupted the evolutionary process of these societies, but they were never the main cause of the emergence of despotism. As mentioned earlier, despotism targets internal forces, not external ones, while governments target both.

Both of the above-mentioned factors—i.e., the lack of progress in private ownership and the conflicts between the migrating and the settled societies—can be considered the results of the water shortage. One can also conclude that the mode of living among Eastern tribes and their politics and religion were tied to the climatic features of their societies. The progress of the Greek civilization, as mentioned before, followed the same rule. The underdevelopment of both modes of production emanated from the need for centralization in productive forces in raising cattle and in agriculture. The mode of agricultural production required more advanced relations, but since this mode was also affected by limitations and the problem of water shortage, it was not able to break free from the limitations of agricultural life and create products in excess of consumption and urban life and trade relations as more advanced relations. For the migrating tribes, trade had no significance. They exchanged goods for goods. Therefore, they were naturally more distant from the growth that appeared in more advanced civilizations. Lack of trade between migrating tribes and more civilized ones was another cause of their underdevelopment. These tribes had tried to dominate agriculture societies throughout history. Many times, they had succeeded, but as Khosravi has written, "when the migrating tribes won the war and got settled in Iran, at first their mode of production became dominant, but after some time this mode was influenced by Iran's (Asia's) ancient mode of production. The same trend has been witnessed among the Arabs (in the first century, A.H. = 7th century C.E.), the Turks (in the fourth century A.H. = 10th century C.E.), and the Mongols (in the seventh century, A.H. = 13th century C.E.)."[84]

As for the reasons for the emergence of Oriental despotism, various explanations have been offered. All of these explanations are related to the water shortage problem. But even after the centralized Kingdom was organized and the danger of the migrating tribes' attacks was removed despotism continued. Monarchy also emerged in Greece, but the king was not a despot. Therefore, the reason that despotism lasted in Iran is a question the answer to which should be sought in the economic relations of the society, not exclusively in external factors. Although the attacks of the migrating tribes obviously inhibited growth and development in Iranian civilization, it is a mistake to think that the formation of a centralized army had exclusively been accomplished in order to defend the land against these attacks or other expansionist attempts. The other function that military forces have served throughout history has been to preserve the superior position of the ruler, and this function still exists. Despotic governments were formed not just to defend the nation against foreigners but also to control the people of the nation as well.

As for why political despotism lasted in Iran, one may add that the ruling political despotism persisted because the social groups failed to resist the absolute power of the government. Such an imbalance in power is the result of a duality in economic power. Either the economy is controlled by the government or the organizations engaged in production are so weak that they can only produce what they need and thus lack the ability to accumulate capital and create a powerful structure that can engage in something other than agriculture. Consequently, they are deprived of social activity and opportunities for political involvement.

However, as was mentioned earlier, there is no general agreement on whether the political and economic relations in Iran should be considered Asian. Because both the features of feudalism in general and the historical landowning system in Iran have been described in previous sections, I will not describe in detail here the views of the proponents of the idea that feudalism existed in Iran. Therefore, only a cursory look at these views will follow, and the interested reader is referred to the works of the experts mentioned.

Ehsan Tabari refers to an entity that is drastically different from Western feudalism.[85] In reality, the system in which all the land in the nation was considered the shah's personal possession and in which even the landowners were not immune to the shah's wrath and could lose both their lives and their land at the shah's will did not resemble European feudalism in any way. The shah at some junctures in history controlled even trade. Tabari discusses the special features of this system without explicitly defending the Asian mode of production.[86]

Iranian "Feudalism"

Other researchers, however, including Mohammad Reza Feshahi, Hamid Momeni, Petrooshefski, and many others, have specifically stressed the existence of a feudal system in Iran. Feshahi believes that the Iranian society has been a feudal society since the Seleucid era. Before the emergence of feudalism, he says, Iran was heavily influenced by the Greeks, and during the rule of the Seleucids organizations that resembled the Greek polis emerged in Iran.[87] But "the influence of the Greeks coincided with the emergence of feudalism in Iran, and that was why the Greek polises gradually disappeared."[88] He adds, "After the arrival of the Sasanian dynasty at the beginning of the third century C.E., the slave system began to disintegrate and the first phase of the feudal society took shape in Iran before the fifth century C.E."[89]

These relations remained intact until the nineteenth century C.E. According to Feshahi, "In the first half of the nineteenth century, the same old land relations existed, and the feudal lords profited from them."[90] With respect to the growth and development of feudal relations in the Seljuq era, Feshahi considers Nizam-ul-Mulk (Malek Shah's wise minister) the "mastermind of the feudal government."[91] At this time, the landowning system and the political system had reached complete centralization, while in a feudal system power and private ownership by feudal lords (not government benefice) are dispersed. Piccolo Sekaya and his colleagues, authors of *The History of Iran*, emphasize that Nizam-al-Mulk (the author of *Siyasatnameh*) advocated centralization of power and was adamantly against the disparity between the feudal lords. They write:

> In this book, Nizam-al-Mulk passionately defends the traditions of the centralized government of Iran. In his opinion, the governments of the Ghaznavid dynasty, the Samanids, the Buyids in the recent past, and the Sasanian in the ancient time were examples of a centralized government. He believes that the internal policies of these governments were the most desired policies, and he vigorously

criticizes the independence, the disparity, and the stubbornness of feudal lords.[92]

Feshahi is well aware of the fact that the presence of tribal life and the dominance of the migrating tribes over Iran have been one of the main obstacles to the growth of agriculture in Iran. The dominance of the migrating tribes, as we saw previously, was in contradiction to the growth of agricultural relations—both feudalist and Asian. With respect to these tribes' attacks, Feshahi writes:

> After the Mongols conquered Iran, the onrush of desert dwellers to Iran started. The "law" of Gangis Khan prohibited the settlement of the desert dwellers in one area. The riders in the Mongol era had more privileges than those in other eras. The immigration of the Mongol desert dwellers thwarted the course of development of the feudal society in Iran for several reasons. Based on their laws, the Mongol desert dwellers forcefully drove the settled farmers away. Thus, the pastures expanded and cattle raising increased. In other words, farms tuned into pastures.[93]

Many Iranian political scholars have followed the general rule of historical materialism[94] in calling the prevalent mode of production after the Sasanian era feudalism, rather than basing their judgments on their own independent research. For instance, Hamid Momeni emphasizes this point in the introduction he wrote for *The Government of Nader Shah Afshar*. He states, "All human societies pass through specific social systems ... feudalism is a social system all existing societies have had at some point during their history."[95] Based on this general conclusion, he essentially concludes that the feudal hierarchy has existed in Iran, too.[96] He finds the features of the feudal regime in the framework of this view, not the other way around.

Ali Mir Fetrus also refers to the "special kind of feudalism" in Iran. Of course, using this term is indicative of the fact that in his view the production systems in Iran and under Western feudalism were different. He writes:

> Feudalism (whether in the West or in the East) has been fed by similar economic and ideological systems, despite some minor differences. The Islamic scholastic (as the superstructure of feudal ideology that evolved in the Islamic Caliphate's kingdom) has quite a few similarities and harmonious views with the European scholastic of Catholicism and feudalism.[97]

Based on this line of reasoning, and using pre-determined clichés about base superstructure, one cannot point to similar economic and ideological systems in Iran and Europe. The scholastic theology of Islam should be considered the superstructure of the tribal economy that originated from the Arabian Peninsula. The Western economy, in contrast, was formed on the ashes of the slave system economy and the decentralized system of landowning, as well as on the scholastic theology of Christianity, which was influenced by the Greek civilization.

Sadeq Ansari and Baqer Momeni, translators of *The History of the Middle Ages*, write in their introduction that Iranian feudalism had two distinct features that were not seen in the West. The first is that "in the Eastern feudalism, the slave system had been preserved in a certain form for a long period of time."[98] The second feature of Eastern feudalism is that "land belonged to the feudal government and the leader of that government—i.e., the Sultan."[99] Although there is no documented proof regarding the first feature—i.e., the persistence of the slave system in Iran—these two features can effectively point to the fact that this system cannot be called feudalism. Max Weber calls Sultanism a maximized patrimonialism, an absolute authority, which is not equivalent to European feudalism.[100]

It is this difference that created an obstacle to the development of the society in the direction of capitalism. That is why this mode of landowning should be considered distinct and why the different effects it has had in subsequent developments should be taken into consideration.

The foregoing are just a few examples of views that have suggested the existence of feudalism in Iran.[101]

Partrimonialism

The main reason for including a short explanation of partrimonialism[102] in this section is to show the similarities that exist between this system and the Asiatic mode of production on the one hand and the differences between it and feudalism on the other.[103] Two main characteristics of a patrimonial system are (1) arbitrary power, and (2) the fact that the administration is directly under the control of an absolute ruler. Norman Jacobs has argued that the source of backwardness in Eastern societies, which continues to affect the political and economic institutions, has been the traditional authority of partrimonialism.[104] It should be noted that partrimonialism should be distinguished from the other traditional form of authority, Patriarchalism. Jonathan H. Turner et al. write:

> Weber distinguishes between two forms of traditional authority, only one of which has administrative apparatus. Patriarchalism is a type of traditional domination occurring in households and other small groups where the use of an organizational staff to enforce commands is not necessary. Partrimonialism is a form of traditional domination occurring in larger social structures that require an administrative apparatus to execute edicts.[105]

In Patriarchalism, which is the earliest and most traditional form of power, the society is formed based on a tribal economic system as a large family, and the power of leadership is traditional and hereditary. On the other hand, the personnel of the state establishment, including the military forces, are considered the personal servants of the leader. The state employees are no longer considered the members of the leader's family but instead become the official servants of the establishment, to the point that certain groups in the society may turn into slaves. This system leaves the boundaries of the tribe's leadership, and the sultan assumes unlimited power over multiple ethnic and tribal groups.

Norman Jacobs, who has done extensive study on the theories and concept of development of Eastern societies, focuses on the role of the patrimonial system as the source of backwardness in these societies. Jacobs indicates that his definition of partrimonialism differs from what his predecessors like Marx and Weber and their disciples, notably Karl A. Wittfogel, contributed to the elaboration of the concept[106]. Briefly, Jacobs' model is based on social rather than material considerations. Regarding the characteristics of his model, he writes: "The patrimonial system is a (model) social type distinct from and parallel to a feudal-cum-successor social type, each with its own stages of social evolvement, *including the present*"[107] However, Jacobs emphasizes that this model is not a substitute for the conventional Eurocentric models, which assume "(1) that all precapitalist or presocialist agrarian societies are feudal; (2) if the patrimonial concept is recognized, that partrimonialism is a stage which existed universally prior to feudalism; or (3) that partrimonialism is Asia's peculiar road to universally shared evolutionary destiny."[108] Jacobs, in his other book, *Modernization Without Development: Thailand as an Asian Case of Study*, argues that there are differences between the feudal land tenure system and that of partrimonialism. Unlike feudal societies, under partrimonialism land is not inherited through family relations, private transformation, or internal group relations, but as in the Asiatic mode of production it is granted as a gift or special privilege to the holders of bureaucratic positions. This right is rooted in the royalty of the king.[109]

In addition, the strong patrimonial system in the East kept the local governors dependent upon the central system. However, in the feudal West the local powers and kingdoms used their independent military forces and broke away from the patrimonial system's limitations.

Max Weber, like many other thinkers in the social sciences, was eager to find an explanation for the initial growth of individualistic capitalism in the West, as opposed to the East. This issue compelled him to do research on the cultural and structural differences between the civilizations in the East and the West. Weber, like Marx, was able to identify the special features of the Asian mode of production. He described the Asian mode of production in the form of partrimonialism, predominantly in Chinese society, as a willful, bureaucratic, and despotic regime of monarchs. These political characteristics in Eastern societies separate them from the West.

On these differences, Weber writes, "Marx has enumerated the special features of the Indian artisans in rural areas. The dependence of these artisans on fixed wages (in the form of commodities) instead of producing for sale in the market, has been the main reason why the Asian people have remained so stable, but also stagnant." Weber considers Marx to be right on this issue.[110] In his studies of the Asian mode of production, Weber considered the religious and political factors (oriental despotism), in addition to economic factors. He described oriental despotism as being based on forced labor and a liturgical, centralized, bureaucratic state. In such a state, the monarch fed, equipped, and led the army and became the absolute landlord and all-powerful ruler.[111] Because this system was bound up with the administrative requirements of river regulation and irrigation, the monarch had successfully separated all administrative officials from control over these key resources. Due to these economic, political, and religious characteristics, Weber observed, "the East and the West show in this respect the usual contrast."[112]

[1] Irving M. Zeitlin, *Ideology and the Development of Sociological Theory*, 6th ed. (New Jersey: Prentice Hall, 1977), 171.

[2] A.K.S. Lambton, *Landlord and Peasant in Persia* (London: Oxford University Press 1953), p. 2.

[3] Karl Marx and Friedrich Engels, *Selected Correspondence* (Moscow: Foreign Languages Publishing House, 1953).

[4] Francois Bernier. *Travels in the Mongul Empire A.D. 1656–1668* (Westminster, UK: Archibald Constable and Company, 1670), 354.

[5] Karl Marx and Friedrich Engels, *On Colonialism: Article from the New York Tribune and other Writings* (New York: International Publishers, 1972), 313.

[6] Ibid., 313.

[7] Max Weber. *The Theory of Social Economic Organization* (New York: Free Press, 1947).

[8] Adam Smith, *An Inquiry into the Nature and the Causes of Wealth of the Nations* (New York: Modern Library, 1937).

[9] James Mill, *History of British India* (Chicago: University of Chicago, 1975).

[10] Richard Jones, *An Essay on the Distribution of Wealth and the Sources of Taxation* (New York: A.M. Kelley, 1964).

[11] [11]Irving M. Zeitlin, *Ideology* op. cit. -, 169. For more details on the views of thinkers such as Aristotle, Francis Bacon, Hobbes, Rousseau, Adam Ferguson, Hegel, etc., see Roni Ambiorenson, "Asia in the Eyes and the Hearts of the Europeans: Analysis of European Theoreticians about Europe, From the Perspective of the History of Sciences and Ideas," trans. Seyyed Mohammad Fazl Hashemi, *Nameye Farhang: Research Quarterly on Cultural and Social Issues*, 6th year, no. 2, 22, Summer of 1975. See also Yadollah Mowqan, "The History of Oriental Despotism," *Negah-e-nou*, No. 23, Azar-Bahman, 1973. In addition, see Qafoor Mirzaie, *Tomorrow a Captive of Yesterday: The History of Iran and the Analysis of the Elements that Construct the Cultural and Governmental Structure* (Los Angeles: Mazda Publishers, 1976), 205–210

[12] Karl Marx, "The British Rule in India," *New York Daily Tribune*, June 25, 1853. See Irving Zeitlin, Chapter 15, ibid.

[13] Friedrich Engels, *Anti-Duhring: Herr Eugen Duhring's Revolution in Science* (New York: International Publishers, 1939).

[14] Karl Marx, "Letters to Sasolovich," in Keyvan Dadfar et al., *The Scientific Socialism and the Class Struggle*, No. 1, (Tehran: Entersharat Sa'di, Farvardin, 1358 (1980)).

[15] Karl Marx, *The Capital*, vol. 3, (New York: International Publishers, 1894), pp. 325–331. Also see *Dynamics of Social change: A Reader in Marxist Social Science*, 3r ed., ed. Howard Selsam et al. (New York: International Publishers, 1975), 238.

[16] Karl Marx, *The Grundrisse*, ed. and trans. David Mclellan (New York: Harper Torchbooks, 1971). Besides Marx and Engels' scattered writings about the special features of the Asian mode of production and oriental despotism,

Marx explained these relations in the notes he wrote in 1875 about the process of initial capital accumulation entitled, "Different Forms of Production Before Capitalism." Marx and Engels first showed interest in these features in 1853 while studying England's policies in India. Marx's pamphlet was first published about a century later in 1939. This pamphlet was entitled, "An Introduction to the Critique of Political Economy." [Two different Farsi translations of this pamphlet were published within a short period in 1353 and 1354, one by the Organizations of the National Front (abroad) under the title "Pre-Capitalist Economic Formations," by Karl Marx, and the other by the Research Group, entitled, "The Scientific Socialism and Class Struggle," a supplement to issue no. 1, Farvardin 1358, edited and written by Keyvan Dadfar et al. This book is a collection of Marx and Engels' views on the Asian mode of production, and it explains the factors involved in this mode and its consequences. Also see the series of essays by Mohammad Ali Khonji about the Asian mode of production in the *Monthly of Political and Economic Information*, 9th and 10th years, 1374-1375].

[17] For the views of Russian Marxists in the Leningrad Conference and afterwards, see Stephen P. Dunn, *The Fall and Rise of the Asiatic Mode of Production* (UK: Routledge and Kegan Paul Ltd., 1982). (Persian trans. by Abbas Mokhber, Tehran: Markaz Publications, 1368).

The above-mentioned writings do not get involved in the dispute among the Marxists about the Asian mode of production. What main theme of the discussion presented by the participants in the Leningrad conference concerned who favored or disagreed with this mode of production as a concept. Although Marx's research and point of view has been used as the view of a creative and reliable researcher, the argument here is based on the principle that "this argument is valid and Marx had adopted it too" and not "Marx has adopted this argument, so it must be valid."

[18] Ernest Mandel, *The Formation of the Economic Thought of Karl Marx* (New York: Monthly Review Press, 1971).

[19] V.I. Lenin, *Collected Works*, vol. 20, 21 (Moscow: Progress Publishers, 1971).

[20] Ibid.

[21] See Karl August Withfogel, *Oriental Despotism: A Comparative Study of Power* (New Haven, CT: Yale University Press, 1957).

[22] Ibid.

[23] Some experts have considered the feudal system in Japan similar to European feudalism. The reason for the development of capitalism in this society has been explained from this perspective. For example, see Peter Duss, *Feudalism in Japan: Studies in World Civilizations*, 2nd ed. (New York: Alfred Knopf, 1976).

[24] See George V. Plekhanov, *Fundamental Problems of Marxism: The Materialism in Conception of History, The Role of Individual in History* (New York: International Publishers, 1975).

[25] Leon Trotsky, "The Permanent Revolution," in Ernest Mandel, op. cit.

[26] Joseph Stalin, "Dialectic Materialism and the Historical Materialism," in *Three Essays by Stalin*, The Marxist-Leninist Organization of Tufan, no. 8, Azar 1348.

[27] Ernest Mandel, op. cit.

[28] Keyvan Dadfar et al., "The Scientific Socialism and the Class Struggle," no. 1 (Tehran: Farvardin, 1358 (1980)).

[29] Friedrich Engels, "Letter to Marx, Manchester, June 6, 1853," in Karl Marx and Friedrich Engels, *On Colonialism*, (New York: International Publishers, 1972), 314.

[30] Keyvan Dadfar et al., op cit., 1358.

[31] Friedrich Engels, [Anti During], vol. 20, p. 590, quoted from Keyvan Dadfar et al., 107.

[32] Keyvan Dadfar et al., ibid., 107.

[33] Ibid., 107.

[34] Max Weber, *The Theory of Social and Economic Organization* (New York: Free Press, 1947), 346.

[35] Ibid., 347.

[36] Ibid., 346.

[37] Ibid.

[38] Ibid.

[39] Friedrich Engels, *The Origin of the Family, Private Property and the State* (New York: International Publishers, 1975).

[40] Marc Bloch, *Feudal Society* (Chicago: University of Chicago Press, 1961), 112.

[41] Ibid., 112.

[42] Will Durant, *Caesar and Christ: The Story of Civilization, part III* (New York: Simon and Schuster, 1991).

[43] . Phillip K. Hitti, *History of the Arabs*, 10th ed. (London: St Martin's Press, 1970), 242.

[44] Bernier Francois, *Travels in the Mongul Empire,* (Westminster: Archibald Constable and Company, 1670), 360.

[45] Max Weber, *The Religion of India*, trans. and ed. Hans H. Gertis and Don Martindale (Glencoe, IL: The Free Press, 1958)

[46] A.K.S. Lambton, *Land and Peasant in Persia*, 1953, p. 2.

[47] The Sumerians, the Akads, and the Babylonians were the first centralized governments in the region, and their history goes back to 2,000 years before the birth of the Christ. These governments in Mesopotamia were among the oldest governments in the world and were considered the basins of civilization. See Akajdan et al., *The History of the Ancient World*, vol. 1, trans. Sadeq Ansari, Dr. Aliollah Hamedani, and Mohammad Baqer Momeni, 4th ed. (Tehran: Andisheh, 1353).

[48] Max Weber, *The Theory of Social Economic Organization*, ed. Talcott Parsons (New York: The Free Press, 1947). Weber sees oikos as one of a wide

variety of different possibilities of partrimonialism and an obstacle to the development of capitalism. He writes: "an *oikos* is maintained by the chief, where needs are met on a liturgical basis wholly or primarily in kind in the form of contributions of goods and compulsory services. In this case, economic relationships tend to be strictly bound to tradition, the development of markets is obstructed, the use of money is primarily oriented to consumption, and the development of capitalism is impossible." (Ibid., 354). Also, see Irving Zeitlin, op. cit., 219.

[49] Ibid.

[50] Irving Zeitlin, 220.

[51] Ibid.

[52] Ibid.

[53] Bahman Nirumand, *The New Imperialism in Action* (New York: Monthly Review Press, 1949).

[54] Friedrich Engels, op. cit.

[55] Francois Bernier, *Travels Containing a Description of the Dominations of the Great Moguls, (Voyages Contenant la Description des etas du Grand Mogol* (Westminster: Archibald Constable and Company, 1670).

[56] Mogul emperor (1659–1707).

[57] Karl Marx, "Letter to Engels in Manchester London, Jane 2, 1953" cited in On Historical Materialism, (Tehran: Vahdat Komonisti, 1358 (1980), 19–20).

[58] Francois Bernier, op. cit., 381–82.

[59] Quoted from the *Correspondences Between Marx and Engels About Historical Materialism,* the Organization of the Communist Unity, 1358, 19-20.

[60] Max Weber, 1947, 379.

[61] See "Decline of the Indian Nation Under the Conditions of Colonization," in *Scientific Socialism and the Class Struggle* (Tehran: Entesharat Sa'di, 1358 (1980)), 82.

[62] Karl Marx, "The Future Results of British Rule in India," in *The Marx-Engels Reader*, ed. Robert Tucker (New York: Norton and Company, 1972), 583.

[63] Bryan Turner, "Citizenship Studies: A General Theory," *Journal of Citizenship Studies*, vol. 1, 1, Feb. 1997.

[64] Ernest Mandel, op. cit.

[65] Ibid.

[66] Max Weber, Max, cited in M. Irving Zeitlin, op. cit., 221.

[67] M. Irving Zeitlin, op. cit., 221.

[68] Maxime Rodinson challenges this view of Weber's that growth in capitalism requires Protestant reforms. He argues that Islam and capitalism have no inherent contradictions. However, he supports Weber in considering Islam a religion of worriers, and he calls Prophet Mohammad an armed prophet. (Source: Ali Mir Fetrus, *Some Considerations in the History of Iran, Islam and the True Islam,* 1st ed. (Canada/France) (Tehran: Farhang, 1988), 58.)

[69] Mohammad Ali Khonji, *An Essay on the Analysis of the History of the Medes and the Source of Diakonov's Theory Along With Other Essays and Notes*, 1st ed. (Tehran: Tahoori, 1358).
[70] Mohammad Ali (Homayoon) Katuzian, *The Political Economy of Modern Iran, Despotism and Pseudo-Modernism, 1962–1979*. Used Persian edition: *The Political Economy of Iran, From the Constitutional Revolution to the End of the Pahlavi Dynasty*, 2nd ed., trans. Mohammad Reza Nafisi and Kambiz Azizi (Tehran: Markaz Publication, 1372). Katuzian is one of the scholars who negate the existence of the feudal system in Iran.
[71] A.K.S. Lambton, *Landlord and Peasant in Persia: A study of Land Tenure and Land Revenue Administration* (London: Oxford University Press, 1953).
[72] Ashraf considers the main obstacles to the emergence of industrial capitalism in Iran to be both external and internal factors. The internal factors in his view originate from the urban, rural, and tribal modes of production, and the external factors from the semi-colonized situation in Iran.
[73] Khosrow Khosravi, *The Rural Society in Iran*, 2nd ed. (Tehran: Tehran University Press, 2535 (1977)); and *The Peasant Society in Iran* (Tehran: Payam, 1957).
[74] Parvis Pooriya, "Obstacles to the Development in Iran: Historical Factors (4)," *Politico-Economic Information*, May-June, 1371. Pooriya presents a clear and distinct view about the existence of the Asian mode of production in Iran.
[75] Sadeq Zibakalam, *How Did We Become We: Looking for the Roots of Underdevelopment in Iran* (Tehran: Roozaneh, 1373).
[76] Habibollah Paymaan, "On the Iranian Despotism," in Javad Mousavi Khorasani, *Towse'a Book*, no. 10, 1974.
[77] Mohammad Ali (Homayoon) Katuzian, ibid., 345 (Persian edition).
[78] Habibollah Paymaan. ibid, 89.
[79] Ibid., 85
[80] Ibid., 85
[81] Ibid., 85.
[82] Ibid.
[83] Some experts consider the source of emergence of states in the East different from that of the West. For instance, Sadeq Zibakalam writes: "If the formation of states in the West was based on conflict (as Marx argues), the source of emergence of states in the East has been mainly 'unity,' or the necessity of collective works" (op. cit., 101). In other words, he believes that due to the shortage of water, the state emerged to unite people to meet the needs of production. Marx, and particularly his colleague Engels, considered the difference between the East and the West in this regard (see *Anti-Duhring*, New York: International Publishers, 1972), but the view that conflict as the source of the emergence of states is shared among many, including Marx and Engels. The state as an apparatus of control initially emerged as a result of the conflict over production surplus. Tribal authority in ancient Eastern societies should not be equated with the state. Also, the state was not a means of production, but the

means of control of production. The state was needed to protect the private ownership and production. In other words, in ancient societies the state was formed because of surplus production, not a shortage of production. But class conflicts were a general and historical factor that led to the emergence of the state. Zibakalam has unjustifiably equated states and societies. What he considers to be the outcome of unity is the society, not the government. For example, he holds that ancient Iranian society emerged following the unity of six tribal groups. However, the state of the Medes in Iran was the outcome of one tribe's domination (the Medes) over the other tribes. In the ancient era, the domination of the tribe led by Herald in Norway resulted in the formation of the government. In Peru, the victory of the Inca nation over the other nations resulted in the creation of a powerful centralized empire that matched the governments of Iran and Rome. See Amir Hossein Aryanpour, *The Background to Sociology*, 7th ed. (Dehkoda, Iran: Pocket Books, 1353).

States are formed when people become settled in an area and specify boundaries for their territories. Managing the affairs of a society requires a leadership and a government. Marvin Harris, adopting an anthropological perspective, has stated that the root of the government is strengthened by an order in which concentrated labor leads to the emergence of products in excess of consumption See Marvin Harris, *Cannibals and Kings: The Origins of Cultures* (New York: Random House, 1977).

This concentrated labor gives rise to the excess value that is the cause of the conflicts among rival groups. The dominant group creates a government as the lever of power to prevent the other groups from gaining access to the resources they have forcefully conquered. The unity of a society is only possible when these class divisions and the new social order are preserved. If the forces of the dominated group do not accept this order, the government will be transformed from a unifying and protecting factor to a repressive one. This phenomenon is universal and historical. To consider the government a unifying factor is to adopt the superficial view that overlooks the depth of the mechanism that produces the government's performance and its relationship with the society.

Let us add that it is not merely Marx or the Marxists who consider class conflicts the main cause of the emergence of governments. For example, Max Weber considered a government as a monopolistic institution that legitimizes violence in the realm of its sovereignty. Or, for example, Daniel Chirot, in discussing the emergence of government in agricultural societies, says, "Governments are born out of growing social conflicts and wars. They continue for the most part of their existence as an exploiting machine that mercilessly exploits the majority of the population, engages in wars with its neighbors, provokes the dissidents, and incites violent competitions among the elite" (ibid., 25). Also see Will Durant, *Our Oriental Heritage* (part I of *The Story of Civilization*), Chapter 3 (New York: Simon and Schuster, Inc., 1935).

These different theories about the emergence of governments all consider it the outcome of conflicts, wars, and expansionist attempts, not a unifying factor. There is no need to go back to ancient history. We need only look around us to better understand the main cause of the existence of governments, in particular despotic governments. The change in the performance of a government, from an agent of control and repression to an agent of unity that protects the boundaries, is only possible if the society moves toward democracy and recognizes the rights of individuals as citizens. Democracy and citizenry are modern and relatively new phenomena. Despotic governments use war as a device to help them consolidate their domination within their societies, not as a tool to help them to defend their country's boundaries.

[84] Khosrow Khosravi, *The Sociology of Iranian Rural Areas*, ibid, 58–59.

[85] Ehsan Tabari, "Some Analyses About Worldviews and Social Movements in Iran," from the publications of the Tudeh Party in Iran, 1354.

[86] The official position Tabari held in the Tudeh Party of Iran and the fact that this party's policies were directly taken from the Communist Party of the former Soviet Union prevented Tabari's multi-dimensional, extraordinarily resourceful views as a capable researcher in contemporary Iran from flourishing freely.

[87] Mohammad Reza Feshahi, *A Short Report on the Intellectual and Social Developments in the Feudal Society of Iran (from the Goths to the Constitutional Revolution)* (Tehran: Gutenberg, 1354).

[88] Ibid., 39.

[89] Ibid., 41.

[90] Ibid., 195.

[91] Ibid., 117. Feshahi has also referred to Rashid al-Din Fazollah as the mastermind of feudalism during the Mongol era and to this period in Iran as the period of the exultation in feudalism. See ibid., 143–144.

[92] N.V. Piccolo et al., *The History of Iran from the Ancient Era to the End of the Eighteenth Century A.D.*, 5th ed., trans. Karim Keshavarz (Tehran: Payam, 1363), 271.

[93] Mohammad Reza Feshahi, ibid, 141. (translated from Persian)

[94] These people refer to a universal linear path of historical development of societies in the following five stages: primitive commune, slavery, feudalism, capitalism, and communism. Russian historians who followed the communist party line wrote their books to justify this framework. Others who were influenced by Russians followed the same path.

[95] Hamid Momeni, in M. R. Aroonova and K. Z. Ashrafian, *The Government of Nader Shah Afshar* (the general outline of social relations in Iran in the fourth and the fifth decades of the eighteenth century), Publication No. 79 of the Institute for Social Studies and Research (Tehran: Tehran University, 1352), 11.

[96] Ibid.

[97] Ali Mir Fetrus, *Hallaj*, 5th ed. (Tehran: 1357), 88. (translated from Persian)

[98] Sadeq Ansari and Mohammad Baqer Momeni, *The History of the Middle Ages*, under the supervision of professor Kaminski, trans. Ansari, Momeni, vol. 4, 4th ed. (Tehran: Andisheh, 1353), 22. (translated from Persian)
[99] Ibid.
[100] Max Weber, *The Theory of Social and Economic Organization.*
[101] For Further information, see Farhad Nomani, "Origin and Development of Feudalism in Iran: 300–1600," Dissertation, University of Illinois, 1972.
[102] See Max Weber, op cit., 346–358. In addition to Marx Weber, James Mill, Karl Wittfogel, and Eric Wolf have studied partrimonialism in the East.
[103] With respect to the role of partimonialism in the development of the East, see Norman Jacobs, "The Condition of Patrimonial Theory in Explaining the Roots of and Guiding Asian Development in the Twenty-First Century: A Theoretical Introduction," *Asian Perspective*, vol. 13, 2, Fall–Winter 1989, 5–34.
[104] Norman Jacobs, *The Korean Road to Modernization and Development* (Chicago: University of Illinois Press, 1985).
[105] H. Jonathan Turner et al., *The Emergence of Sociological Theory*, 4th ed. (New York: Wadsworth Publishing Co., 1989), 174.
[106] Norman Jacobs, op cit., 1989.
[107] Norman Jacobs, op. cit., 1985, 4.
[108] Ibid., 4.
[109] Norman Jacobs, *Modernization Without Development: Thailand as an Asian Case Study* (New York: Praeger Publications, 1971).
[110] M. Irving Zeitlin, op cit., 218.
[111] Not all patrimonial leaders are divine. For example, see Norman Jacobs as he describes a Thai patrimonial ruler. He writes: "…Thai leadership, although it is absolute, is not divine…" (Jacobs, op. cit., 1971, p. 28).
[112] Max Weber, *General Economic History*, trans. Frank H. Knight (New York: Collier Books, 1961), cited in Irving M. Zeitlin, op. cit, 20.

Chapter 4
Why Did Capitalism Not Grow in Iran?

In order to answer the question of why capitalism did not grow in Iran, we need to first address the reasons why the rise of the bourgeois class, the development of independent cities, and the division of labor—which all happened in the West—did not happen in Iran. The short answer is that there were obstacles to development of these characteristics in Iran. Principal among them were the non-feudal land tenure system, tribal domination, the integration of agricultural and commercial activities, and political despotism.

Comparison Between the East and the West

As was discussed earlier, agriculture is the main pillar of feudalistic production, and it depends upon water and fertile land. The amount of available water in agriculture accounts for the most notable difference between the East and the West, as far as production (the foundation of the society) is concerned. The abundance of water in the West and the shortage of water in the East, along with the poor quality of the soil in the East, have resulted in different social, political, and cultural consequences in these regions. While in the West the availability of water was a comfort to the human work force, in the East the major part of a peasant's energy was devoted to securing water. Due to the facts that securing water was both costly and difficult and that it was not a task that an individual could undertake independently, the centralized power of the state had to organize and manage the human forces necessary to secure water.[1] As a result, two forms of ownership (state and collective) originally came into existence and were extended in several forms. In the East, agricultural land was worthless without irrigation. Therefore, land ownership was largely determined by the ownership of water resources. Thus, states (ruled by kings), having the monopoly control over the military forces, became the most powerful landowners, and peasants mostly became the king's work force. The motto in Iran that "the land and the peasants both belong to the king" stems from this reality.

After the emergence of Islam, as discussed in Chapter 3, a new form of landholding—i.e., *iqta* (benefice)—became more common in Iran. Land was usually given as an *iqta* to regional rulers or to someone else the king controlled. *Iqta* usually changed ownership during a generation, and normally the king was free to seize back the land he had given away and transfer it to someone else when he so desired. In the 9th century, during the Seljuq dynasty, *iqta* was changed into *soyurghal*, or military and administrative *iqta*.

In the West, land that was allocated to feudal lords was no longer in the king's possession. Feudal lords had special military forces bestowed upon them in return for a piece of land they transferred to military officials as feud. Unlike the West, in the East the king determined the nature of the relationships he had with landholders and peasants. With regard to the dispersion and the independence of different regions in Germany, Engels presented his views as follows: "...Germany was divided into various independent provinces that were completely isolated from one another. As a nation, this country had to endure a situation in which each province was divided into numerous divisions."[2] In the West, the allocation of power was the basic principle. In the East, power was concentrated in the hands of a despot. The nature of the landowning system they had, in the East or the West, determined the nature of each society.

The independence that the feudal lords enjoyed in the West, and the peasants' dependence upon the land in the East, stemmed from two different types of landholding: private ownership by feudal lords in the West and state (king)-controlled or collective ownership by the peasants in the East. While the former led to the distribution of political power among hundreds of feudal lords, the latter placed the political power in the hands of the kings and paved the way for absolute despotism. Such relations could lead to the Asiatic mode of production or to a patrimonial system, both of which were politically different from feudalism. Collective ownership also created the village organization, which deprived the peasants of their individual freedom and inhibited the emergence of free labor. In Europe, the king's authority was limited, and he relied predominantly on the support of feudal lords. In the East, regional rulers played no role in electing the king. Sometimes these tribal rulers attempted to engage in military attacks in order to seize the power of the king or another local ruler, but military aggression against other rulers or the king was not done with the aim of reducing the centralized power of the king. Instead, it was an attempt on the part of a ruler to expand the realm of his own power. The establishment of these two ownership modes and political and cultural behavior naturally led to two different types of futures. In the West, along with the development of cities a bourgeois class arose that eventually defeated the feudal lords economically and built its own financial kingdom. In the East, in contrast, confronting the centralized power of the king, who held a monopoly on the military forces and controlled a major portion of the trades, turned out to be an impossible task. This was the case particularly because of the fact that monarchy was considered a divine trust. Of course, in some eras in the history of Iran a certain type of feudal society was formed, but it only bore the fruit of intensified tension and military confrontation between different tribes and regional rulers. Contemporary Western civilization was the fruit of the attempts made by the bourgeoisie to ensure the disintegration of feudalism and the growth of commodity relations, which replaced the natural, self-sufficient economy.

In the East, the king, the caliph, or their subordinates generally controlled the regional rulers. In the West, by contrast, feudal lords controlled the king. In the East, the king enjoyed absolute power and was able to replace rulers readily, while in the West feudal lords owned the land they ruled over. The absolute power of the king in the East was the outcome of state ownership of the land, the main source of income. In the West, agricultural land was operated privately, and feudal lords were its principal owners. In the East, the king stood at the head of the only organized army, which had the responsibility of preserving the king's absolute power and maintaining control over the land that he dominated. In the West, feudal lords enjoyed the support of the fighters they controlled. In the East, the king's laws governed the country, whereas in the West feudal lords made the laws governing the territories they controlled. In the East, the centralized despotic power was in the hands of one individual, while in the West the despotic power was distributed among feudal lords, kings, princes, and the church. In the East, the integration of religion and state was the existing order, whereas in the West the church establishment, like a feudal lord and powerful landowner (which it was), was separate from the local power of the lords and a rival power to the monarchical authority. For several centuries, popes in the Catholic Church tried to impose themselves as the faultless representatives of God on earth. They considered themselves the "soul" of society and considered monarchs to be its body. By this division, the Popes reached the natural conclusion that soul was superior and demanded that the kings follow their orders. This rivalry was due to the feudal land tenure system in Europe.[3]

Why Did Capitalism Grow in the West?

> The economic structure of capitalistic society has grown out of the economic structure of feudal society. The dissolution of the latter set free the elements of the former. K. Marx[4]

So far we have dealt with the reasons that feudalism emerged in the West, why it did not emerge in the East, and the differences between the Asian mode of production and feudalism. This section, in an abstract and pinpoint format, deals specifically with the factors that led to the originator of contemporary Western civilization—capitalism.

The first area in which capitalist production grew was the industries of spinning and weaving in England in the eighteenth century. In these industries, merchants decided, for the first time, to buy two types of commodities at the same time. One was the equipment and the raw materials, and the other was human labor.[5] Before the emergence of capitalist production, laborers (peasants) also worked for wages, but in the capitalist mode of production, except for sharecropping, this turned into a focal principle. The workers became a class that depended upon wages to survive. In other words, this meant the transformation of peasants who depended upon the land into free workers who were dependent upon wages earned from their labor.

Thus, the capital had to provide the peasants with another job, either along with their main job as farmers or as a replacement for their dependence upon the land. Also at issue was forcing the landowners to leave the peasants alone so that they could make decisions for themselves. Of course, the material conditions governing the lives of the peasants, both before and after the emergence of capitalism, were out of the peasants' control. The merchants who had capital purchased the land and caused the peasants who depended upon the land and the landowners who controlled them to be separated, thus freeing the peasants and allowing them to be drawn to non-agricultural workshops, first in rural and then in urban areas. This was how the initial accumulation of capital—which combined a free work force (wage workers as opposed to farmers who received shares) and technology (the means of production) with cash capital (the mediator)—was formed.

The key to the emergence of capitalism, in other words, was the development of working for wages. One has to ask why this situation came about in the West and not in the East. Although the *tuyul*[6] system surfaced during some periods in the East, the conditions were still not ripe for their development into capitalism. What should have occurred, but did not, was the freeing of the peasants from the land. The share-holding system (sharing of the products) remained dominant throughout the history of Iran. What would have been necessary to bring about the emergence of capitalist relations in Iran was not only the feudal system but also the necessary conditions for the growth of the phenomenon of free peasants (free from the landlord's yoke and free from any type of ownership, either public or private), so that they could become wage-earning workers.[7] This was what happened in the West.

We may say that the secret of the development of capitalist relations in the West can be summarized as follows:

1. Unlike their Eastern counterparts, the Western merchants were drawn to production. In Iran, trade still enjoys priority over production, as it does in all pre-capitalist societies. In modern societies, this relationship is reversed.[8]

2. In the West, during the period before the breakup of feudalism, the political power was not centralized. Rather, it was dispersed, and the holders of the power, unlike in the East, were weak.[9] The remoteness of the cities from the areas where the feudal lords resided on the one hand, and the existence of independent military establishments on the other, had disrupted the concentration of power. The relationship between the political, military, and trade forces was vague and even hostile. In the East, these three forces were concentrated in one establishment (the central government).

3. In the West, feudal landowners prevented the merchants from investing in land. They knew that the ownership of land was the foundation of the ruling class and its power.[10] The feudal lords needed the merchants (more than the central governments did) to exchange their excess products for other strategic products. The central governments in the West used tax money to pay for their expenses, while in the East ownership of the land performed this function.

4. By prohibiting the merchants from investing in land and obtaining political power, the feudal lords forced the merchants to invest in less-secure investments. Therefore, the merchants invested their

capital and excess products in concentrated and open trading. This opportunity allowed them to accumulate money, not land, and their capital was invested in different areas of business activities. Of course, trade was prevalent in all areas of the world, including Iran, but nowhere did trade automatically turn into the capitalist mode of production.[11]

Major Characteristics of Capitalism in the West

To facilitate understanding of the material presented in this chapter, an abstract is presented here.

- Capitalism was the originator of contemporary Western civilization.
- The factor that gave rise to capitalism in the West was the presence of feudalism as an unprotected system. Europe had been divided into many pieces dominated by the feudal lords.
- Capitalism first appeared in England, because this country was the main center for the production of a key product in capitalism—wool.
- The first industries that served the manufacturing of this product and made it international were spinning and weaving.
- The advance of science was revolutionary—this would not have been realized without the bourgeois revolution.
- The Industrial Revolution was a great development within capitalism, not vice versa. It led to the industrialization of capitalism. However, capitalism would not have survived without industrialization.
- Capitalism started in rural areas, but the force that transformed villages came from the cities. Thus, village life lost its dominance over life in the cities.
- With the increase in population and the resulting need for more commodities, capitalism turned into an effective system to meet this need.
- Profit was the incentive that motivated growth in capitalism, but without social, religious, political, and cultural developments in civilized society the incentive for profit making could have turned into slavery. The revival of the ancient Greek intellectual and philosophical legacy and the judicial relations of Rome created the ground for this development.[12]
- Securing cheap labor would not have been possible unless the peasants had gained freedom in both labor and ownership). The

separation between labor (the force of production) and property (the means of production) is essential for capitalistic development.

- Capitalism could not have been transmuted into the main power of society if the serf system had not disintegrated. The private ownership based on personal employment had to be replaced by private ownership based on the employment and exploitation of others.

- The ground for the emergence of the Industrial Revolution could not have been established without the incentive for individual profit, production for sale in the market, and competition between producers. Also, without the Industrial Revolution capitalism could not have become an international system.

- The basis for the accumulation of capital and the growth of capitalism could not have materialized without the cruel exploitation of workers, in much the same way that without slavery the Greek and Roman empires would not have been built.

- Capitalism would not have gone through a revolutionary development unless the commercial economy had been transformed into the industrial economy (merchants becoming industrialists)—i.e., unless the exchange of commodities had changed to become the process of production.

- Capitalism would not have grown unless capital and the use of the world's natural reservoirs and resources, such as precious metals, had become international.

- These developments did not take place in Iran. People remained dependent upon agriculture for the production of the necessary means for their survival. Suitable land and accessible water to increase production were scarce. Artificial irrigation in Iran took from the farmers and from society all of the energy and time they had. As already mentioned, the main obstacles to the emergence of capitalism in Iran were the landowning system, the presence of migrating tribes, and the unity of trade and agriculture (i.e., commerce and agriculture).

- As far as the social, political, and cultural dimensions are concerned, revolution in its classic meaning did not occur in Iran, while such revolutions took place many times in the West. Upheavals mainly occurred in order to force the authorities to rule on the basis of traditional values, not to change them for new values. The events that happened in Iran were mainly tribal, sectarian, and religious wars, and this was primarily because of the unequaled power of the state and the disparity of social groups, due to the climatic and the land situation in Iran.

How the Agrarian Economy and Tribal Relations Blocked Independent Commerce in Iran

The Western economy was marked by independent commercial activities from ancient times. The Iranian economy, on the other hand, was dominated by agriculture in ancient times and tribal relations after the invasions of the Central Asian tribes.[13] These were the two major obstacles to independent commerce in Iran. The need to meet people's basic requirements for food and other essentials of life in Iran diverted the major part of the work force into the agricultural sector. Cities were distanced from one another and separated by deserts and mountains, a situation that made trade less attractive. In addition, the centralized government followed policies based on the concentration of forces in the agricultural sector and discouraged people from engaging in trade, as if such activity were morally corrupt. Therefore, unlike ancient Greece and Rome, where trade constituted the major part of the economy and was itself an indication of society's progress, Iranian people respected agriculture and reproached trade. Daniel Chirot writes: "Trade and commerce, generally considered inferior occupations in the high imperial cultures that ruled most of the agrarian world, were actually the greatest bearers of change and adaptation."[14] Mohammad Ali Islami Nadooshan, in a description of the ancient civilization in Iran, writes that "Commerce and trade were considered undesirable professions. People believed that merchants and businessmen had to tell lies and this sometimes contaminated society."[15] On the same topic, he adds, "King Darius's appeal to God to protect Iran against the three vices of lies, drought, and the enemy (quoted from Bistoon, section 3) was in fact an expression of the people's wishes at that time. Iran has suffered from these vices more than from anything else."[16] Darius again claimed, based on his epigraph in Persepolis (*Takht-e-Jamsheed*), "God protected his country of believers against the enemy's army, famine, and lies."[17]

As it is further explained in the forthcoming sections, the word "lies" is used here as a synonym for trade. The fact that Iran has long been considered one of the important passages of trade between the East and the West is not in contradiction with the fact that internal trade has not been very prevalent in Iranian society itself. Also, Iran was not a center of trade like the ports in Greece.[18] Instead of directly reproaching merchants, the ethics of trade were criticized. So, the three main enemies of ancient Iran were actually trade, drought, and invasions—other ethnic groups' invasions to take over Iranian territory, including agriculture and the work force. Herodotus, the Greek historian, wrote, "Iranians hate buying and selling and market trades, because they do not want to be forced to lie and cheat. They are also reluctant to borrow and lend, because they are afraid they will not be able to pay back their debts and therefore would be forced to lie."[19]

In response to questions about his reluctance to attack Greece, Cyrus has been quoted as saying "If I set out to conquer Greece, I would never feel bad about killing people who commit lies in their markets every day."[20]

Nadooshan added that agricultural and military jobs in Iran were the most desired of all professions.[21] This quite clearly points to the importance of agriculture and of the military that defended it. Furthermore, Darius's direct reference to drought points to the shortage of water as one of the three main problems in that society. In the works written by the Zoroastrians, we read, "Anyone who does not do agricultural work and does not plow the land is cursed by the land. Those of you who do not work on the land, be aware that you will someday stand at people's doorstep begging for a piece of bread and depending upon other people's leftovers."[22] In fact, according to the Zoroastrian book *Avesta*, "anyone who planted a seed of wheat was actually planting the seed of piety and helping the promotion of the religion of Mazda. Such a person's rewards were equal to a hundred prayers, and this act was a thousand times more reasonable than performing religious rituals. It was a hundred thousand times better than offering sacrifices."[23]

Trade and the Development of Thought

Trade created cities and vice versa; all brought not only the exchange of commodities but also new ideas, scientific thought, and technology, which led to further creativity and development. The growth of cities indicates the presence of surplus production and social development. In fact, the growth of the cities in the West was directly related to the development of commerce and industry, and thus capitalism. In contrast, the above-stated evidence about Iran indicates the importance of agriculture in that society and the degree of the society's dependence upon agricultural products. Therefore, the culture and the knowledge of the society had not gone beyond the closed environment of rural life, and people remained underdeveloped and rigid-minded instead of thinking about how to make urban life better. The growth of urban life in the Greek civilization, it should be noted, opened new horizons to human beings and brought about an intellectual revolution. In Iran, however, philosophical dictates and the admonitions of the political and religious establishments that the people should remain in agriculture were indicative of the need for the concentration of human forces in the agricultural area. Life in rural areas, based on the prevalent traditions, not only impeded intellectual progress but also made people dependent upon superstitions supported by the all-knowing governments and religions.

There were, then, religious and state support and encouragements for the rural and agrarian activities. However, Rumi, the greatest mystical poet of the Persian language, aware of the qualitative difference between rural and urban life, wrote:

> Do not go to the village; the village makes one dense,
> It blurs one's mind and reasoning.
> Spending one day in the village,
> Is enough to distract you for a whole month.[24]

The above-mentioned points also reflect the problem of water shortage. The holiness of water in ancient Iran was the direct result of its shortage. In the *Avesta*, Khordad Emshaaspand is the angel and the guardian of water. Aabaan was another angel of water. Accordingly, Anahita or Nahid was the maintainer of Oxus and Jaxartes (two major rivers). The two words "aabaadaan" and "biabaan," which refer to the place where water exists and the place where it does not exist, respectively, show the relationship between water and development. Water was nothing less than the origin of development because it provided the possibility of transformation from cattle raising and migratory life to settled life and agriculture. The relative abundance of water was the decisive factor in production in excess of consumption in societies and in the development from rural to urban life. Urban life has had and still has certain characteristics and features that are different from those of rural life and, by implication, tribal life. In the following pages and chapters, these points will be discussed at greater length.

Abundant examples and historical evidence with regard to the prominence of water—and its holiness—exist in Iranian culture. According to the *Avesta*, "It appears that water and everything related to it have been considered holy by the Turks of Turkistan."[25] A quick comparison between Iranian, Greek, and Arab cultures shows that the degree of accessibility to water not only affected the form and mode of living but also influenced the value systems of these societies significantly. In the civilization of desert-dwelling Arabs, one's significance depended upon the will to avoid agriculture and trade and adopt the hard life of the desert. For the Arabs who had to live in a dry land, due simply to the prevailing natural and climatic conditions, there was no other choice but to justify their living situation and attempt to encourage and persuade people to make use of nature in earning their living. While a sector of the non-desert dwelling, tribal society devoted itself to agriculture and trade, the rest of the people in the desert had to confront natural disasters. Therefore, their social values were focused upon communal and tribal life and upon preventing individuals from leaving the tribe. In fact, the concept of "individual" does not have a meaning and does not make sense in desert-dwelling Arab culture. In Iranian culture, the attempt to keep the individual in a group was motivated by the goal of promoting agriculture. The government taxed group production and groups, not individuals. In ancient Greek culture, by contrast, individuals and individualism had gained a meaning. Urban life and engagement in trade and industry were the requirements for such values.

The construction of irrigation networks that used the bulk of the work force constituted the basis of the economy in the East. The development of these very expensive irrigation systems required a centralized organization and special management skills. The organization and its management could not be run or handled by a single person or even a group of people but rather required powerful establishments such as a state to run and control them. As described earlier, this arrangement eventually led to a situation in which the kings controlled the fates of their societies. This was the real reason that monarchies in areas such as Egypt and Mesopotamia came into existence. War between regional powers such as the Medes, Sumerians, and Babylonians, culminating with the final victory of the Medes, started with the aim of conquering the irrigation canals and the agents who constructed and maintained them—i.e., the people.[26] These high-cost wars, which were fought for the protection and expansion of the power of the kings, were the salient cause of the failure of these civilizations. The masses had to perform forced labor, regardless of who ruled them, because "land, as the king's possession, was occupied by communal societies in which people worked."[27]

The Absence of a Bourgeois Class in Iran

Two other relevant factors are important for the growth of capitalism: the emergence of a bourgeois class (middle class) and the independent growth of cities. In Iran, when state ownership and the king's property were modified by *soyurghal* (benefice), more land began to be shifted toward private ownership. The *soyurghal* (*tuyul* system) was the beginning of the formation of land ownership by private landlords, and it has been the predominant form of ownership until recent eras. However, the dependence of the private landholders on the king, the collective form of agricultural cultivation, and the involvement of landowners in trade were factors that prevented the formation of a bourgeois class, and in particular an industrial bourgeoisie, which is the key to capitalistic development.

In the East, the landowners who lived in the cities often had to travel to the villages to oversee agricultural activities on their land. The fact that they lived in the city and kept their lands in the village was an obstacle to the growth of independent trade and urban activities. That is, they refused to give up their land and transfer their capital to the cities to be used in urban production. Owning agricultural land allowed the Iranian khans (landlords and tribal leaders) to influence the politics and to invest in trade and urban services. Unlike in the West, trade activities in Iran were not exclusively the domain of merchants According to Ashraf, "Rulers, governors, and government employees also engaged in trade."[28] In fact, even the king and his associates were involved in trade. This was the prevailing situation in Iran until the land reforms of 1961 —i.e., four centuries after the disintegration of feudalism in the West.[29]

In Eastern societies, again unlike the West, trade was heavily dependent upon centralized states, and they largely controlled it. Also, trade did not enjoy the necessary security. According to Eric Wolf, in Eastern societies the seeds of capitalism existed, but what did not exist was the capitalist mode of production. Before the development of an industrial economy could be achieved, the capitalist mode of production had to grow. Wolf also states that what is notable about the society of England, for example, is that businessmen were quickly and inevitably drawn to the realm of production.[30]

The West's discovery of new geographic areas in the world in the sixteenth and seventeenth centuries was undoubtedly a revolution in the realm of trade. This was a revolution that facilitated and accelerated the development of trade capital, which was one of the important factors in the transition from the feudal system to the capitalist mode of production.[31] The natural economy or agrarian production did not have such a capacity.

The transition that took place in the realm of politics in the West started from the feudal aristocracy and moved to the trade aristocracy, the industrial aristocracy, the banker aristocracy, and finally the present-day information aristocracy. In Iran, what did not occur was the development that could result in the flourishing of the economy at each stage. The growth of capitalism in twentieth-century Iran was limited to the commercial sector. The reason for this limitation was the fact that the landholders and the merchants were the same people. Of course, the feudal aristocracy in the West also represented a rather static system, but what caused the change in the West was class conflict between the bourgeoisie and the feudals, which led to the disintegration of feudalism.

Marx concisely explained the emergence of capitalism in the West in his book *Pre-Capitalist Economic Formations*. With respect to this idea, he has referred to three factors: (1) the real accumulation of capital, (2) the change from use value to exchange value and the production of surplus value, and (3) the objective conditions (or the freedom of the work force from being tied to the land and the feudal lords—the dual freedom).[32] Comparative study of the East and the West suggests that these elements did not appear in the East. The obstacles to the emergence of these factors were discussed in previous chapters. The formation of capital basically does not depend upon land ownership. Rather, it depends upon trade relations in the cities and capital loaned at interest. This capital makes access to cheap labor possible and frees the peasants from the land. Capital, in the sense that it could enable wealth in the form of cash to circulate and employ the free, cheap labor force in the field of production, did not come into existence in Iran. Peasants remained dependent upon the land, and money did not find the objective conditions needed for real accumulation as happened in the West.[33] By real accumulation, we mean the circulation of money in the social production process.

The two principles of free work and a free market are necessary for the growth of capitalism in that they are prerequisites for the growth of industrial capital. Once again, these two factors did not appear in the East because the peasants continued to be dependent upon the land.

Free work means working independently of the restrictions of the feudal system and being "free" from any form of ownership of the means of production. In fact, free workers own only their labor. This development is possible when work and the concentration of capital, or, as Weber described it, work and the concentration of power—including administrative, military, scientific, and technical management power—are separate from each other.

In contrast to the West, the importance of competition between the freedom of the workers and the dependence of peasants on the land was never appreciated in the East. In Iran, the merchants were also landowners, while in the West the merchants and the feudal lords were considered rivals as far as the employment of the peasants' labor was concerned.

With regard to production, the transformation of the production process from the use value to the exchange value is a necessary condition for the growth of monetary and capital relations. In societies in which nature divides and isolates the populations, as in Iran, this process basically does not take form, and production remains at the level needed for only consumption. In addition to low surplus production, due to the difficulties of transportation and communication, trade is less beneficial in these societies. In many of them, only colonization was able to break this framework and convert production for consumption to production for exchange.[34] But even then the colonizer's capital was an obstacle to the emergence of production capital. As was mentioned earlier in relation to India, the capital was based on competition at this juncture, and Eastern countries were not in a position to compete with the West. This happened because of the force of global capital, which dominated a global market, dictated the quality of goods, and supported technological advancement in the capitalist societies.

Of course, Max Weber believed that capitalism—or concern with profits—had already shown some of it signs in other regions of the world. What was exclusively found in the West was a very different form of capitalism that he called rational capitalism. This type of capitalism was based on the organization of free labor. Aside from this, Weber considered two other factors to be important in the formation of capitalism in the West. One was the legal separation of business from private ownership, and the other was rational accounting, both of which are now considered features of modern economic life. In the East, however, a concentrated effort was made to unite business with affairs related to family. The characteristics described by Weber were actually the product of the organization of free labor. The application of accurate calculations (rationalism) to all other financial affairs only becomes possible through free labor.[35]

Furthermore, the legal, official, political, and economic bases of autonomy and the rational organization of industry and trade did not appear in the East. Although the utilization and control of rivers in China, Egypt, and other Eastern civilizations led to a kind of economic autonomy in these societies, religious and other cultural features of despotic rule kept this autonomy very limited.

In addition, the "feudal" systems in the East and the West did not have the same features, as discussed earlier. The landlordism in the East enjoyed the benefits of the concentration of power in the despotic government, while in the West this power was dispersed, and different areas enjoyed relative autonomy and self-sufficiency. Also, in the era of the emergence of the cities and the growth of industries and trade the development that took place in these two geographical areas was affected by different climatic and productive conditions and different political systems. In Europe, the central power had disintegrated following the demise of the Roman Empire, and the government had fallen into the hands of barbaric kings who were not capable of defeating one another. Government, as such, did not have its present form and was divided into small, local units run by the leaders of the feudal aristocrats. In other words, the general affairs of these societies were operated by a limited number of feudal lords. By contrast, following the decline of ancient civilization in the East, new centralized despotic states replaced the old ones and sustained the integration of the territories.

To clarify the role that the central, despotic governments played in inhibiting the growth of a bourgeoisie, we will consider an example from China. In the fifteenth century, China—more than any other country, including Portugal—was quite active in the fields of trade and navigation. The Chinese engaged in navigation and sailed in the waters of the southern part of East Asia, the Indian Ocean, the newly discovered African seas, and Arabian Peninsula. Their commercial ships were far bigger and more advanced than the ships belonging to the Europeans. But due to the fact that this country was worried about the Chinese merchants' increased power, these activities were labeled dangerous, and bureaucratic obstacles were created to stop them. The Chinese government prohibited the construction of transatlantic ships under the pretext that pirates threatened them.[36] Such was the role of a despotic, centralized government in holding back the society. In Europe, on the other hand, lack of a central government with absolute power gave the merchants relative freedom and prevented the feudal governments from stopping the merchants from making bold plans for advancement. Thus, European merchants undertook trade and the colonization of other countries, and whenever they faced the opposition of feudal establishments, they overthrew them.

The European merchants debilitated the feudal lords by making the circulation of money possible. This was a turning point at which development in the East and the West diverged.[37] Daniel Chirot recounted that before the Portuguese reached the new regions in Asia and Africa, the Chinese had been there. "But the Chinese generally gave up their colonizing activities in favor of preserving their old system."[38] Chirot believed that if China had not been afflicted by the misfortune of having a centralized, despotic government and had been able to engage in trade activities freely, without the bureaucratic limitations the government power imposed on them, it probably would have been the first society to discover the modern sciences and industrial production. Unfortunately, China did not have this opportunity.

The Absence of Autonomous Cities in Iran

To analyze the growth of capitalism in the West, Weber conducted a comparative economic study. He considered the emergence of cities, such as Florence in Italy, a result of the financial growth by the government, something the Eastern governments were not able to achieve. The cities in the East, as Bernier reports, were nothing but military garrisons, and therefore they did not enjoy the autonomy that cities had in the West. Domination of Iran by the Central Asian tribes in tenth and eleventh centuries caused the composition of the population to become more tribal and less settled, so that three-fourths of the total population became tribal.[39] This provided less security for the market in the cities and undermined agricultural production by the people whose activities were pastoral and horticultural. In addition, as far as trade was concerned, roads became less secure for transportation of the commodities. Tribal rule continued to exist in Iran until twentieth century.

In contrast, Western cities were able to use their political autonomy to establish local military forces, which grew to the point that they were able to defend the cities. Thus, the cities were not dependent upon the support of the bureaucratic forces of the central government and were not subject to the political control of merchants and craftsmen, as in China. In contrast, in places like China, the cities did not become establishments separate from the central government. Independent legal contracts—whether economic or political—were not drawn up. And in China, particularly, despite the existence of a rich civilization, the bourgeois class did not form in autonomous cities. J. Turner et al., in analyzing Weber's view, argue: "because of early unification and centralization of the Chinese empire, cities never became autonomous political units. As a result, the development of local capitalistic enterprises was inhibited."[40] Because of this situation, a monetary system did not emerge, and instead of calculative legal procedures a "substantive ethical law" dominated.[41] In the West, the cities were the product of a prolonged struggle between urban businessmen and craftsmen on the one hand and regional rulers on the other, which resulted in successive local riots. Of course, the history of the East's social development also contains many social disturbances, but these events were often meant simply to replace one ruler by another or involved religion or attempts to modify the laws and traditions within the existing system, rather than to free the cities from the limitations imposed on them by a central power.[42] None of the mass movements in Iran can be considered a movement against large landowners in favor of a new class or a new socioeconomic formation. There was no alternative to the agrarian system. Peasant protests concerned issues such as economic oppression, harsh tyranny by the rulers, or a change from one ruler to another. The main reason for this is that the residents of Eastern cities were never considered citizens with specific rights, as they were in the West.[43] Ahmad Ashraf writes:

> The reason urban societies did not develop into societies in which citizens enjoyed solidarity and autonomy—features that have played a crucial role in social development—was that political power was situated in the cities and dominated the urban society. The establishment of the government in the cities hindered the development of autonomous trade councils and similar organizations. Not only did the people not elect the city government and not representative of them, but the cities also did not have independent rules, regulations, constitutions, and courts elected by their citizens. Thus, Islamic cities only had two of the five characteristics Weber considers necessary for the formation of autonomous cities. The Eastern cities had a military and a market, but they did not have independent councils, a concrete constitution and courts to represent the citizens, and an autonomous government elected by the people. On the other hand, the economic and social features of Islamic cities confirm, to a large extent, Karl Marx's view on lack of development in the social division of labor in agriculture, exchange, and industrial production."[44]

Cities in the West had their roots in the ancient era, and they were trade centers that established trade activities with cities overseas (polises). But in China, for example, trade was usually an internal affair and aimed at preserving traditions, and external trade was limited to the Canton port. Industrial development was also absent in Chinese urban centers, even after it existed in the West. Ironically, it is a known fact that industrial development was a reality in the East before it was realized in the West, prior to the emergence of capitalism, but capitalistic relations had to emerge to foster industrial development as it eventually happened in the West. These relations were absent in the East.

Between the fifth and the fifteenth centuries, China was more advanced than the West technologically. The establishment of a printing industry, the discovery and utilization of gunpowder, and the invention of the compass were among China's technical achievements in this period.[45] Thus, if industry alone was the factor that led to the formation of Western civilization, China had the potential to build this civilization for itself as well. So, the secret behind the growth of Western civilization was not industry but rather the capitalist relations for which China was not prepared.

How Tribal Relations Restrained Social Classes in Iran[46]

Engels and Weber referred to several large-scale social revolutions in the West that determined the fate of Western civilization. These were the revolution that took place in Italy in the twelfth and thirteenth centuries and led to the Renaissance; the revolution that occurred in Denmark in the fifteenth century that challenged the feudal domination; the revolution in Holland that founded a republic; the revolution that took place in England, which replaced the feudal aristocracy with an urban middle class that developed into a bourgeois aristocracy; and the revolutions that occurred in the United States and France in the eighteenth century, which severely challenged the domination of the church and opened the gates for democracy.

The first revolution is considered the source of the subsequent revolutions in Europe. The basis for this revolution was a conflict that existed between the church and the feudal lords over sovereignty and over who would control the other. In subsequent centuries, the newly established bourgeois class (middle class) advocated the elimination of the dominant roles of both the church and the feudal lords in general and the economic and legal relations in particular. The continuation of this trend led to the emancipation of the entire continent of Europe from the limitations that the church and the feudal system had imposed on it. Following the disintegration of the feudal system, the weakening of the church, and further growth of the bourgeoisie class, the industrial economy, and the philosophy of liberalism, the religious establishment was separated entirely from the government establishment. The nature of these revolutions was a class struggle between the growing bourgeoisie and declining feudalism over sovereignty in Europe.

Although the church controlled massive wealth as late as the sixteenth century, its role in the affairs of the secular Christian governments diminished due to the emergence of the Reformation movement and the separation of the Church of England from the Roman Catholic Church. The center of the Reformation was Germany, where, according to Will Durant, the church at one time owned one-third of the wealth (along with one-fifth of the wealth of France).[47] Despite the conflict, the Church was the strategic ally of the feudal lords. Therefore, Engels writes, "every struggle against feudalism, at that time, had to take on a religious disguise, had to be directed against the Church in the first instance."[48] The Reformation led to the confiscation of the church's properties and decreased its power considerably.[49]

Such a development did not occur in the East. Tribal relations were an obstacle to the development of social classes. Tribal relations maintain a patrimonial hierarchy, which is a dominant system in the East. Social and class revolution was a phenomenon of modern times. Political and military conflicts and the struggles against the ruling powers in agrarian societies were not based on class conflicts but on tribal, regional, and religious differences. As Barfield writes: "In terms of political legacy and cultural patrimony derived over the course of the whole millennium, it could be said that the modern nation of Iran itself was the by-product of the struggles between successive dynasties and tribal confederations within and outside on Iran."[50] The bourgeois class did not grow, and religion and the state were not separated in these societies. The unity between these two establishments was constantly an obstacle to the development of intellectual independence and human creativity, since everything was considered predetermined. People could not, and were not expected to think and behave outside this framework. As stated earlier, the history of the East has basically manifested itself as the history of religions.[51] Within this structure, people were born to serve God or divine rulers who were God's representatives on Earth. Therefore, individuals had obligations but no rights.

Although Eastern religions inhibited the growth of the society in general and the emergence of industrial capitalism in particular, this was the case only in specific circumstances and historical eras. When economic interests become an issue, then religious obstacles are removed or modified. Irving Zeitlin drew attention to an important comment from Max Weber, in which Weber stated that when Western forces began constructing the railroad system and some factories in China the Chinese geomancers demanded that they take special care when constructing buildings and institutions near certain mountains, forests, rivers, and cemeteries so that the spirits' peace would not be disturbed.[52] Weber added in a footnote to the same section that "as soon as the Mandarins realized the chances for gain open to them, these difficulties suddenly ceased to be insuperable; today [1920] they are the leading stockholders in the railways."[53] Weber goes on:

> In the long run, no religious-ethical conviction is capable of barring the way to the entry of capitalism, when it stands in full armor before the gate; but the cat that it is [now] able to leap over magical barriers does not prove that genuine capitalism could have originated in circumstances where magic played such a role.[54]

In other words, religious, ethical, or superstitious beliefs can, at specific historical junctures, turn into significant obstacles to growth. However, at other historical junctures (e.g., the sixteenth century in Europe) these obstacles can easily be surmounted. Here, the important point is the role that economic interests and relations can play in removing religious obstacles.

In Iran, religion turned into a very powerful instrument for preserving the established political power structure. The kings, whose power had its roots in the traditional modes of landowning, not only did not face any opposition from the religious establishment but they also considered it a factor that reinforced their power. In Europe, only the bourgeois class's interests stood in opposition to the traditional religion, which was based on feudalism. Yet, in Iran the bourgeois class did not emerge to gain such power. The conflicts between different sects and religious interpretations were essentially the product of conflicts of power within the same agrarian economy.[55]

Thus, unlike in the West, in Iran most of social upheavals, instead of being based on class interest, were religiously motivated. In modern times, aside from the anti-West Tobacco Movement (1889),[56] which was led by clerics, one can only refer to the Constitutional Revolution (1905–09),[57] which represented a turning point in the social awareness of the Iranians in the contemporary era. But even this revolution could not stay away from religious disputes and was finally led astray. The Constitutional Revolution in Iran was essentially a challenge against the despotic rule of the shah, not a class struggle. The bourgeois class in Iran was not strong enough to lead the revolution and enforce a state of law to replace *shari'a* (religious laws). Also, the commercial bourgeoisie (as distinct from an industrial bourgeoisie) made no demands for socioeconomic change and participation in the political power structure. Religious leaders were active in the revolution, but they split over the nature of constitutionalism. One faction saw constitutionalism as a protest against the despotic rule of the shah, so it had no conflict with *Shari'a* and therefore became actively supportive.[58] Another religious faction was led by clergyman Sheikh

Fazlollah Nuri, who stated that "constitutionalism cannot be *shari'a*" and opposed it in favor of traditionalism. About three hundred clergymen were behind him.[59] Nuri was right, however, not to precede society, but to maintain a reactionary state of traditional laws. Actual constitutionalism would have meant the replacement of the *Shari'a* by man-made codes of law, but that was not what the progressive religious faction wanted. The conflict between two factions became very tense and hostile, and in the end Nuri along with four others were convicted as traitors and hung.[60]

In the West, the anti-church protests in Europe were based on class relations and were undertaken against the most powerful feudal lords associated with the church. In contrast to such protests, the riots in Iran predominantly had tribal and sectarian motivations. Yet, this argument does not negate the class-based nature of some of the social movements and peasant struggles in Iran. Still, because of the fact that a new class did not emerge—i.e., a bourgeois class—to seek its interests in another socioeconomic formation and confront the economic, political, and religious power of feudal lords, the peasant movement did not result in a social revolution. Traditional Islam has constantly been worried about the advancement of the sciences, the extension of national literacy, and, in particular, development in philosophy, and there was no organized bourgeoisie class to demand scientific development. Yet, it is a known fact that the expansion of capitalism was not possible without the growth of the sciences.

New scientific discoveries during the European Renaissance dealt another blow to the credibility of the church, the power of which had been considered divine. Before the advent of the bourgeoisie and social revolutions, new scientific achievements were subjected to attacks by the church and religious officials. Therefore, the economic conditions in the West were intertwined with its social revolutions and revolutions in the fields of science. Religion ultimately contributed to these developments. In Iran, on the other hand, economic conditions did not lead to the growth of a bourgeois class that advocated political independence and putting an end to the power of the religious establishment. On the contrary, the long-lasting tie that existed between landowners, merchants, and the religious and political establishments remained intact until the twentieth century, when, following the deep influence of Western capital in Iran, these relations lost their classic form. Therefore, the West—independently of the East—made progress due to the internal developments that had occurred there, while similar developments did not occur in Iran.

Lack of Competition, Technological Growth, and Social Division of Labor in Iran

Another difference between a capitalist economy and a pre-capitalist economy is based on three factors: the levels of competition, technology use, and the division of labor. The differences between Iran and the West with regard to these factors, and the different outcomes that resulted, will be discussed here.

Levels of Competition

In backward societies, traditional "wise leaders" prevent rationalism, intellectual competition, and human creativity because they consider themselves the source of all knowledge. Competition in the field of production in the capitalist system is a mechanism that has an individualistic base, but it can turn into a massive social and even historical development in specific circumstances. Under this situation, competition moves from the individual domain to the structural and social realm, and then it becomes integrated with legal and political relations. If competition remains exclusively within the confines of the individual's characteristics, it acts as a monotonous force throughout history. In pre-modern agrarian systems, competition had no significant role in causing the individual's intellectual and productive activities to lead to social production.[61] In modern capitalist society, the personal feature of competition gains a social function. There is no doubt, for instance, that competition in modern societies has extended itself from the economic domain into other realms of life such as culture, literature, the sciences, religion, and art.[62]

Technology Use

The second difference between capitalist and natural economies is the role of modern technology. In a capitalist society, people and financial agencies involved in production resort to the creation of new technologies so that they can gain more profits and the control of the market through the utilization of new instruments that are not yet available to their competitors. In other words, competition in this field leads to the discovery and invention of new devices aimed predominantly at increasing profits, but these discoveries also have social and historical advantages. In other words, individual profit can lead to the development of a society.

Although technological development restricts the function of the labor force, it also causes consumption to increase, so that new fields of work and labor opportunities are created. Therefore, although growth in technology appears to be in contradiction with workers' usefulness—and this may very well be true initially—the trend in development will practically increase the demand for the labor force in new areas and compensate in the end for its negative effects in the short-run.

The Division of Labor

Pursuant to the growth of technology and the emergence of new professions, the social division of labor increases, and economic activities become more and more specialized. Thus, the scope of bureaucracy expands, and new regulations are devised to ensure individual rights. In an industrial economy, unlike in a natural economy that is dependent upon climatic factors, production comes to depend upon new factors such as management, the consumption market, supply and demand, distribution mechanisms, internal and international financial interactions, and so on. In a natural economy, factors outside human control mainly determine the outcomes of production. The mode of production in both urban and rural Iran prevented the social division of labor between agriculture, commerce, and industry. This caused the urban and rural communities to mobilize into larger regional, economic, political, social, cultural, and religious communities. It also led to the notification of the cities and the villages. Such characteristics prevented development of autonomous cities and a bourgeois class. Both religious and political institutions had prevailing positions over the cities and their business activities.[63]

The new production system, as exemplified by the West, requires a new legal order. Therefore, establishments that devise laws, such as parliaments, come into existence and enforce the laws of the elected and periodical governments. Thus, also, an independent judicial establishment is created. In the realm of politics, like the economy, competition plays a key role and eliminates the tribal and ethnic monopolies. In pre-modern systems, traditions often play the role of laws, and collectivism functions instead of competition.

Such developments as mentioned above only take place in capitalist societies. In Iran, due to the fact that the bourgeois class did not appear officially, the consequences that are associated with the existence of such a class—i.e., the social, political, and legal consequences—were practically absent. In addition, when an attempt was made to copy the Western patterns in the realm of politics, such as instituting democracy and the rights of citizens, the society faced a big challenge from traditional forces, and these attempts met frustration. In the West, developments in the social, political, legal, and cultural domains resulted in the establishment of further economic activity. In Iran, because of the fact that the economic structure of the pre-capitalist society did not move toward capitalism, any efforts undertaken in the realms of politics and social activities were doomed to failure.

For example, the Constitutional Revolution in Iran was an attempt to overthrow the despotic regime and to restrict the power of the royal family and its foreign allies. Constitutional states in the West influenced the constitutional movement in Iran. Yet, it was not a movement aimed at overthrowing the ruling class of the landlords. Unlike the Western examples, the necessary social and class force— i.e., a bourgeois class—had not been formed in Iran, and thus concrete demands associated with such a class were not made. Majlis, the National Consultative Assembly (or, as the clergy who participated in the movement preferred to call it, the House of Justice) did not succeed in functioning like European parliaments, first, because of the lack of capitalist relations and a strong bourgeois opposition that could rise to lead the movement, and, second, because the constitutional laws did not have an economic and class base. None of the leading groups in the constitutional movement were representative of a bourgeois class. For this reason, and because of the occurrence of a sectarian war in various parts of the country afterward, a new form of dispersion resulted and, subsequently, a military dictatorship became a necessity to bring unity to the country as a nation again. In the chaotic situation, the British government picked Reza Khan, later Reza Shah, a military commander, to lead a coup d' Etat.[64] He began to launch a series of reforms, including measures aimed at nation-state building. If we consider Reza Shah's measures the beginning of the demands of a bourgeois class movement, there is still the problem that the leadership of this movement was not associated with an industrial bourgeoisie but with a military whose methods of government were not liberal but dictatorial. This was an attempt from the top to launch some features of modernism in Iran.

Thus, despite many attempts since the Tobacco Movement, a parliament similar to a European parliament was not formed in Iran. Forces beyond the control of this establishment, even when people's true representatives participated in it, always preempted its performance and created a gap between its function and its true nature. So the political development depended upon economic development of the country because a class of wealthy people with interests tied to the existence and strength of an elected parliament was not there to support it. An opportunistic commercial bourgeois class whose interests lie in overt and covert business dealings cannot perform the same function as that played by an industrial bourgeois class whose interests lie in the strength of an internal legal system and the growth of a working class. Therefore, what contributed to Iran's underdevelopment in the modern era was the growth of the non-production-related and non-industrial bourgeois class in the heart of conservative or so-called commercial capitalist, agrarian, and even tribal relations. Neither political nor economic competition exists in such a system, which is ruled and dictated to from the top. Technology does not need to grow, since commercial capitalism is not dependent upon technologic advancement. Also, without technological development, the social division of labor does not appear. Even the imported version of capitalism remained barren at the core of the society, as trade dominated the economy.

[1] Because of its significance, there are very complicated regulations on the usage of water in Iran. I have purposely avoided discussing the details in this book. For information, see Ann Lambton, *Landlord and Peasant in Persia*, Chapters IX and X (New York: Oxford University Press, 1953).

[2] Friedrich Engels. *The Peasant War in Germany* (Moscow: Foreign Languages Publishing House, 1965), 93.

[3] For the conflict and the rivalry between the church and the monarch, see Seyyed Javad Tabatabaei, *The Concept of Jurisprudence in the Political Thought of the Middle Ages* (Tehran: Pegah, 1980 (2002)).

[4] Karl Marx, *The Capital*, vol. 1, (1867), 714.

[5] Eric Wolf, op. cit.

[6] Tuyul was an estate that the shah used to give as a reward to an individual who rendered him a service. For details, see Hosein Mir Haydar, *Az Tuyul ta Enqelab-e Arzi* (from *Tuyul to the Agrarian Revolution*) (Tehran: Amir Kabier, 2535 (1955)).

[7] The traditional land tenure system in Iran continued to exist until the mid-20th century. An American-ordered land reform program was launched in Iran in the 1960s that had multiple purposes. It abolished the old land tenure system; it revealed the peasants as a labor force and dispatched them to the cities, where the newly established industry demanded cheap labor; and it neutralized the potential for any peasant revolt against the landlords. The process, which had not naturally and historically occurred in Iran, was imposed from the top by the shah and his ally the United States. The new labor force was supposed to meet the needs of the new foreign and domestic investments in industry. For details, see Kazem Alamdari, "The Socioeconomic Effects of the Land Reform Program in Iran 1961–1981," (Dissertation, University of Illinois, 1982).

[8] Ibid.

[9] The land belonging to feudal lords in France, as in England, was divided into numerous small pieces, but the existing conditions were much less desirable. Terriers were formed in the 14th century, and their number rose until it exceeded 100,000. These Terriers paid different leases in the form of cash or goods, from one-fifth to one-twelfth. Terriers were divided into several categories depending upon their value and size (fiefs, arrier-fiefs, and so on) and sometimes did not consist of more than a few arpan (each arpan was about 4,200 square meters, or less than half an acre). These Terriers had different degrees of judgment rights over the residents in their domains. The pressure these cruel owners exerted on the people living in rural areas is understandable. Monteil states that at that time 160,000 courts existed in France, while today only 4,000 courts suffice (including peace courts). See Karl Marx, *The Capital*, vol. 1, p. 1065f.

[10] Max Weber, *General Economic History*, trans. Frank H. Knight (New York: Collier Books, 1961).

[11] Eric R. Wolf, "The Emergence and Expansion of Industrial Capitalism," in op. cit., ed. Stephen K. Sanderson.

[12] Karl Marx and Friedrich Engels, *The German Ideology*, ed. C.J. Arthur (London: Lawrence and Wishart, 1974).

[13] See Thomas J. Barfield. "Turk, Persian, and Arabs: Changing Relationships between Tribes and State in Iran and along Its Frontiers" in Nikki Keddie and Rudi Matthee, *Iran and the Surrounding World*, (Seattle: University of Washington Press, 2002).

[14] Daniel Chirot, *How Societies Change* (Thousand Oaks, Ca: Pine Forge Press, 1994), 49.

[15] Islami Naddooshan and Mohammad Ali, "Parsi: The Basin of the First Empire in the World," quoted from Ettela'at Daily, *Azar,* 1375, copied from the Iranians' News Peyk, no. 75, 7th Year, April 1999 (Farvardin 1378 h.), 30.

[16] Ibid, 1999, 30.

[17] Herodotus, cited in Mobed Rostam Shahrzady, *The Zoroastrian Worldview* (Tehran: The Organization of Foruhar Publications, 1367 h.), 60.

[18] The political and religious establishment's reproach for trade and admiration for agriculture are indicative of the fact that of necessity the society has concentrated its work force in the agriculture sector. It does not seem that Iran had a significant role in marine trade. I V. Pygorluska et al., in *History of Iran*, op. cit., state that "during Sasanian, Iran had almost no sailors" (p. 242). This may be used as further evidence to confirm the insignificance of marine trade in ancient Iran.

[19] Mobed Rostam Shahrzady, op. cit. 1367 h., 61.

[20] Ibid, 1367, 61.

[21] Mohammad Islami Nadooshan, op. cit., 1978.

[22] Mobed Rostam Shahrzady, op. cit., 1367 h., 106.

[23] Avesta, *The Book of Vandidad, The Third and Fourth Fargard*, quoted from Ibid, 1367 h., 106–107.

[24] Rumi (1207–1273), the author of *Mathnavi*, migrated to Anatolia in fear of the Mongols' brutality. His poetry has had significant influence throughout the Islamic world.

[25] *Avesta*, op. cit., 106.

[26] Max Weber, *The Agrarian Sociology of Ancient Civilization*, trans. R. I. Frank (London: NLB, 1976, orig. 1909).

[27] A. Kajdan, et al., Ibid, vol. 1, *The East*, 256.

[28] Ahmad Ashraf, *Historical Obstacles to the Development of Capitalism in Iran During the Qajar Period* (Tehran: Zamineh (Payam), 1959 h.), 26.

[29] In recent Iranian history, the 10-year-long struggle between the proponents of land reform and the landowning Khans was finally resolved by the pressure the U.S. put on the Khans and by the Americans' ability to convince the Iranians that investing in urban trade was more profitable.

[30] Eric Wolf, op. cit.

[31] Karl Marx. *The Capital*, vol. 3, in op. cit., eds. Howard Selsam et al. (New York: International Publishers, 1975).

[32] Ibid.

[33] Ibid.

[34] Ibid.

[35] Max Weber, *The Theory of Social and Economical Organization* (New York: Free Press, 1997), 186–212.

[36] Ibid. Also see Joel Mokyr, *The Lever of Riches: Technological Creativity and Economic Progress* (Cambridge, UK: Oxford University Press, 1990), 231–2.

[37] Daniel Chirot, op. cit.

[38] Ibid.

[39] Ahmad Ashraf, *The Historical Obstacles*.

[40] Jonathan Turner, et al., op. cit., 169.

[41] Ibid.

[42] In Iran, mass movements predominantly occurred to support one central establishment against another. For example, Abu-Muslim Khorasani's movement, a national movement in Iran, supported the Abbasid Caliphate against the Umayyad Caliphate. This pattern was prevalent throughout the history of Iran.

[43] Max Weber, *Religion of India*, in Irving Zeitlin, *Ideology and Development of Sociological Theory* (New York: Prentice Hall, 1977).

[44] Ahmad Ashraf, op cit, 34. (translated from Persian)

[45] Daniel Chirot, *How Societies Change* (Thousand Oaks, Ca.: Pine Forge Press, 1994).

[46] Here we mean the growth of social classes as developed in the West; otherwise, ultimately, every society is composed of social classes.

[47] Will Durant, *The Reformation: Part VI of the Story of Civilization* (New York: Simon and Schuster, Inc., 1957). Durant writes that this situation created haters against the church on one side and caused corruption within the church on the other, so that internal reforms were necessary.

[48] Friedrich Engels. *Socialism: Utopian and Scientific*, Introduction to English Edition, (1892), *Collected Works of Marx and Engels* (New York, International Publishers, 1968), 387.

[49] See Jerome J. Langford and O. P. Galileo, *Science and the Church* (New York: Desclee Company, 1966).

[50] Thomas Barfield, op cit. 85.

[51] Karl Marx *Correspondence Between Marx and Engels on Historical Materialism, the Organization of Communist Unity*, 1358 h.

[52] Irving Zeitlin, op. cit.

[53] Max Weber, *General Economic History*, trans. Frank H. Knight (New York: Collier Books, 1961), 245, cited in Irving Zeitlin, op. cit., 237.

[54] Ibid, 237.

[55] For example, Ayatollah Azari Qomi's position, when he had his share of power, was considerably different from the position he took after he was expelled from the state establishment. When he was at the peak of his power in the government, he stated, "If the *faqih* (jurisprudence) decides, and if his decision is in conformity with the expediency of the state, he can dismiss the principle of monotheism (God)." Quoted from an interview with Mr. Bazergan, cited in *Religious Modernism: A Talk Between Hasan Yosefi Eshkevari and Bazergan*, ed. Hasan Yosefi Eshkevari (Tehran: Qasideh, 1377 h.), 36. Azari Qomi altered his view after his religious rival ousted him from his official state position.

[56] For details, see Nikki Keddie, *Religion and Rebellion in Iran: The Tobacco Protest of 1891–1892* (London: Frank Cass, 1966), and N. Keddie, *The Roots of Revolution: Religion and Politics in Iran* (New Haven, CT: Yale University Press, 1981). For more information on the role of the clergy in politics, see the following sources: Said Amir Arjomand, ed., *The Political Dimensions of Religion* (New York: State University of New York Press, 1993).

[57] For details, see the following: Mongol Bayat, *Iran's First Revolution, Shiism and the Constitutional Revolution of 1905–1909* (New York: Oxford University Press, 1991); Janet Afary, *The Iranian Constitutional Revolution, 1906–1911* (New York: Columbia University Press, 1996).

[58] This faction was led by two grand ayatollahs—Tabatabaie and Behbahani. For details, see Said Amir Arjomand, *The Shadow of God and the Hidden Imam: Religion, Political Order, and Social Change in Shiite Iran From the Beginning to 1890* (Chicago: University of Chicago Press, 1984).

[59] Hossein Abaadian, Hossein, *The Theoretical Base of Constitutional and Shari'a Governments* (Tehran: Ney, 1374).

[60] Sheikh Fazlollah Nuri, one of the leading figures of the religious establishment in Iran, advocated against the constitutionalism and was hung by the order of the court and religious proponents of the constitutional revolution. See Ervand Abrahamian, *Iran Between Two Revolutions* (Princeton: Princeton University Press, 1988).

[61] Referring to the factors responsible for the rise of capitalism, Weber writes about the maintenance of a nationwide competitive examination in China. It should be noted that such an examination was held to identify the best-qualified individuals for the state bureaucracy, which inhibited capitalist development.

[62] For a discussion of the relationship between religious competition and development, see Peter Berger, *The Sacred Canopy, Elements of a Sociological Theory of Religion* (Garden City, New York: Doubleday and Company, Inc., 1967).

[63] Ahmad Ashraf, Ahmad, *The Historical Obstacles*.

[64] Reza Khan, a Cossack Brigade Commander, launched his coup d' etat in February 1921. He was later appointed Commander-in-Chief of the Iranian Army and Minister of War. In October 1923, he became

Prime Minister, and in October 1925 the National Assembly deposed the Qajar Dynasty. On December 12 of that year, Reza Khan was sworn in as the Shah of Iran.

Part II
The Imposed Capitalism

A Modernization Project

The Socioeconomic Effects of the Land Reform in Iran (1961–1981)[1]

Introduction

As was explained in the first part, capitalism was the engine of modern development in the West. The land tenure system in Iran, in contrast to the West, was an obstacle to the development of capitalism. Understanding this, some Western developmentalists (see Chapter 1), in an attempt to remove this obstacle, justified a project of engineered "modernization" that involved imposing capitalism from the top down. Under this project, developing countries under the influence of the West were advised to launch land reform programs to modify the obsolete traditional land system. Iran was one of these countries. We will now examine how this project was implemented and what its consequences have been.

In Part One (Chapters 2–4) we looked at the macro level of structural backwardness in Iran. In Part Two (Chapters 5–10) we will present a micro-level study covering a short period of time from 1961, the point at which the land reform program began, to 1981, which saw the beginning of the Islamic system in Iran. The difference between "modernity" (what occurred and became institutionalized in the West over several centuries) and "modernization" (what was imposed from the top and dictated by the West after World War II in undeveloped societies such as Iran in order to modernize them and introduce capitalism) has been discussed in Chapter 1. I would call a modernization project an "imposed capitalism" with multiple purposes, not the least of which is creating a new market for the West. The results of this type of development have been different from what happened in the West as it achieved modernity. One of these results was a cultural backlash, or what might be called a cultural gap or cultural identity crisis. Modernization exclusively modernized economies and kept the political institutions under autocratic systems. Peasentization of urban areas was another result that occurred due to mass migration of peasants from villages to the cities. In Iran, these things happened when the land reform program left many peasants jobless and pushed them toward urban areas. Such movement eventually led millions of deprived and unsatisfied peasants into the Islamist revolution.

Chapter 5

I. Theories and Causes of Land Reform

This part examines the nature of the land reform program in Iran. Following the 1953 coup d'etat in Iran, and preceding a continuous political tension, economic stagnation, and unresolved land questions, the U.S. government launched a land reform program in Iran. Land reform had two principal aims—one political and one economic—and the economic one had priority. At the time of ratification of the Land Reform Bill, the two leading countries involved, England and the United States, constituted the main political and economic influences in Iran. Great Britain, as the traditional supporter of the Iranian landlords, opposed the plan because the implementation of such a program meant strengthening the capitalist faction of the regime, which was mainly pro-American, and weakening the landlord faction that was the British base in Iran. The contradiction between the U.S. and England was rooted in the period of nationalization of the oil industry in 1951. The rivalry between the two powers finally ended in favor of the U.S. and its land reform program.

The program was carried out in three related stages, each monitored by the new Iranian minister of agriculture. It aimed to abolish the outdated socioeconomic system of *Muzara'eh*,[2] and it was successful in this regard. The results of the reform have shown that it transformed the old tenure system into a capitalist one that connected landlords to urban business. The traditional markets were opened up to consumer and manufactured goods. In addition, the launching of the land reform program released more than five million workers from bondage to the land and forced them to migrate to urban areas. The new land tenure system brought new and different agricultural enterprises, such as agro-industrial companies and joint-stock agricultural companies. With regard to the political aim, the program succeeded in neutralizing the centers of potential peasant revolt in rural areas, but it transferred these centers into the cities. The land reform program did not improve either the peasants' living conditions or the country's agriculture. The shah's regime was eventually overthrown, but the agrarian question remains unresolved.[3]

The Necessity of Land Reform

In general, land reform occurs because an old and outdated agrarian system is no longer applicable. The historical events that result in reform include two major types: (1) destruction of the existing agrarian system from the bottom, and (2) change in agrarian production relationships imposed from the top.

In the destruction of an existing agrarian system, land reform is followed by a "revolt from below" by the peasants against their rulers. If successful, the authority of landlords is replaced by a new and more progressive agrarian system. The land distribution following such political conversion is usually drastic and ends the economic dominance of the old rulers and establishes a new social order. In the classic case, the champions of the struggle are the middle classes, especially bourgeois democrats such as those who destroyed the fundamental social and political institutions of feudalism[3] and established new ones, including a land tenure system. The land tenure system in Iran was one in which (1) the natural economy was the domi-nant productive relationship in the countryside; (2) production was mainly for domestic consumption and mostly in the traditional manner; (3) cultivation was based on both share-cropping and tenancy; (4) the *corvee* (free labor service), and other traditional agricultural dues were common; (5) landlords controlled the political power in the country; (6) there was no linked or organic economic relationship between landlords and the world market; and (7) cultivation proceeded through the use of traditional agricultural equipment rather than machinery. This system acted as an obstacle to the development of capitalism, and it was this system that the 1961 land reform program sought to abolish. Because the best-known example of this type of reform is the French reform after the great 1789 Revolution, this is known as the French route.

During the twentieth century, many underdeveloped, dominated societies (i.e., colonies) also experienced radical land distributions following their liberation from colonial rule. Such reforms were part of the liberation movements in Vietnam, China, Algeria, and Mozambique. In addition, during World War II, many anti-fascist movements in eastern European countries' leading parties and organizations succeeded in seizing political power. These communist organizations began land reform programs immediately after victory. By distributing agricultural land to the poor and landless peasants, such movements temporarily gained massive support for the revolution. However, those were not the first communist land reforms. The most radical land distribution of this type was introduced in the Soviet Union just after the 1917 social revolution.[4]

The second major type of land reform, characterized by the change of an outdated and traditional land tenure system from the top down, is known as the Prussian or "absolutist" route. This method involves a gradual transition in political, economic, social, and military institutions of the society toward a more advanced society. However, it does not include destruction of the old system. In this case, landlords and capitalists form a partnership and dominate the major institutions. By accepting new and more advanced relations of production and by employing new techniques in the agrarian system, the government is able to neutralize the possibility of peasant revolt. In addition, through various reform measures, peasants are mostly channeled into the newly created labor market. Classic examples of this method can be found in some European countries during the late nineteenth century, especially in Prussia; hence it is known as the Prussian route to modernization.

After World War II, the Prussian method of land reform was used wherever authority recognized that the existing socioeconomic order in the countryside was either unstable or inefficient and that it was necessary to replace the traditional agrarian system with a more stable and productive one. The bourgeoisie and its foreign supporter, the United States, used this method in Iran, for example, because the experiences of revolutionary land reform, especially in Southeast Asia, had liberated some countries from the bondage of the landlords' rule but had left them on the side of the socialist bloc. This forced the West—particularly the United States—to initiate land reform programs from the top wherever they could in order to thwart agrarian revolution from below. The United States also blamed the communists as "quick to exploit this dissatisfaction [i.e., rural discontent] for political purposes. As a means to seizure of power, they promise land to the landless cultivators."[5] Ironically, declarations by the United States government indicate a similar purpose, albeit with a different quality. According to a U.S. State Department document,

> . . . in many areas present unsatisfactory institutional arrangements are a source of persistent discontent and unrest . . . we favor efforts to improve such agricultural economic institutions wherever possible in order to lessen the cause of agrarian unrest and political instability and as a key to improving rural standards of living.[6]

This American policy was first implemented in Japan in 1945, then in South Korea in 1946, and subsequently in Taiwan in 1948. In this connection, Dr. Christodoulou, the UN-FAO agrarian reform policy officer, wrote:

> As is well known, the U.S.A. was instrumental in promoting a radical land distribution programme in conquered Japan and in South Korea and Taiwan in the 1940's in order to reduce the power of militarist groups who drew their strength from conservative, quasi-feudal landlord interests dominating the countryside on the one hand, and in order to broaden the political power base through the creation of millions of cultivators with a small stake in land on the other.[7]

After these experiences, the United States pressed the issue of land reform at the General Assembly of the United Nations in 1950.[8] Consequently, the United Nations' General Assembly in November 1950 gave specific attention to land reform.[9] During the 1950s and 1960s, and with the same goals, the American strategy was also implemented in other countries in which the U.S. had strong influence, such as the Philippines, South Vietnam, and some Latin American countries.[10] As Christodoulou noted, "in the early 1950s the U.S.A. was strongly advocating land reform in the Philippines to help defeat insurrection which was threatening the newly independent republic."[11]

Latin American countries that introduced land reforms under the influence or initiation of the United States government during the sixties and seventies have continued to be especially plagued by agrarian problems. Christodoulou has stated that "the defects of the agrarian structure in Central and South America are perhaps the most pathological known today and have caused some of the worst misery and rural underdevelopment of recent decades."[12] Similarly, Iranian land reform, initiated by the United States and implemented from the top, has been unable to resolve the agrarian problems of that country. The reasons for this will be analyzed specifically in the present work.

Different Approaches to Land Reform

The stated objectives of all land reforms have been to make more or less direct changes in the existing character of land ownership and in the distribution of wealth, income, or productive capacity. In this regard, Dr. H. Kunert, the senior officer of FAO-UN, wrote the following in 1976:

> In short, *agrarian reform* covers mainly the following three structures: land tenure, production, and supporting services. The main feature of an agrarian reform is the change in the land ownership, which with its supplementary measures is leading toward an integrated rural development process. (Italics original)[13]

Still, there is no uniform or common definition of land reform, because different countries and various agencies, on the basis of particular economic and political purposes, define the concept differently. The U.S. Department of State has emphasized that "many persons mistakenly identify land reform solely with land redistribution. While land reform in some localities may require an adjustment of land holdings, either by division or consolidation, such an adjustment may or may not have a part in a particular land reform program."[14]

This definition is fundamentally different from those describing radical land reforms, which aim to reconstruct new relations of production. Apart from this, such definitions do not make clear who will be favored by the adjustment of land. It was based on such an impression that the Technical Cooperation Administration carried on the Point Four Program with a major emphasis on agriculture. This program, proposed by President Truman in January 1949, aimed at sending technicians and specialists to those countries in which U.S. influence was paramount, to help the population increase production and to improve the economic and social conditions of rural life.[15]

Henry Bennett, the head of the Point Four Program, at the conference on the World Land Tenure Program at the University of Wisconsin (October 8, 1951), said, "We are putting major emphasis on agriculture because we know it is fundamental . . .. So we believe the Point Four Program must be concerned first and foremost with agriculture and especially with *man's ability to produce more food.*"[16] (Emphasis added.) Actually, this was the policy that the U.S. government had followed after World War II in some countries in order to neutralize the material conditions of a radical agrarian reform. But many countries that were covered by such programs or "green revolutions" have been forced to design, sooner or later, a land reform program. For instance, the implementation of the Point Four Program in Iran began in 1950s, but it did not resolve the land question, and thus the U. S., despite the will of the ruling power, instituted a land reform program beginning in 1961. However, because such land reforms aimed only at adjusting the dominant land holding system, they were not able to respond to the agrarian question. For a better understanding of different approaches to land reform, a few more definitions will be reviewed.

According to Warriner, land reform means "redistribution of property or rights in land for the benefit of small farmers and agricultural labourers."[17] This is a simplified and incomplete definition of land reform, although it does demonstrate a more radical approach than the one mentioned above. However, this definition is not universally applicable to situations in societies having different levels of development. Indeed, Warriner's definition is mainly applicable to pre-capitalist societies in which redistribution of land is a step upward under any circumstances. Bergmann has defined such land reform as "measures taken for the radical redistribution of property and/or the disposal and utilization of land (and water) in favor of the effective primary producer (cultivator, tiller), and consequently a redistribution of land rent (the agricultural surplus product)."[18]

Some scholars believe that a political revolution must precede the implementation of a land reform program because landholders in agrarian societies are usually the political rulers.[19] This is the course that many revolutionary land reforms have taken. Other theoreticians think that land reform means the elimination of large-scale land holdings and the establishment of small peasant proprietorships. Although we agree that this is the first step of a land reform program in many pre-capitalist countries and countries under foreign domination, we consider that it is actually a backward step in more advanced capitalist societies.

This is because, from the author's point of view, a genuine land reform program should achieve a number of objectives. Evidence from ineffectual land reforms indicates that in agrarian societies landlords are the major obstacle to genuine reform. (Later discussion will indicate how landlords in a "legal land reform" frequently maintain their socioeconomic status in new positions.) Thus, political and socioeconomic disposal of landlords is a primary factor in a successful land reform program. In addition, it is necessary to destroy the dominant traditional land tenure system and to abandon outdated relations of production. Third, changes from the traditional system of production to a more advanced economic system must be followed by some supplementary supportive services. Development of a true land reform program should include the following objectives: (1) development of productive forces, and (2) an alteration in the relations of production in favor of the tillers. By placing the major emphasis on the first factor (i.e., improving equipment and the peasants' productive capacity, without considering termination of the landlords' rule or development of more progressive relations of production), land reform only maintains the problem in a new form. By emphasizing the first objective to the exclusion of the second, many Western theoreticians have limited their reform proposals for underdeveloped countries to such measures as the "green revolution," the "white revolution,"[20] and the administration of technical and administrative aid.[21] However, United Nations' studies of such societies, which stress such measures, have shown that these societies are still faced with serious agrarian problems.[22] In particular, existing social relations are not changed in favor of peasants because reform is intended to stabilize and not undermine the position of the landowners in society. This is so even though many land reforms have "radical" stated objectives. Such was the case in Iran.

For these reasons, we believe and will attempt to demonstrate that the objectives of land reform cannot be uniform but must differ from society to society in accordance with the dominant socioeconomic situation at a particular stage of historical development. The key determining factors are (1) the mode of production as defined by the forces of production (such as levels of skills, the organization of labor, and the level of technology); (2) the relations of production (such as methods of extracting the surplus); and (3) ideological conditions in areas such as culture, law, and religion. It is for this reason that the Soviet Union and China, having similar political motivations, were bound to have different agrarian reform, since, at the time of the land reform, the former was a capitalist society, whereas the latter was a pre-capitalist, dominated, and backward society.[23] This will be taken into account in our discussion of the Iranian case.

A Concrete Study in a Concrete Situation

Because the Iranian land reform program is a specific case, it is best studied within its particular concrete situation. This is important, I believe, because the socioeconomic results of the program cannot be judged as either a failure or a success unless they are evaluated in relation to the concrete situation in Iranian society.

We will attempt to show concretely how the two specific elements (productive forces and the relations of production in Iran) in a period before the beginning of the land reform project primarily determined the outcome of Iran's land reform. Several things must be considered, including the techniques used on plantations (irrigation systems, the introduction of plowing and harvesting equipment); the types of labor organizations in agriculture (peasants' communes, peasants' unions, collective farms); the existing relationships between landlords and tillers; and the methods of extracting surplus value in the countryside (capitalist vs. pre-capitalist modes). However, we will also examine the positive and negative influences of some cultural aspects of life—e.g., ideology, religion, and law—because we believe that they play secondary but significant roles in socioeconomic development.

Similarly, I believe and will attempt to show that environmental conditions (the type of land, the amount of rainfall and surface running water, the presence of mountainous areas, etc.) also play pertinent roles in determining the success or failure of land reform.

The Process of Land Reform

As Warriner states, all land reform programs contain two phases or processes, which can be described as (1) abolition of the existing structure and (2) establishment of a new structure. The first phase involves expropriation, exemption, and compensation, while distribution occurs in the second phase.[24] For example, in revolutionary land reform, there is no compensation—or, at most, very low rates of payment—for land, whereas in some non-revolutionary cases the compensation rate is full payment. An examination of the stated laws and objectives of a particular land reform program and its implementation through these stages, therefore, is one way of examining the nature of reform, and we propose to employ this method in the current study.

II. Environmental Conditions

Introduction

The backwardness of Iranian agriculture has been due to varied human and environmental factors. If we regard the growth of modern agriculture elsewhere in the world as being based on the development of a bourgeoisie,[25] such factors as the persistence of the traditional Iranian political authority, colonial penetration, and the existence of tribal groups in the countryside can be considered as principal obstacles to the development of agriculture in Iran.[26]

Nevertheless, the underdevelopment of Iranian agriculture is also partly due to some geographical factors, which include the region's climate (insufficient rainfall, a shortage of water) and the mountainous nature of much of the area. The existence of such problems potentially makes agricultural conditions poor, and thus a consideration of these factors is needed in any study of the agrarian question. Hence, although the solution to the agrarian problem is related primarily to political and socioeconomic measures, geographical conditions constitute the material basis of Iran's agricultural problems today. Therefore, ecological studies of society—e.g., the study of patterns of relations between rural people and their environment—can help us learn the importance of geographical factors. In addition, relevant productive forces such as the level of irrigation techniques and peasants' organizations in Iran prior to the time of the land reform program also matter, and they too will be considered in this section.

Geographical Background

Iran is a large country consisting of 164.5 million hectares (636,000 square miles) confined by a long frontier with Pakistan and Afghanistan on the east, Iraq and Turkey on the west, and Armenia, Azerbaijan, and Turkmenistan on the north. In the south are the Oman Sea and the Persian Gulf. Several high mountain ranges that cross the country and surround the vast central plateau function as natural barriers to the sea moisture. Part of the Iranian plateau is covered by huge expanses of salt deserts (the Dasht-i Kavir and the Dasht-i Lut), which are inhospitable to almost all forms of life. These deserts are considered the most arid in the world.[27]

The Zagros mountain chains extend from the northwest part of the country, Azerbaijan, to the southeast, Baluchistan; the Elburz run from the northwest to the northeast of Khurasan province; and the volcanic Kuh-i Damavand, exceeding 18,500 feet, extend along the Afghanistan border from the north to the south. While Iran has various natural geographical dry or semi-dry areas, summers are mostly hot and dry except in places where they are hot and humid. Temperatures during the days reach 100° to 110° F on the plateau, but nights are relatively cool.

Like the summers, winters vary in the different areas. The coastal plains and the oil field province of Khusistan have mild winters, but most of the country has cold weather (even below zero) with heavy snows and strong winds.

Rural Demography

Statistics for 1979, the year of Islamist Revolution, show Iran's estimated population as 36.3 million, with an average annual growth rate of 3%.[28] On the eve of the land reform (1962), 69% of the people lived in villages, and 49.6% of them were engaged in agricultural activities. These rates changed to 46.7% and 40%, respectively, in 1973.[29]

According to Dr. Valian, the Minister of Cooperative and Rural Affairs in 1972, the total number of villages just before the land reform was estimated at 66,745.[30] This figure changed to 65,180 in 1975.[31] Apparently between 1962 and 1976 as many as 1,565 villages were vacated as a result of the land reform program. The *Iran Almanac*, one of the official publications of the Iranian government, stated that "statistics released in April 1976 showed that in the past decade (1966–1975) some five million rural inhabitants have moved to towns and cities," adding later, "Many small holders no longer find farming profitable; hence, they leave their villages and go to cities and towns in search of work in industry."[32]

Most Iranian villages have small populations. Of the total of 66,745 villages, only 8,725 have a population of more than 200 households (1,000 persons). More than half of the entire rural population lives in 8,725 villages; the remainder occupy 58,031 villages. Of these, some 21,624 (26,000 according to the 1976 statistics) have fewer than 250 persons each.[33] Table 1 shows these details.[34]

Table 1
Number and Size of Villages, 1966[35]

In Iran

Size of Population	Number of Villages[a]	Percent of All Villages	Total Population	Percent of Population
50 or less	21,624	32.4	484,140	3.1
50–250	27,367	41.0	3,595,785	23.3
251–500	10,140	15.2	3,588,185	23.2
501–1,000	5,170	7.7	3,561,320	23.1
1,001–2,000	1,862	2.8	2,511,150	16.2
2,001–5,000	593	0.9	1,708,290	11.1
Total	66,756	100.0	15,448,870	100.0

[a] According to the official statement, any area with no more than 5,000 inhabitants is defined as a village.
SOURCE: Statistical Center of Iran, cited in K. Khosravi, *Jame'eh-i shinasi-i rustaei-i Iran* (Tehran: University of Tehran, 1978), p. 9, with adjustments.

The Water Problem

Climate plays an extremely important role in the life of Iran's peasants, determining the method of farming, the system of irrigation, and the type of product grown. In general, rainfall is insufficient, and with the exception of the southern shore of the Caspian Sea it is seasonal.[36] The heaviest rainfall area is the narrow strip beside the Caspian Sea, with 150 cm of precipitation annually. The driest part—Sistan and Baluchistan—receives only 5 cm of rainfall each year. Apart from the Caspian littoral, the rest of the country can be divided into two geographical regions, the eastern and the western. The western section, including the Azerbaijan province and the coastal plains of the Persian Gulf, receives 30 cm of annual precipitation. The eastern part, constituting 73.6% of the total land area of the country and including the desert region, receives less than 30 cm per annum, a seriously insufficient amount of rainfall. The western region actually receives 2.6% more than the eastern part,[37] but in general the average annual precipitation in Iran is 28 cm.[38] Of this amount, 28% occurs over 4% of the area of the country and 73% over the remaining 96%.[39]

Water is a formidable factor in agricultural development anywhere, but it has had so crucial a role in Iran that it merits further comment. It can be said that many social, political, and religious characteristics of Iran, especially in the rural communities, are dependent upon the amount of available water. The method of irrigation depends upon the types of sources for water as well as the annual rainfall. In many areas, the ownership of water has been as important as the ownership of land[40] because land without water is virtually worthless.

It becomes obvious, then, that in many areas of Iran agriculture is possible only through the use of artificial irrigation. Lambton states, "irrigation, indeed, is the great limiting factor to agricultural development in Persia (Iran)." [41] But in spite of the importance of irrigation, more than half of all cultivations are *daymi* (dry farming) that depend upon rain rather than irrigated agriculture (*abi*).[42]

Huge salt deserts, arid climate, and high mountain ranges present further barriers to cultivation in almost half of the 164.5 million hectares of total land area in Iran. The total amount of land under annual and permanent cultivation, either *daymi* or *abi,* is 7.1 million hectares. In addition to this amount, about 11.9 million hectares of agricultural land is called *ayish* (fallow land). Usually any non-dry farm land (*abi*) will be rotated between *ayish_*and *abi* fields every three years. However, from the 7,650,000 hectares total of annual and permanent fields, 3,450,000 hectares (45%) have been appropriated to *abi* cultivation and 4,100,000 hectares (53%) remain *daymi* fields.[43] The eastern region of the country, being drier, has more *abi* fields, and consequently irrigation systems there are more numerous than on the western side.[44] Table 2 illustrates the proportions of the different land areas in Iran.

Table 2. Land Utilization at the Beginning and End of the Fourth Plan in Iran (in thousands of Hectares)

Type of Land Utilization	Area	1968 (End of third Plan) Percentage of Total Land Area of Country	1972 (End of Fourth Plan) Area	Percentage of Total Land Area of Country
1. Total land under cultivation, including:	19,000	11.5	19,000	11.5
a. Area under annual, permanent cultivation	7,100	-	7,650	
Area under irrigated cultivation	(3,150)	-	(3,450)	
Area prepared for cultivation beneath dams		-	(100)	
Area under dry farming	(3,950)	-	(4,100)	
b. Area temporarily fallow	11,900	-	11,350	
2. Permanent pastures and meadows	10,000	6.1	10,000	6.1
3. Forests and copses	19,000	11.5	19,000	11.5
4. Uncultivable land capable of reclamation and development	31,000	18.8	31,000	18.8
5. Uncultivable land (mountains, deserts, lakes, swamps, cities, roads, etc.)	86,000	52.1	86,000	52.1
Total	165,000	100.0	165,000	10.00

SOURCE: Plan Organization, *Fourth National Development Plan 1968-72* (Tehran, Iran, 1968).

Irrigation Techniques

The crucial importance of irrigation has led to use of different irrigation methods in different parts of the country. Sources of irrigation are rivers, streams, springs, and wells. The methods are *bands* (dams), canals, and *qanats* (man-made underground water channels).

1) Bands (also called *weirs*) have been used historically for two purposes in Iran. First, because most of the rivers and streams do not carry water all year round, *bands* were built to store water during the winter for use later when needed for agriculture. Second, because most rivers and springs run in the mountainous areas where there is not enough flatland suitable for cultivation, *bands* were built to raise the water to a level high enough so that it could be channeled along riverbeds or canals toward areas where cultivable land was located.[45]

2) Qanat, a second method of irrigation, is found mostly in the central part of the plateau. This old irrigation system, which is unknown to many other societies,[46] is a technique to bring underground water to the surface. A *Qanat* or *kareez*[47] is an underground conduit that carries water from below to the surface. Using the slopes of a mountain, *qanat* are dug into the soil toward the foot of the mountain, where the water can be reached. *Qanats* start from the *madder chap* (mother well), through the open spot, from which they reach the surface. Several vertical wells (*qanats*) are dug through the length (over 10 kilometers) between two spots, in order to lift to the surface the excavated soil at the time of construction. These wells are also to be used for later maintenance of *qanats* when mud should be removed from the underground conduit. Because of their depth and length and the difficulty of their construction, *qanats* require especially skilled workers.[48] Keeping the *qanats* constantly active with a high flow rate also requires annual clean-ups. *Qanats* were built with cheap labor in rural communities, using very primitive tools, and the loss of many lives has indeed been one of the real costs of these combinations of long horizontal tunnels and vertical wells. Based on recent studies, however, the average monetary cost per kilometer in recent decades has been $10,000.[49]

Based on the author's personal knowledge, there are many *qanats* with depths exceeding 400 *zar* (*zar* = 104 cm = 43 in.). Goblet, discussing *qanats*, writes, "Some are only a few hundred meters long and do not go deep down, but there are some in the Yazd region that are over 43 kilometers in length and others, near Gunabad, that reach down to more than 300 meters. A length of 5 to 10 kilometers, with a

depth of the order of 100 meters, is a common average."[50] The total
number of *qanats* in Iran has been estimated at 46,000.[51]

3) Wells. In recent decades, beginning even before the 1962 land
reform, a number of wells, both deep and shallow, operated by gasoline
or electric pumps, have been sunk.[52] Usually these wells are sunk by
town-dwellers as a new business. Later in this study, this new operation
and its consequences for the destiny of the peasants in the villages will
be discussed further. In addition to the three methods mentioned,
construction of modern dams has supplied water to new agricultural
fields. Before this time, landlords had a two-fold monopoly on water
and land, especially in those areas such as Yazd (on the desert's edge)
where the land is almost worthless without water. Storage cisterns have
been used in some regions, but they are not common in many areas.
They usually function as a supplementary source and are used for small
plots and private homes.[53]

Peasant Organization (*Buneh*)

In previous sections, the importance of water in agriculture in Iran
was discussed, and it was shown that the quality and quantity of
production, the size of population in a region, the methods of irrigation,
and the types of plantations depend upon the amount of water available
in any particular area. The type of peasant organization is an additional
variable affecting the vital element, water. Due to the conditions
described, and in order to maximize the usage of available water, a
particular type of peasant organization had been in existence in the
eastern and central parts of Iran for many years. The organization,
called *buneh* (peasant teamwork), provided a form of collective or
multifamily production. It had different names (such as *sahra,
haratheh*) in various parts of the country, but in spite of some
differences in form the general characteristics remained the same.[54]

A typical village was divided into several *buneh,* depending upon
the size of the village and the amounts of available water and arable
land. The size of any *buneh* was determined by *joft* (an area that could
be plowed by two oxen in one day). Each *buneh* usually had four to six
members, with membership depending upon such factors as the
distance of residence from the village, farming ability, and, most
important, the consent of the landowner or his or her agent in the
village—i.e., the bailiff (*mubashir*).

Each *buneh* was administered by the most experienced and eligible
peasant, the *buneh* head *(sar-buneh)*. He also mediated between the
landlord or his agent in a village and the peasants in a relationship

called *arbab-ra'yat i*. This person often had received a larger share of land than had the ordinary peasants, and the landlord usually devoted to him a piece of land cultivated by peasants freely.[55] Social and economic mobility within the *buneh* from a simple peasant to the *buneh* head was possible.[56]

Crop-sharing peasants were engaged in two different ways. The first was when one peasant with his family independently tilled a piece of land for which he paid a "landlord share," keeping a share for himself. The second was when he was a member of a *buneh* and all members of the *buneh* tilled the *buneh* land collectively, with each peasant receiving a share of the one- or two-fifths of the crop allotted to the *buneh* and the remainder going to the landowner. In both individual and collective farming, the peasant held a particular right on the land, called *haq-i nasaq* (or cultivating right). These crop-sharing peasants were called *nasaq-dar* (title holders), and peasants usually had a right to transfer their *haq-i. nasaq* by inheritance. The next chapter will show that *haq-i nasaq* became one of the criteria in redistribution of land among the peasants during the land reform.

Each *buneh* was called by the name of its *buneh* head. The members of each *buneh* usually resided in one part of the village, sometimes having their own mosque and cemetery. The *buneh* head played a particular role in the rural community, having a significant voice in any community decision.[57] Indeed, this form of organization had operated to strengthen the ceremonial form of communities in rural areas.

Due to the land reform program, this type of organization—the natural consequence of existing conditions in rural areas—was abolished. But because the difficulties of irrigation remained, peasants continued to maintain some sort of cooperative work arrangements within their groups for a few years after the initiation of land reform. Gradually, individual farms replaced the organization of the *buneh*.

In addition to the members of *buneh* just described, usually the village blacksmith, the village carpenter, the village barber, and the public bath keeper had provided the necessary services for several *buneh* and their members in several villages. In return, they would receive a specified percentage of the harvest each year.[58]

Additional Barriers to the Development of Agriculture

The traditional techniques of irrigation and, more broadly, the traditional methods of cultivation in Iran, especially before the 1962 land reform, presented barriers to developing production. However, this was only one obstacle to the growth of agriculture. The domination of the *Muzara'eh* system (the dividing of the harvest based on the five agricultural elements of land, water, seed, labor, and plow animals) and tenancy were equally important elements in keeping agriculture in a state of backwardness. The small plots of the peasants could not accommodate the use of productive machines, and those who controlled vast lands with abundant labor forces of *barzigaran* (landless peasants) and sharecroppers showed no tendency to use any machinery. Statistics show that even in the most highly cultivated areas, such as the Gilan and Mazandaran provinces and the Khusistan plain, the use of productive machinery was very limited.[59] Only 5.17 of these areas were mechanized,[60] while about 87% were covered by man and animal husbandry and 6.87 by a combination of these.[61]

In addition, the arid climate created a situation in which 7% of the rural population—those not involved in agricultural activities—lived in temporary settlements. These nomadic people migrated with their animals (sheep, goats, camels, and donkeys) and their primitive and portable furniture from one place to another during the summer and between their summer and winter pastures.[62] Such nomadism itself has been another barrier to agricultural development. Because many nomadic tribes have apparently lived an autonomous existence, apart from the mainstream family life style, they have lived in miserable conditions. As far as the land distribution program is concerned, they have actually been excluded.

The Rural Community

In spite of the nation's huge annual oil revenues, the average rural family has lived in conditions not much better than those of the nomad people. They usually lived in a mud-constructed room with a wooden roof but no windows, and most often there was neither electricity nor running water. In spite of considerable propaganda by the government, many villages had no school, no health services, no transportation services, and no clean water. Their food was very simple and restricted to only a few items. Normally they ate bread and cheese or bread and yogurt—very rarely meat. Their typical main food was wheat or barley bread, and a high percentage of the agricultural lands were dedicated to the production of these items. Thus, from the 7.1 million hectares of cultivated land, 4 million hectares (73.2%) were used for production of just these two foodstuffs.[63] (See Table 3.)

Table 3
Area Under Cultivation of Wheat and Barley

| (In Thousands of Hectares) | | | | | |
Irrigated	%	Dry Farming	%	Total	%
Wheat	1,400	19.7	2,600	36.6	4,000	56.3
Barely	330	4.6	870	12.3	1,200	16.9
TOTAL	1,730	24.3	3,470	48.9	5,200	73.2

SOURCE: Plan Organization: *Fourth National Development Plan, 1968-72.*

One reason that nearly 70% of the cultivated areas produced such items is the large domestic demand, but dry farming, which is not applicable to all kinds of cultivation, is a second reason. As Table 3 shows, almost two-thirds of the total cultivation relies on dry farming (*daymi*).[64]

The headman, *kadkhuda*, who is selected by the landlords or elected by the peasants and approved by the local political authority, manages the village's primary social and judicial affairs. He is the representative of the landlord and the government in the village. If a landlord selects him, he functions as the landlord's intermediary in the village.[65] In the case of an absentee landlord, however, that landlord "may appoint an agent to take care of his personal affairs and be his personal representative in the village(s)."[66] In addition, the headman plays a semi-official role in the absence of a government representative in the village. For instance, he helps the authorities in the induction of village youth into the armed services whenever a gendarmerie station is not available. In recent years, before the land reform program, with the growth of political tensions, the government has hired some headmen and given them the responsibility of reporting any changes taking place in the village.

Peasants facing administrative problems have been compelled to go to provincial capitals. For example, official transfer of land, or any investigation of a lawsuit, must be handled in the major cities. In any case in which a landlord has been involved, the judgment has been based on the report of local gendarmes (frequently bribed by the landlord); peasants have been the victims of most disputed cases. However, bribery of officials, including gendarmes, even by the peasants themselves, is not uncommon in Iran.[67]

In addition to the headman, to whom an annual percentage of the crop has been paid by the landlord or the peasants (or both), there are other village officials to whom the peasants pay a share of the crop.

These include the *dashtban* (the man responsible for protection of agricultural fields from any human or animal aggression) and the *mirab* (the man responsible for control of the precise distribution of water in irrigated areas).[68] Finally, peasants must consider the "rights" of the village *mulla* (clergyman). Clergymen in villages are representatives of Islam and are responsible for guiding villagers in accordance with the Islamic codes. Either the landlord or the peasants, or both, pay them. This unproductive group had special privileges among the habitually religious people.

[1] Following chapters are adopted from my doctoral dissertation written in 1981.

[2] Muzara'eh is a sharecropping contract between two parties—i. e., peasant and landlord—based on the agricultural elements (land, water, seed, the plough, animals, and labor).

[3] See: *Enqelab Islami* (daily newspaper), 23rd Day 1359 (January 1981); 14th Bahman 1359 (February 1981); 25th Esfand 1359 (March 1981); 16th Bahman 1359 (February 1981).

[4] T. Bergmann, "Agrarian Reforms and Their Functions in the Development Process," *Land Reform, Land Settlement and Cooperatives*, FAO-UN, no. 1, 1978.

[5] United States Department of State, *Land Reform—A World Challenge* (Washington, D.C.: U.S. Government Printing Office, 1952), l.

[6] Ibid., 6.

[7] D. Christodoulou, "Agrarian Reform in Retrospect: Contributions Dynamics and Related Fundamental Issues," *Land Reform, Land Settlement Cooperatives*, FAO-UN, no. 2, 1977, 19.

[8] Poland also raised the issue of land reform in the U.N. at the time, but of course it was not supportive of the American plan.

[9] United States Department of State, *Land Reform*, 1952, 1.

[10] For example, see R. P. Dore, *Land Reform in Japan* (London: Oxford University Press, 1959). Also see *New York Herald Tribune*, 13 November 1945, pp. 1, 34.

[11] D. Christodoulou, 19. In the case of the Philippines, Christodoulou concludes that "The Philippines seem to have tried all known evolutionary means toward an effective agrarian reform and all parallel roads toward elimination of mass rural poverty, such as package programmes and the 'green revolution,' but these efforts have hitherto proved inadequate and the problems still remain" (p. 4). For details about this program and consequent programs in the Philippines, see A. Guerrero, *Philippine Society and Revolution* (Hong Kong: Ta Kung Pao, 1971), and *People's War in the Philippines* (Union of Democratic Filipines: KDP, 1975).

[12] Christodoulou, p. 9. For information regarding the results of land reforms in Latin American countries, see "Peasants, Capitalism and the Class Struggle in Rural Latin America," *Latin American Perspectives*, Part I, V (3) (1978), and Part II, V (4) (1978).

[13] H. Kunert, "Criteria for the Evaluation of Agrarian Reform and Rural Development Programmes," *Land Reform, Land Settlement and Cooperatives*, FAO-UN, no. 1 (1976): 89.

[14] U.S. Department of State, p. 41.

[15] G. H. Bennett, "Land and Independence, Americans' Experience," in *Land Reform*, ed. H. K. Parsons (Madison: The University of Wisconsin Press, 1956).

[16] Ibid., 37.

[17] Warriner, xiv.

[18] Bergmann, 2.

[19] United Nations, *Progress in Land Reform*, 4th Report, 1966.

[20] By a "green revolution" it refers to technological improvements in traditional agriculture in some countries such as India and Indonesia, and "white revolution" was a tag used by the Shah of Iran for a series of reforms, including the land reform program. The details will be discussed in coming chapters.

[21] Other western sociologists, who believe that social and cultural elements bring about economic growth, have developed similar theories concerning undeveloped societies. They suggest that lack of development in these societies is due to the specific social and cultural characteristics these societies, and, hence, they propose to replace certain existing "backward" social and cultural factors with social and cultural factors of the modern advanced Western societies. For examples, see Talcott Parsons, *Social System*, 1951, and Bert F. Hoselitz, *Social Structure and Economic Growth*, 1953.

[22] Christodoulou.

[23] For details about the similarities and differences between these two types of agrarian reform programs, see Bergmann, 17, Table 2.

[24] Warriner, 16–22.

[25] Development of the bourgeoisie is associated with the modern growth of both productive forces and relations of production in all economic sectors, including agriculture.

[26] For details of the obstacles to the growth of the bourgeoisie in Iran, see A. Ashraf, "Historical Obstacles to the Development of Bourgeoisie Iran," *Iranian Studies*, II (2-3), (Spring-Summer 1969): 54–79.

[27] *Iran Almanac*, 1976, 59.

[28] *The 1979 World Population Data Sheet* (Washington, D.C.: Population Reference Bureau, Inc., 1979).

[29] *Iran Almanac*, 1976.

[30] M. Muhammadi, *On the Agrarian Policy of Iranian Government and for a Democratic Solution of Agrarian Problems* (Tehran: Tudeh Publishing Center, 1973).

[31] *Iran Almanac*, 1976.

[32] Ibid., 1976, 321 and 181, respectively.

[33] *The Iran Almanac* (1976) indicates that 20,000 villages have fewer than 10 households (50 persons) each.

[34] As K. E. Abbott writes and Charles Issawi also emphasizes, "It seldom happens in Persia that two statistics on one subject, even when derived from official sources, are found to correspond: (cited in Charles Issawi, *The Economic History of Iran, 1800–1914* [Chicago: University of Chicago Press, 1971], 20). This is so because Iranian government statistics are not based on fact but usually have political purposes. Such statistics have mostly been propaganda statements rather than realities. This problem makes conclusions confusing when others wish to use such data.

[35] Only 9% of the agricultural land in Iran has sufficient rainfall. The remaining 91% requires artificial irrigation, Fourth National Development Plan (1968-1972), *Plan and Budget Organization of Iran*, (Tehran: the Imperial Government of Iran, 1968).

[36] Based on the Islamic code, any estate property is divided into six *dongs* (parts). Thus, each village contains six *dongs*: according to the code, not only each village, but each house, orchard, well, tree, etc. contains six *dongs*.

[37] J. Safi-Nejad, *Buneh (The Systems of Cumulative Farming) Before and After Land Reform* (Tehran: Tolls Press, 1353 (1975). In Persian.

[38] The average for the entire world is 86 cm per annum.

[39] K. Khosravi, "Irrigation and Rural Community in Iran," *Journal of the Social Sciences*, 3, no. 1 (February 1970): 48–57. In Persian.

[40] N. Jacobs, *The Sociology of Development: Iran as an Asian Case Study* (New York: Praeger Special Studies in International Economics and Development, 1967).

[41] A. Lambton, *Landlord and Peasant in Persia: A Study of Land Tenure and Land Revenue Administration* (London: Oxford University Press, 1953), 2.

[42] The shortage of water limits the expansion of agriculture in Iran. However, because of the use of the most traditional methods of irrigation, such as *qanats* (underground water channels), which extract permeating water all year round even though it is not needed during several months of the year, and because of the lack of a relevant agricultural plan, much available water continues to be wasted.

According to official estimates, total water received annually fluctuates from as little as 300 billion to as much as 590 billion cubic meters. About half this amount is lost through evaporation. Less than 20% (100 billion cubic meters) is surface flow in the forms of various rivers. Only one-fifth of this 20% is used for irrigation purposes. From the 60 billion cubic meters of permeating water, only 7% is extracted and utilized. (*Plan Organization, The Fourth and Fifth National Development Plans*, 1968–72 and 1973–77).

[43] The remaining 2% has been "area prepared for cultivation beneath dams." The total amount of land under annual and permanent cultivation before the land reform program (1962), as we have stated, was 7.0 million hectares (*Plan Organization*, 1968, p. 103, Table 4).

[44] Safi-Nejad.

[45] The dams were usually built through cooperation between *ra' yats* (crop-sharing peasants) and small farmers, and they were maintained by the community.

[46] Issawi, in this connection, writes, "Before the Arab conquest, *qanats* spread from Iran to neighboring lands and countries under Persian rule—for example, the Oasis of Siwa in Egypt. In the Islamic period, the technique was carried to North Africa, where they are known as foggaras" (1971, p. 213). Nomani writes that "this system spread from the Near East to North Africa, Spain, and Sicily in Roman times" (F. Nomani, "Origin and Development of Feudalism in

Iran: 300–1600 A.D.," Dissertation, University of Illinois, 1972). In Iran itself, wherever agriculture could rely on rainfall, rivers, or springs, as in north and southwest Iran, *qanats* were not found.

[47] *Kareez* is the other name of *qanat* used in Iran.

[48] For more details about qanats, see G. Cressey, "Qanats, Kareez, and Foggaras," *Geographical Review* 48, no. 28 (1958): 231–254; Issawi, 213; Lambton, 217; and Nomani, 99.

[49] Issawi, 213-4; Lambton, 221-22.

[50] Cited in Issawi, 213.

[51] *Iran Almanac*, 1976.

[52] A. Lambton, 1953. She mentions that as a result of this new method of extracting ground water, water prices have fallen slightly. But she adds discussion of a fear that the price of water could be relatively low at first, in order to encourage peasants to invest money and labor. Once they have invested in their gardens, the cost of water would be raised and the peasants would be faced with either a high payment for water or the option of leaving their gardens to ruin.

[53] Nomani; Lambton.

[54] For further details, see Safi-Nejad, 238–261.

[55] Safi-Nejad.

[56] Each peasant might change his *buneh,* or the *buneh* head could transfer any peasant to another *buneh* in the same village.

[57] Khosravi.

[58] Safi-Nejad.

[59] Keddie has called the area below the Caspian Sea (i.e., Gilan and Mazandaran) the "prosperous province" (1968, p. 72).

[60] By using the term "mechanized farms," we mean those agricultural sectors that use any type of machinery, even one tractor.

[61] Tahqiqat-E Eqtesadi, *Quarterly Journal of Economic Research*, Institute for Economic Research, Faculty of Economics, University of Tehran, no. 9-10 (September 1965/Abaan 1343), and nos. 11 and 12 (August–September 1966/ Shahrivar 1344).

[62] E. J. Hoogland, "The Effects of the Land Reform Program on Rural Iran, 1962–72," (Ph.D. Dissertation, Johns Hopkins University, 1975). Nomads have different ethnicities in different areas.

[63] Statistics show that the total amount devoted to these two products before the land reform was 79.6% of the total land under cultivation. This means that the differentiation changes under industrial plants. (See following chapters.)

[64] The average yield per hectare in dry farming of wheat is 490 kilograms (about 1,079 pounds); with irrigated wheat cultivation, it is 1,150 kilograms (about 2,533 pounds). (*Plan Organization*, 1968–72, and *Statistics Yearbook*, 1961.)

[65] Jacobs.

[66] Ibid., 136.

[67] Ibid.
[68] Lambton.

Chapter 6
The Conditions Prior to the Land Reform

I. The Land Tenure System Before the Land Reform

Introduction

The land reform program was a radical approach to the traditional landholding system in Iran, even though gradual changes had been taking place during the half-century after the 1905 Constitutional Revolution. The social relations of production, however, still remained either the *Muzara'eh* system (sharecropping based on the five agricultural elements, to be discussed below) or tenancy.

This chapter intends to explain the land tenure system from the early twentieth century to the pre-land reform program. In this regard, various forms of land ownership, all dominated by the two above-mentioned types of production relations, will be briefly described, as they existed throughout the country. The chapter will also show the existing relationships between landowners and peasants, the shares of each in cultivation and harvest during this time period, and the method of extracting surplus value. The purpose of such a discussion is to show the characteristics of the old agrarian system, which affected the land reform laws.

This section is not intended as an analysis of the dominant socioeconomic formation of Iranian society prior to land reform. Instead, we will discuss the forms of land ownership that affected land distribution, as distinct from the dominant relations of production, although both had to be changed during the 1962 land reform project.

Forms of Land Ownership

Study of the forms of land ownership in Iran is important for two main reasons. First, some of the agricultural land had been sold to peasants on the basis of the form of land ownership existing before the 1962 program. For instance, sales of state land to peasants had begun gradually as early as 1931, and crown land had been sold to peasants beginning in 1949. Second, the form of land ownership was a criterion for exempting some land, such as endowed land, from distribution in the first stage of the 1962 land reform program.

In Iran prior to the 1962 land reform there were five forms of land-holding:[1]

1.   *Melk* or *arbabi* (private landed estates)
2.   *Khaleseh* (state lands and public domain)
3.   *Amlak-i saltanati* (crown lands)
4.   *Vaqf* (plural *ouqaf*, endowment lands)
5.   *Khurdeh maliki* (peasant proprietorship).

With the exception of peasant proprietorships, the two types of socioeconomic relations—i.e., *Muzara'eh* and tenancy—largely dominated these forms of land ownership.

Within the various forms of land ownership, the following groups were big landowners. The first group included members of the ruling family, both military and civil high-ranking officials. This group of absentee landlords obtained their lands by conquest, inheritance, gift, and purchase, and they were the most powerful in Iran. As discussed in a previous chapter, Reza Shah himself (father of the last shah) became the biggest landowner during his reign through the first-stated way. The second group was the tribal leaders, who acquired their land in various ways. Some of them were absent from their estates and lived in the larger towns, while others lived among their people in tribes, ruling as the regional rulers. They had special military forces to defend their properties and to force the people to pay them. Third were the village merchants whose landed properties near the villages were acquired in two ways: (1) through the transfer of land from those peasants who borrowed money from the merchants and were unable to pay their debts when they were due, and (2) through direct purchase. This group also consisted of absentee landlords. Finally, there were the clergymen, a remarkable group whose land holdings were derived from grants and pensions from the state, inheritance, or purchase. This group also controlled the *vaqf* properties that will be discussed later.[2]

1. Melk or arbabi (large-scale private land ownership) was the major and most important form of land ownership in Iran. According to existing statistics, before landlords, constituting only 1% of the villages' populations, dominated reform, about 56% of the total agricultural land.[3] In addition, tribal heads owned about 13% of arable land.[4] Thus, traditional landlords, who were usually members of the various high-class social groups—absentee landlords, tribal leaders, and clergy—who had varying attitudes toward the land, owned about 69% of all agricultural land. Still, their social, political, and economic status depended upon the amount of land they owned, and the biggest landowners had the most influence in social and political affairs. They owned the best types of land in various parts of the country, and they had always held the majority of seats in the *Majlis* (National Consultative Assembly). During the 40 years preceding land reform, an average of 57% of *Majlis* deputies were landlords.[5]

In summary, 52% of the land was in the form of *melk*. The owners themselves seldom cultivated such lands, which were either rented out to peasants or cultivated according to the *muzara'eh* system. In the latter case, the crop was divided into shares according to the five agricultural factors: land, water, work, seed, and plowing. In the rental form, the landlord would require rent to be paid in cash or in kind.[6]

In the case of an absentee landowner, a third person (the bailiff, or *mubasher*) acted as intermediary between the peasants and the landowner. An owner who preferred to free himself of the need to administer his property would hire a *mubasher* to collect his rents in the villages. In some cases, the landowner might rent his land to a third party, receiving a fixed annual amount of rent, but having no responsibility in the village. This renter, in turn, either rented the land to peasants or exploited them directly in the form of sharecropping. This form of land ownership remained unchanged until the 1962 land reform program, but it was affected by the first stage of the land reform laws.

2. Khaleseh (state lands), or lands that belonged to the government, constituted 6% of the total agricultural land in Iran. These domains were dispersed throughout about 3,000 villages.[7] This very old form of state ownership had existed since pre-Islamic times in Iran, and the land had mainly been confiscated for arrears of taxes and other debts. The government itself administered some of it, but other parts had been given to individuals for personal use for a period of time, with a right of transfer.[8] Sometimes the possession of this land carried with it an obligation of military service to the central government. Any *khaleseh* with such obligation was called a *tuyul* (land assignment), and the person who used the land was named a *tuyul dar* (*tuyul* holder). This form of landholding was called *tuyul-dari*. A definition of *tuyul* is thus land given to a high echelon of the military or civil service for loyal service to the court. A *tuyul*, a source of income for the *tuyul-dar*, was similar to the fief in European feudalism. In some cases, land was given to state officials as pensions.[9] From the state land administered by the government itself, the revenue collected was also distributed to military or civil officials as pensions. *Tuyul-dari* came under attack during the Constitutional Revolution, and the National Consultative Assembly abolished *tuyul* in 1907.[10]

Khaleseh had been sold to peasants since 1931. For this purpose, the *Majlis* passed several bills during the 1930s and 1940s. Finally, in 1955, in spite of the stated objective, this land was mainly sold—not to the landless peasants but to the newly emerging urban and rural bourgeoisie.[11] Some of this land, however, was distributed among the nomadic people in Luristan in order to settle them,[12] because these nomadic people with their constantly changing living locations were creating problems for the government.

The amount of *khaleseh* land varied from dynasty to dynasty because of the constant distribution and confiscation of land by the government. For instance, during the Reza Shah's reign, although some state land was sold, the Shah "legally" confiscated many landlords' and rebel tribal khans' landed properties in different areas for alleged arrears of taxes.[13] (How this confiscated land, under the name of the state, became the personal property of Reza Shah was explained in the previous chapter)

Finally, let us briefly note the various types of *khaleseh*. There were three: (1) *khalesehjat-i intiqali* (transferable land),[14] or land that had been handed over to individuals for life or for a stipulated period, with the right of transfer; (2) *khalesehjat-i tuyuli*, or land for which the holders were obliged to furnish military service; and (3) *khalesehjat-i divani,* or land under full possession of the government. The major portions of these lands had been sold to peasants before the land reform program, with the remaining lands being subjected to distribution in the first stage of land reform.

3. *Amlak-i saltanati* (crown lands). Historically, crown lands belonged to the private estates of kings, caliphs, or khans. There were, however, no major differences between state and crown land for powerful rulers.[15]

After the Arab invasion and before the Reza Shah's domination in Iran, there was no way to distinguish crown land from state land. In this study, we mean by "crown land" those pieces of land that Reza Shah had gathered by confiscation of private and state lands and then named "crown lands." This possession made him the biggest landowner in Iran, as well as one of the richest men in the world.[16]

For a better understanding of how an ordinary man became the biggest landowner in Iran, a few of the many pertinent existing documents will be summarized. First, Jaami states:

> Reza Shah was placed upon the throne in 1925. Before that time, he had nothing of his own such as estates, factories, or money invested in foreign banks.

> When Reza Shah could no longer rule the country through force and violence, he had to rein in his power. But by this time, in contrast to 1925, he was the owner of the most fertile land in Mazandaran and Gilan provinces. Because of his investments in the banks of England, America, and Germany, he was considered one of the richest men in the world.[17]

How could such an enormous amount of money be collected in such a short time? One risks the loss of objectivity in describing a man's rise to riches, but from sources available to researchers, these facts seem to indicate a simple answer: at the beginning, the Ministry of Finance issued an order to the owners of the land that, since they could not own the land, it would be necessary for them to sell their land to a "qualified person" (whose qualification was decided by a government commission). If they did not abide by the order, their land would be confiscated. During most of this time, the Ministry of Finance acted as the "qualified person" and seized the lands or used force to buy them. The land was then turned over to Reza Shah. A series of examples of what was done follows.

According to the heirs of Jafar Quli Asad:

> Since you are not supposed to own any land or property in the Khuzistan region, you are to sell all of it to persons whose qualifications have been approved by a commission in your area. Meanwhile, you should act within a year; otherwise the Ministry of Finance will confiscate all of your property and in return you will be given some pieces of land of lesser value.

Mr. Loatfali-Khan (Salar) Malik Marzban states:

> Since you are bound to leave your personal property, you must transfer all of your belongings to your new residence. If you do not act within the date set, all of your property will be seized without payment.

Loatfali-Kahn sent an open letter to the National Consultative Assembly about Khalarestan (seized by Reza Shah), which reads as follows:

> Khalarestan, which had 134 summer and winter quarters [residences], pastures, and forests, was seized by the Ministry of Finance and Estate. The same thing happened in Kojour, Tankabon, and later on in Mazandaran, Gorgan, and parts of Gilan. Some of the landowners were jailed in Qasr prison. Their families were sent in different groups to the towns.[18]

One of the exiles from Shiraz writes:

> Dear Sirs: Kamineh lands located in Kalege village, Kajarestan, Kojour, and Mazandaran were confiscated. They were neither sold by the owners nor bought from them. The confiscators did not give the owners a notice concerning the confiscation of the land.

Jaami writes:

> When Reza Shah Pahlavi stepped down from the office two and a half months ago and fled to India and Mouris Island through Kerman, he revealed a fact in Kerman. The fact was mentioned to two of the residents where he was received: "I collected seven thousand million tumans[19] to teach the people that anything can be achieved through effort and that we should not be satisfied just by owning meat and bread.[20] This amount was equal to 5,400 kharvars gold [roughly, 1,620,000 kilograms] with the rate of the day.[21]

Reza Shah left this land to his son Muhammad Reza Shah (the last Shah of Iran) as the crown land. Muhammad Reza Shah began to sell the crown land, through a complicated arrangement, to peasants in 1949, but two years later, when Dr. Mosaddeq came to power as the national prime minister, he was able to return all the remaining crown lands to the control of his government, in order to remove the shah's authority over the land. This remainder, according to Lambton, consisted of

> ...some 1,277 villages wholly belonging to the *vaqf*; 706 villages belonging to it in part; 1,975 pastures; and 2,381 pieces of real estate other than cultivated land or pastures. They were situated mainly in the Caspian provinces [i.e., the most fertile region of the country]; some were in Kirmanshahan, and a few were in Khurasan. Their gross annual revenue was alleged to be some 88 million r_s. [400,000 British pounds].[22]

There were about 250,000 peasants engaged in agricultural activities on that part of the crown land, which was sold to peasants in 1949–50; about 300,000 inhabitants lived on the remaining parts.[23] Although the shah had been able to convert the major portion of the crown lands to hard currency before the 1962 land reform program, the remaining part was sold to the peasants during the first stage of the land reform program.

4. *Vaqf* Lands (endowments). Land under this category had been given to religious institutions, holy shrines, and their administrators, for charitable or personal purposes. Such holdings represented a total of 6,000 endowed villages, or about 12% of the total arable land in the country.[24] Since the institution of *vaqf* (pl., *ouqaf*) is essentially Islamic, high-ranking theologians, religious judges, and their servants, as well as curators, would receive an important part of the income of *vaqf*.[25] For instance, the holy shrine of Imam Reza in Mashhad[26] had 400 villages in its name.[27] This explains why Lambton says, "on different occasions in the past the government in power has attempted control of the administration of *ouqaf*."[28]

Two kinds of *ouqaf* were recognized in Iran: (1) *vaqf aam* (general endowments) for public interest, and (2) *vaqf khass* (special endowments), which were endowments in name only. These kinds of land, especially the private *vaqf*, were constituted for private purposes.[29] Landowners converted their land into *vaqf* for several reasons. First, the personal landed properties, as was discussed earlier, were always endangered by confiscation by the government or by more powerful landlords. Land was declared *vaqf* in order to insure it against such confiscation.[30] Second, as Nomani writes, "the turning of an estate into *vaqf* was an indirect way of avoiding too strict a division of property under the law of succession and of retaining for the male members of the family an undivided farm estate that otherwise would have been split up or alienated."[31] Third, by such maneuvers, owners were able to avoid paying taxes on the land.[32]

According to Islamic law, any *vaqf* must have a *mutavalli* (administrator). The same law said that the *waqif* (founder) could designate himself or another person as *mutavalli* for a lifetime or for a stipulated period.[33] Inasmuch as the relations of production on *vaqf* lands were the same as on any private farm estate, the *mutavalli* was able to exploit peasants even more strongly than an ordinary landlord.

In addition to agricultural land, there were many pieces of real estate and movable properties related to the religious institutions that the Department of *Ouqaf* held under its control as *mutavalli* when it was established after the Constitutional Revolution.[34] The endowed land, in contrast to the state and crown lands, was untouched until the 1962 land reform program. Although the special endowments were included in distribution during the first stage of the reform program, general endowments remained until much later.

5. *Khurdeh Maliki* (peasant proprietorship). There is a lack of accurate information about the actual size of the holdings of peasant properties. One source indicates that small proprietors owned 5% to 6% of the land.[35] According to the 1339 (1960) survey, 60% of the peasants owned no land, 23% owned less than one hectare of land, and 10% held between one and three acres each. Thus 93% of the peasants owned either no land or very small tracts, and only 7% of the farmers owned more than three hectares of land.[36]

These tracts of land were found in various areas of the country, especially where ownership of land was separate from ownership of water.[37] In most cases, holdings were too small to support a family adequately, so most peasants engaged in supplementary work such as carpet weaving or flock keeping. In the absence of a supplementary source of income, many were forced to leave their villages and migrate to the cities in search of work, especially when a holding was broken up by inheritance into separate units.[38] Peasant proprietors in such situations were often on the edge of bankruptcy, and thus their lands were an easy channel of investment for those who had surplus capital and were interested in land purchase. Jacobs writes:

> Village merchants, who through clever manipulation of the advance sale of crops from those marginal peasant proprietors who owned small tracts of land, sooner or later could foreclose for debt, thereby reducing the peasants to tenants.[39]

Many of the peasants sought loans from money lenders at an interest rate of about 50% for living expenses during the winter and for beginning their cultivation in the spring.[40] They had to pay exorbitant prices for their simple daily needs—tea and sugar, for example. Prices for such items were sometimes more than double the usual cost.[41] A narrow stratum of better-off peasants, who owned 10 to 20 hectares of land each and lived comfortably, will be discussed later.

During the implementation of the land reform program, some of the peasant proprietors who were also *nasaq* holders received some land in cases of distribution of lands in their areas.

The Dominant Social Relations of Production

The vast majority of the rural population owned nothing except their labor. This group was composed of landless peasants, tenants, and agricultural laborers. The relations between peasants and landlords were mostly based, as has been indicated earlier, on the *muzara'eh* (sharecropping agreements) or a fixed rent, and only rarely on a wage-paid relationship.[42] The two dominant types of relations are further described below.

1. *Muzara'eh* System. Based on local custom, the *muzara'eh* system was ratified constitutionally and explained by 24 articles in the Iranian Civil Code.[43] According to Article 518 of that Code,

> A *muzara'eh* is a contract in virtue of which one of the two parties gives to the other a piece of land for a specified time so that he shall cultivate it and divide the proceeds.[44]

Traditionally, division of the crop was on the basis of five the agricultural elements *(avamel-e keshavarzi)*: land, water, draft animals, seed, and labor. One share was allotted to each element and would go to the provider of that element.[45] Thus, those peasants who contributed only one element (for instance, labor) would acquire only one-fifth of the yield. This was not, however, the common rule in the entire country. Accompanying and dependent upon the geographical situation, the allotment of shares for each side would differ. In some areas, for example, the landowners would receive two-thirds and the peasant one-third of the harvest.[46] In such regions, the peasant was sometimes able to provide two elements.

In some areas, such as Dizful, draft animals were provided by a third party in the person of a *gaavband* (the person who owned the oxen), and in that situation the *gaavband* would take a share.

The common relationship between peasant and landlord has been called *arbab-ra'yati*. Based on this relationship, peasants, either individually (as was common in some regions) or collectively (several families), were involved in a specific "rural community"—i.e., buneh (team work). Buneh is described in detail in Chapter 6.

2. Peasant Tenancy. A peasant might undertake to pay a fixed rent, in cash, in kind, or both, instead of engaging in crop sharing. According to Demin, "Rates of rent payments varied sharply and ranged between 10% and 30% of the crop."[47] In a fixed rent agreement, the peasant had more independence, to the extent that any increase in output remained in his own possession. More enthusiasm in cultivation was thus often shown. Apparently, this kind of agreement was more progressive than the *muzara'eh* system, but since most peasants usually did not own all the productive elements they were compelled to pay for these elements with some of their products, in addition to the fixed rent. Most often, the owner of such elements was again the landlord.

Sometimes urban capitalists rented a whole village from the landlord and then, in turn, divided the village land into smaller portions that they either rented to peasants or made into sharecropping lands based on the *muzara'eh* system. This was frequently the case for *vaqf* and state lands.

3. Peasant Extra Services *(bigari).* In addition to paying sometimes as much as 80% of the crop as share or rent, peasants were also obligated to perform various chores for the landlords. The government in Article 520 of the Civil Code legalized such extra payments, which stated:

> In a *muzara'eh* it is lawful to make a condition that one of the two parties should give to the other party some other thing in addition to a share from the produce.[48]

The number and form of these chores varied from place to place, the most common form being *bigari* (*corvee,* or labor). For example, it might be the duty of the peasant to transport the landowner's share of the harvest from the threshing floor to the granary[49] or to work on construction sites or as servants for the landlord.[50] Also, "for the poultry they reared in their shacks or the grapes they dried in the sun within the confines of their houses, they were obligated to pay dues in kind."[51] The important thing is that such *bigari* and various other dues acted as additional barriers to the growth of productive forces in Iran. Through gradual changes in the relations of production in the countryside and relaxation of the *muzara'eh* system, many of these labor services diminished.

4. *Khwush-neshin.*[52] In addition to those peasants involved in crop sharing or rental farming, there were other people working on agricultural land just as laborers for the landowners or renters.[53] These landless people, including agricultural laborers and non-farmers who engaged in various rural commercial services but who lived in the villages, have been called *Khwush-neshin.* They were not a homogeneous group; they were from different classes. As Hoogland states, there were among them "some of the wealthiest, as well as some of the poorest of all villagers."[54] Anyone who did not hold a *nasaq* (cultivating right) was a *Khwush-neshin.* Included were the *barzigar* (landless peasants), *pilevars* (peddlers), *baqqals* (village shop keepers), *rebakhars* (local money lenders), bazaar merchants (wholesale dealers), *mirabs* (water officials), *dasht-i bans* (field watchers), *asiyabans* (grinding millers), *salmanies* (barbers), *hammamies* (public bath house attendants), *ahangar* (blacksmiths), *mesgars* (coppersmiths), *najJars* (carpenters), *kaffash* (shoemakers), and *muallems* (teachers). These groups constituted 40% to 50% of all villagers, and they received no land during the land reform program.[55]

II. Social, Political, and Economic Background

Introduction

This section offers a response to the specific question: Why was the land reform launched at this particular moment in Iranian history? A brief review of the social, political, and economic history of Iran will be given, because it is believed that the old society received the first challenge to its order (i.e., the activities of the Constitutional Revolution) in the early twentieth century. Those social, political, and economic actions, which had an effect on the evolution of the pre-reform status quo, such as the regional movements against landlords, will be reviewed. Finally, we will discuss the situation after the 1953 coup d'etat and those factors that accompanied the proposal of the land reform program. This section will discuss the roles of the governments of the U.S. and Britain, the two dominant powers in Iran, as their roles affected land reform and the position of the clergy in this period.

Constitutional Revolution (1905–1911)

The Constitutional Revolution as a national movement against court despotism and its foreign allies[56] took place in the early twentieth century in Iran. Some believe the Revolution was also against the feudal order,[57] but the lack of participation by the peasant stratum in the movement and the lack of a specific demand by them for land would seem to show that claim to be incorrect. Although it was true that many peasants lived in an inhumane situation, suffering injustices and cruelty from many local landlords and the central and local governments, B. Mu'Mini, writing about the situation on the eve of the Constitutional Revolution, concluded:

> The feudal lord robs him [the peasant] of everything; the new landowner exploits him; the clergyman feeds off him; and the government snatches away his last penny. Everybody is against him, and the urban petty bourgeoisie supports him only in words. Nobody calls on him to join the movement, and he himself does not expect any gains from the movement.[58]

The merchants, intellectuals, and clergy against the oppression and injustice of the Qajar dynasty, the main obstacle to the growth and development of capitalistic relations of production, and also against supporters of the ruling classes—i.e., Russian czarism and British domination—led the movement. In such a situation, there was also no protective immunity for the capital investment and trade relations of the national bourgeoisie.[59] B. Jazani describes the situation:

> Sometimes a prince confiscated the whole of a businessman's movable assets. There was no real security for capital, and real wealth was often represented only by large inherited property. Therefore, not only was the bourgeoisie unable to use public resources for its own benefit, but the self-seeking manner in which the landlords behaved was a constant threat to its very existence.[60]

The bourgeoisie needed to end this uncertain status quo that had been created and was supported by Court despotism. The bourgeoisie started the movement, but in general it could triumph over the ruling class only if the fundamental role of the peasant in such a revolution was considered. It was a big mistake that little or no attempt was made to attract the peasant to the revolution, but for the Iranian bourgeoisie, contrary to the European case, there was no motivation to mobilize the peasant.

The lack of growth on the part of the industrial bourgeoisie prevented the full growth of the contradiction between the bourgeoisie and the agrarian system of production. The commercial bourgeoisie was not in need of a plentiful supply of labor or the land owned by feudalists (as in the West) to produce the raw materials that would otherwise have been needed by industry. Indeed, the bourgeoisie itself was deeply involved in land ownership. Therefore, at that stage of its development, the bourgeoisie's contradiction was merely with the political superstructure of feudalism and its allies. It was this contradiction that was the cause of the Constitutional Revolution.[61]

Merchants and intellectuals and a faction of the clergy strata sought to establish a constitution and a parliament and to restrict the autocratic power of the shah. The first result of the Constitutional Revolution was a National Consultative Assembly, one of the most important sociopolitical institutions favoring capitalism in Iran. This newly established Assembly succeeded in abolishing the *tuyuls* (land assignments)[62] and in providing conditions for a modern tax administration that was the main source of revenues for the central government. The new legal measures restricted the autocratic power of the shah, but according to Lambton they "did not materially alter the structure or personnel of the landowning classes; . . . they ensured greater security of tenure to landowners."[63] Thus, the ruling class was still predominantly composed of landowners.[64] And while the Constitutional Revolution was a step forward in opposing political despotism and the tribal system in Iran, the peasants gained nothing from the revolution.

Regional National Democratic Movements and the 1921 Coup d'Etat

The revolutionary movement, with its many ups and downs, brought about a compromise between the landowning class and large-merchant capitalism. It was temporarily suspended in 1911, but it continued in the form of regional movements and finally destroyed the Qajar Court. If the larger movement was originally started against court despotism, these regional movements primarily opposed the landowners and the corruption of the provincial administration. Two important national movements that were influenced by the 1917 Russian socialist revolution will be briefly reviewed.

The first example is the Jangali movement, led by Mirza Kuchik Khan in the wooded area of Gilan in the northern part of Iran. Jangalis (woodsmen), who began their struggle in 1915 and were in control of Gilan and parts of the nearby provinces,[65] started an anti-landlord program in the liberated areas. It was through this struggle that in June 1920 the Soviet Republic of Gilan was established.[66] The Jangalis first abolished dues and labor service, and then they modified the crop-sharing system in favor of the peasants.[67] Lambton writes, "The complaints of the peasantry were investigated by the Jangalis, control of water for irrigation was assumed, and landlords were compelled to disgorge their wealth and pay to save their estates from confiscation; in some cases landlords were kidnapped and held for ransom."[68]

In the Azerbaijan national democratic movement, the leader, Sheik Muhammad Khiabani, proclaimed a revolutionary government in 1920. The government established by the Democratic Party of Azerbaijan immediately launched its reforms, including a land reform program.[69]

> The land reform program of the public committee provided for unconditional distribution of all state land among the peasants. However, most of the privately owned land remained in the hands of the big landowners and clergy.[70]

These revolutionary measures did not meet with the approval of either the landlords or their supporter, the British government. It was in this situation that Reza Khan (later Reza Shah), under direct management of the British and with their strong military support, staged a coup d'etat in 1921. Following this coup, Reza Shah undertook two main tasks: (1) to destroy the national democratic movement,[71] and (2) to terminate the local khans' authority. At the same time, a "modernization" program was proclaimed. The coup d'etat regime was the close ally of British imperialism, and it represented the interests of the landlords and the comprador bourgeoisie.[72] However, Halliday states, "the state he [Reza Shah] created provided the context for the later capitalist development of Iran."[73] Because Reza Shah himself, by seizing landlords' lands, gradually became the biggest landholder in the country,[74] it was perhaps natural that "he made no attempt to alter agrarian relations in Iran."[75] The central government, however, extended its control over the outlying areas of the country and restricted the social and political power of local landlords.[76]

The Beginning of Mohammad Reza Shah's Reign (1941)

At the beginning of World War II, because of Reza Shah's sympathy toward the fascists, allied forces invaded Iran and the shah's dictatorial regime collapsed. In the absence of the dictatorship, new political and economic elements emerged in Iran. For one thing, the new situation facilitated the return of the landlords to their seats of power. On the other hand, however, the progressive and opposition forces, such as the Tudeh party and founder elements of the National Front, were also able to grow as well.

All land that had been confiscated by Reza Shah during his reign was first placed, after his abdication, in the hands of the state. Later, during a conspiracy by the Majlis (parliament), these lands were passed immediately to his son, Mohammad Reza Shah (the last shah).[77] Mohammad Reza Shah in 1329 (1949–50), as we have indicated earlier, began to sell the land that had been known as the Crown land.

By the end of World War II, the peasant movement had grown up again in the Gilan, Kurdistan, and Azerbaijan provinces. In December 1945, the Soviet-inspired autonomous Republic of Azerbaijan, under the premiership of Ja'far Pishevari, was proclaimed.[78] It immediately began various reforms, including a land reform program. First initiated was the redistribution of state land among the peasants;[79] then landlords' lands were expropriated.[80] Some similar programs took place in Kurdistan, but about a year later, these new republics (Azerbaijan and Kurdistan)[81] were invaded by the autonomous republics (i.e., the shah's military forces).[82] Thus, the landlords regained their power in these areas. After this bloody suppression by the central government's invasion, the government and the shah himself became more and more powerful, and as Jazani states, "After the suppression of the peasant movement in Azerbaijan in 1946, all such movements died down."[83]

As we have stated, the shah obtained official control over the Crown lands in 1327 (1948), but the people were organizing against the Court and the landlords in various groups and parties. Despite tightening his power, the shah's status suffered from this situation. The *Darya* newspaper anticipated a dangerous situation and wrote, "It seems that the smell of gunpowder has had an effect on the minds of these people, for they realize that a dangerous future faces them."[84] Meanwhile, the shah himself, and the reasonable sector of the bourgeoisie, realized the dangerous situation of the time, and for that reason the shah decided to sell the Crown lands and convert them into hard currency for deposit in foreign banks in case he had to flee the country.

If we have concentrated on the political motive of the shah's measures, let us not forget the economic motives behind his actions. The shah, owner of the largest landholdings in Iran, was becoming associated with the bourgeoisie, and these measures facilitated the transformation of landlords into a bourgeoisie. Also, in this period an increase in American influence in Iran became apparent, and American policy provided financial aid to help with the transformation. Both the domestic bourgeoisie and its foreign—especially American—supporters were concerned that other landlords be similarly, peacefully transformed. It was in this connection, and in order to try to save the whole system from possible revolt, that H. Arsanjani,[85] the bourgeois liberal editor of the *Darya* newspaper, wrote:

> The Shah should begin. He should instruct that all those 1,500 villages that are for the movement among the Pahlavi endowments be immediately distributed among the peasants. Then His Majesty should summon all the big landowners of the country and say, "I started myself. You must imitate me." Then he should have the government present a land distribution bill to Majlis.[86]

Bill adds, "Less than a month after this editorial, the Shah of Iran handed down his decree calling for the distribution of the royal lands."[87] Based on the above political and economic factors, the sale of the Crown lands began in 1329 (1949–50). The program lasted several years, and as a result of it some 25,000 peasants received agricultural land.[88] Along with the growth of the movement, in 1951 Dr. Mohammad Mosaddeq, with strong support of the people, formed a new government. The program of the Mosaddeq government represented the interest of the national bourgeoisie[89] and the petty bourgeoisie (middle class) in Iran, confronting all those who represented the old system, including the shah, and, through the shah, the United States and England. Because Mosaddeq[90] had the support of the people, he was able to challenge the shah's power. Consequently, the shah's land measures—which benefited only the shah—were suspended. The new government took over control of the Crown land, and a new progressive program under Mosaddeq leadership began. It is felt by many that the confrontation with the U.S. and England was the cause of the Mosaddeq government's overthrow in a coordinated coup d'etat on August 6, 1953, led by the British intelligence service and the United States C.I.A.[91]

The two-year period of Mosaddeq premiership (1951–1953) was marked by other reforms, including the nationalization of the oil industry.[92] In the case of land, Lambton writes: "The sale of the Pahlavi estate was suspended by Dr. Mosaddeq's government," and "it was stated that the government would hand the land over to the peasants on 99-year leases."[93] Mosaddeq issued two decrees: first, he reduced the landlord's share of the harvest by deducting 20% of the total crop (10% in favor of the peasants cultivating the land and 10% for rural construction); and second, he abolished all dues in the form of sheep, *roughan* (clarified butter), and *bigari* (labor service).[94] After these decrees, landowners were compelled to pay for any extra work done by the peasants. However, many of these dues and labor services were revived in some regions after Mosaddeq's fall.[95]

In addition to these reform measures, for the first time various village and district councils were formed to empower the peasants against the landowners. In the rural areas, these councils were to be responsible for social and provisional affairs, such as schools, public baths, drinking water, mosques, clinics, and roads. In order to give financial and technical support to the peasants, the Agricultural Bank and the Seven Year Plan Organization were developed.[96] But again, like other reforms, most of these measures were cancelled after the 1953-reactionary coup d'etat.[97] This coup was engineered by the C.I.A. when the U.S. government realized that Mosaddeq was not going to be "their man."[98] Mosaddeq had started to run the country independently of any foreign power. Although he did succeed in his program, relatively speaking, his dreams blinded him to the fact that the army was heavily dependent upon the U.S. It was this army that, with capitulation to the C.I.A. and the conspiracy of the Court, ultimately launched the coup on August 6, 1953 that resulted in the fall of the Mosaddeq government.

The 1953 Coup d'Etat: The Conditions Preceding the Land Reform

After the coup, a tremendous wave of terror swept the country, and all of Mosaddeq's social, political, and economic reforms were cancelled with the coming to power of the new military government of General Zahedi. Zahedi abolished Mosaddeq's land measures by holding that the transfer of the Crown lands to the state was not valid.[99] Less than a month after the coup, an initial package of financial aid was given to the shah by the U.S. government.[100] At the same time, aid under the name of Point Four was expanded. Although the activities of the Point Four programs had begun in October 1950,[101] the fundamental aid program began after the coup. According to Richards,

> Year by year, the grants were $85 million in 1954, $76 million in 1955, and $73 million in 1956.... Official U.S. figures for 1953–57 show that Iran received a total of $366.8 million in economic aid.[102]

U.S. aid and loans reached a total of one billion in six years.[103] By that time, U.S. influence in Iran greatly exceeded that of its rival, the British. The new oil agreement was no longer with the British-owned Anglo-Iranian Oil Company, but with the Anglo-American Consortium. Halliday writes,

> The exploitation of Iranian oil was until 1951 in the hands of a British-owned company, first known as the Anglo-Persian Oil Company, then as the Anglo-Iranian Oil Company, and now as British Petroleum.[104]

However, through increasing U.S. influence in Iran after 1953,

> The most important change was that BP lost its monopoly position. A new consortium was established in which U.S. capital now had a share. B.P. retained 40 percent, Shell acquired 14 percent, CFP 6 percent, and the remaining 40 percent was divided among the five main U.S. companies (with 7 percent each) and a group of smaller U.S. firms (sharing the last 5 percent). [See Table 4]. It was above all this internationalization of oil operations that distinguished the pre-1951 position from that which followed 1943.[105]

Table 4
The Major Shares Held by Iranian Oil Participants (IOP)

Company	Percent of Share
British Petroleum (BP)	40
Shell	14
Exxon	7
Mobil	7
Gulf Standard Oil of California	7
Texaco	7
Compagnie Francaise des Petroles	6
Iricon Agency Limited*	5

Source: Iran Almanac, 1969, p. 323.
*Iricon is a partnership of Atlantic Richfield, Getty, Standard
Oil of Ohio, Charter, and American Independent.

This status was established after the nationalization of the British-
owned Anglo-Iranian Oil Company. Such anti-British action could not
have succeeded, at that time, if the national bourgeoisie (Mosaddeq)
had not utilized the existing competition between the United States and
Britain as well.

The Competition Between the U.S. and Britain

Competition between the United States and Britain in Iran began
during and after World War II, when the allied forces occupied the
country. The north part of the country went under the control of the
Soviet Union, while U.S. and British forces controlled the south. By the
end of the War, all military forces left the country, but Britain, which
had politically been in Iran for at least a century, actually maintained its
influence inside the country by receiving support from the landowning
class.

Yet, it is clear that the final winner was the U.S. because it had not
been one of the battlefields of World War II. Britain, because of war
destruction and damages, was not able to maintain its world supremacy
any longer, and that position was then left to the most powerful
country, the United States. However, both the U.S. and Britain
maintained their political and economic influence in Iran until 1950, the
time of nationalization.

By the end of World War II, the competition between Britain and
the United States in Iran had grown, and each power tried to strengthen

its political ties and influence through domestic elements within the country. At that time, Ahmad Qavam, a senior Iranian politician who was prominently pro-American, was the prime minister of Iran, having earlier been the second prime minister after the British-backed coup in 1921. Later exiled by Reza Shah (another figure of the coup) when he showed his sympathy toward the U.S. by inviting American advisors to Iran, Qavam became prime minister again in 1944. Britain then attempted to defeat Qavam's cabinet through pro-English Majlis deputies. Majlis had to confirm any cabinet. The shah himself was in agreement with Britain at the time.[106] Finally, the dispute between the two factions of Majlis, and through them between the U.S. and Britain, ended with the fall of Qavam's government in September 1945.

The pro-American cabinet, which was supposed to be given a loan of $250 million from the International Bank for the purposes of purchasing weapons from the United States and spending on a "Seven-Year Plan," was replaced by a pro-British one led by Abrahim Hakimi.[107] When Hakimi took office, the dominant political atmosphere began to favor Britain.

Meanwhile, as the British were ruminating on how to lower their profile in Iran, the Americans were doing everything in their power to increase theirs. Britain's background had become undesirable in Iran, while the U.S. had not yet been tested. After a time, the U.S. signaled a threat of having the promised loan by the International Bank cut off, and in the absence of the influence of the powerful pro-American figure Ahmad Qavam the shah himself gradually turned toward the United States. To counter this, British Foreign Minister Anthony Eden invited the shah to England.[108] After this visit, which resulted in some agreements between the British government and the shah, the U.S. sent another warning to the shah threatening to have the loan terminated. The shah then sent his brother, Ali Reza Pahlavi, to Washington with a private message.[109] During his visit, a mutual agreement was signed in which 56 American advisors were to be employed by the Iranian government for the purpose of implementing the Seven-Year Plan. Following this agreement, George Allen, the Deputy Secretary of State of the U.S., arrived in Tehran and informally visited the shah.[110] Following these visits and agreements, the shah finally became convinced he should try to keep both the U.S. and Britain satisfied, but rivalry between the two major powers continued. The conflict intensified with the nationalization of the oil industry.

The rivalry extended to the Iranian military organizations. General Ali Razm-Ara, who was pro-British, controlled the army. But because the modern gendarmerie had primarily been established by the

American army and was still under control of American military officials led by Colonel Norman Schwarzkopf, General Razm-Ara made an attempt to bring the gendarmerie under army control. In this connection, the *New York Times* wrote,

> Should the gendarmerie be taken over by the army, the American Gendarmerie Mission would not continue its task. . . . The person who is behind this transformation is General Ali Razm-Ara, the Chief of Staff of the Iranian Army.[111]

Razm-Ara became prime minister and remained in office until he was assassinated by an Islamist group (Fedaian-Islam). The United States had tried to gain supremacy over British influence in Iran while Britain owned the oil industry. The National Front raised the issue of nationalization of the oil industry in Majlis and with the people. At the same time, Mosaddeq, the unchallenged leader of the National Front and champion of the oil nationalization movement, in an attempt to gain support from the U.S. against Britain, showed his tendency to favor the United States. It was after displaying this tendency that Mosaddeq appealed to President Truman for a loan of $120 million.[112] Due to this maneuver, the U.S. as a strategic ally of England, temporarily distanced itself from the crisis, even showing sympathy for the nationalization of the oil reserves. Although the nationalization was the people's demand, it apparently satisfied the U.S., too. According to Barbee et al.,

> When the British Ambassador made a last-ditch effort to delay the Shah's signing of the nationalization bill by appealing to the U.S. Ambassador to intervene, Grady [the U.S. Ambassador] could only reply that he had no instructions.[113]

This so-called "neutral" position became clearer when "the U.S. pressured the British to accept the 'principle' of nationalization. In Tehran, Ambassador Grady simultaneously assured Mosaddeq of continued U.S. aid to Iran, including the prospect of a $25 million Export-Import Bank loan."[114] It seems evident that the United States favored nationalization of the oil industry because it meant nationalization of the dominant power of its competitor. Because the defeat of Britain in this "battle" meant the loss of its power base in Iran, Jazani writes, "the commercial and bureaucratic sections of the comprador bourgeoisie, dependent on the North Americans, as well as the conservative and opportunistic sections of the bourgeoisie, also supported Mosaddeq."[115] Use of the basic competition between the

U.S. and Britain ultimately won for Mosaddeq his six-year battle against the British, and he was able to gain Iranian sovereignty over the country's oil resources. As Jazani states,

> Indeed, it was largely the support given to Mosaddeq by the U.S. and its allies inside Iran which helped bring about the nationalization of oil and in a relatively short time eliminated direct British control over Iranian oil. [116]

After the nationalization of oil, and in the absence of British influence, the relationship between the U.S. and Iran strengthened. However, because of the domination of the national government and the elimination of pro-American elements such as General Zahedi and Ali Amini from the cabinet, the status of both landlords (dependent upon Britain) and comprador bourgeoisie (dependent upon the U.S.) was endangered. So also were the interests of the rival powers, the U.S. and Britain. The national bourgeoisie resented both the landlords, who were seen as the main obstacles to the growth of capitalism, and the dominance of Western capitalism, represented by the comprador bourgeoisie, because they were unable to compete with advanced capitalism in the market. It was because of these contradictions that the rival powers reached the conclusion that the national government of Mosaddeq had to be overthrown. According to Jazani,

> The pro-British and pro-American elements within the cabinet immediately after the coup were actually cooperating with each other, although the U.S. supporters like Zahedi and Amini were, albeit temporarily, playing a more important role. [117]

Zahedi became the prime minister and Amini the oil negotiator in the coup cabinet. Immediately after the coup and the downfall of Mosaddeq, economic, political, and military relations between the U.S. and Iran developed rapidly.

Two years after the coup, a pro-British cabinet again replaced the American-backed cabinet of General Zahedi, [118] but this situation could not last for long. The landlords still remained the close ally of Britain, and the comprador bourgeoisie was the ally of the United States. The national bourgeoisie was becoming polarized with regard to the comprador bourgeoisie.

Economic Crisis Before the Land Reform Program.

Several things facilitated the deep economic penetration of the U.S. in Iran. These included different forms of American aid; the polarization of the national bourgeoisie into two different sections; rapid growth of the comprador bourgeoisie, led by Ali Amini with support from certain U.S. monopolies; and the unprecedented decline of the British-backed landowning class in the entire society. In a short period of time, Iran received hundreds of millions of dollars in different forms of loans, such as bank credits. The United States' economic and technical assistance to Iran between 1953 and 1963 amounted to $796,112,000 (see Table 5). Military assistance to Iran between 1950 and 1967 totaled $895 million, and aid given under the food heading reached $122 million in the same period.[119] This penetration occurred along with a rapid importation of foreign commodities, which accompanied the bank credits. The imported commodities, in many cases, remained unsold because of a lack of buying power among the people of Iran. Jazani describes the situation of the economy after 1953:

> During the period of 1953 to 1963, the majority of the old factories were threatened by bankruptcy. Due to the importing of unlimited and unconfined amounts of foreign commodities such as textile fabrics, the old factories went bankrupt. For example, several wool-spinning factories such as Esfahan, Vatan, Kazerouni, and the Esfahan curriery factory, which were threatened by bankruptcy and collapsed, were taken under government control. Changes in the consumption system and the abundance of foreign manufactured goods caused many workshops to reach liquidating conditions. [120]

These factors as a whole created a stagnation of business in the bazaar. Neither the government nor the private sector was able to charge ordinary prices. The sick economy needed deep changes to end the prevailing crisis.

Ettela'at wrote on March 20, 1963,

> During the last year the market struggled against economic stagnation . . . . However, the general situation of transactions was somehow better than during the preceding year. In 1961–62 many cases of bankruptcy and breach of contracts were recorded, but last year there were no important bankruptcies. [121]

Table 5
United States Economic and Technical Assistance to Iran 1953–1963:
Figures in U.S. dollars

Technical Assistance, Administration Year	Grant Aid	Loans	Agricultural Commodities	Totals
1952/				
1954	20,326,000	103,212,000		237,000	123,775,000
1955	6,917,000	34,937,000	84,982,000	949,000	127,835,000
1956	7,542,000	32,962,000	12,500,000	10,827,000	62,831,000
1957	7,779,000	21,053,000		1,586,000	30,418,000
1958	7,119,000	15,456,000	23,695,000	3,284,000	49,554,000
1959	7,587,000	10,671,000	46,110,000	902,000	65,270,000
1960	6,781,000	30,534,000	30,200,000	658,000	68,173,000
1961	4,684,000	22,190,000	62,913,000	16,056,000	105,843,000
1962	5,393,000	30,000,000	39,177,000	12,754,000	87,024,000
1963	4,482,000	1,323,000	17,400,000	50,884,000	74,089,000
Total	78,610,000	302,388,000	316,977,000	98,137,000	796,112,000

Source: Iran Almanac, 1963.

The toiling urban masses suffered the greatest pressure from this economic crisis, but the situation in the villages was hardly better than that in the urban areas, as Jazani describes:

Iranian villages were heading toward ruin; there was no increase in agricultural production; the feudalists were making no attempt to plough back some of the agricultural income into new or even old irrigation systems; and there was no mechanization. The attitude of most large federalists toward their villages in this period can be likened to a highwayman who at the last moment of his raid takes anything that is going. The feudalists were failing to discharge their conventional financial and administrative responsibilities to the peasants and were also failing to take steps in times of drought or calamity, thus offering no support to the peasants. In some important parts of the country, peasants who had lost their crop left the land and became vagrants. A section of the large-scale feudalists found new financial interests: they entered commerce, built large urban properties to let, built hotels and cinemas, entered into partnerships with banks, and, of course, salted away cash in foreign banks. This was the general policy of the privately owned villages, crown lands, and religious endowments. [122]

The expanding economic crisis had two major effects on the society. First, it caused an increase in the existing tensions between landlords and the comprador bourgeoisie in the ruling class. Second, it promoted the development of protest activities among the people. The government began losing stability. The remaining part of the national bourgeoisie, with some support from the petty bourgeoisie of the bazaar, made its final effort to revive the struggle around its banner. At the same time, members of the clergy were appearing to lead the movement.

In this situation, some of the big landowners began to sell their land. The Court had already sold the major part of its lands. This was the situation when the U.S. government had the Iranian government implement a land reform program in order to end the crisis. Halliday, with regard to the U.S. policy for land reform, writes:

> Since the Second World War the U.S. government had encouraged land reform in countries under its influence. The initial thinking on this was developed in relation to Japan, where a group of sociologists including Talcott Parsons saw the need for a stable state to have a contented peasant class. Subsequent to the reforms in Japan, U.S. advisers helped supervise reforms in China (prior to 1949), Korea, Taiwan, the Philippines, Egypt, Bolivia, and Iran. All of these reforms had an explicitly conservative aim: even where, as in both Japan and Iran, there was no immediate threat from a peasant movement, the U.S. advisers realized the need to reorganize the countryside in order to produce long-term stability. [123]

Although the peasants were living in miserable conditions, due in large part to numerous suppressions by the Pahlavi regime after 1921, they remained passive during these years, so there was no *immediate* threat of a peasant revolt. Big landowners closely connected with the Court, who had received prior warning about the coming land reform, took some measures to save their properties. Others began to take a defensive position against any reform. Landlords who had relied on the traditional support of Britain still maintained a dominant position in the Majlis and were a big obstacle to any bill relating to land reform. It was also a crucial time for the British government to maintain its traditional domination through the landowning class in Iran. This class was represented by Prime Minister M. Eqbal and his successor, Sharif Emami (about whom it was said that "the U.S. wanted him out" [124]).

The newly strengthening comprador bourgeoisie, led by Ali Amini, with full support of the U.S. government, urged passage of the reform bill. The Court, and especially the shah himself, was at that time the connecting point between the two ruling class factions (i.e., the landowners and the bourgeois compradors), and in general disagreed with the principle of land reform. The British government and its ally, the landlords, stood against land reform. For them it meant the loss of England's hegemonic political status in favor of the United States and its ally, the comprador bourgeoisie. It was, indeed, a critical point for the long-time dispute between the two factions of government and their supporters.

The U.S. government had threatened the landlords and the Court through a coup attempt led by General Qarani, chief of the Second Bureau of the Iranian Army, in 1958. [125] The U.S. also put the Iranian government under economic pressures when the Iranian economy became more and more dependent upon American financial aid. President Kennedy believed that communism would grow wherever there was poverty, corruption, and injustice. In Mach 1961, he dispatched his special envoy, W. Averill Harriman, to Iran along with a package of social, and economic reforms. [126] In this connection, Halliday writes:

> The Iranian economy had been in recession since 1958, the budget was in deficit, and the Shah was in conflict with a number of civilian and military officials. In January 1961, the Kennedy Administration came to office in Washington and let it be known that it would only continue to support the Shah on condition that he put through a programme of reforms. A $35 million U.S. loan was made dependent on certain policies being implemented. [127]

Many landlords, not able to understand the role of land reform as a mechanism for their peaceful transition to capitalists, put up resistance to the program. As we said in Chapter 1, this type of transition was the new strategy of world capitalism promoted by the U.S. government. Some countries passed through this stage successfully, while other dominated countries were just beginning the process.

The Position of the Clergy vis a-vis Land Reform, and the Massive Uprising of 1963

Except for a small section of the clergy that had ties with Mosaddeq, the bulk of it was an effective ally of the regime both during the 1953 coup d'etat and in post-coup years. While the masses of the lower sections of this stratum were of petty bourgeoisie origin, the great majority of high-ranking clergy represented feudalism and the comprador bourgeoisie. [128]

Large numbers of the high-ranking clergy had direct and indirect interests in maintaining old relations. Apart from those clergy who had control over the endowment lands *(vaqf)*, which constituted 12% of all arable land, many of them were landlords in clerical robes. Not only their direct and indirect ownership over the land, but also their social status was dependent upon the existing order. They realized how expansion of the capitalistic mode of production and the penetration of Western culture would destroy their status rather quickly, and they were, thus, strongly opposed to any reform.

When the initial proposal for land reform was given to the National Consultative Assembly, Ayatollah Burujirdi, the leading religious dignitary of the day, wrote to Majlis deputies that "he had informed the prime minister personally, and the Shah in writing, that such a step would be contrary to the laws of Islam." [129] The social and economic necessity for land reform was very serious, so the "laws of Islam" were not given much consideration. Thus, the protest against the reform continued.

Because the clergy did not represent a homogeneous stratum, their protest against the land reform program came from different positions. Basically, the clergy's interest had two elements—class economic and sectional economic (clergy caste) interests. The social action of this stratum as a whole, however, was mainly in accord with its own sectional economic interests.

At the time of the introduction of land reform, sectional economic interests as a whole were endangered, but the protest from the clergy against the plan was from a different position. Unlike the upper clergy, the lower clergy largely favored the lower-class masses. Rather than defending popular interests, however, they mainly followed the leading religious dignitary—in other words, they supported their own sectional economic interests rather than those of the lower class.

In the case of land reform measures, Jazani says, "The clergy, almost without exception, opposed the whole land reform project." [130] Two grand ayatollahs, Burujirdi and Behbahani, officially opposed any land reform program because they saw it as an action against *shari'a* (the canon law of Islam). [131] Both their land interest and their social and economic status were at stake. They therefore declared the land distribution unlawful and any distributed land as *qasbi* (usurped land). However, they would accept a land reform program if (and only if) the land was purchased from the owners and sold to the peasants. They failed to convince the peasants, so between the land and religious decrees the peasant chose the land. Thus, a few years later, in spite of opposition from the clergy, the reform was begun, although clergy's conditions were met. Land was purchased by the state and sold to the peasants if they agreed to pay off the purchase price in installments.

Land reform was only one of a series of reforms. There were other minor actions, including a literacy corps, a health corps, profit sharing in industry, reform of the electoral laws to include women—all under the umbrella of the so-called "white revolution." Objective conditions for a people's uprising were already present, but the last-mentioned point provided the clergy with the necessary excuse to excite and mobilize the people against the regime. [132]

They used their usual weapon—emotion—to overcome the reforms. N. Jacobs has correctly said, "The weapons of the Iranian clergy are emotions which lead only to rioting." [133] And rioting did occur, because "religion and political authority were interlocked" and "the clergy perform religious roles in the social order." [134]

With the fall of Mosaddeq and the dominance of the military government, the people still did not give up the struggle. The protest continued, to a lesser degree, in the years following the coup. Several times people took to the streets, organized or spontaneously, but suppression of all types of political organizations and trade unions created a four-year drought of political expression. Then, in 1959, two important massive street protests, one by brick-kiln workers and the other by taxi drivers, broke the political silence. During the years of economic crisis, the National Front and other opposition groups such as student organizations became active. At the same time, the conflict between the two factions of government—the landlords and the bourgeois compradors—entered a new stage. While the pro-American bourgeois compradors urged launching of the land reform program, the British-backed landlords were strongly opposed to it. When the shah himself agreed to support the program and became the leading figure in land reform, the clergy, who were against the land reform program, raised the anti-dictatorship slogan, covering it with religious overtones. They succeeded in mobilizing different sections of middle- and lower-class people such as shopkeepers, tradesmen, the deprived, and the self-employed strata of petty bourgeoisie, as well as the workers, against the shah's regime. [135]

Within a short time, the movement spread throughout the country. People in some cities such as Tehran, Qom, and Varamien (east of Tehran) were more active. The revolt intensified during the passion holy days of Moharram (February and March 1963), but the regime did not retreat, responding to the movement with strong suppression. It has been said that in a massacre around June 5, 1963 numerous people were killed. [136] Although the clergy succeeded in leading the struggle against the shah, their participation was only for their own narrow sectional interests. [137]

After the shah's suppression of the movement, the clergy separated themselves from and opposed the masses—except for a small group, they even supported the regime. By the time the shah's reforms began, many clergymen had joined the regime, supporting the shah and dependent (i.e., foreign-controlled) capitalism.

Among the rare clergymen who remained opponents of the shah's dictatorship even after the establishment of dependent capitalism in Iran was the Ayatollah Khomeini. During the 1960–63 fights, he was able to lead the anti-shah dictatorship movement for a short period. In this connection, Lambton writes:

> A mujtahid, named Khomeini, a man of reputed honesty and progressive ideas, became the leader of the movement of revolt. After an outspoken attack on the Shah (not, however, on grounds of the land reform), he was arrested on June 4, 1963. This provoked demonstrations and disturbances in Tehran and the provinces the following day. They were ruthlessly suppressed. [138]

After the government gained full control of the movement, Khomeini was exiled, and this exile was to last for 15 years. More than a decade of political repression followed, but then once again, through a massive movement against the shah's regime, Khomeini as a religious leader was able to gain leadership of the struggle for the following reasons: (1) lack of any popular political organization; (2) his good record—Khomeini had never collaborated with the shah and had remained a militant figure throughout the movement; (3) lack of a well-known, popular political figure; (4) the existence of traditional institutions such as mosques and religious schools, which acted as the only connective network during the struggle, given that no political party remained after the shah's suppression; (5) the political role of religion within Iranian society; and (6) the active participation of the bazaar as a traditional support for the clergy during the struggle. When

Khomeini gained control of the entire society, the shah fled the country forever.

At the very beginning of the land reform program, suppression was possible because the regime had already succeeded in uniting the ruling classes, while the people's movement was dispersed and unorganized. Under such circumstances, the land reform program, together with its supplementary activities, was launched. The next chapter will provide further details on this tumultuous period in Iran's history.

[1] For details about these forms of land ownership before the Constitutional Revolution, see F. Nomani, "Origin and Development of Feudalism in Iran: 300–1600 A.D." (Dissertation, University of Illinois, 1972), Chapter III. Also see A. Lambton, *Landlord and Peasant in Persia: A Study of Land Tenure and Land Revenue Administration* (London: Oxford University Press, 1953).

[2] For further details, see A. Lambton, *The Persian Land Reform* (Oxford, UK: Clarendon Press, 1969), Chapter I, and Lambton, *Landlord and Peasant in Persia*, Chapter XIII.

[3] H. Muhammadi, *On the Agrarian Policy of Iranian Government and For a Democratic Solution of Agrarian Problems* (Tehran: Tudeh Publishing Center, 1973. In Persian.

[4] Ibid.

[5] M. Muhammadi.

[6] O.I.P.F.G., *Land Reform and Its Direct Effects in Iran* (London: Iran Committee, 1974). These types of relations of production will be discussed in the following pages.

[7] Ibid. Other statistics show the number of state villages to be 2,109 (M. Muhammadi, 1973).

[8] For descriptions of different types of *khaleseh* and their origins, see Lambton, *Landlord and Peasant in Persia*, Chapter XII, and Nomani, Chapter III.

[9] Lambton, *Landlord and Peasant in Persia*, Chapter XII.

[10] Lambton, *The Persian Land Reform*.

[11] Ibid.

[12] According to the 1958 law, about 26,894 hectares of *khaleseh* land in 59 villages were sold to peasants, each one receiving at most either 10 hectares of irrigated land (*abi*) or 15 hectares of dry land (*daymi*), (M. Muhammadi).

[13] Lambton, *Landlord and Peasant in Persia*.

[14] *Khalesehjat-at* is the plural of *khaleseh*.

[15] F. Nomani.

[16] Jaami, *Gozashteh Cheragh-i Rah Ayandeh* ("The Past as a Guiding Light for the Future" (Tehran: Liberation Front of the Iranian People, 1977. In Persian.

[17] Reza Khan (later Reza Shah) was a Gazaq officer who, according to the order of Ayron Side in 1920, became *Sardar-i Sepah* (chief of military staff) and a few years later called himself Shah of Iran. Ayron Side was the commander of the English forces in Iran at the time. Jaami, 88.

[18] *The Tajaddud Newspaper of Iran*, no. 3278, Abaan 1320 (1941), cited in Jaami, 90.

[19] Seven tumans = $1.00 (in 1980).

[20] Bidari Kerman, no. 20, 17 Azar 1320 (1941), *Setareh Newspaper*, no. 1164, 8 Mehr 1320 (1941), and *Iran Newspaper*, no. 6683, 4 Mehr 1320 (1941), all cited in Jaami, 99.

[21] Jaami, 99.

[22] Lambton, *The Persian Land Reform*, 54.

[23] E. Tabari, *Iranian Society During the Absolute Reign of Reza Shah* (Tehran: Tudeh Publishing Center, 1977), 81. In Persian.

[24] O.I.P.F.G., 1976.

[25] F. Nomani.

[26] Mashhad is a city in the northeastern part of Iran. Lambton writes, "The office of administrator of the *ouqaf* is vested in the reigning monarch. This is also the case with the *ouqaf* of the Sipahsalar and Shah Chiragh mosques in Tehran" (1953, p. 234). [Shah Chiragh mosque is in Shiraz.] The *ouqaf* of the Shrine of Imam Reza in Mashhad were under the Reza Shah and later the Muhammad Reza Shah administrations, a situation that is frequently offered as one of the main reasons that the clergy hated the Pahlavi dynasty.

[27] O.I.P.F.C.

[28] Lambton, *Landlord and Peasant in Persia*, 230. Finally, after the Constitutional Revolution, the Department of *Ouqaf* was set up to control *ouqaf* properties.

[29] Ibid.

[30] O.I.P.F.G., 1976, and F. Nomani, *Origin and Development of Feudalism in Iran: 300–1600 A.D.*, Dissertation, University of Illinois, 1972.

[31] F. Nomani, 35.

[32] Ibid.

[33] Lambton, *Landlord and Peasant in Persia*.

[34] O.I.P.F.G.

[35] H. Richards, "Land Reform and Agribusiness in Iran," *MERIP Reports (Middle East Research and Information Project)*, 43 (December 1975).

[36] M. Muhammadi.

[37] Lambton, *Landlord and Peasant in Persia*.

[38] Ibid.

[39] N. Jacobs, *The Sociology of Development: Iran as an Asian Case Study.* (New York: Praeger Special Studies in International Economics and Development, 1967), 143.

[40] N. Keddie, "The Iranian Village Before and After Land Reform," *Journal of Contemporary History* 3, no. 3 (1968): 69–91.

[41] The situation was not changed in the years prior to the land reform.

[42] M. Muhammadi.

[43] See Lambton, 1953, Appendix I.

[44] Lambton, 1953, 402.

[45] Ibid., Chapter XVII.

[46] A. I. Demin, *Basic Forms of Tenure* (Moscow, 1967), 44–50, cited in *The Economic History of Iran, 180–1914*, ed. C. Issawi (Chicago: University of Chicago Press, 1971), 223. Demin comments that in the fertile lands "in the neighborhood of Isfahan, peasants contributing draft animals and seed received only one-third of the crop, instead of 2/5."

[47] Ibid., 51.

[48] Lambton, 1953, Appendix I, 402.

[49] Ibid., Chapter XVIII.

[50] O.I.P.F.G., 1976.

[51] Ibid., 20. It is notable that in 1952 Prime Minister Mosaddeq abolished all feudal dues. After his downfall, many of them became common again. See also Lambton, *The Persian Land Reform*, 36–43, and Chapter 6 of this study.

[52] In the principal Iranian language, Farsi, *Khwush-neshin* means "those who sit comfortably."

[53] For details about different cultivator and non-cultivator strata in Iran, see Keddie, 1968.

[54] E. J. Hooglund, "The *Khwush-neshin* Population of Iran," *Iranian Studies* VI, no. 4 (Autumn 1973): 229.

[55] For further details about *Khwush-neshin,* see E. Hooglund, 229–245.

[56] The first anti-colonialist struggle was the Tobacco Movement in 1891. The national bourgeoisie led this struggle against the British government, which had monopolized the tobacco trade in Iran. England had acquired such monopoly power by bribing the Qajar Court (Naseredien Shah). See Nikki Keddie, *Religion and Rebellion in Iran: The Iranian Tobacco Protest of 1891–1892* (London: Frank Cass and Co., Ltd., 1966).

[57] B. Momeni, "Iran on the Eve of the Constitutional Revolution," trans. S. Azad, *RIPEH (The Review of Iranian Political Economy of History)* 1, no. 2 (June 1977): 80–92.

[58] B. Momeni, 86. For details about the Constitutional Revolution, see A. Kasravi, *The Constitutional Revolution* (Tehran: Amir Kabier, 1973); M. Ivanov, *The Constitutional Revolution of Iran* (1975); B. Mu'Mini, *Iran on the Eve of the Constitutional Revolution,* (1358/1979); F. Adamiyat, *Social Democracy Thoughts in the Constitution Movement of Iran* (1355/1976).

[59] By using the term "national bourgeoisie," we mean the part of the bourgeoisie that had characteristics as follows: (1) it came into existence in the second half of the nineteenth century, and (2) it was left weak when, after the Constitutional Revolution, the upper section of the bourgeoisie compromised with colonialist powers through the Shah's Court. This part of the bourgeoisie

[60] B. Jazani, *Tarikh-e See Saleh-e Iran (Thirty-Year History of Iran)* (No publisher indicated, 1353 (1974)), 16–17. In Persian.

[61] Ibid., 17.

[62] A. Lambton, *The Persian Land Reform* (Oxford, UK: Clarendon Press, 1969).

[63] Ibid., 32.

[64] Ibid.

[65] G.H. Razi, "Genesis of Party in Iran: A Case Study of the Interaction Between the Political System and Political Parties," *Iranian Studies* 111, no. 2 (Spring 1970).

[66] Their movement was formed by direct participation of communist groups, and later their leadership brought in some very radical programs, including a

drastic agrarian reform. Such an approach to the situation was regarded as too extreme and was criticized by various groups. See Speer Zambia, *The Communist Movement in Iran* (Berkeley, CA: University of California Press, 1966), Ch. 1.

[67] Lambton.

[68] Ibid., 33.

[69] Y. Benab, "Tabriz in Perspective: A Historical Analysis of the Current Struggle of Iranian Peoples," *RIPEH (The Review of Iranian Political Economy and History)* 11, no. 2 (June 1978): 14.

[70] Ibid. Leaders of both the Gilan and Azerbaijan movements had been active during the Constitutional Revolution.

[71] The Azerbaijan national movement was almost suppressed by the central government before the coup. Reza Shah was commissioned to complete the job.

[72] Bijan Jazani,1974. The term "comprador bourgeoisie" is used in this study to indicate bourgeoisie with these characteristics: (1) they were born under the influence of colonialist power after the Constitutional Revolution; (2) the group correlates directly with the development of a relationship with Western capitalism; (3) they co-existed in power with the landlords in Iran, as commercial and bureaucratic bourgeoisie, for three decades (1921–1953); (4) after the 1953 coup, the group grew rapidly, taking control of the main productive forces in Iranian society; (5) their economic life has been dependent upon direct support by imperialist countries, which has included capital, basic materials for production, management and technician forces, and markets; and (6) this group has represented the interests of international monopolies in Iran.

[73] F. Halliday, *Iran: Dictatorship and Development* (London: Penguin Books, 1979), 23.

[74] One source reported his personal estate at 2,400,000 hectares of land in nearly 2,300 villages, with 300,000 peasants being involved in these lands. See B. Jazani, *An Outline of Sociology and the Foundations of the Strategy for the Revolutionary Movement in Iran, Part 1: Economics*, 1979. In Persian.

[75] Halliday, 23.

[76] Lambton, 1953.

[77] Jaami, *Gozashteh Cheragh-e Rah-e Ayandeh (The Past as a Guiding Light for the Future)* (Tehran: Liberation Front of the Iranian People, 1977), documents this conspiracy. In Persian.

[78] For details, see Benab.

[79] Ibid.

[80] Lambton, 1953.

[81] There appears to be no documented information concerning the agrarian program in Kurdistan.

[82] Jazani, 1974. Also see J. Sadeeq, *Meliyat and Enqelab dar Iran (Nationality and Revolution in Iran)*, No publisher indicated, 1973.

[83] B. Jazani, *Capitalism and Revolution in Iran* (London: Zed Press, 1980), 32.

[84] *Darya* (daily newspaper), 25 Day 1329 (1951), cited in A. J. Bill, *The Politics of Iran: Groups, Classes, and Modernization* (Columbus, OH: Charles E. Merrill Publishing Co., 1972), 137.

[85] Later, Dr. Arsanjani was appointed as the First Minister agriculture, to implement the land reform program of 1961.

[86] Bill, 137.

[87] Ibid. Years afterward, the Shah himself declared that "my program of land distribution was intended not only to benefit the peasants on Crown lands, but also to set an example for the big private landlords" (M. R. Pahlavi, Shah, Mission for My Country, 1960), 204.

[88] *Darya* (daily newspaper), 25 Day 1329 (1951).

[89] Between the years of 1950 and 1953, under leadership of the National Front, while oil revenues were almost cut off, the national bourgeoisie grew rapidly. All domestic factories were operating at full capacity, and many traditional industries, such as glass-blowing, soap-boiling, and curriery, developed (Jazani, 1980, 36).

[90] Dr. Mohammad Mosaddeq was born into an upper-class family. He graduated from law school in France. His first governmental position was as governor of the Fars province before the 1921 coup d'etat headed by the Reza Shah. Mosaddeq was the Finance Minister in the second cabinet after the coup, under the premiership of Ahmad Ghavam. He was, however, effectively restrained from all types of political activity by the dominance of the Shah's dictatorship. Mosaddeq returned to politics as a Majlis deputy after Reza Shah abdicated in 1941. Years later, he raised the issue of nationalization of the oil industry in the Majlis, and the effort ultimately reached fruition in March 1951. After this victory, he achieved power enough to form a bourgeois and national government in April 1951, but his government was overthrown by a coup in August 1953. Mosaddeq was then sentenced to three years in prison by the military government. He died in 1966 while he was being forced to live in the small village of Ahmad Abaad.

[91] For documented information about the coup, see Jazani, 1980 and 1353 (1974); H. Richards, "American Shah Shahanshah's Iran," *MERIP Report (Middle East Research and Information Project)* 40 (1975); Halliday, 1979; F. J. Cook, "The Mystery of One Billion Dollars," *The Nation*, 12 April 1965.

[92] For details of the oil industry nationalization, see Stephen Kinzer, *All the Shah's Men: An American Coup and the Roots of Middle East Terror* (New York: John Wiley & Sons, 2003); Jebhe Melli, *Karnameh-i Mosaddeq va Hezb Tudeh* (The Record of Mosaddeq and the Tudeh Party) (USA: Mozdak, 1973; and B. Nirumand, *Iran, the New Imperialism in Action* (New York: Monthly Review Press, 1969), Chapter 2.

[93] Lambton, 54–55.

[94] Ibid., and O.I.P.F.G., Land Reform and Its Direct Effects in Iran (London: Iran Committee, 1976).

[95] Lambton.

[96] Ibid.

[97] Discussion of the progressive efforts of Dr. Mosaddeq's government during his two years in office is not within the sphere of this study. For further information, see Mazdak (Edition), *Karnameh-i Mosaddeq va Hezb* (Tehran: Tudeh, 1953).

[98] Anthony Iden, the Foreign Minister of England said, the U. S. was worried that Mossadeq leaned toward the Soviet Union. See Iraj Afshar, ed., *Khaaterat va Ta' alomat Mosaddeq (The Memories and Afflictions of Mossadeq)*, (Republished by the National Front of Iran, abroad, 1365 (1967)), 190.

[99] Lambton.

[100] H. Richards.

[101] Utah State University, *Iran and Utah State University: Half a Century of Friendship and A Decade of Contracts: Point 4* (Logan, UT: Utah State University, 1963).

[102] Richards, 7.

[103] Jazani.

[104] Halliday, 141.

[105] Ibid., 142.

[106] Jaami.

[107] Ibid.

[108] Ibid.

[109] Ibid.

[110] Ibid.

[111] The New York Times, 24 April 1948, cited in Jaami, p. 459.

[112] Lynne Barbee et al., "Iranian Nationalism and the Great Powers: 1872–1954," *MERIP Report No. 37* 1975, p. 24.

[113] Ibid., 23.

[114] Ibid.

[115] Jazani, 28. A small number of pro-American bourgeois compradors, such as Ali Amini and General Zahedi, were able to get positions in the first cabinet of Dr. Mosaddeq.

[116] Ibid., 27.

[117] Ibid., 33.

[118] Ibid.

[119] *Iran Almanac*, 1970. The government-to-government agreement for military sales to Iran from 1950 to 1979 reached $24,454,102,000. (See *MERIP Report No. 71*, 1978, 22–23.

[120] Jazani, 43.

[121] Cited in *Iran Almanac*, 1963, 228.

[122] Jazani, 1974, 73–74.

[123] Halliday, 134.

[124] M.R. Shah Pahlavi, *Answer to History* (New York: Stein and Day, 1980), 22.

[125] Jazani.

[126] Azienfar, Hasan. "A Review of the Land Reform in Iran and its Consequences" *Rahavard (A Persian Journal of Iranian Studies)*, 58 (Fall and Winter 2002): 161–186.

[127] Halliday, 26. See also M. R. Pahlavi (1980), 22–23, and *The New York Times*, 3 August 1961.

[128] Jazani, 1980, 62.

[129] Lambton, 1969, 56.

[130] Jazani, 1974, 117.

[131] Azienfar, Hasan, op. cit.

[132] Jazani, 1980, 63–64.

[133] N. Jacobs, *The Sociology of Development: Iran as an Asian Case Study* (New York: Praeger Special Studies in International Economics and Development, 1967), 223.

[134] Ibid., 218.

[135] Jazani, 1980.

[136] There is no confirmed figure for the number of people killed in this movement. Religious people tend to say up to 15,000 people were killed, but they provide no documents for this claim. Recent study indicates that the figure was not in thousands, or hundreds, but in tens. See Emad al Deen Baqi, *The Study of the Iranian Revolution* (Tehran, 1370 h. (1992)). Baaqi gives a total number of 34 killed during the uprising in 1963. For the summary of this study see www.Iran-Emrooz.de, July 30, 2003.

[137] Jazani, 1980.

[138] Lambton, 112. This statement by Lambton was written years before Khomeini achieved power. During his rule he demonstrated a suppressive policy.

Chapter 7
The Land Reform Law

Introduction

In this chapter and the next we will specifically explore the nature of the land reform program. While this chapter examines various parts of land reform legislation, Chapter 9 will focus on the operation of these laws. The laws of this project, in addition to two annexing laws, were ratified in three phases, covering a ten-year period from 1962 to 1972. When the laws of the first stage were half completed, the laws of the second stage were begun, and both the first- and second-stage laws were in progress when the third stage was initiated. All three stages were near completion when the annexing laws—i.e., the Law Relating to the Sale of Religious Endowments and the Law Relating to the Sale of Ghares Maleki Orchards—were ratified by the Majlis (parliament) in May 1972 and May 1973.

The purpose of this chapter is to explain the objectives of the land reform program by reference to the laws that are part of any land reform—that is, the laws dealing with expropriation of land, the laws of exemption, the laws of compensation, and the laws of land distribution.

Objectives of the Land Reform Program

The objectives of the land reform can be discussed from several points of view. While the government has stated official objectives as the "real" objectives of the reform, there has been much controversy among opposing groups in Iran concerning the actual objectives of land reform. In this chapter, I will attempt to elucidate the differences between these points of view.

As mentioned in the previous chapter, the land reform program was proposed and imposed by the American government. Following the acceptance of such order by the Iranian government, high-ranking officials in support of land reform acted as if the reform was at the shah's personal initiation and agreed that Iran was to be one of the first countries in the world to initiate a land reform program.[1] However, Dr. Arsanjani, the first Minister of Agriculture at the time of land reform, confessed, "Iran perhaps is one of the rare countries that has not launched a land reform yet."[2]

A few years later, when the shah was convinced that he should lead the program, he proclaimed that the purpose of the program was "to put an end to all the social inequalities and factors which caused injustice, tyranny, and exploitation."[3] But in 1966, the United Nations' publication *Progress in Land Reform* concluded, "it is, indeed, the explicit intention of the reform not to establish equality, but to create an extended tenure ladder."[4]

In opposition to the government, there was no uniform view regarding the objectives of land reform. While one group believed that a propaganda campaign had occurred,[5] a second group described the program as the shah's retreat from his position in favor of the peasants' demands.[6] A third group, however, analyzed the land reform program as a social, political, and economic measure aiming toward the elimination of pre-capitalist relations of production. According to this group, expansion of capitalism in the villages was the first aim of the land reform, and opposition to any possible peasants' revolt was a secondary goal.[7] The present study favors this view, which will be elaborated in the following pages.

The land reform program was intended to terminate the dominant economic and political crisis in Iran through two main objectives: first, to expand capitalist relations of production in outlying urban and rural areas, and, second (and to a lesser degree) to neutralize any possible peasant unrest against the landowners. At the beginning of the land reform in Iran, the *New York Times* wrote, "Some of the landlords, who had long been the most powerful and dominant group in Iran, recognized the inevitability of the breakup of their estates and have been trying to shift their resources to trade and industry."[8] That was a very clear and understandable point, and it was the reason the United States pushed the landlords to accept the land reform program. The same American newspaper, in an interview with a businessman in Iran, added, "If he [the shah] can just carry this through, he will succeed in saving Iran from a red revolution."[9] So, the American media recognized both main objectives of the land reform program, at least indirectly.

In truth, as stated earlier, a rush of foreign investments, imports of foreign commodities, and bank credits created the economic crisis, which dominated the whole country between 1958 and 1963. This crisis created a situation in which the urban middle and lower classes organized a new phase of protest against the Court and the government. Because the people's uprising against the shah's regime corresponded with the United States' pressures for the land reform program, British-backed landowners, such as Prime Minister Sharif Emami, labeled the people's movement an "American-made conspiracy against the Iranian government!"[10] The shah himself, who had remained silent for a long time during his rule after the reform, finally exposed the matter when he was ousted from the country, in this manner:

> At the time, Prime Minister Emami took the brunt of the animus, as was his legal responsibility. The U.S. wanted him out and its own man in as prime minister. This man was Ali Amini, and in time the pressure became too strong for me to resist, especially after John F. Kennedy was elected president. John F. Kennedy was never against me. I considered him a friend, although we had little direct contact. I remember so well my first meeting with the Kennedys at the White House: Jacqueline Kennedy spoke of Amini's wonderfully flashing eyes and how much she hoped I would make him prime minister. Eventually I gave Amini the job. There have been rumors that Kennedy offered me a $35 million aid package as an inducement. These rumors are totally unfounded, for it was Amini who obtained this money from the United States after he became prime minister. But he mismanaged affairs so badly that he was soon asking the Americans for another $60 million, which was refused.[11]

In this context, Halliday writes: "The Kennedy administration believed that for political reasons the only way to preserve the pro-Western (i.e., capitalist) states in the third world was to put through a reform program within which land reform held a special place."[12]

Again, in order to state the main purpose of Dr. Ali Amini's mission, The *New York Times* explicitly wrote, "Land reform is the foundation of Dr. Amini's program to save Iran from what he has called economic chaos."[13] At any rate, it was America's position, and if the shah and his groups wanted to remain in power they had to follow the order.

Finally, the shah and the big landowners bowed to the U.S. proposal, and Dr. Ali Amini became the prime minister of Iran. He immediately constituted his cabinet, but it was still threatened by the landlords and their military allies. Amini was chosen by the United States to carry out their new policy. At the time, Andrew Tally, who had worked for the CIA, called him "one of the C.I.A. boys."[14] In order to ease the political crisis, Amini formed a government that included ministers with links to Dr. Mosaddeq, or at least ministers without bad records. His minister of agriculture was Dr. Hasan Arsanjani, a young, liberal, and almost unknown man from a religious family. Arsanjani, who had previously proposed a land reform program to the shah through his newspaper *Darya*, expressed the objective of the land reform program as follows: "The objective of this law is to save the 15 million population of this country. It is to save the *landowners themselves and their capital* in those areas where they have left the dispersed land idle" (emphasis added).[15]

After this carrot-and-stick approach, big landowners gradually bowed to the Amini-Arsanjani land reform program. They agreed to sell their estates to the government for redistribution to the peasants. The *New York Times,* writing about these big landowners and their holdings, noted, "Among those authorizing the sale of their estates to the government was Mehdi Batmanqilij, who contends his holdings cover an area larger than Switzerland."[16] Meanwhile, the United States agreed to establish a $35 million loan fund—$26 million in development aid and the remaining $9 million for military supplies.[17] The International Bank for Reconstruction and Development also granted $15 million in credits.[18]

On the eve of the land reform program, the Court relented and changed its position. Its acceptance of the land reform program eased the conflict with the new pro-American bourgeoisie. Now it was the shah's turn to convince other landowners to support the program. To justify his new position at the beginning year of the plan, he wrote,

> Only a few years ago, these landlords [including the shah, himself] became very bitter when anybody broached the idea that their vast holdings should be divided, but many have now come to realize that in terms of social justice their position is untenable. Moreover, with the expansion of alternative investment opportunities, landowning as such no longer commands quite so much profit or prestige/value as formerly. Obsolete production methods are commonly in use on the great estates, and the introduction of modern techniques would require heavy investments, so that many landlords are finding that

they can get quicker returns from investing in Persia's expanding industry and commerce.[19]

Thus, with the acceptance of the plan by the landowners, both ruling factions were ready to face the political crisis and leave no material base for the people's movement that had potential to develop. If pressure from the U.S. government was one factor that compelled the landowners to accept the program, the threat of a social movement that could endanger the whole monarchy system was quite another. Therefore, in order to save the whole system, the two ruling classes— i.e., the landlords (pro-British) and the new bourgeoisie (pro-American)—united.

The Major Points of the Land Reform

After a boom in the late 1950s, followed by a severe economic and political crisis,[20] an abortive land reform law was passed by the Majlis in April 1960 (1339-2-26). Because of dissidence from powerful landowners in both the cabinet and the Majlis, the law remained on the books until January 9, 1962. On May 6, 1961, Dr. Ali Amini, with direct support of the U.S. government and with a very clear and specific mission to advance the land reform program, became prime minister.[21] He attempted to implement the law passed by the Majlis in April 1960, but his cabinet was threatened with overthrow by the military generals who were supportive of the big landowners and their representatives in the Majlis. Before any action by the landowners, however, the Majlis was dissolved by a decisive move of the new government. In the absence of the Majlis, Amini, as the prime minister, issued a cabinet decree for land reform, and the law initially ratified by the Majlis in 1960 was finally ratified. As Zonis stated, "On January 15, 1962, Arsanjani announced that the Land Reform Bill had become law, by royal proclamation."[22]

Later, in support of the bill, and in order to threaten both the progressive groups and the landowners, a referendum was held throughout the country by the government. This referendum, in support of a six-point Reform Program that included land reform, took place on January 26, 1963. All opposition groups, including the National Front, urged the people to boycott the referendum. The National Front announced a mass demonstration on January 25 to protest the shah's tactic. In order to clarify its goal in this matter and to distinguish its line from that of the dissident landlords, the Front issued a manifesto with the slogan, "Land reform, yes. The arbitrary rule of the shah, no."[23] However, in spite of the popular boycott, Zonis writes, "the government announced overwhelmingly popular support for the referendum."[24] After this referendum, the six-point Reform Program (land reform, nationalization of forests, sale of state-owned factories, profit-sharing plan for factory workers, enfranchisement of women, and establishment of a Literacy Corps) apparently received support enough to go into operation.

Following a broad propaganda attempt and a "Farmers' Congress" held by the government, the peasants gradually came to believe that some reform measure was under way. When all factions of the government accepted the program, the capitalist element (the group that most benefited) used all its power to present the land reform program as the most significant measure in history.[25] Along with several additional laws and regulations, the cabinet decree was ratified by the Majlis and later recognized as the first stage of the land reform program. During this period, all factions of the ruling class bowed to agrarian reform.

We will now review the first stage of this program in more detail. The land reform laws were enacted in three stages, with each stage having a different, but related, purpose. The purpose of the first stage was to limit large-scale ownership of agricultural land, while the second stage aimed, according to Halliday, to strengthen "the peasant movement that was coming into being."[26] The third stage was a move toward expansion of capitalism in remote rural areas and, as Halliday writes, "against the smaller proprietors in order to boost production."[27] To reach these goals, each stage included several laws and regulations; however, the main laws of land reform were stated in the first stage. These laws were published in nine chapters, as follows:

1. The definitions
2. Land ownership limitations
3. Lands subjected to distribution, and related regulations
4. Estimation of value of land and manner of payment
5. Regulations of land distribution
6. Regulations of distributed lands
7. Peasant-landlord relations
8. Fiscal regulations
9. Regulation of technical aid.

The first chapter was devoted to the definitions of terms and concepts such as *dih* (village), *malik* (landowner), *zari'a* (peasant), etc. Up to then, these terms had different meanings in different regions, and thus it was necessary that each expression be defined objectively so that they applied equally to all landowners. Still, the definitions were clearly biased in favor of the landowners. For instance, the definition of a landowner was "a person who owns land but is not, personally, engaged in agriculture." [28] This definition included only absentee landlords. Obviously, this is not an objective definition of the term "landowner" but rather one that is in opposition to the stated purpose of the first stage of the program (i.e., to limit large-scale land ownership). According to this definition, any landowner who was involved in agriculture directly, no matter how much land he or she owned, could not actually be defined as a landowner. Thus, the land was not subject to distribution. This definition allowed many landowners who owned thousands of hectares of agricultural land to remain big landlords. On the basis of this definition General Riyahie, the second minister of agriculture after the beginning of the land reform program, said "all who produce the country's wealth via agriculture can be called *zari'a* (peasants); so we can say that one landowner can own 40 hectares, or 4,000 hectares, or 400 hectares."[29] Riyahie first made *zari'a* synonymous with landowner, and then he failed to consider any limitations on the size of the land each landowner could hold. Here, General Riyahie revealed that, according to him, the primary purpose of the land reform was not to distribute large lands among the landless peasants but to encourage the landowners to get involved in agribusiness. However, Dr. Arsanjani, the first minister of agriculture, would give equal value to both the distributing land to meet the needs of the peasants and to replacing the traditional land tenure system with modern capitalist relations. The type of distortion General Riyahie created was not limited to only the definition of landowner. The government changed any concept related to the land reform that would serve the landowners. Article I of the Land Reform Law defined *Zari'a* (peasant) as "one who is not the owner of land but, possessing one or more of the 'agricultural elements,' individually or with the help of members of his family cultivates land that belongs to a landowner, to whom he gives a portion of the crop in cash or kind."[30] According to this definition, approximately 40% of the peasants were not defined as *zari'a* and were simply excluded from the distribution of land.

As explained in a previous chapter, the *muzara'eh* system in Iran was dependent upon the five agricultural elements. Also, we learned that any person who owned one or more of these elements would be allotted a share of the crop. Those peasants who were cultivating lands based on this order could receive *nasaq* (cultivation right). In the land reform laws, the peasant was, as mentioned, defined as a person who possessed one or more of the agricultural elements, but as we have also seen there were many people working on agricultural land who did not receive *nasaq*. These people were called *Khwush-neshin* (landless settlers). Based on available statistics, the total number of *Khwush-neshin* before the land reform program was 1.3 million families, in comparison with 1.9 million families of *nasaq* holders and small holders.[31] Thus, about two-fifths of the peasants were legally excluded from land distribution by definition.[32]

The land reform law specified that those groups of peasants who were not *zari'a* (a peasant who owns one or more "agricultural elements") but were *barzigar* (a cultivator who owns none of the agricultural elements but who provides labor for which he receives a share of the crop in cash or kind from the landowner),[33] or *Kargar-i keshavarzi* (an agricultural worker who neither owns nor provides any of the agricultural elements but who receives a wage in cash or kind for specific agricultural work) would not be eligible to receive land.[34] This law demonstrates that the main purpose of the land reform was not to answer the demands of the landless peasants because a major part of the landless peasants (i.e., *barzigaran* and *kargaran-i keshavarzi)* were already participating in wage-paid labor capitalist relations and thus were excluded from the land reform measures.

Following the first chapter on definitions, the remaining chapters of the laws of the first stage were organized according to the steps of the land reform process. Throughout these chapters, laws related to the expropriation and exemptions of land reform, compensation, and land distribution are discussed.

According to Article II of the first-stage laws, any landlord could hold one *shesh-dang,*[35] irrespective of size, and leave the others, if any, for sale. The landowner was free to choose one *dih* (village) as his *dih-i intekhabi* (chosen village). He or she might choose different parts of separate villages to total six *dongs*. This method enabled landowners to circumvent the law in several ways because, as Lambton wrote, "to decide what constituted a village was not . . . always as simple as might at first sight appear."[36] To justify such irrational and nonscientific methods, Dr. Arsanjani, then the minister of agriculture, claimed that the government would have to pay 700,000 *toman* (one *toman* roughly equals 1/7 U.S. dollar) for cadastral surveys, which might take as long as 30 years.[37]

Apart from the alleged technical problems, however, the primary factor that mitigated against the choice of a systematic survey was the influence of powerful landowners. It was through this process that the landowners retained most of the best land and maintained their influence in different villages for the future.

The members of a landowner's family, who included a wife and children who were under the care and guardianship of the head of the family, were, by the terms of the law of the first stage, regarded as one person. Later, the Land Reform Council[38] reversed this law and decided that all children and wives, irrespective of their dependency, could hold the maximum amount of land permitted by law.[39]

Following this decision, many landowners were able to retain their lands. In addition, female landowners, regardless of their husbands' positions, could hold land as independent persons, whereas hundreds of thousands of female peasants, working shoulder to shoulder with their husbands, or even independently, were prohibited from purchasing agricultural land under the land reform law. Similarly, children of landowners could hold land without regard to age, while hundreds of thousands of peasants' children, working on farms in miserable conditions, were forgotten.

Thus, the law provided landowners with several means by which to retain their lands. For example, a landlord with several children could hold several villages. In addition, laws relating to the exemption of land such as dih-intekhabi (the chosen village), the freedom to select six *dongs* in various villages, and the absence of limits on holdings of "mechanized" land permitted landlords to retain their lands during the first stage. They were given additional time to change their old, traditional relations with peasants in favor of capitalist relations and thus to retain their lands forever. In 1966, the United Nations summarized the outcome of the laws of the first stage as follows:

> There was nothing to prevent landlords from reordering the cultivation pattern in their villages before the land reform reached them in such a way as to ensure that the best land—or indeed any land at all—went only to their friends, relatives, and loyal dependents. Again, landlords who exercised their option to retain a collection of parts of villages might contrive to retain the best of each and even, perhaps, those parts that dominated the water supply for the rest of the village.[40]

Apart from the above advantages for landlords, law exempted certain categories of land. They were orchards, grazing farms, tea plantations, groves, woodlands, suburban villages, mechanized lands, and those lands that had been rented out before December 5, 1959 (i.e., before ratification of the land reform bill). In the case of rented lands, the decision was conditioned on a period of five years or less; otherwise the lease was to be considered void after a period of five years. In the case of mortgaged land, the government undertook to pay its value on the due date.

Mechanization of land was another way to avoid land distribution. According to the Land Reform Law, mechanized land was land on which wages were paid for cultivation or on which a tractor was used for plowing.[41] As the author of *Land Reform and its Direct Effects in Iran* writes,

> Mechanization or motorization were, in reality, frequently used for window dressing and employed by the landlords to avoid land distribution. When we asked some village women what motorization or mechanization was, they replied, "Motorization means that they give you 8 pounds of wheat and one toman (roughly about 1/7 dollar) a day; and mechanization means that you should sign the wage slip at the end of the month."[42]

Professor Lambton also writes, "the regulations for the additional Articles stated that cultivated land would be considered mechanized if it was plowed by tractor and labor employed received a wage in cash or kind."[43]

Clearly, declaring that a piece of land as being mechanized was very easy if the landowner realized the true main objective of land reform. Landowners had been given enough time to make a decision as to whether they wanted to keep their land any longer. Based on the law, 930,000 hectares (i.e., nearly 1/7 of all the arable land) of the most fertile land were exempted from sale to the government.[44]

In addition, landowners were given warning as early as 1959, two years prior to the implementation of the program. Thus, according to Keddie, landowners "had had two years to transfer ownership of their villages to their wives, children, and relatives."[45] Also, if their villages were subject to sale, they received good money for them.

Compensation was based on the tax each landowner paid before January 9, 1962. However, the price was multiplied by a number of coefficients determined by the Ministry of Agriculture for each region.[46] Finally, landowners who had paid little or no taxes[47] received a price ranging between 100 and 180 times the amount of tax paid.[48] In the case of *vaqf* lands (religious endowments), the law separated the *vaqf khass* (private endowment) from the *vaqf aam* (general endowment). *Vaqf aam* was untouched in the first stage of the land reform.[49] The rules regarding *vaqf khass* were the same as those applying to private ownership of land. Like other landowners, the *mutavalli* (administrator of the endowment) could hold the maximum amount of land permitted by the law. In the case of the distribution of *khaleseh* (state lands) and *amlak-i saltanati* (crown land), no separate laws were provided. However, it was notable that these two types of land were divided into plots of a given size and that some sold before the final announcement of the 1962 Land Reform. The remaining state lands were distributed according to the land reform laws, while the remaining Crown lands, which qualified as mechanized lands, were exempt from distribution.[50]

The Agricultural Bank compensated landowners in ten annual installments (later changed to fifteen). In order to provide money for the price of land, the government issued special land reform *qubuz* (bills of exchange, or promissory notes). These *qubuz*, which were exempt from taxation, earned 6% interest. Landlords were encouraged to invest bills of exchange in any productive unit such as industry, mining, or agriculture; to purchase shares in government factories; or to put the bills, discounted, into the Agricultural Bank. Qubuz were also used in payment of taxes and dues claimed by the government. Through such uses, some landlords stepped forward into urban business activities. Western-type capitalist relations thus replaced traditional agrarian relations.

The government played the role of mediator between the landlords and the peasants. The purchased lands were to be sold to eligible peasants by the government. The peasants had to pay the original price of the land, plus 107 administrative costs, during a period of 15 years. We will see later that a majority of peasants could not afford the prices determined by the government. A study by the Research Group of the University of Tehran showed that the peasants were unsatisfied with the determined prices and believed that "lands were sold out to the government at higher than their real prices."[51] Similarly, the daily newspaper *Etela'at* wrote, "The landowners in Gilan Province sold out their lands to the government for 33,500,000 rials (roughly about $419,000) higher than their real prices."[52] However, it was not the government, of course, that paid extra money to the landlords. Peasants who received some of the land were required to pay the original price that had been paid to the landlords, plus bank interest and administrative expenses. In other words, the extra charges fell to the peasants—whose average annual per capita income was approximately $14.[53]

Distribution of land among the peasants was based on the existing *nasaq*—i.e., the amount of land that any peasant cultivated at the time of transmission, either individually or collectively in the form of *musha'* (undivided shares). The *nasaq* holders were usually members of the traditional agricultural units (*buneh*) of the village. They had to be residents of the village and own at least one of the five "agricultural elements" (land, water, seeds, oxen, or labor).

According to Article 16 of the Land Reform Law, land could be transferred to members of the following groups: (1) the *nasaq* holders (but only the heads of families); (2) the heirs of peasants who had died within a year before land distribution in the village; (3) *barzigaran* (share-paid agricultural workers) who were engaged in cultivation but did not own any of the agricultural elements beyond their labor; (4) *kargar-i kishavarzi* (wage-paid agricultural workers) who, like *barzigaran,* did not own other agricultural elements; and (5) those groups who were volunteer agricultural workers. In accordance with Article 16, priority was given to peasants who owned resources in addition to labor. However, this was in theory. In practice, none of these groups except the *nasaq* holders received land. Thus, virtually 47.5% of the peasants who owned only their own labor were excluded from land distribution.[54]

In addition, only peasants who were members of the New Cooperative Society could purchase land. Membership in this society meant that one had to pay an annual membership charge, but it seemed to lead to no advantages because, as a United Nations report stated, "it is certain that many of these were cooperative in name only."[55] If any peasant failed to satisfy the requirements issued by the Society—e.g., the payment of three land installments—the purchased land had to be returned.[56] Everything seemed to be against the peasant. When he was fired with the fever of become a small landowner, the big landowners took advantage of him, with the support of the government. For example, according to the law, irrigated land was to be sold to peasants with related water rights. In some cases, however, water was sold to peasants separately, so that they paid twice for a piece of land.[57]

This was the situation of the prosperous peasants—i.e., those who were considered eligible to purchase land. Both *barzigaran* and *kargaran-i kishavarzi* (share- and wage-paid agricultural laborers), who realized that something was happening around them, prepared to ask for their rights, but the government was very careful not to incite a reaction from the peasants in the villages. It was government's fear that peasants throughout the country might initiate actions against landlords, as they had done in a few areas.[58] In some cases, landlords had been attacked physically and expelled from villages. According to Lambton, "By the summer of 1962, the peasants in many areas, especially in Azerbaijan, were withholding the payment of the landowner's share of the crop from land which had not yet been transferred or was not subject to transfer."[59] Peasants were encouraged by slogans such as "The land belongs to the person who cultivates it."[60]

Realizing the dangerous atmosphere, which it had, in part, created, the government stopped propaganda against the landlords and threatened the objecting peasants. In one of his speeches on clarification of the purpose of the land reform, Dr. Arsanjani, the minister of agriculture, stated, "if some of the younger men in the field sometimes talked against the landlords and advised the peasants to resist their impositions and to withhold their dues, it must be remembered that there was often strong provocation."[61] Thus, the government made a firm decision to oppress peasants' reactions against the landlords, and, by such decision, land reform began with no attention paid to landless peasants who objected.

The primary laws and regulations of the land reform were given to the Land Reform Organization. In order to supervise implementation of these laws and the preparation of any further regulations, a council was formed. Under the chairmanship of the minister of agriculture, the council was composed of five high-ranking officials, including the head of the Land Reform Organization. This group, called the Council for Land Reform, made the first steps toward executing the land reform.

[1] B. Momeni, "Iran on the Eve of the Constitutional Revolution," trans. S. Azad, *RIPEH (The Review of Iranian Political Economy of History)* 1, no. 2 (June 1977): 80–92.

[2] H. Arsanjani, 1940, cited in B. Momeni (1979), 105.

[3] M.R. Pahlavi, Shah, *The White Revolution*, 2nd ed. (Tehran: Kayhan Press, 1967), 15.

[4] The United Nations, *Progress in Land Reform, Fourth Report* (1966), 26.

[5] This group (i.e., those who believed the land reform program to be a propaganda campaign) based their reasoning on the following argument: "Feudalism is the governing system in Iran, and feudal relations of production form part of the society's infrastructure. A fundamental transformation of the society capable of destroying the system and doing away with the old infrastructure can only be achieved in a revolution. If we accept that the land reform has succeeded in abolishing feudalism, then we must also accept that a revolution has taken place. And since no revolution can come about without a revolutionary force and revolutionary leadership, then we are inevitably led to believe that the [Shah's] regime in Iran has a revolutionary character. However, since it is abundantly clear that the regime does not possess such a character, then feudalism, with some minor changes, is still the ruling system, and the semi-colonial, semi-feudal system of government is, as previously, still dominant." Cited in B. Jazani, *Capitalism and Revolution in Iran* (Tehran: Zed Press, 1980), 49.

[6] B. Jazani, *Capitalism and Revolution in Iran.*

[7] Ibid.

[8] *The New York Times*, 3 August 1961.

[9] *The New York Times*, 30 May 1961.

[10] M.R. Pahlavi, Shah, *Answer to History* (New York: Stein and Day, 1980).

[11] Ibid., 22–23.

[12] F. Halliday, *Iran: Dictatorship and Development* (London: Penguin Books, 1979), 26–27.

[13] *The New York Times*, 23 May 1961.

[14] A. Tully, *The Inside Story About Our Government's Most Secret Organization—The Central Intelligence Agency* (New York: A Crest Book, 1962), 76.

[15] Arsanjani, personal interview with Pars Press, 25 Dey 1340 (January 1961), cited in M. R. Soudagar, *A Study of the Iranian Land Reform (1961–66)* (Institute for Social and Economic Research: Tehran, 1979), p. 9. In Persian.

[16] *The New York Times*, 25 May 1961.

[17] Ibid., 3 August 1961.

[18] Ibid.

[19] M.R. Pahlavi, Shah, 204.

[20] N.R. Keddie, "The Iranian Village Before and After Land Reform," *Journal of Contemporary History*, 3, no. 3 (1968): 69–91.

[21] *Etela'at* (newspaper published for Iranians abroad). no. 10019, 23 October 1977.

[22] M. Zonis, *The Political Elite of Iran* (Princeton: Princeton University Press, 1971), 74.

[23] Ibid.

[24] Ibid., 75. In part, the National Front Manifesto read: "We warn the people that our country is now on the verge of being officially changed from a democratic parliamentary regime to one of reaction and despotism. We must, therefore, say YES to the abolition of the feudal system, land and water for the farmers and better rewards for the worker, sovereignty for the nation and freedom for all, and destruction of colonialism and exploitation. But we must say NO to the arbitrary rule of the Shah, his interference in the affairs of the state, the rule of terror and Savak [secret police] atrocities, colonial domination of the country, police violations and gendarmerie oppression, and the overlordship of government officials in towns and villages." (Zonis, 74).

[25] B. Momeni.

[26] Halliday, 125.

[27] Ibid.

[28] Land Reform Law, Article I (viii), 1962. Cited in M. Mohammadi, *On the Agrarian Policy of Iranian Government and For a Democratic Solution of Agrarian Problems* (Tehran: Tudeh Publishing Center, 1973). In Persian.

[29] *Etela'at* (daily newspaper), 23 Aabaan 1343 (Oct.–Nov. 1964), cited in M. Mohammadi, 1973, p.17.

[30] Land Reform Law, Article I (ii), 1962.

[31] O.I.P.F.G., *Land Reform and Its Direct Effects in Iran* (London: Iran Committee, January 1976).

[32] This percentage includes the small non-cultivators *(Khwush-neshin),* such as the village barber, blacksmith, bath keeper, etc.

[33] Land Reform Law, Article I (iv), 1962.

[34] Land Reform Law, Article I (v), 1962.

[35] A village is divided into six parts or *dongs (shesh dongs). Dong* means one sixth part of any piece of real estate.

[36] A. Lambton, *The Persian Land Reform, 1962-1966* (Oxford, UK: Clarendon Press, 1969), 65.

[37] The Ministry of Agriculture, *Land Reform in Iran* (Tehran: Ministry of Agriculture, 1963).

[38] The Land Reform Council is discussed in following pages.

[39] Lambton, 1969.

[40] The United Nations, 26.

[41] Lambton, 1969.

[42] O.I.P.F.G., 1976, p. 49.

[43] Lambton, 1969, p. 261.

[44] M. Mohammadi, 1973. Professor Lambton adds: "There were frequent complaints in some areas, notably Kirmanshahan, that much of the best land in

the villages subject to sale to the government under the first stage and to settlement under the second was declared to be mechanized when in fact it was not, and that the land reform officials had connived at such declarations. It was also alleged that in Arak the landowners had in many cases taken the best land of the village away from the peasants and begun to cultivate it by means of tractors. Similar cases were alleged in Isfahan and elsewhere." (pp. 261–262).

[45] Keddie, 82

[46] Lambton.

[47] N. Jacobs, *The Sociology of Development: Iran as an Asian Case Study* (New York: Praeger Special Studies in International Economics and Development, 1967).

[48] Mohammadi.

[49] O.I.P.F.G.

[50] There is no indication related to the distribution of crown lands in released statistics.

[51] The Research Group, *Quarterly Journal of Economic Research*, nos. 17 and 18 (April–September 1969) 273. (In Persian.)

[52] *Etela'at*, 9 Ordibehesht 1346 (April 1967), cited in Mohammadi, 20. (In Persian.)

[53] Research Group, 174–175. In this relation, they explain that the 184,400 rials annual revenue of the village of Qar was to be divided among 42 families, which meant each family would receive 4,390 rials (roughly $59). If this amount were divided into the average number of members of a family (4.2 in this village), the annual income is 1,045 rials, or about $14.

[54] N. Keddie.

[55] United Nations, 27.

[56] M. Mohammadi.

[57] Research Group, *Quarterly Journal of Economic Research of University of Tehran*, nos. 15 and 16, Bahman 1346 (February 1968).

[58] O.I.P.F.G.

[59] Lambton, 100.

[60] Ibid.

[61] Ibid., 99.

Chapter 8
The Land Reform in Practice

Introduction

This chapter aims to explain and analyze the process of implementation of the land reform program. Since reform took place in several stages, with different but related goals, the chapter is intended to study these stages as they actually occurred in practice. Also, in order to provide a better understanding of the nature of the land reform, statistics, data, and figures are included in this chapter.

In addition to the three major stages, two supplementary laws were ratified and implemented to complete the program, and this chapter examines these laws to the extent that they throw light on the entire process. Finally, one of the declared objectives of the project was diminution of large-scale land ownerships. This chapter attempts to show what end results have actually been.

To complete the land reform program, supplementary measures under the umbrella of the "White Revolution" took place. Understanding the objectives and nature of Iranian land reform depends partly upon an analysis of the principles of the shah's White Revolution. Therefore, study of these principles is the final purpose of this chapter.

The First Stage of the Land Reform

Operation of the land reform began with a number of propaganda speeches against landlords. Dr. Arsanjani, the minister of agriculture, headed the campaign. Maragheh, one of the most fertile regions of Azerbaijan, was chosen as the place for the first steps of execution of the land reform. Then, aside from a few regional exceptions, the operation began in all provinces throughout the country.

As described earlier, five types of land ownership within the *muzara'eh* system were common traditionally in Iran. According to Article 2 of the land reform law, four out of the five—i.e., *arbabi* (private landed estates), *khaleseh* (state lands and public domain), *amlak-i saltanati* (crown lands), and *vaqf* (endowment lands)—were affected by the first stage of the land reform program. *Vaqf* lands existed in two forms: (1) *vaqf khass* (private endowment), and (2) *vaqf amm* (general endowment). The latter form was untouched in the first stage, and, needless to say, the fifth type—*khurdeh maliki* (peasant proprietorship)—was not subjected to distribution at all.

The exact number of villages in Iran has been a mysterious subject for a long time. At various times, the number has been announced in a range between 48,000 and 66,000.[1] In 1972, it was stated as 55,030 villages and 21,863 *mazra'eh* (hamlets).[2] According to information released by the Statistical Center of Iran (1976), a total of 14,962 *dih* (villages) and 868 *mazra'eh* (hamlets) were affected by the first stage of the land reform throughout the country. Among them, 3,967 villages and 103 full hamlets (six dang), and 10,995 villages and 765 partial hamlets (less-than six dang) were purchased and sold to 707,000 farmers, with 3,565,000 members of farming families being settled on their so-called "own lands."[3] (See Table 6.)

It is not clear, however, how many hectares of land were purchased and distributed in the first stage. In addition, official statistics have not clearly stated the percentage of purchased land under the category "less-than-six-dang villages." Indeed, it could be 5/6 of a village, 1/6, or even less. According to Iranian economist H. Mahdavi,

> Even if one-hundredth of a village were to be sold to the government, in most statistics issued by the government that village would be classified as "reformed."
>
> . . . If only a fraction of a village is sold by one landlord, the entire household of the village is claimed to have benefited from the reform. If a second landlord sells another fraction, the entire village household is counted as having benefited from land reform.[4]

With considerable caution, then, we conclude that villages and hamlets in the category of "less than six dang" can range between 1/6 dang and 5 dang. In the absence of reliable data, we will assume an average of 3 dang for each partially purchased village or hamlet, meaning that two partially purchased villages or hamlets would equal one that had been fully purchased. Consequently, we found that 9,464.5 six-dang villages and 485.5 hamlets were purchased from the land-owners.[5] Based on this assumption, the total number of affected villages and hamlets in the first stage was 9,950. In contrast, Dr. Arsanjani in 1962 estimated that about 15,000 villages belonged to landlords with more than five villages, and the government stated that 400 to 450 large landlords owned 57% of all Iranian villages.[6] This number was roughly 1/7, or 15%, of the total number of villages existing at that time. Needless to say, this 15% included the worst of the agricultural lands, since it was what had remained after the landlords had made their choices wherever they wished. According to the law, landlords were free to choose the best six-dang village, or six dongs of the best parts of their different villages. In addition, since there was no limitation on landholding in terms of total hectares, it is conceivable that the purchased villages and hamlets were the smallest, as they were the least arable lands with the least water available for them.[7]

Table 6
Implementation of the First Stage of the Land Reform
From the Beginning to the End of 1353 (1974–75)

Number of six-dang villages purchased	3,967
Number of less-than-six-dang villages purchased	10,995
Number of six-dang hamlets purchased	103
Number of less-than-six-dang hamlets purchased	765
Value of all lands purchased (paid to landowners) (in millions of rials)	10,350
Number of peasant households receiving land	707,000
Number of peasant family members receiving land	3,565,000

Source: Plan and Budget Organization, Statistical Center of Iran. *Statistical Yearbook of Iran*, June 1976.

It should be mentioned that although the number of peasants who were able to purchase land seems relatively high (about 707,000), the official statistics are not reliable, according to Mahdavi, because "they include many-fold counting."[8] In addition, there were many cases in which each peasant received only about one-half hectare of land, or even less.[9] For example, in one village named Ghalaah Garden, in

Mazandaran province, 20 hectares of land were sold to 32 peasants, which meant that each peasant received about 0.62 hectares.[10]

Priority in the sale of land was given to those peasants who provided more than their labor for cultivation (e.g., oxen or seeds or both); thus approximately 47.5% of the peasants, who could provide only their labor, were actually excluded from acquiring any land.[11] The remaining 52.5%, called *nasaq* holders, received land in different sizes in proportion to their *nasaq* rights. In the principal Iranian language, this group is called *ra'iyat* (peasants who own at least one of the five agricultural elements in addition to their labor). The amount of *nasaq* of peasants was not equal, so some peasants received too little land to support even their household living expenses.

Statistics show that before the land reform, 40% of the peasants (or 749,000) had been cultivating a piece of land of less than two hectares and owned just 5% of the total arable land.[12] In contrast, only one percent owned 13.5% of the lands.[13] Different studies show that those people who owned less than four hectares of land (except in those regions with sufficient rainfall and good soil, like the southern shore of the Caspian Sea) were not able to support an average family in the rural areas.[14] This group contains 55.6% of all peasants. Obviously, many people who were "benefited" by the land reform program were in this category. When landless peasants were actually informed that they had to be agricultural workers or go somewhere else to find new jobs, this group was placed in an almost untenable situation. The small piece of land was an obstacle to moving to another location. The peasant did not wish to leave his small piece of land, but it could not provide for his family's living expenses.[15] Sooner or later, most of the peasants in this group were forced to leave the land, even their own villages. This was precisely expected to happen in responding to the need for a cheap labor force in the cities, where the new and growing capitalist economy needed more workers.

About 18% of the peasants who owned more than five hectares in the Caspian Sea plain, or between 10 and 20 acres in other regions, could get good benefits from the land reform program.[16] Most of these well-to-do peasants raised animals on their farms as another source of revenue.

However, the lands of the country's most fertile region (i.e., the southern shore of the Caspian Sea) were mostly "mechanized" and consequently less affected by the law. Only 12.5% of the land of this region was affected by the first stage.[17] Table 7 shows implementation of the first stage of the land reform in different provinces.

Table 7

Implementation of the First Phase of the Land Reform in Rural Areas By Administrative Divisions for the Period Through 1352 (1974)

Administrative Divisions	Number of villages and farms distributed					Payment by the farmer		farmer
	Farm Dang		Less than six dang		Value of land purchased (Million rials)	Payment by the Land Reform Org. to landlords for 1st installment (Million rials)	Households receiving land (1,000)	Family members receiving land (1,000)
	Village	Farm	Village	Farm				
Total	3,967	103	10,957	765	10,350	3,128	707	3,565
Markazi (Central)	220	0	618	432	1,164	345	50	277
Khorasan	222	0	1,069	0	515	144	26	132
Esfahan	60	0	338	0	192	43	22	111
East Azerbaijan	510	0	1,305	0	1,726	774	123	615
Khuzestan	256	4	452	297	287	38	22	112
Mazandaran	175	70	559	36	836	91	74	379
Fars	247	0	1,405	0	454	57	63	317
Gilan	57	0	683	0	1,163	318	41	211
West Azerbaijan	402	0	447	0	820	195	35	173
Kerman	97	0	454	0	168	38	6	23
Kermanshahan	487	0	1,214	0	716	151	59	295
Coastal	3	0	13	0	5	0.4	0.2	1
Sistan and Baluchestan	1	0	3	0	2	0.1	+	0.2
Kurdistan	163	0	492	0	271	59	32	158
Hamedan	189	0	647	0	1,177	614	81	405
Luristan	99	0	447	0	226	79	17	83
	169	3	429	0	356	148	20	101
	0	0	15	0	0.6	+	+	0.4
Bushehr	49	0	132	0	54	6	6	30
Chaharmahal and Bakhtiyari	6	0	102	0	39	10	6	30
Semnan	10	0	59	0	29	6	0.7	3
Ilam	210	0	89	0	117	9	10	48
Boyer Ahmad and Kohkoliyeh	335	26	43	0	31	1	12	62

Source: Plan and Budget Organization, *Statistical Yearbook*, June 1976.

According to the released statistics, among the villages affected by the first stage of the land reform there were 1,535 six-dang villages, 41 six-dang hamlets, 245 less-than-six-dang villages, and 141 less-than-six-dang hamlets affected that belonged to the state and Crown lands.[18]

Khosravi (1980) indicated that, overall, between 700,000 and 800,000 peasants had been benefited, in different ways and at different levels, by the end of the first stage.[19] This part of the rural population, however, received just 15% of the agricultural land available in Iran.

The Second Stage of the Land Reform

Table 8
Summarized Implementation of the Second Phase of the Land Reform

Number of villages implemented	54,833
Number of hamlets implemented	21,850
Number of peasants receiving land	213,551
Number of landowners operating their land	793,871
Number of peasants' households whose status was clarified	2,519,155

Source: Plan and Budget Organization, Statistical Center of Iran. *Statistical Yearbook of Iran*, June 1976.

The laws of the second stage of the land reform were ratified as a cabinet decree on January 17, 1963, while the Majlis was closed because of conflict. These laws became known as the "annexed Articles" of the land reform. Apparently, this stage was designed to complete the first stage and aimed to do away with the remaining *muzara'eh* system. Contrary to the first phase, which was a serious challenge to big landlords, this phase was indeed a retreat in favor of them.

In 1963, one year after the beginning of the program, the shah took steps to blunt the trend of the first stage by appointing a military man who, according to Bill, "represented the ideal guide for a program designed to preserve traditional relationships."[20] The liberal minister of agriculture, Dr. Arsanjani, was dismissed, and General Riyahie was appointed in his place. Arsanjani had actually favored launching a land reform that would replace the *muzara'eh* system with a capitalist system, but his plan was stopped by influential elements in the ruling class. Still, government had no option but to continue the capitalist trend.

The second stage was put into operation in August 1964. Landowners were legally free to hold 30 to 150 hectares of non-mechanized land, depending upon the region, and for the rest of their holdings they were given five alternatives as follows:

1. Rent the land to customary tenants for 30 years on the basis of the average of the net income of the three previous years, regardless of the tax and in accordance with local custom. The lease was subject to revision every five years.
2. Sell the land to the peasants at a mutually agreed price.
3. Divide both the irrigated and the dry lands with the peasants on the basis of the former division of the crop, and receive 2/5 of the value of the land on a 10-year installment plan.
4. Set up a joint-stock agricultural unit with the peasants, in which each side's share would be equal to the former division of the crop.
5. Purchase the peasants' cultivating rights (*haq-i nasaq*) and then employ the peasants as paid laborers.

Official statistics released by the Plan and Budget Organization in 1976 show that landlords mostly preferred the first alternative. In the second phase, from the beginning to the end of 1352 (1974), a total of 232,366 landlords rented out their lands to a total of 1,243,961 peasants.[21] (See Table 10.)

Table 9
Figures Relating to All Provisions of the Second Stage as Implemented

Provisions	Landowners	Explanation of Subject	Peasants
1	248,409	Rented their land to	1,417,065
2	3,202	Sold their land to	13,374
3	24,359	Divided their land with	157,598
4	81,292	Formed JSAU with	122,907
5	8,989	Purchased cultivating rights of	13,374

Source: Plan and Budget Organization, Statistical Center of Iran. *Statistical Yearbook of Iran*, June 1976 (with adjustment).

As we have said, all charitable vaqf (general endowments) were exempted in the first stage of the land reform. In the second stage, the law required that all general endowments were to go to rent to those peasants who had been working on these lands.

Table 10
Implementation of the Second Phase of the Land Reform
up to 1352 (1973–1974)

Provisions		Distribution of the Subject	
I. Rent	A.	Number of landowners who rented out their land	232,366
	B.	Number of tenant peasant households	1,243,961
	C.	Number of rented charitable *vaqf* (general endowment) estates	8,564
	D.	Number of *mutavalli* (*vaqf* land administrators)	13,633
	E.	Number of tenant peasant households in these lands	137,173
	F.	Number of rented estates and hamlets of *vaqf khass* (private endowments)	957
	G.	Number of *mutavalli* (*va f khass* land administrators)	2,410
	H.	Number of tenant peasant households in these lands	35,931
II. Division	A.	Number of landowners who agreed to divide their land with peasants	25,359
	B.	Number of peasants who acquired land through division	157,598
III. Selling	A.	Number of landlords who sold their land to peasants	3,202
	B.	Number of peasants who were able to purchase land	55,953
IV. Form JSAU	A.	Number of cases	41,615
	B.	Number of villages JSAU was built in	39,952
	C.	Number of peasants involved	81,292
	D.	Total number of shareholders	122,907
V. Purchasing	A.	Number of landlords who purchased peasants' use-rights	8,989
	B.	Number of peasants who sold their use-rights	13,374
VI.		Number of landlords operating their lands	393,871
VII.		Number of whole villages mechanized	1,225
VIII.		Number of deserted whole villages	6,236
IX.		Number of orchard villages	2,083
X.		Number of peasant-householders whose statuses were clarified by the second phase	2,519,155

Source: Plan and Budget Organization, *Statistical Yearbook,* June 1976

The leases were to run for 99 years and were subject to five-year revisions. Based on this article of the law, a total of 8,564 villages and hamlets were rented by 137,173 peasants.[22]

In addition to the general endowments, 957 *Roqabat* (estates) of *vaqf khass* (private endowment) had remained from the first stage. These lands, also, were rented to 35,931 peasants in the second stage. (See Table 8.) The total number of peasants who became new tenants of different types was thus 1,317,065.[23] In comparison with the other provisions, this number is very high (e.g., 1,417,065 tenant peasants compared to 179,971 peasants who received land either by repurchase or through division), but the reason is simple. By this method, landlords were, first, able to retain some of their common privileges, and, second (by using various possible tricks), able to charge a good rent.[24]

Use of the second alternative was quite low—only 3,202 land-owners agreed to sell their lands to 55,953 peasants.[25] It seems clear that these lands were among the non-fertile ones the owners had been anxious to dispose of.

The third alternative was to divide the cultivating lands. In 25,359 cases, the lands were divided between landlords and the peasants who had traditionally been cultivating them,[26] on the basis of the amount of shares each owned. Usually, a landlord owned three (or, more likely, four) of the five shares (agricultural elements). Thus, the landlord owned 3/5 of the land alone, while the remaining 2/5 was to be shared by all of the peasants. Clearly, in such conditions, the landlord was able to continue as landowner because of his or her larger number of shares, whereas each peasant would receive only a small plot of land—so little that sooner or later he would be compelled to sell that small portion and leave the village to seek work elsewhere.

In the case of the division of land, peasants were obliged to pay two-fifths of the price of the land they were receiving as their own share. For instance, if the peasant's share of a previous arrangement had been two-fifths of the total harvest of a certain area, he would receive two-fifths of the land. But he had to pay two-fifths of the price of the portion he acquired. Since peasants usually did not have cash in hand, landlords chose to get some additional land in return for providing the peasants with cash; therefore, the peasant, in such a case, would actually receive less than two-fifths of the land. According to the *Statistical Yearbook of Iran*, based on such agreements some peasants "acquired as little as 1/4 of a hectare of land."[27] There is no question that the landlord chose to keep the best-quality portion of the land. However, in the second phase 157,598 peasant households did receive land by this agreement.[28]

According to Article 17 of the land reform regulations, landlords could choose to set up a joint-stock agricultural unit (JSAU) with the peasants, as the fourth alternative. Under this alternative, 3,952 agricultural units were formed, with 81,292 peasants being engaged in cultivation of these units.[29] This was another method by which the landlord could continue his domination in the relationship with the peasants. Under the new capitalist form of relations, nothing major had changed to benefit the peasants.

The fifth alternative was the purchasing of peasants' rights. Based on this agreement, the landlord had to buy the peasants' use-rights (*haq-i nasaq*). As mentioned earlier, 13,374 peasants "chose" to sell their use-rights to 8,989 landlords. Peasants traditionally had clung to their land unless deprived of it by force, and in many cases they were indeed forced or tricked into transferring their cultivating rights to landlords. For example, in cases of contact with several peasants, it was said that "they were taken to the registry office (*mahzar*) and made to sign documents, the nature of which they did not understand. Only afterwards did they realize that they had sold their *nasaq* (use-rights). Before being taken to the registry, they would occasionally be given a good meal."[30] This group of peasants then faced the same two choices faced by many other peasants: continue as a daily paid laborer working for the landlord, as many other landless peasants did, or leave their village to move toward the cities in order to find another job. Both cases favored capitalistic relations in the villages and the cities.

The second stage was proclaimed completed in January 1967, but, as was the case with the other phases, it was continued for years afterward. According to cumulative statistics available, overall about 1.7 million peasants were covered by the varying measures of the second phase of the land reform.[31] Of that number, 82%, or 1.4 million peasants, were involved in some form of tenancy.[32]

In addition to the two major laws passed at the beginning of the second stage, a few others were passed while the first two measures were in progress. The legislation relating to distribution of orchards was ratified in June 1964 as the 27th and 28th Articles of the land reform regulations. According to these articles, all orchards and groves, where *arseh* (land and water) belonged to the landlord and *a'yan* (tangible property), trees, and buildings belonged to the peasants or were jointly shared by landowner and peasants, had to be divided between them on the basis of their current rights, or one of them should purchase the other's share. However, these articles were not implemented until seven years later (May 1971), when it was passed as The Law Relating to the

Sale of Gharas-Maleki Orchards. This law will be discussed later in this chapter.

Also at the end of the second stage, the law related to the joint-stock agricultural companies was ratified. It will be discussed in detail in the next chapter. Finally, it should be noted that while 707,000 peasant households acquired land in the first stage of the land reform, only 213,551 peasant households became landowners in the second stage.

The Third Stage of the Land Reform

If the first stage of land reform was a challenge to large-scale land ownership and the second stage was a retreat in favor of the landowners' interests and an expansion of tenancy, the third stage was an action against tenancy, new tenants, and the remaining old relationship between landlords and peasants—in favor of the expansion of capitalist relations of production into remote areas. In other words, the laws of the third stage, which were ratified in March 1968, aimed to break down those relations that had been legalized in the second stage—i.e., tenancy and the new form of crop sharing in the joint-stock agricultural units.

To carry out these laws, a new minister of agriculture, Dr. Valian, a military colonel and one of the top officials of the SAVAK (the shah's secret police), took office.[33] He was appointed to solidify the interests of the new and growing class of bureaucrats and technocrats in the agricultural sector of the economy. The program of this stage (which included 20 Articles), like those of the former stages, was apparently designed to increase agricultural production and improve the standard conditions of the peasants' lives. Not only were such aims not achieved, but, as statistics show, "approximately one in three tenants (or roughly 500,000 cultivators) lost their rights on the land under the third phase and became landless laborers or migratory workers."[34]

The law of this phase contained two main provisions—distribution or sale of rented farms, and distribution or sale of the land in JSAUs. As with the former phases, it was the landowner who chose between the options.

According to the law, all rented farms (except general endowments) were to be either sold to tenants or divided between landowners and tenants in proportion to share-cropping. If selling, landowners were required to sell both land and water rights to the peasants. The price of land was fixed at either 10 times the annual rent for cash transactions or 12 times the annual rent if the land was sold on a 12-year installment plan. In the case of distribution, which was in proportion to the share-cropping ratios, the landlord was to receive two-fifths of the price of the peasant's portion on a 10-year installment plan. All JSAUs were to be replaced in identical manner.

Table 11
Summary of Implementation of the Third Stage of the Land Reform

Provision	Number of Landowners Covered by the Law	Number of Peasants Whose Legal Status Was Clarified
Division	35,403	110,347
Sale	316,372	1,154,578

Source: Plan and Budget Organization, Statistical Center of Iran.
Statistical Yearbook of Iran, June 1976.

As mentioned, according to the statistics, there were 1.7 million peasants covered by the second phase of the land reform, in which 82%, or 1.3 million, were engaged in the 30-year tenancy agreement.[35] The third-phase laws were supposed to clarifying the status of these 1.7 million peasants. Of this group, 57% (800,000) acquired a piece of land regardless of size. The remaining 47% (600,000 peasants) received nothing.[36]

According to official figures released by the Statistical Center of Iran in June 1976, the total number of peasants whose legal status had been clarified to that time was 1,264,921.[37] The same source shows the number of involved landlords as 351,775.[38] Among them, 110,347 peasants and 35,403 landowners were covered by the division provision, while the remaining numbers were related to the second alternative, the provision for sale.[39]

It appears that the government did not seriously urge implementation of the third phase. Execution of this phase lasted several years, but less than one year after ratification of the third phase law (February 1969) the government declared that the three stages of the land reform program had been completed and that no additional bills would be introduced. However, since the intended program was still ongoing, in spite of the government statement, additional laws relating to the sale of religious endowments and the sale of the orchards were ratified. They are discussed below.

The Law Relating to the Sale of the General Endowments

It was three years after the ratification of the third stage laws of the land reform and the government's declaration that all phases of the reform were completed that a law called The Transformation of Tenancy into a Better State of Affairs, and the Transfer of Endowed Villages and Farms to Tenant Farmers was passed. According to this law, all tenant farmers of the general endowment were to purchase the land under their cultivation. The available statistics show that by the end of 1352 (March 1974), 1,237,173 peasants rented 8,564 *Roqabat* (estates) of *vaqf amm* (general endowments), which had been controlled by 13,633 *mutavalli* (administrators).[40] According to Khosravi, (1980), 13,000 peasants became owners of these lands through 99-year leases.[41]

The Law Relating to the Sale of Gharas-Maleki Orchards [42]

In May 1964, in the early years of the second phase of the land reform, regulations related to the distribution of the orchards were ratified, but little attention was then paid to these Articles. According to the regulations, in cases in which the *arseh* (land and water) were owned by the landlord and the *a'yan* (trees, buildings) belonged to the peasant, two options were offered: division of the orchard between landlord and peasant based on their existing shares, or purchase by either landlord or peasant of the other's share.[43] Because this law had been ignored for several years after its ratification, the government drafted another bill in January 1972 to emphasize the earlier Articles. The new bill was passed by the Majlis and sent for implementation. The law held that if landlords and peasants failed to reach a mutual agreement in terms of either sale or distribution of the orchards by August 1972, the government itself would take action. This law affected two types of landlord-peasant relationships. First, in those cases in which the peasant owned the total *a'yan* and the landlord the total *arseh,* the peasant would receive three-fourths of the area of the orchard along with the water rights. In a case in which the landlord owned the *arseh* but the *a'yan* was shared between him and the peasant, each side would receive a half-portion of the orchard along with all related rights. Neither of these two appendix laws has played a large role in the nature of the land reform program.

Has Large-Scale Land Ownership Diminished?

The land reform program, first presented as a program to break up the existing large-scale land holdings and to create a middle range of farmers, in practice became a tool by which large-scale land holding stabilized itself in a new form with new relationships. Study of the different phases of this reform shows that in the early years the general policy was to break up large-scale holdings in the old tenure system of *muzara'eh*, whereas in the later years of the program different projects under the names of joint-stock agricultural companies and agro-industrial companies established many huge, private agricultural ownerships. Along with mechanization of lands and new methods of cultivation, many areas went under irrigation available from the newly constructed dams. Most regions that had traditionally been cultivated by indigenous peasants were taken over by both domestic and foreign investors. The new agriculturists succeeded in developing the cultivation areas and increasing agricultural output at the expense of the migration of thousands of peasants and their families to urban areas. For example, Fischer (1979) stated that in Khuzistan plateau, under the Dez dam, in order to build modern agricultural units "some 38,000 peasant families were expelled from 140,000 acres and were paid below-market prices for their land if they owned it."[44] Only 68 families were kept on farms as wage-paid laborers.[45] There are many other examples, such as Dasht-i naz Farm, owned by the shah's brother Gholam-Reza Pahlavi, where hundreds of peasant families were ousted from their homes by the armed forces.[46]

These projects might have been considered development projects if the peasants had benefited and if the programs had been implemented to serve internal needs. But in fact, as Fischer (1979) indicated concerning the Dez irrigation project, "it was the peasant farmers of Khuzistan that suffered most from the project, and national elites or international corporations that benefited most."[47]

In the context of ownership, statistics show that almost nothing has changed in terms of the size of land holdings as a result of an expensive and long-term project of land reform. If, as claimed, land reform had aimed to diminish large-scale land ownership, the figures indicate that it failed—the status quo has continued to dominate. In order to clarify this statement, two groups of related figures are compared in Table 12.

As Table 12 makes clear, large-scale land ownership—for instance, over 100 hectares in 1960—represented 8.5% of the total cultivatable land, which was in the hands of 0.5% of the landlords. By 1974, thirteen years after the beginning of the land reform program, the amount of large-scale land ownership using the same standard (i.e., more than 100 hectares), was 15% of the total cultivatable lands in the hands of only 0.4% of landowners. That is more than twice as much concentration of land in the hands of landlords as existed before land reform began. While the average coefficient for each landlord was 17 (i.e., 8.5: 0.5 = 17) in 1960, it had become 37.5 (15: 0.4 = 37.5) in 1974. (See Table 12.) Another source has indicated that the average land holding of more than 100 hectares is equal to 256.77 hectares for each holder.[48]

On the other hand, only 26.5% of the peasants held less than one hectare of land in 1960. In 1974, 30% of peasants owned less than one hectare. In addition, those 26.5% owned 2% of the available lands in 1960, whereas the latter group held just 1.5% of the total available lands in 1974. At that time, the average holding of a big landlord was 256.77 hectares, and the average for the small holder was just 0.35 hectare.[49] There was a gap of 733.6 times between the average holding of a large and a small landholder by the end of the three phases of land reform in Iran.

The results of the three stages of land reform in Iran show that in spite of its initial claims this program expanded large-scale land ownership. It was, however, able to diminish the old, out-dated relations of production (muzara'eh). My assumption, as it was defined at the beginning of this part, is that if a genuine land reform had been held it would have had to alter the old relationships of production in favor of the cultivators. Iranian land reform succeeded in replacing the old relationship with a new one, but it did not serve cultivators. Rather, it stabilized the economic status of big landowners through an expansion of capitalist relations of production to remote rural areas, and it eased the way for landlords to become urban capitalists.

Table 12
Comparison of the Sizes of Land Ownership in Two Different Periods of Time

Size of Land Holdings in Hectares	Number of Land Holders				Areas of Used Lands			
	1339 (1960) Absolute	%	1353 (1974–75) Absolute	%	1339 (1960) Absolute	%	1353 (1974–75) Absolute	%
Less than 1	492,306	26.5	734,274	30%	198,939	2	259,886	1.5
1–2	256,496	13.5	322,192 13	13%	371,846	3	443,675	3
2–5	474,457	25	541,592 22	22%	1,553,906	14	1,732,868	10.5
5–10	340,037	18	427,934 17	17%	2,413,042	21	2,953,447	18
10–50	301,371	16	428,074 17	17%	5,263,713	46.5	7,500,741	45.5
50–100	8,446	0.5	16,269	0.6%	563,805	5	1,073,697	6.5
More than 100	4,086	0.5	9,553	0.4%	991,003	8.5	2,452,906	15
TOTALS	1,877,199	100	2,479,889	100	11,356,254	100.	16,417,221	100

Source: Kh. Khosravi, *Masa'leh-i dehqani va masa'leh-i, Arzi dar Iran*, 1980, pp. 47, 61 (with adjustments).

The "White Revolution"

Land reform objectives—either officially stated or real—could not be achieved without some supplementary measures. With land reform as a cornerstone, some reformist social, economic, and political measures had been proposed. Like that cornerstone, they were embellished with charming words and slogans, in addition to the facts. Thus, on January 9, 1963—one year after the official declaration of the land reform and the appointment of a new minister of agriculture—the shah inaugurated his "White Revolution." He wrote a few years later (1967), in his book entitled *The White Revolution of Iran*, that

> ...the realization came to me that Iran needed a deep and fundamental revolution that could, at the same time, put an end to all the social inequalities and all the factors which caused injustice, tyranny and exploitation, and all aspects of reaction which impeded progress and kept our society backward.[50]

Indeed, it was another disguise that covered the real goals of a series of measures that had been taken to complete the initial move. It was true that the realization came to him to bring about some reformist changes in society, not to end the social inequalities and injustice as he said, but to stabilize the existing inequalities through a modern economic relation. The shah's reformist measures did not even lessen the exploitation, but expansion of the capitalist relations of production did open the doors of investment to hundreds of foreign corporations. It was following this "revolution" that, as official data show, the number of foreign companies in Iran exceeded 2,000 by 1976. In spite of the shah's claims, this policy made Iran politically and economically more and more dependent upon foreign powers, even though the shah boasted that "the most important result of the White Revolution has been to enable us to pursue a completely independent foreign policy."[51]

The shah's White Revolution contained several principles that he called *ousol-i Enqelab* (principles of revolution). These principles, beginning with six points, totaled 19 items at the time of his downfall, but they had been announced in several groups at different times. In the first step, on January 9, 1963, a six-point reform program was proclaimed that consisted of the following:

1. Land reform
2. Nationalization of forests
3. Public sale of state-owned factories to finance land reform
4. Workers' profit sharing in industry

5.   Reform of electoral law to include women
6.   A literacy corps.
     In order to put the six points into official existence, a referendum
was held. Despite objections from several political and religious
groups, especially *ulama* (clergies), the shah took steps to accomplish
his program.
     Three more principles during 1964 and three more on October 6,
1967 enlarged the six-point program, as follows:
1.   Formation of the health corps (January 21, 1964)
2.   Formation of the reconstruction and development corps
     (September 23, 1964)
3.   Establishment of the rural houses of justice (October 13, 1965)
4.   Nationalization of water resources (October 6, 1967)
5.   Establishment of a program for urban and rural reconstruction
     (October 6, 1967)
6.   An educational and administrative revolution (October 6, 1967).
     Along with the growth and development of capitalism, some new
principles were offered to provide the necessary supplementary
measures. At the same time, these principles challenged the residual
agrarian and traditional culture of the society. These measures were:
1.   Employee and public ownership in state-owned enterprises
2.   Price stabilization and a campaign against profiteering
3.   Free education and a daily free meal for all children from
     kindergarten to the eighth grade
4.   Free nutrition for infants up to the age of two
5.   Nationwide social security, especially for rural inhabitants.
     With increases in oil revenues, some social reforms took place in
the name of the shah's principles. Mostly, these principles would insure
the already completed investments, making the country a secure and
fruitful center for any type of investment.
     In December 1975 the shah announced his two last principles of
revolution, as follows:
1.   A fight against land and housing speculation
2.   A fight against corruption.
     However, despite of these economic and social measures to secure
his reign, he did not reform political power to remove the political
tension built after his coup d'etat of 1953. He also mentioned possible
additions, but the angry people of Iran left him without opportunity to
inaugurate any further "revolutionary principles." The February 1979
revolution, in one sense, made clear that without political reform these
changes could not satisfy the society and could not secure the economic
reform and a good market for secure investment. Experience in the

West proves that economic development must be secured by political reforms that provide opportunity for the majority to participate in the process of democratization of the society. The shah, however, tightened his autocratic rule while moving toward economic development. One of the reasons was that the economic reform was imported and aimed to serve foreign investors, without whose support the shah could not survive.

The shah, in trying to win over his landlord allies, who were opposed to any reform, justified the offering of these supplementary measures as follows:

> The evolution of mankind toward unification and toward the elimination of discrimination and differences is something which will happen, whether we like it or not, in conformity with the dictates of history. Experience has always taught us that if we go out to meet inevitable events, we get better results with less risk of danger than if we simply let them overtake us.[52]

Although he confessed that these reformist measures were taken due to historical experience, he did not forget to add, "My goal in revolution was simply to increase their [the people's] prosperity and welfare."[53] Yet, he did not understand that the people's prosperity includes their political freedom and social justice, which were absent from his "White Revolution" project. Whatever his claims, no change happened to the existing facts. Later events, indeed, showed that neither were these measures intended for the people's prosperity nor had he himself learned from history.

From this author's point of view, the White Revolution, with its nineteen principles, was a collection of measures devoted to serving the main goal of the reform program—that is, expansion of capitalism and elimination of the cause of any possible revolt in the future. This "peaceful revolution" had the mission of paving the way for Iran to become one of the prime bases for the interests of world capitalism. It was in this sense that Iran became the biggest market for the shipment of the most sophisticated arms; one of the most important spy bases in the world against its neighbor, the former Soviet Union; and the gendarme of the region, sending troops to the Persian gulf and even to Vietnam to fight communism. The shah was one of the closest friends of the West and the second largest oil producer for its industries,[54] but the Western powers did not trust him to rule his country properly. Also, the shah did not pay attention to the cultural lag, the cultural identity crisis, and the cultural conflict that were the outcomes of his one-dimensional reform within the society.

If the first principle of the shah's "White Revolution," the land reform, aimed to destroy the old landholding system, the others accelerated the transition period and paved the way for the traditional landlords to move into the capitalist orbit. The growth and development of capitalism, once capital is accumulated, is dependent upon a sufficiently free labor force and an open market. The execution of the land reform itself, as we are seeing, created both mass labor forces and new markets in the cities and towns. As the shah himself agreed, some of the principles were closely related to the first one—land reform.[55] For instance, public sale of state-owned factories to finance land reform played a two-fold role in this respect. The first role ensured the landlords' compensation, and the second funneled their capital directly into the factories and other economic institutions with absolutely dominant capitalist relations of production. The "released lands" sold to peasants in the first stage of reform became capitalized by "new" investors later (discussion will follow). The maneuver of the transformation of land to peasants ironically made thousands of them jobless and led them toward the newly created urban markets to sell their labor (see chapter 10 of this book).

The fifth principle created hundreds of thousands of cheap, integrated members of the labor force. The "reform of electoral law" to include women was indeed a challenge to the traditional culture that had kept half the labor force at home. However, this principle provided enough excuse for those religious leaders who were against any reform at all to incite prejudiced people to revolt.[56] Although the regime was faced with a serious situation, retreat was never made on this vital aspect of the reform.[57]

The Literacy Corps intended to extend literacy to the village children as part of educational reform. This measure was part of the shah's social reform, which benefited deprived people in the country as well. These people, however, were supposed to be future workers in the factories. So there was mutual benefit for the education of the new generation in a period of economic development. Typically, capitalism needs workers with at least a minimum education, so they can handle machinery. This project made them ready to work whenever they wanted to sell their labor in cities. But the official goal of this project had been stated as "the propagation of knowledge and culture."[58] Again, there is no doubt that this program, like other reformist measures of the White Revolution, did have some positive effects on the villagers.[59]

The decree of the Reconstruction and Development Corps was issued when the second phase of the land reform program was begun in villages. The Corps, composed of high school graduate groups with four months of special training taken simultaneous with their military training, had been extended to the villages, as the shah wrote, in order "to complete the program that began with the execution of the land reform"[60] and "to increase the technical knowledge of farmers and farm workers."[61] But the Corpsmen knew little about agriculture. Villagers with many years of experience in their work could better handle their own current problems. The peasants' problem was not shortage of technical knowledge at that time. They suffered from a lack of available land, a lack of money for paying land installments, cruel behavior on the part of government officials and gendarmes, exploitation, shortage of water, and a lack of financial aid. The Iranian government was able to support peasants and to improve agriculture not merely by sending technically trained Corps members but also by distributing land free (or at least with easy conditions) and providing free technical assistance and low-cost financial aid.

The purpose of the Reconstruction and Development Corps was, indeed, to open and extend the market for new manufactured goods, either imported or made by Western-installed factories in Iran. The Corpsmen, in close association with the Rural Cooperative Companies, taught the villagers how to use the new industrial goods. In short, they were partially the carriers of capitalism and its ethic into the countryside. It should also be said that the positive effect of such projects on the peasants' lives—such as opening a new world to the frequently closed-minded peasants—was not popular.

The twelfth point of the shah's revolution consisted of two parts— "revolution" in education and "revolution" in administration. The first part intended to build educational units to train the newly required cadres for the more complicated system. Newly constructed plants and economic institutions would need more technicians, engineers, and managers. In this regard, in a short time—ten years—hundreds of business, technical, and vocational training schools at different levels were established. The number of such institutions increased from 130 in 1964 to 339 in 1974, and the number of students in these areas rose from 12,894 to 69,682.[62] By the end of the Fifth National Development Plan (1976), the number reached 80,000 students, and the shah estimated that by the end of the Sixth National Development Plan, in 1982, it would reach 550,000 students.[63]

In the area of higher education, the number of colleges and students increased dramatically. In addition, many students were sent to more advanced countries to receive training in order to support the growth of capitalism of Iran. Due to the good market and the demands of business, many students were encouraged to study such things as business administration and engineering.

With reference to the second part of the twelfth principle, the shah wrote,

> The objective of the administrative revolution was a decisive and comprehensive attempt to fight against "bureaucracy" and to destroy any kind of anarchic behavior in the departments, to create a sense of duty and honesty, to adjust administrative regulations, and to allow easy circulation of the country's affairs.[64]

This principle intended to sweep away the static and outdated "feudal bureaucracy" and establish a dynamic relationship in which capital would circulate better. It happened, not based on the "sense of duty and honesty," as the shah had said, but in as debased a manner as possible in the absolutist bureaucratic orbit of capitalism. A sense of social responsibility was hard to establish when the higher up one looked the more corruption one saw.[65]

However, in order to remove causes of corruption, a few other "revolutionary" principles were issued. For example, the shah stated that points fourteen and nineteen were designed to reduce corruption.[66] In addition, point fourteen was also intended to fight against the high level of inflation. It was the case, however, that the existing inflation was a natural consequence of economic development, high oil revenues, and the importation of commodities from the West, particularly nonproductive goods such as expensive military hardware and facilities. As a result of the heavy and expensive arms purchases, the shah's military became the fifth largest in the world. These sources of economic inflation could not be removed by issuances of principles from the top.[67] A few other principles (such as free education, free nutrition for infants up to age two, and social security for all Iranian citizens, especially rural inhabitants) were issued. In spite of all such measures, both the rural inhabitants and agriculture in general were ignored.

Overall, the implementation of the principles of the White Revolution brought about some fundamental economic changes in both urban and rural areas, but it did so largely in the service of the capitalist class and its foreign supporters. The shah did not relax his autocratic rule, despite some achievements, and in the end his rule collapsed when his main supporter, the United States, during the Carter administration, compelled him to open Iranian society politically. Indeed, the land reform program, without these supplementary principles and political reform, was never to be completed.

[1] The Research Group of the Institute for Economic Research has declared the number to be 48,592. Institute for Economic Research, *Tahqiqat-e Eqtesadi, Quarterly Journal of Economic Research* (Tehran: University of Tehran Faculty of Law, Political and Economic Sciences, 1969), Nos. 7, 8, p. 186. *Iran Almanac* (1976) stated it as 66,438 in 1966. Since other data have the same problem, there is confusion when using different sources.

[2] Kh. Khosravi, *Mas'aleh-i dihqani va Mas'aleh-i Arzi (Peasants' Questions and Land Questions in Iran)* (n.p., 1980). *Mazra'eh* means farms without any dwellings that have been cultivated by peasants from nearby villages.

[3] Plan and Budget Organization, *Statistical Yearbook of Iran* (June 1976), 210.

[4] H. Mahdavi, *Iran's Agrarian Problems,* cited in N.R. Keddie, "The Iranian Village Before and After Land Reform," *Journal of Contemporary History*, 3, no. 3 (1968), 82–83.

[5] See Table 6.

[6] Keddie, 195.

[7] O.I.P.F.G., *Land Reform and Its Effects in Iran* (London: Iran Committee, 1976).

[8] Mahdavi, cited in Keddie, 83.

[9] O.I.P.F.G.

[10] Research Group, 1964, nos. 11, 12.

[11] Keddie.

[12] Khosravi.

[13] Ibid.

[14] M.R. Soudagar, *Barasi-e Eslahat Arzi (A Study of Iranian Land Reform (1961–66).* (Tehran: Institute for Social and Economic Research, 1979).

[15] Ibid.

[16] Ibid.

[17] Research Group, 1964, Nos. 7, 8.

[18] Plan and Budget Organization, *Statistical Yearbook of Iran*, 1976.

[19] Khosravi.

[20] J. Bill, *The Politics of Iran: Groups, Classes, and Modernization* (Columbus, OH: Charles E. Merrill Publishing Co., 1972), 143. Dr. Arsanjani was appointed as the Ambassador to Rome, probably in order to separate him from his rural and urban connections, which were bases for his growing power. This mission did not last long. Several months later, in August 1964, he was called to Tehran and ignored for the rest of his life. He died suddenly in May 1969 because of a heart attack or, as some people believe, by poisoning by the government. See H. Richards, *America's Shah Shahanshah's Iran (MERIP Reports*, no. 40, 1975).

[21] Plan and Budget Organization, *Statistical Yearbook of Iran*, 1976.

[22] Ibid.

[23] Ibid.

[24] O.I.P.F.G., 1976.

[25] Plan and Budget Organization, *Statistical Yearbook of Iran*, 1976.

[26] Ibid.

[27] Ibid.

[28] O.I.P.F.G., 1976.

[29] Plan and Budget Organization, *Statistical Yearbook of Iran*, 1976.

[30] E. Ajami (1970) cited in O.I.P.F.G., 1976, p. 47.

[31] Khosravi.

[32] Ibid. Mention should be made that this new form of tenancy was reached by involving a third party as intermediary between the landowner and the peasants. The resulting relationship was completely capitalistic. Peasants became daily wage laborers, and production was made for the market. See O.I.O.F.G., "On the Remains of Feudalism," *Iran: Politics and Revolution, A Theoretical Journal*, 1 (August 1977): 19–47. (The Journal is published by the Eugene Iran Committee).

[33] Khosravi

[34] H. Richards, 1975, 8

[35] Khosravi.

[36] Ibid.

[37] Plan and Budget Organization, *Statistical Yearbook of Iran*, 1976.

[38] Ibid.

[39] Ibid.

[40] Ibid.

[41] Khosravi.

[42] Gharas-Malik orchards were those orchards with lands and waters that were owned by landlords but whose trees were usually planted by peasants. In such cases, peasants and landlords owned orchards jointly. Commonly, landlords owned *arseh* (land, water) while peasants owned *a'yan* (trees, buildings). The orchard output would be divided between the two parties based on the local common practice

[43] Articles 27, 28, of the Land Reform Law.

[44] M. Fischer, *Cultural Survival, Khuzistan*, Unpublished research (second draft) (August 1979) 2.

[45] F. M. Javansheer, *Political Economy, Capitalist Mode of Production* (Tehran: Tudeh Party, n.d.), 120.

[46] Ibid., 120–121.

[47] Fischer, 32.

[48] *Mubarezien Rah Arman Tabaqeh-e Kargar, (An Analysis of the Situation of the Rural Community in Iran)* (Tehran, 1980), 57.

[49] Ibid.

M. R. Shah Pahlavi, The *White Revolution*, 2nd ed. (Tehran: Kayhan Press, 1967), 15.

[51] Ibid, 151

[52] M. R. Shah Pahlavi, 1967, 175.

[53] Ibid., 16.

[54] For details, see F. Holliday, "Iran: The Economic Contradictions," *MERIP Report* no. 69 (1978).

[55] M. R. Shah Pahlavi, 1967.

[56] See Chapter 7 of this study. Khomeini himself was among the religious leaders who openly opposed women's participation in elections. In the 1979 revolution, however, he strongly encouraged women to participate in the revolution, and later, after the fall of the Shah and the formation of the Islamic Republic of Iran, women were allowed to run for the parliament.

[57] Although the main goal of women's freedom was to use their cheap labor in the market, there is no doubt that engaging women in productive activities was a positive outcome and a step forward in development.

[58] M.R. Shah Pahlavi, 1967, 103.

[59] See Chapter 10 of this study.

[60] Ibid., 134.

[61] Ibid., 135.

[62] Plan and Budget Organization, *Statistical Yearbook of Iran*, 1976.

[63] M.R. Shah Pahlavi, *Toward the Great Civilization* (Tehran: Offset Company, 1978), 139

[64] Ibid., 177–8.

[65] There are many reliable sources about corruption in Iran during the Shah's regime. These are samples: *Fortune Magazine,* October 1974; *New York Times,* 4 March 1976; *Herald Tribune,* 4 March 1978; *Le Monde,* 4-5 March 1972; *The Nation,* 12 April 1965 ("The Billion-Dollar Mystery"); *Le Monde Diplomatic,* May 1975; *Newsweek,* no. 16, June 1975.

[66] M. R. Shah Pahlavi, 1978.

[67] At the time of the shah's fall, Iran had a pre-paid deposit of about fourteen billion dollars in international banks. The U.S. government at the time of the hostage crisis seized this deposit. For details, see Mahvash Alerassool, *Freeing Assets: The USA and the Most Effective Economic Sanction* (New York: St. Martin's Press, 1993).

Chapter 9
The Economic, Social, and Political Consequences of Land Reform

The General Results of the Land Reform Program

The outstanding result of land reform in Iran has been abolition of the dominant, out-dated socio-economic system of *muzara'eh* in the countryside. But reform could never have taken place under the manifest factors of the old non-operative order of *buneh* (peasant teamwork or peasant organization) and *nasaq* (peasant cultivating rights). Land reform challenged these two elements. Both *nasaq*, considered as the natural border of distribution, and *buneh*, formed by *nasaq* holders, were marked for dissolution because of the land reform law.

Buneh was replaced first by a new form of teamwork, and then by individual peasant land ownership. The latter form, due to its nature,[1] was doomed to destruction, sooner or later, because of the growing competition between the large (landlords) and small (peasantry) capital holdings. The destruction process took about a decade.

The second indicator—*nasaq*—was dissolved as land distribution took place. Nearly half of the villages' inhabitants, as we have mentioned, were excluded from land distribution since they were non-*nasaq* holders. From the remaining part, 83% held *nasaq* of less than 10 hectares.[2] Due to the poor quality of the soil and especially to the insufficient water in many regions, those peasants who acquired less than 10 hectares could not benefit greatly from land reform. Therefore, only 10% of the peasants really benefited from land distribution.[3] The major portion of the remaining 90%, plus those peasants who received nothing, were faced with two alternatives—to stay in the village and work as agricultural workers, if such work were still available, or to leave the village and seek another job in the city. Indeed, according to Weinbaum, "Land reform hastened the process as large numbers of peasants excluded from the land redistribution chose to become urban rather than rural proletariat. Many other peasants, given title to parcels of land too small to be profitable, sold their property and migrated."[4]

For the growing number of capitalists and their foreign supporters, however, the adopted policy created a new situation with at least three advantages. First, the *muzara'eh* system, as carrier and retainer of the old traditional land holdings, and also as the main obstacle to growth of productive forces, was dissolved because, as Halliday said, "the pre-capitalist landowning class had to be eliminated as such since it constituted an economic and political block to capitalist development and to state control of the countryside."[5] Second, the architects of the Iranian agrarian reform sought to provide a group of well-to-do peasant landholders as the social basis of the government in the countryside. The reform did succeed in creating this minor group (about 10%) as supporters of the regime against the majority of the village inhabitants.

The third outcome of the designed and adopted policy was the releasing of masses of peasants from the land and their traditional relationships, leaving them to serve urban needs. Within a short period, a majority of these people left their villages for the cities, although some of them were hired by the newly built agricultural enterprises in the villages. Thus, a context for capitalist relations developed in both urban and rural areas simultaneously. The process of development in urban areas was rapid because the overwhelming majority of available credit and capital funds were devoted to trade, industry, the financial sector, and construction. The heavy urban investment, especially noticeable after the flow of oil revenue began, caused neglect of the agricultural sector.

However, many domestic and foreign investors (with considerable governmental aid) developed new agricultural firms in the best regions of the country, such as areas beneath the newly constructed dams and those with sufficient rainfall and good soil. These agricultural companies became the basis for the new form of large-scale land holdings. These forms are discussed in detail later in this chapter.

Another consequence of the land reform has been the extension of commodity production into the countryside. This capitalist factor affected agriculture only to a limited extent, although it challenged the self-sufficient consumption in villages.

Following elimination of the *muzara'eh* system and encouragement of landowners to use agricultural machinery, chemical fertilizer, and pesticides, a great market was opened to consumption of these goods. The inauguration of new forms of peasant cooperatives and the availability of manufactured goods to peasants acted as a positive step toward the extension of commodity production. Despite the past, yield was produced largely for supplying urban markets. The peasants' travel back and forth between towns and cities, the migration of young villagers, the penetration of urban culture and standards into the countryside, the constitution of different forms of enterprise and showcase farms, the construction of roads and dams, the growth of wage earning and other monetary relations—all these were factors the villages and villagers had not previously encountered.

The new relations liberated hidden unemployment and labor forces that were remaining idle in the countryside. This manpower that was being exploited by landlords had been dependent upon land and cultivation tools for many years. The new order freed them, letting them go wherever they wanted in order to sell their labor. Some of them were absorbed into the new mechanized agricultural sectors, and the rest went to fill the demands of the new industries in the cities.

The reform program not only encouraged landlords to mechanize their land, but also forced them to do it. As mentioned earlier, one of the exemptions from distribution of land was the mechanization of land. Many landlords were quick to employ such a profitable way to avoid distribution. In addition, a supportive policy of financial and technical aid accelerated the mechanization process.

Another result of the land reform has been the expansion of orchards. Since orchards were one of the exceptions to land distribution, at least in the first ten years, many landowners chose this way to retain their land. For example, many landlords in Rofsanjan developed their land into pistachio orchards, with the result that the total production of pistachio nuts went from 6,000 tons in 1960 to 36,000 tons in 1968. Production of apples and pears increased from 60,000 tons in 1960 to 356,000 tons in 1968, and citrus fruit production rose from 80,000 tons to 254,000 tons during the same period.[6] The second reason for expansion of orchards was an increase in the demand for fruits.

In spite of the expansion of agricultural lands from 11,356,254 hectares to 16,417,221 hectares, mechanization of some parts of the agricultural lands, increased use of chemical fertilizers and pesticides, and provision of technical, financial, and administrative support, Iran has been forced to import agricultural products more and more.[7] According to statistics released by the U.S. Department of Agriculture, Iranian agricultural production fell in the years immediately after the land reform. This is not unusual; many other countries have faced similar problems due to internal changes, but in Iran the small growth of 2.5% in agricultural production has continually run behind the population increase of 3.2%, and food consumption has risen at an average rate of 10% per annum.[8]

Iran before the land reform program could export agricultural products, such as cotton, tobacco, rice, and wheat, and it could thus obtain substantial foreign currency. After the land reform program, it was faced with a food shortage and became a food-importing country. That trend continued so that the total food imports per year had risen to $2.6 billion by 1977.[9] In this connection, the *Christian Science Monitor* wrote: "In 1982, Iran's total food imports will grow to between $4.5 billion and $5 billion from $3.5 billion last year and $2.8 billion in1980."[10]

The main reason for this shortfall in output was the basic policy behind agriculture—that is, the government policy of importing agricultural products rather than supporting the peasant to make Iran a self-sufficient country. Based on that policy, $1.5 billion annually was spent to subsidize the difference between cost and selling price in order to keep the prices of domestic products lower than current market prices.[11] The purposes behind this policy were two: (1) in order to neutralize the potential for revolt, the government wanted to keep the prices of food low and affordable to low-income families; and (2) importing goods was a profitable business for some people in the government. Overall, this policy damaged the agriculture sector.

The dependency policy worked as follows. Financial and technical aid were put behind wealthy foreign or domestic landlords while small peasants were ignored. The most profitable lands were centralized and placed in the control of a handful of capitalists. As a consequence, five million peasants were forced to migrate to cities in a ten-year period.[12] This was about 1/7 of the total population of the country.

There seems little doubt that under this policy the huge oil revenues have played, even in the historical dimension, a negative role in the success of agriculture. It is true that while many countries have not been able to improve their agriculture due to a shortage of financial resources, Iran could not improve its agriculture—at least partially—*because* of the extra available money. Under this policy, the government devoted $2.5 billion to import its needed food, whereas the total credits for agricultural development during the Fifth Plan (1972–78) was 266.85 billion rials ($762 million annually), or about 2/7 of what was spent to import food in 1977.[13] If one adds the $1.5 billion related to the differential between the buying price and the selling price of imported foods, the total of annual credits for agricultural development represented only one-fifth of the importing expense. It is no surprise that, in terms of both the value and the volume of imported food, the United States held the superior position, as was the case in the other sectors of the economy.[14] Although historically the geographical factors were the main causes of the shortage of food, during this period it was political and economic factors that kept Iranian agriculture in backwardness. One may argue that the financial support from oil could have allowed Iran to meet its agricultural needs by importing, which would, in turn, have allowed the country to spend the capital in industrial development. Lack of sufficient infrastructures such as ports, roads, and bridges, however, showed that the government was not truly concerned about real development in Iran. Therefore, the oil revenue was mainly spent wherever the people in the government could financially benefit.

The New Capitalist Form of Large-Scale Landholding

The first stage of the land reform, as we have said, challenged the traditional large-scale land holdings by providing for mechanized lands, wage-paid cultivation, and a capitalist form of relations. But if the first stage was challenging, the second—and especially the third—stages deliberately facilitated the achievement of this goal. It was near the end of the second stage and throughout the third stage that the government, lawfully, promoted a new form of capitalist landholding by providing financial and technical aid, almost gratuitously, to investors. Therefore, different agricultural arrangements using different names but with similar natures appeared. The following introduces some of them.

1. Joint-Stock Agricultural Companies[15]

In February 1968, six years after the beginning of the land reform program, the newly formed Ministry of Land Reform and Rural Cooperation announced the constitution of joint-stock agricultural companies (JSACs). The Majlis (parliament) ratified the bill related to this form of agribusiness company. According to this law, the government was authorized to form mechanized farm cooperatives through collection of the lands of peasants in each region. It also specified that constitution of any companies must be preceded by the written request of the peasants of a region. However, regardless of peasants' demands, the government chose some of the best areas for such purposes.

The stated objectives of this expensive project were (1) to mechanize and expand the scale of agricultural operations, (2) to introduce modern methods of cultivation to peasants, (3) to increase usage of manpower in both agriculture and industry, (4) to extend cultivation into barren and dead lands, and (5) to stop the fragmentation of lands into small portions, which had been common after the land distribution, or any division due to death.[16]

These objectives were announced following the visit of some government officials from kibbutzim in Israel and collective farms in Eastern Europe and the Soviet Union. Apparently, the Iranian government was seeking to use some experiences of both socialist and capitalist countries on its own land. However, despite spending millions of dollars for this project, the result was unsuccessful.[17]

One of the reasons for the lack of success of this project is the fact that in spite of the basic support needs of millions of poor, landless peasants, these companies were established in areas where peasants were already doing well in terms of the amount of land held, and in the regions that had the best fertility of soil and supply of water. If the government had really intended to improve the conditions of peasants and to increase agricultural output, these supports should have gone to small holders and should have made barren lands available to landless peasants. Not only did such provisions not cover poor and landless peasants, but there was also some limitation for peasants wishing to be members of these companies.

Membership was legally confined to peasants who had acquired land during the first and second stages of the land reform, either through purchase or division. Landlords, without exception, could participate in such a company, no matter whether they were absentee landowners, their lands had been exempted from distribution, or they were not even involved in agricultural activities. Cultivators of plantations and orchards whose property had not been affected by the first two phases of land reform were included. That was the legal appearance; in practice the government acted as it preferred. For example, according to law the constitution of each JSAC was dependent upon the written request of the peasants and 51% of their votes. Despite some governmental aid, peasants opposed entering JSACs, mainly because they wanted to remain independent landowners and not be controlled by the government. However, the government did not respect the peasants' wishes, forming JSACs at any place where the government decided to do so.[18] In some cases, when the peasants resisted the creation of a JSAC on their land, the government threatened them. It seems that peasants felt that it was a way to expel them from their lands. Despite such resistance, in the first year the government was able to create 15 companies throughout the country.[19]

The government led management of these companies, although sometimes regulations were passed to the contrary. According to the law, a JSAC's actions were to be managed by its General Assembly at annual meetings and by its Board of Directors during the year. The General Assembly, which consisted of all shareholders, was to elect three members to the Board of Directors. In addition, the officer of the Reconstruction and Development Corps (*afsar sepahi-i tarvij va abadani*) and the teacher of the Literacy Corps (*sepahi-i danesh*) or the principal of the village school would be members of the Board of Directors.[20]The government paid all of these persons. However, although legally the General Assembly and the Board of Directors were responsible for making decisions, it was, according to Richards, the government-selected manager who "usually made most of the decisions."[21]

In addition, a JSAC has a professional bookkeeper, a few accountants, livestock and agricultural specialists, a few *sepahi-i tarvij va abadani* "inspectors," and various technical personnel whose salaries are all paid by the government.[22]

Peasants received shares based on the value of the holdings (including land and any other properties) that each had placed at the disposition of the company. The official personnel of the Ministry of Land Reform and Rural Cooperation estimated the value of land or other properties. In addition to their shares from the yield, peasants could be hired as wage-paid laborers and receive a monthly payment. Those with special skills like tractor driving had more opportunities to receive higher wages, but due to the increasing use of machinery many peasants who had previously been cultivating lands of the company lost their jobs and were forced to seek other employment in the village.

Thus, the revenue to shareholder peasants came from two sources—their labor wages and their divided shares. In the case of a loss, the shareholder peasants lost part of their income. According to various studies, most of these companies lost money. For example, according to Field, "In 1971, one corporation in Western Iran lost 50% of its village."[23] A study by O.I.P.F.G. showed that the benefits to the shareholder peasants were less than their income prior to the formation of JSAC.[24] And M. R. Soudagar summarized: "According to the available information, most of these companies have incurred loss."[25] He continued: "The main reason could be found in mismanagement and taking advantage of the properties of the company by its Board of Directors."[26]

However, a JSAC was a privilege for those landlords who participated with large amounts of land and other properties in their companies, because the government spent considerable money to create good showcases as signs of the success of the land reform program. The government provided these companies with new housing complexes, schools, clinics, public baths, mosques, and the like. These and other facilities were provided just for the use of the shareholders. But the small shareholder, due either to losses of the company or to further regulations such as minimum permissive landholding in the company—in one case, 40 hectares of non-irrigated land and 20 hectares of irrigated land—was forced to leave the company. Virtually all of the provided facilities under the name of peasants remained for landlords.

The high expenditures for these companies meant that government could not establish them in large numbers. The total number of such companies throughout the country reached 89 by 1980.[27]

According to available information, the total number of JSACs by 1974 had reached 65 units. This number included 525 *mazra'eh* (hamlets). The amount of land under the control of these companies was 258,162 hectares, with only 87,012 hectares under cultivation. The total shares of all these companies were 306,950, controlled by 22,778 shareholders, including the government. It should be compared with the 199,366 persons who resided in these areas.[28]This differentiation shows that many people residing on the domain of these companies were apparently ignored. (See Table 13.)

It is notable that between 1973 and 1978—i.e., the period of the Fifth Development Plan—only 34 units of JSAC were built. More than 48 billion rials (or about 13% of the total agricultural credits) had been devoted to development of these companies.[29] While Iran had about 60,000 villages, these companies covered only about 600 villages and farms—one percent of the total existing villages. There is no doubt that these villages were chosen from among the best land areas, which likely were not in serious financial need, while thousands of villages and their inhabitants needed just a water supply or another basic item. The aim of this wrong-headed policy will be clear when we study how these credits were spent, and for what, below. In order to get a clear idea of this type of agricultural company, the first established unit will be reviewed as a case study. It was named the Aryamehr Joint-Stock

Agricultural Company, and it has been one of the best showcase farms. Its name is one of the shah's titles of honor, and it is located close to the tourist area of Persepolis, in Shams-abaab in the Fars province.[30] The area consists of two villages and one hamlet, with a total population of 862 persons (427 men and 435 women) in 150 peasant families. Out of the 150 peasant families, 80 had been *nasaq* holders who were able to receive land during the land reform program. The 70 remaining families were *Khwush-neshin* (village inhabitants who were neither landowners nor *nasaq* holders), so they received no land. Thus, the company got its farm with both landholders and government help.[31]

Table 13: Individuals' Shares Plus Those of Government

Status of Joint-Stock	Agricultural Companies		1347–1352		(1968–1973)	
Description	1347	1348	1349	1350	1351	1352
Number of farm corporations	15	20	19	27	43	65
Number of villages and farms falling within	80	109	109	157	217	525
Areas within the boundaries of corporations (hectares)	60,789	82,519	82,519	109,077	191,777	258,162
Land area (hectares)	58,139	77,653	77,653	99,450	169,863	231,759
Area under cultivation when corporations were established (hectares)	13,770	19,271	19,271	28,468	53,215	13,770
Usable water when corporations were established (liters per second)	9,377	10,726	10,726	18,828	39,069	9,377
Cultivation program in this year (hectares)	...	...	...	...	...	87,012
Population covered (persons)	43,171	54,996	54,996	76,921	134,313	196,366
Shareholders (persons)	24,429	33,241	33,241	47,489	81,375	123,881
Number of shareholders (individuals)	4,698	6,169	6,169	8,689	15,250	22,778
Government	1	1	1	1	1	1
Number of shares: (thousands of individuals)	161,143	228,141	228,141	342,221	640,922	306,950*
Government	36,770	40,648	40,648	40,847	44,012	...
Nominal value of capital shares (million rials)	198	269	269	383	685	992
Credits: Subsidies (million rials)	214	230	173	343	...	...

Table 13: Individuals' Shares Plus Those of Government

Status of Joint-Stock	Agricultural Companies 1347–1352 (1968–1973)					
Description	1347	1348	1349	1350	1351	1352
Loans (million rials)	69	70	73	106	...	...
Repayment of Loans (million rials)	...	...	...	66	...	...
Gross Revenues (million rials)	...	...	...	496	797	1,767
Expenditures (million rials)	...	...	...	312	522	1,065
Net Profit (million rials)	...	...	...	185	275	702
Reserves: Depreciation reserves (million rials)	...	...	...	110	167	274
Other reserves (million rials)	...	...	...	108	185	556

Note: In 1970, two JSACs in Lower and Upper Nim Bloc, Birjand were merged under the name of Shahabad-e-Qaenat JSAC.

-Area of lands of JSAC has partly been calculated through survey of the lands and partly through estimation.

-Repayment of loans comprises total amounts repaid up to and including 1971.

-Twelve JSAC were established before 1971.

Source: Ministry of Co-operatives and Rural Affairs, released by Plan and Budget Organization, *Statistical Yearbook, 1976.*

The government has spent much to provide facilities for both the company and the shareholders. It built 80 units of houses for residences of the shareholder peasants, each with two rooms, one storage area, a shower, a kitchen, and a washroom. The residences also came with electricity and piped-in water. The government faced difficulties in transferring village families into the newly built houses because peasants did not know how to raise and keep their animals in the new places. In addition, the government constructed two schools, two public baths, one clinic, one mosque, one nursery center, one cultural center containing a library, and one conversation room with a TV set. For the government officials, the government built four special houses, an office for the Board of Directors of the company, a house for residence of the Reconstruction and Development Corps representative, a working area, a stable, barns, and a repair shop. In addition, the company was furnished with different types of agricultural machinery such as tractors, earth-tilling discs, jeeps, a truck, combines, cultivators, motorcycles, and the like. Drainage ditches were also constructed.

Despite all of this spending for the company and the availability of the services of agricultural specialists, the average per capita peasant income for the first year was about $150.[32] This was equal to the one-month income of a teacher. Although in comparison with many other villages this amount seems high, when we consider the amount of land for each peasant—20 hectares of high-quality land in this company—it is quite low. It must also be noted that unlike the other regions, peasants in this area had been able to own about 20 hectares of land each.[33]

Such large holdings of land have not been usual in other JSACs. Since the companies had been instituted to create a group of well-to-do peasants, the government passed a law indicating that shareholders in JSACs must keep up their irrigated land.[34] That meant that the typical shareholder peasants, whose holdings had been less than 10 hectares, had no choice but to give up his share to larger landholders and remain as wage earners in the enterprise.

Therefore, we conclude that these plans were designed to change even those to whom some land was transferred into wage-paid agricultural workers and to support middle-range landholders as the social basis for the regimes in the villages. It is also clear that all of the technical and financial support of the government benefited the landlords and the newly created middle-range land-holders, not the poor peasants. In addition, creation of these mechanized companies created many "jobless" peasants and, consequently, further migration to the cities. Finally, however, establishment of such agricultural enterprises increased rural-urban relations, which meant expansion of monetary relations and the consumption of industrial products.

2. Agro-Industrial Companies

When the second stage of the land reform was apparently almost completed and the third stage was at its beginning step (1967), a bill relating to formation of agro-industrial companies was ratified by *Majlis*. According to this law, the areas beneath dams, which are among the best agricultural lands, were subjected to rent for both eligible domestic and foreign investors. In addition, the government itself was permitted to participate in these companies. However, like other sorts of agricultural companies, the government's usual share was to provide necessities and give different forms of aid. In this context, apart from direct aid, the government provided some infrastructural programs like road construction and provision of electricity. Specifically, two governmental ministries were authorized to undertake these tasks. Richards has written:

> Their industrial half, if any, falls under the supervision of the Ministry of Economy, and the agro half under the Ministry of Water and Power, which provides canals for units over 100 hectares and roads for units over 1,000 hectares. The rest, including minor canalization and the employment of labourers, is left to the companies under a 30-year lease. Their shares may be bought by foreign companies as well as by Iranians.[35]

In order to establish such companies, indigenous peasants lost their land as the project continued to expand. As we have said, for example, 38,000 peasant families were expelled from their homes in the project under the Dez dam in Khuzistan province.[36]

According to available statistics, the 213 units of such agro-industrial forms were established within a domain of 238,000 hectares of land.[37] Seven units of this number, with 134,000 hectares of land, were controlled completely by the government, and 202 units were given to the private sector.[38] Some of them were run by internal and some by external agribusiness, while some were under mixed investment. For instance, mixed companies owned 61,000 hectares of the area beneath the Dez dam. Table 15 shows the agro-industrial companies involved under the Dez irrigation project.

These companies have been the most profitable agricultural units in Iran. They usually have received large loans with low interest.[39] For example, Hashem Naraqi, who held 51% of the shares of Agro-

Industries of Iran and America under the Dez irrigation project, with more than 20,000 hectares of land, earned millions of dollars annually. Naraqi, an Iranian capitalist who resides in the United States, invested only $15 million in the first private agro-industrial company in Khuzistan province. His American representative in Iran in 1970 said, "We will be able to gain 160 million *tomans* (roughly about $23 million) from only the exportation of alfalfa per annum."[40] In contrast, Critchfield has written: "All the villagers got progressively in debt as Khuzistan was modernized, so badly in debt that when KWPA (Khuzistan Water and Power Authority) came to buy their lands, the net gain of the villagers was almost nothing."[41]

Of course, alfalfa was not the only product of his company. It was producing several other products, such as asparagus, for export, because Iranian people were not familiar with that vegetable. Indeed, these companies mainly produced for foreign markets, whereas at the same time Iran imported several billion dollars worth of agricultural and livestock products annually, including wheat, rice, barley, corn, sugar, meat, oil, and eggs.[42]

In addition to direct investment, many foreign capitalists were able to invest in different areas related to the agricultural plan. For example, in dam construction for the creation of electric power, in the building of irrigation systems, and of course in the selling of agricultural machinery, various foreign corporations earned huge profits. However, some of these agro-industrial companies pulled out after they got what they wanted and after experiencing what the biggest shareholder (Naraqi) called "creeping nationalization."[43]

Alongside these private agro-industries, some government-owned companies like the Haft Tapeh Sugar-Cane Project that was producing for domestic consumption were built and developed. However, they were controlled by capitalist-bureaucrats and benefited the whole ruling class.

3. Farm Corporation

The farm corporation was another form of large-scale landholding after the land reform. Some former landlords and a minor group of selected elites extended their capital into the agricultural sector. Some high-ranking officials relied on their official status (with different tricks such as making false documents, purchasing land cheaply, or even using force) to expel peasants from their lands. Others had been given barren lands, using large, government–sponsored, low-interest loans to irrigate lands through sinking deep wells. They frequently used their official authority in order to construct roads and provide electricity at the expense of the state for their private lands. Some military officials have even used soldiers as free farm workers on their lands.

Among the owners of corporations were several members of the Royal family, and military generals.[44] In addition, several ministers, ex-ministers, and senators occupied lands in one of the most fertile regions of the country, Dasht-i Gonbad.[45] The shah's brothers and sisters had special status permitting them to own several thousand hectares of land in the southern and eastern parts of the area near the Caspian Sea, where most of the Crown land was located. For example, two of the shah's brothers, including Pars Shah, Kian Shah, and Dasht-i Naz, owned several farm and livestock corporations, and the shah's nephew owned the Sherkat-i Omran-i Rustae-i. Sherkat-i Sahami-i Alah Abaad belonged to General Riyahie, the shah's minister of agriculture during the second phase of the land reform, and Sherkat-i Sahami-i qand-i Dizful belonged to a deputy minister of the Court.[46]

The Tehran Economist, an Iranian pro-shah journal, in praising one of these agro-businessmen (the shah's brother, who owned some of these farms, including Dasht i-Naz with its 3,700 hectares of land[47]), wrote: "The prince, who is an economist, a scholar, an unparalleled hunter, a toiling farmer, and a perfect human...,"[48] had "20 tractors, 9 combines, 13 trucks, 80 pieces of light and heavy agricultural equipment, 6 silos, and 2 live-stocks."[49]

Existing large-scale units of farm corporations show better the aims of the land reform program. The owners of these corporations, expecting their political influence to gain them such favors as large loans with low interest rates, obtained exemptions for their businesses from any kind of taxes.[50] For example, while peasants were fortunate to receive a few thousand rials as a loan (7,000 R = $100), and then with numerous difficulties,[51] landlords had not only been given different types of government support but were also able to receive loans of at least five million rials in 1970.[52]

To grant such loans to this type of corporation, two banks were used: (1) The Agricultural Development Bank of Iran that was established during the Fourth Plan (1968–72) for loans above one million rials, and (2) The Agricultural Cooperative Bank of Iran, which granted loans below 500,000 rials.[53] Peasants were not able to request loans from these banks. The Rural Cooperative Societies had been developed for peasants' loans, but peasants could not borrow unless they first became members of these cooperatives. In order to do so, they had to buy shares in such a cooperative; then each peasant was eligible to receive about five times the amount of his shares as a loan.[54]

If he had the ability to purchase ten shares of cooperative holding, he became eligible to borrow about $50.

Changes in Social Stratification

The land reform program sharply changed social stratification in both rural and urban areas—among the peasants, the major social group, but also among the landowners and even among the "national bourgeoisie" and petty bourgeoisie—which altered the between- and within-class structures in both the ruling and the ruled sectors. Following these changes, some of the old classes and strata were eliminated and some new ones appeared.

After the elimination of the *muzara'eh* system, polarization within social classes began. On one side, many landlords, some voluntarily and others by force, were paid for their lands and invested the money in recommended urban activities. Still other landlords, who remained as absentee landlords, changed their relationships with the peasants. Some of them became new large-scale rental landlords in the villages.[55] However, many of them gradually realized that in the newly created context of economic activities urban markets were more profitable; hence, they preferred to be urban capitalists rather than rural ones. As a result, the old traditional landlordism was mostly broken into two sections, urban and rural capitalism. In addition to these groups, some of the landlords who were able to retain their lands through the exemptions of the land reform continued exploitation of peasants based on the old *muzara'eh* system. Many landlords who owned orchards or tea plantations were in this category. Some peasants under the pressure of poverty were forced to accept whatever agreement the landlords proposed, and many landlords in areas with poor soil and insufficient water preferred to continue the *muzara'eh* agreement, and they did so.

In addition to the already-mentioned groups and strata, another group was created by the reform—the water sellers, who had not owned agricultural land but who controlled the water supply. This group controlled certain water sources either through *qanats* or by sinking deep wells on their properties and selling the water to whomever wanted it.

The land reform program, nonetheless, affected those people who either did not own any land or owned very small amounts. In general, before implementation of reform, peasants were divided into two large categories: those who worked as agricultural workers and who owned nothing, and those who owned something. If the first group constituted almost a homogeneous group, the latter group included a range of socioeconomic statuses. While the members of the "upper" group usually owned enough land to support their families, the members of the "lower" group—the major part of this social stratum—owned only small plots that did not even cover living expenses.

To summarize, land reform pushed the landless peasants into becoming semi-urban and rural proletarians. They constituted almost half of the village populations. A small fraction of those who owned or acquired land during the land reform (about 10% of the rural population), who were satisfied with the reform, created the stratum of "better-off" peasants, loyal to the shah's regime. The residual groups, however, were unsatisfied with the shah's reforms; many of them lost whatever they had acquired during the land distribution and out of necessity joined the rural and urban wage earners.

In cities, the millions of rural exodus peasants joined the existing urban proletariat to supply the labor force needed for the new, growing, imposed capitalism. On the other hand, the rush of foreign and domestic investment into various economic sectors created an organized, strong capitalist class. With such changes, the traditional small bazaar capitalists and the wide-ranging petty bourgeoisie were bound to become polarized sooner or later. Under the circumstances, these groups faced two alternatives—to retain and associate themselves with the growing capitalist ranks or to side with and join the deprived classes. On the one hand, the small bazaar capitalists were able to join other factions of the ruling class, whereas the petty bourgeoisie was polarized into two sections: (1) the better-off petty bourgeoisie who benefited from the new consumption emanating from the development of dependent capitalism and who consequently supported the new capitalist relations, and (2) the lower—and of course the major—part of the petty bourgeoisie, who urged retention of traditional relations because they had lost whatever they had previously owned due to the new capitalist production relations. The latter group must be regarded as dissidents against the new order.[56] In fact, because of its life-or-death situation, this group played an important role in the overthrow of the shah's regime. Its traditional culture was an identity that mobilized the traditional population of the society. This cultural conflict will be discussed in the next chapter.

Growth in the General Awareness of the Villagers

At the very beginning of the land reform, the Iranian government decided to mobilize peasants to serve the government's purposes by implementing a propaganda campaign concerning its "revolutionary" decisions. By such a maneuver, the government made the peasants aware of their rights against landlords, and that is why, in many regions, peasants who had believed the government's promises not only refused to pay the landlords' shares of crops but also kicked them out of the villages. However, according to the O.I.P.F.G., "the gendarmerie's bayonets soon taught them that the government was not behind them."[57] They saw that the government took the landlords' side in almost any disputed case. Such behavior and decisions, along with other measures related to the land reform, had a number of significant effects on the peasants' minds.

First, and foremost, the villagers became disillusioned about the concept of ownership. In the past, especially, an alleged religious principle that ownership was holy was used to prevent peasants from confiscating land. Second, during the process of implementation of the land reform program, peasants who had never been involved in any kind of official affairs were involved with different arms of the government and soon realized that corruption dominated the entire system.

It was through processes similar to this that peasants found the links between the government and the landlords and realized that one could not trust the government. Thereafter, it was government officials who came to the village, asking peasants to pay their debts or to do this or that—not the landlords or their agents. In other words, the peasants truly came face to face with the government. Now, the bank agent replaced the moneylender. Almost all peasants were indebted to a bank, and now they were exposed to the nature of banks personally.

In addition, the peasants now were acquainted with towns, the use of modern equipment, the expansion of money relations, and the consumption of manufactured goods, and all of these things further widened the peasants' sights. Now, they were gradually realizing that the world was not confined to their villages and that there were things behind the mountains that could reach them.

The Relationship Between the Land Reform and the 1979 Revolution

Introduction

The shah's land reform program, of course, was not the direct cause of the 1979 insurrection, but both positive and negative aspects of the program played their roles, along with other factors. The intention here is not to analyze the 1979 Revolution. This historical socioeconomic, political, and ideological subject requires much deep study.[58] But considering both objective and subjective conditions following the land reform program, some socioeconomic consequences of the project can be considered as contributing in direct and material ways to the people's uprising in 1979. In the relationship between the land reform program and the 1979 uprising, three results will be considered briefly: migration, the expansion of slums, and the bankruptcy of agriculture. It was through these processes that the issues that prompted rural revolt were transferred to political, cultural, and ideological causes in urban areas, where the first popular demonstrations and mass violent uprisings took place. In other words, the rural economic failures fed the urban political revolts.

Migration

Historically, migration is a direct consequence of industrialization and modernization. During the 1960s, Iran was among many developing societies adapting to imported and imposed modernization without political reform. Therefore, migration from rural areas to cities happened in Iran regardless of the nature of the land reform. In general, migration takes place because of both "push" and –"pull" factors. In this case, the push factor includes the shortage of land or jobs in rural areas, and the pull factor includes the availability of jobs and attractions in the cities. However, a correct policy might have reduced the negative outcomes of pushed migration. In particular, migration could have been predicted as the government began the implementation of the land reform program.

Land reform was the cornerstone of the economic reform, or modernization, in Iran. As we have said, land reform in action ignored the majority of poor and landless peasants. It was indeed a land distribution for those peasants who had already owned some land or who had specific rights (cultivation rights) over agricultural land under the old *muzara'eh* system. But the ignored peasants were faced with the choice of finding jobs in the village and working as agricultural laborers, if such jobs could be found, or leaving the village in search of work in the cities. The cause of the migration of this group was absolutely economic. These mostly young villagers were ready for any work, wherever it was to be had, to ensure subsistence for their families.

Thus, migration of the rural population to the cities was a direct socioeconomic effect of land reform. Rural exodus can be considered a consequent phenomenon of the growth and development of capitalism as a whole and of the mechanization of agriculture in particular. But migration from Iranian villages to cities also had its unique rationale— namely, the standards of distribution of land, which created a group of more than a million peasants who held no land (or excessively small amounts), the domination of an open-door importing policy, a high differentiation between rural and urban wages, and a government policy of supporting landowners rather than small landholders. According to available information, the boom of migration began a few years after the beginning of land reform implementation with both landless peasants and those who owned only a few hectares of land. Sixty percent of peasants who owned less than 1.5 hectares and 27% of those who owned more than 4 hectares migrated to cities.[59] To these should be added 66% of migrated *Khwush-neshin* (landless cultivators and non-cultivators).[60]

Water in many regions of Iran is more important than land itself, because land without a water supply is worth nothing. This was especially true when irrigation used to be by *qanats* (underground canals). Thus, if for any reason the water source to a piece of land dried up, no matter how large the piece of land, it became worthless. "Drying up" was a method allegedly used by landlords to expel peasants from their lands. For example, in some parts of the plateau, according to Lambton, "the landowner, in order to cultivate the land he retained more intensively, might sink a deep or semi-deep well (perfectly legally) in his land, which might dry up the *qanats* that watered the land kept by the peasants."[61] In one reported case, the landowner dried up the water source, absolutely intentionally, by filling up the *qanat* with ballast carried in by truck.[62] In such cases, peasants had to purchase water for their lands from their landlords or sink a well. Neither alternative was possible for many peasants, and thus their only option was to forget the land and dispose of it to a person willing to undertake the peasant's debts.

Through this practice, many *Khwush-neshin* found themselves dispossessed of whatever they had. Some small landholders had gone bankrupt through competition with larger landowners, and much against their personal desires they inevitably left their homes for the cities. Simultaneously, the high demand for laborers in the cities, especially in the service sector, together with urban privileges on one side and low income in villages in miserable living conditions on the other, led many peasants—even some who owned more than 4 hectares of land—to migrate to the cities. Consequently, migration was rooted in both the urban and rural economies.

Migration rose under a two-headed policy—first, to support the newly built modern, mechanized farm companies that were producing either the basic materials for industry (oil seeds, cotton) or exporting yields (alfalfa, asparagus); and second, to import those agricultural products of which Iran traditionally had had enough to export (wheat, barley, rice). With inflation, the prices of most goods rose, but the prices of domestically produced grains remained remarkably low. This remained true even as wage rates increased to three or four times their earlier level. In many cases, the cost of the labor to reap the harvest was higher than the total revenue from selling the yield. In such circumstances, many peasants preferred to be urban workers rather than (so-called) rural owners.

Official statistics released in 1976 show that "in the past decade, 1966–1975, some five million rural inhabitants have moved to towns and cities."[63] This number was more than one fourth of the rural population. (Compare it with the country's total population—33.5 million in 1975.) Of course, this figure does not show the number of migrants during the five-year period immediately following the beginning of land reform, nor the years of continuous migration after 1975.

The migrated population carried within itself the characteristics of village life, such as poverty, illiteracy, religiosity, traditionalism, and naivety. This process can be called the peasantation of the cities. In the new situation, migrated peasants found themselves at odds with the city culture, so they settled outside the cities in economically and socially deprived areas. This made them the potential targets of manipulation by others, especially clerics whom they knew well from the past. The cities were in process of being "modernized" or Westernized, creating cultural conflict that left millions behind with their traditions—a situation ripe for the growth of political Islam. Many of these people became the foot soldiers of the revolution.

Expansion of Slums

The overwhelming majority of these migrated peasants settled in the slums constructed in the large cities, forming a destitute and under-employed proletariat.[64] Being impoverished, they would necessarily settle in the poorest and most densely populated sections of towns or outside cities where there were no basic services or facilities of urban life (running water, electricity, schools, public baths, medical centers, etc.). This was not surprising, since these migrants had left situations no better in the rural areas, but it led to new districts characterized by very small, old-fashioned houses constructed of junk materials, tin cans, or mats, and by mud huts and tents. The people of these communities usually worked in the cities, traveling back and forth daily, and they were mostly male and young. Married men often left their families in the villages for a time in order to find employment. Young boys who had grown up in the villages but who had no chance to work on the land after the destruction of *buneh* (teamwork) joined the "out-cities" groups. The existence of these groups was essential for the growth and development of the kind of capitalism being created in Iran, and the capitalist apparatus benefited considerably from the migration of these people to the industrial cities.

Thus, as an immediate result of the "White Revolution," the migrants created a great semi-urban proletariat with great revolutionary potential. They shook the foundations of the shah's regime in 1979 with a massive insurrection, integrating themselves into the city fabrics by joining the revolution.

The rural "transplants" became engaged mostly in construction work and in the service sector. Many former landlords, having heavy investments in construction and services, realized high levels of return. Statistics show that as many as a million of the young male construction and service workers became jobless, again, when these sections of capitalist activities were shut down due to the overthrow of the shah's regime. These people were among the most unfortunate groups in the society during the former regime. The slums continue to exist.

The Malfunction of Agriculture

Migration did not occur accidentally, as we have seen. It arose, at least partly, because of an increasing need for a massive, liberated labor force. Thus, in spite of difficulties, the new rural liberated labor force was absorbed into the urban capitalist market just after the beginning of the land reform program. This process was aided by the increment in oil prices and the consequent growth of deposits of foreign currencies, as well as by the growth in the volume of money in the Iranian market as boom conditions altered the existing situation. In addition, many foreigners at varying levels of skill and education were invited to participate in the dependent capitalist "honeymoon" that had arrived. Several thousand foreign companies became involved in the Iranian economy.[65] The invitation included military, economic, and political advisers from the most advanced capitalist countries, including the United States, Japan, Germany, England, France, and Italy, but also some of the surplus unemployed labor forces from the world's capitalist peripheries such as the Philippines, Thailand, Pakistan, and India.

There was no rational plan to use the huge oil revenue to improve the economy. Oil revenue was mainly distributed to foreign interests and among a tiny portion of the ruling class, including the high-ranking military and civil officials. The inevitable consequence of such distribution of money, at different levels, was high inflation and a large gap between haves and have-nots.

In such circumstances, nobody seemed to care about keeping the agricultural sector productive unless high profits were guaranteed. There seemed to be enough foreign currency to import anything, including agricultural goods. Wheat, rice, corn, barley, vegetable oil, meat, dairy products, and various industrial goods were being imported, even at several times the domestic production costs. The government devoted billions of dollars of its oil revenue to the purchase of agricultural products from abroad, at high prices, selling them to consumers at lower prices in order to keep prices down. More peasants who were still cultivating wheat, barley, etc., concluded that it was better to let the land lie fallow, go to the cities, and become wage earners—or, if they had any cash in hand, to create a small business.[66]

Although the growth of trading, construction, and service sector activities developed because of the dominant open-door import policy, the resulting inflation became especially damaging when the entire capitalist world faced increasing inflation.

A tiny group headed by the royal family, and especially by the shah himself, monopolized not only political affairs, but also economic activities. Trade was one of the most lucrative and convenient activities under the prevailing import policy and the increasingly unreliable situation because, unlike in other sectors, there was no need to invest in fixed capital such as land, buildings, or machinery. Thus, everything could be transferred into money and credits rapidly, in case of a need for flight. Moreover, there was no need to face workers' unrest and less risk of nationalization.

Thus, no one was interested in agricultural business unless he had considerable government technical and financial aid. As we have learned, this support was limited to mechanized enterprises. Even those small landholders to whom land was transferred through the reform program had very little chance to survive against the competition of joint-stock agricultural companies, agro-industrial companies, and farm corporations, which enjoyed the government financial aid. In addition, as we have mentioned, in order to keep prices of agricultural goods low under its open-door import policy, the government appropriated $1.5 billion annually to make up the difference between the import and consumption prices. Thus, the costs of domestic agricultural production were higher than existing prices in the market.[67] It seems a fair conclusion that both peasants and agriculture were forgotten.

The bankruptcy of agriculture had one simple result: the migration of villagers to the cities. But if peasants had not made trouble for the government in the countryside, they created the potential of a nucleus of opposition in the cities, where they were absorbed by the capitalist economy. Because many of these rural migrants were young and active—almost 45% were between the ages of 15 and 35 years[68]—they were especially affected by the contradictions of their new environment.

The new economic environment received great benefits from migrants while giving them very little. Although the government tried to keep down the prices of bread, cheese, sugar, tea, etc. (fundamental staples of subsistence for poor people) by devoting extra budgetary resources to them, the needs and demands of these former agricultural workers were changed to correspond to their new material conditions in the cities. As discussed earlier, the urban environment also changed their attitudes toward life and brought them political awareness. The government was not in a position to reply to their growing needs; quite to the contrary, it continually oppressed them.

Agriculture eventually suffered virtual bankruptcy. The former rural workers, now in the cities, saw the gap between themselves and the rich continue to widen, and their revolutionary potential developed. Occasional skirmishes against the government—for example, when the workers' junk-made houses were bulldozed—increased. And when the political conflict deepened, when the objections of intellectuals and depressed petty bourgeoisie alike were openly stated, and when the religious factor and the Carter Doctrine as applied to Iran came to the fore, the former agricultural workers participated as the pioneers and the active stratum in the anti-shah movement of 1978–9.

[1] J. Safi-Nejad, *Buneh (The Systems of Cumulative Farming) Before and After Land Reform* (Tehran: Tous Press, 1975), 171–189.

[2] Kh. Khosravi, *Masa'leh-i dihqani va Masa'leh-i Arzi dar Iran (Peasants' Questions and Land Questions in Iran, (n.p. 1980)*.

[3] M.R. Soudagar, *A Study of the Iranian Land Reform (1961–66)* (Tehran: Institute for Social and Economic Research, 1979).

[4] M.G. Weinbaum, "Agricultural Policy and Development Politics in Iran," *The Middle East Journal* 31, no. 4 (Fall 1977): 453.

[5] F. Halliday, *Iran: Dictatorship and Development* (London: Penguin Books, 1979), 133

[6] O.I.P.F.G. (Organization of Iranian People's Fedaian Guerrillas), *Land Reform and its Direct Effects in Iran* (London: Iran Committee, January 1976).

[7] Khosravi.

[8] M. Fischer, "Cultural Survival, Khuzistan" (Unpublished research, second draft, August 1979).

[9] F. Halliday.

[10] *The Christian Science Monitor*, 10 January 1982.

[11] M. Kayhan, "Rural Community of Iran: On the Eve of the Land Reform," *Donya, Political and Theoretical Organ of the Central Committee of the Tudeh Party of Iran*, no. 12, March 1977, pp. 42–52.

[12] Echo of Iran, *Iran Almanac, A Book of Facts*, 1976.

[13] Plan and Budget Organization of Iran, *The Fifth Development Plan*, 1973–78.

[14] M. Weinbaum writes: "In value terms, the United States holds the position of major supplier. Imports from the U.S. in 1974-75 amounted to 656.2 million dollars, or just about half the value of all Iran's agricultural imports. In that year, the U.S. furnished some 87 per cent of the total grains and cereals purchased abroad and almost 70 per cent of animal and vegetable fats and oil." *The Middle East Journal* 31, no. 4 (Fall 1977): 455.) Also see the journal *The Middle East and Africa*, 1970–78.

[15] Joint-Stock Agricultural Companies (JSAC) differ from the Joint-Stock Agricultural Units (JSAU) discussed in an earlier chapter.

[16] O.I.P.F.G., *Study of Joint-Stock Agricultural Companies*, published by the Iranian National Front Abroad, Middle East Section, 1974, p. 3; and Organization of Mojahedeen of People of Iran (O.M.P.I.), *A Study of the Aryamehr Joint-Stock Agricultural Company*, published by CISNU, 1974, p. 2.

[17] Ibid.

[18] O.I.P.F.G.

[19] Ibid.

[20] Ibid.

[21] H. Richards, "Land Reform and Agribusiness in Iran," *Middle East Research and Information Project (MERIP) Report No. 43* (December 1974): 11.

[22] The government had agreed to pay them for a period of five years; after that, the company itself had to pay them.

[23] M. Field, 1972, cited in Richards, 12.

[24] O.I.P.F.G.

[25] Soudagar, 59.

[26] Ibid.

[27] Khosravi.

[28] Plan and Budget Organization of Iran, *Statistical Yearbook*, June 1976.

[29] Plan and Budget Organization of Iran, *The Fifth Development Plan (1973–1978)*.

[30] Because this area was close to Persepolis, an ancient tourist area, many foreigners would get an opportunity to visit this showcase farm.

[31] The information about the Aryamehr JSAC has been taken from the reports of two field studies published under the titles (1) "Sherkat hay-i Sahami-i Zera'ei," ("Joint-Stocks Agricultural Companies") by O.I.P.F.G. (Organization of Iranian People's Fedaian Guerillas), 1974, and (2) "Rousts va Enqelab-i Sefeed," ("Village and the White Revolution") by O.M.P.I. (Organization of People's Mojahedeen), 1974.

[32] O.M.P.I., 1974.

[33] Compare this amount with the average holding of small holders (0.39 hectare each).

[34] M. Muhammadi, *On the Agrarian Policy of Iranian Government and For a Democratic Solution of Agrarian Problems* (Germany: Tudeh Publishing Center, 1973).

[35] H. Richards, 14.

[36] Th. Brun Fischer and R. Dumont, "Iran: Imperial Pretensions and Agricultural Dependence," MERIP Report, No. 71 (1978).

[37] Khosravi.

[38] According to official information, only about 68,000 hectares of Dez Dam irrigated land was given to the private sector. *Iran Almanac*, 1975, p. 218.

[39] Plan and Budget Organization of Iran, *Fifth National Development Plan (1973–78)*.

[40] *Kayhan* (daily newspaper), 1 Ordibehesht 1349 (May 1970), cited in Muhammadi, 38.

[41] R. Critchfield, "How Lonely Sits the City," cited in Richards, 14.

[42] According to the *Iran Almanac*, in 1974 Iran purchased 2.5 million tons of wheat, more than 300,000 tons of rice, and 220,000 tons of vegetable oil. *Iran Almanac*, 1975, p. 214.

[43] Richards, 17.

[44] The Turkman Peoples' Political-Cultural Center, Headquarters of Turkman Peasants' Councils, Life and Struggle of the People of Turkman, Bahman 1358 (February 1980).

[45] A list of 109 such individuals appears in ibid.

[46] M. Muhammadi.

[47] Sohrab, *Okhtapous-i Sad Pa*, (n. p., 1978).

[48] *The Tehran Economist*, 21 Mordad 1351 (1972), cited in Sohrab, 6.

[49] M. Muhammadi,

[50] Ibid.

[51] Statistics for 1970 show that the peasants who received small loans at high rates of interest, due to their inferior financial conditions, spent the major part of the loan for living expenses rather than for productive agricultural investment, so 55.3% of loans received by the peasants were spent for subsistence allowances and only 27.5% were devoted to agricultural expenditures. The remainder was spent thus: 6.1% for animal husbandry and 11.2% for other expenditures. Kh. Khosravi, *Rural Sociology of Iran* (Tehran: University of Tehran Press, 1976), p. 157.

[52] Plan and Budget Organization of Iran, *The Fifth Plan (1973–78)*, 1972.

[53] Ibid.

[54] O.I.P.F.G., 1976.

[55] In relation to the new form of tenant farming in Iran, O.I.P.F.G., in an article entitled "On the Remains of Feudalism," wrote: "In general, in the Iranian economy and agriculture there are two different kinds of tenants. Farmers exist: petty and large-scale tenant farming. The sort of tenant farming that we are concerned with here is a kind of feudal production relation and is not very different from sharecropping. This sort of tenant farming was expanded a great deal during the second phase of the land reform, but during the third phase the government struggled against it and it was almost eliminated . . . .. Large-scale tenant farming in reality is a sort of capitalist investment in the agricultural sector. After the implementation of the land reform (second and third phases), large-scale tenant farming has flourished a great deal. This can be explained by the fact that many feudal lords, under the newly emerged production organization, were not capable of managing their share of land exempted from distribution. Thus, necessarily, new managers, as tenant farmers, entered the stage and rented the lands from feudal lords. These tenant managers have made investments in the land they have rented, and by doing so they introduced capitalistic productive relations. In this sense, their productive organizing contains no remains of feudalism." (*Quarterly Journal of Asre Amal* (Fall 1975): 54–70. In Persian.) The new tenant farmers, in their turn, hired landless peasants as daily wage-paid agricultural workers and produced for urban markets.

[56] B. Jazani, *Capitalism and Revolution in Iran* (London: Zed Press, 1980).

[57] O.I.P.F.G., 1976, 87.

[58] For information about the roots of the 1979 Revolution, see Nikki Keddie, *The Roots of Revolution: An Interpretive History of Modern Iran* (New Haven, CT: Yale University Press, 1981); Farhad Kazemi, *Poverty and Revolution in Iran* (New York: New York University Press, 1980); Ervand Abrahamian, *Iran Between Two Revolutions* (Princeton, NJ: Princeton University Press, 1988); and Hamid Dabashi, *Theology of Discontent: The Ideological Foundation of*

the Islamic Revolution in Iran (New York: New York University Press, 1993), among others.

[59] Mubarezien-i Rah-i Arman-i Tabaqeh-i Kargar, *An Analysis of the Situation of the Rural Community in Iran* (Tehran, 1978) 63.

[60] Ibid.

[61] A. Lambton, *The Persian Land Reform*, 1962–66 (Oxford, UK: Clarendon Press, 1969), 243.

[62] O.I.P.F.G., *Land Reform and Its Direct Effects in Iran* (London: The Iran Committee, 1976).

[63] *Iran Almanac*, 1976, p. 321.

[64] Th. Brun and R. Dumont, "Iran: Imperial Pretensions and Agricultural Dependence," *MERIP Report (Middle East Research and Information Project) No. 71*, 1978.

[65] After the Revolution, American companies filed 3,836 claims for damages against Iran. (Bahram Tehrani, *A Research in the Economy of Iran* (1354–1364)/1976–1986, vol. 1 (Paris: Khavaran, 1365 (1986))).

[66] There is no doubt that one of the reasons for importing agricultural commodities was the higher consumption that the Iranian production could not satisfy. The main reason, however, was the low productivity of the agricultural sector.

[67] M. Kayhan, "Iranian Rural Community on the Eve of the Land Reform," *Donya, Political and Theoretical Organ of the Central Committee of the Tudeh Party of Iran*, no. 12 (1977): 42–52.

[68] A. Niek-Aain, "A Study of Some of the Causes of Rural Migration," *Donya, Political and Theoretical Organ of the Central Committee of Tudeh Party of Iran*, no. 11 (February 1978): 36–45.

Chapter 10
The Land Question After the
1979 Revolution

Introduction

A study of land problems under the Islamic Republic government requires another separate investigation.[1] Therefore, this chapter intends to review briefly the continuation of the land reform after the revolution. I consider this chapter to be the conclusion to the study of half a century of struggle for the resolution of the agrarian question in Iran.[2]

The shah's regime was overthrown while the agrarian question remained unsolved; peasant poverty continued, and agriculture did not improve as much as had been hoped. After the 1979 Revolution, the peasants' demands for land increased. With the legalization of the Islamic Republic, the once-hidden socioeconomic conflict between landowners and peasants broke out in bloody confrontations. The demands and the clashes were clear indications that (1) the shah's land reform program had not responded to the needs of the peasants, and (2) the legal ownership of land in Iran had yet to be finalized after years and even centuries.[3]

In response to events in the countryside, post-revolutionary Iran has seen a succession of land reform policies, each corresponding to political maneuvers by different social and economic groups. The new government had to respond to several contradictory proposals, back and forth, between liberal, conservative, and radical agendas, to find its way to a permanent land policy. Also, unlike the pre-revolutionary time, the Islamic Republic created several, sometimes parallel, organizations to resolve the agrarian question. These organizations included the Ministry of Agriculture, the Ministry of Jihad-e Sazandegi, the Foundation for Dispossessed People, the Sevener Commissions, the Imam's Relief Committee, and the Martyr's Foundation. Several plans and policies were introduced by these organizations.[4] Among them, there were three primary policies, the first of which was led by Mehdi Bazergan, a pragmatic prime minister during the period of the constitution of provisional government. The next came during the period beginning with the hostage crisis and take-over of the American Embassy in 1980, the resignation of the provisional government, and the domination of the Revolutionary Council. The third came after the presidential and parliamentary elections. The new government after the revolution had to stabilize a clear land reform policy to match the Islamic laws and to address the economic and political revolutionary situation. While peasants were not aware of the possibility of a radical land reform, in a revolutionary situation the leftist political organizations awaken them to their rights in a genuine land reform program. By the time the shah fell and the big landlords fled, leftist organizations had begun land distribution among the peasants wherever they had influence, such as in the ethnic provinces of Turkman-Sahra and Kurdistan in the north and west parts of the country, and to a lesser degree in Khuzistan in the southwest of Iran. These measures, however, were suppressed, and the lands were taken back by the government to determine the owners. Legalizing the squats took the government seventeen years.

In Western eyes, probably the most notable aspect of the Iranian Revolution has been the immense power of the clergy in Iranian politics. It is important, then, to see that the Islamic clergy in Iran rejected the shah's land reform plan either from a more reactionary point of view or with a "progressive" outlook. Yet, they offered no alternatives to the shah's plan. It is conceivable that many clerics were against any reform of the land system, either because of their own material interests or because of their interpretation of Islamic laws. Since the clerics opposed land reform, the shah was able to open propaganda campaigns, accusing the religions leaders—with partial justification—of wanting to return the "distributed" land to the old "feudals."

In the countryside, the small portion of peasants who had benefited, even slightly, from the shah's land reform and who had acquired enough land to survive during the agricultural development hesitated to join the growing revolutionary movement led by their former neighbors who had fled to the urban areas. Such divisions within the peasantry were augmented because of several traditional problems in organizing peasants: a low level of political consciousness, a generally conservative nature, a scattered population, and landlord intimidation.

This split in the peasantry and the propaganda campaigns against the clergy both aided the shah, but with impermanent advantages. Suspicions about the feelings of the clergy seemed to clear when the Ayatollah Khomeini, as head of the opposition, announced in May 1978 his support for a genuine land reform.[5] With expansion of the mass revolutionary movement, however, participation from across the whole spectrum of the peasantry increased gradually; it was not confined to those who went to the cities and joined demonstrations there. Political activists were now able to organize villagers all over the country.[6] A few months before the insurrection, peasants began trying to expel corrupt landlords, many landowners fled to other cities or to other countries, and many lands were revolutionarily confiscated. Divisions among the peasantry seemed to disappear as peasants from various sectors of the country fought together during the serious revolutionary period. Describing the participation of different strata of peasants, the OPIFG wrote,

> The poor and landless peasants' dreams of acquiring a piece of land were being materialized, so they vigorously participated in the struggle. The middle stratum of the peasantry who wanted to free themselves from the yoke of the bank loans and interest payments participated in the movement. The upper stratum of the peasantry also joined the movement in order to strengthen their own positions in the village and prevent possible confiscation of their own land by the poor.[7]

Revolutionary confiscation continued, especially in those regions where lands were owned by the military and high-ranking civil government officials (including all lands controlled by court favorites who had fled the country earlier). Almost all of these lands had been fully mechanized and were managed by modern capitalist methods.

To enforce their demands and to protect their gains, peasants armed themselves when necessary. According to Azad, "In Kurdistan and Turkman-Sahra (northern Iran), armed peasants seized army and gendarmerie posts, expelled local corrupt rulers, and expropriated lands owned by absentee landlords or local Khans."[8]

After the shah's downfall, in order to maintain and manage the lands, Peasants' Councils were established by the left-wing organizations, especially in the two areas of Turkman-Sahra and Kurdistan.

> Aided by locally based left-wing groups (in Turkman-Sahra, the Organization of Iranian People's Fedaii Guerrillas [OIPFG]; in Kurdistan, the Kurdish Democratic Party; and the Toilers Organization of Komaleh), they set up councils to control themselves and their land, and to improve their living conditions.[9]

The Central Headquarters of the Turkman Peasants' Councils, in a published report, wrote: "The peasants' councils confiscate lands not to divide them among peasants but to own and cultivate them collectively."[10] This was one of the leftist organizations encouraging the adoption of the Soviet model of collective farms instead of individual ownership.

All of these things had been done without the approval of the religions leaders who were in the process of taking power. There was no authority to control peasant actions, once the old regime melted away and the new one had not yet solidified. After victory, the peasants expected that the new government would legitimize their revolutionary action and that the demands promised by the Ayatollah Khomeini before the February 1979 insurrection would be met. This did not take place. The revolutionary government militarily attacked the peasants' organizations and their headquarters and regained control of the confiscated lands. Under the revolutionary situation, the Islamic government, however, was under political pressure to implement a land reform program.

The First Land Distribution Bill

The new government took form with the participation of three main factions—the liberal bourgeoisie,[11] the radical Islamists, and the conservative clerics[12]—and excluded other groups, especially the leftist revolutionary organizations that had played a vital role in overthrowing the shah's dictatorship. In the beginning, after the revolution, it was not easy for the new government to ratify a solid land reform bill because political tension dominated the society and, as Schirazi has written, the "Islamists were poorly informed and gave little thought" to the question of the land reform program.[13] Therefore, various groups within and outside the government had their own interpretations of the objectives of the revolution in general and land reform in particular to satisfy the peasants and to secure the economy.

Within two months after the victory over the shah's regime, conflicts between the Peasants' Councils and the new government in both Turkman-Sahra and Kurdistan resulted in the deaths of several peasants and government troops. One source wrote,

> Because of the division in the government and in the Revolutionary Council, some of the fanatic Islamic groups intervened in defense of the landowners. They did this in Turkman-Sahra, in Gonbad-i Kabous, and in Kurdistan. In the name of Islam they formed themselves into units of Revolutionary Guards and, instead of defending the peasants, came in on the side of the landlords.[14]

Due to the continuing atmosphere of turmoil, the government did not relax its defense of the landlords against the peasants, although there was conflict within the new government over this problem. For example, following bloody clashes between landlords, or khans, and peasants in East Azerbaijan, Nour al-Din Gharavi, the governor of that province, wrote to Akbar Hashemi Rafsanjani, head of the Majlis, in a letter since made public: "As I have pointed out in the meeting of the Revolutionary Council on the 4th Day of 1358 [December 25, 1979] in the presence of all the members, I absolutely disagree with the idea of seeking the assistance of the khans and tribal heads to protect our borders."[15] To protect the borders, the government had to arm the khans and landlords, which meant protecting the landlords against the peasants. Rafsanjani, an influential cleric in the government, was himself a landlord. A report by M. Bahadoran, special envoy of the Ayatollah Montazeri,[16] concerning bloody destruction of a village named Qarna, in Kurdistan, by landlords and their guards, stated, "The Ministry of Defense has distributed arms among the feudals of the region in order to suppress peasants."[17] Bahadoran acknowledged, "the wars (in both Kurdistan and Turkman-Sahra) were the result of the common cooperation of regional feudalists and Mr. Chamran, the minister of defense."[18] Large and medium landowners were the mainstays of the resistance. They organized themselves into Agricultural Councils, which had been reinstated by the Bazergan government. They received effective support from the conservative clerics, among them such grand ayatollahs as Golpaygani, Qomi, and Rohani, who in their *fatwas* and other pronouncements declared restrictions on legitimate land ownership to be illegal and even communist."[19]

With confrontation continuing, it was clear to both factions of the government that the situation in the countryside could not be allowed to continue, yet neither the economic liberals nor the conservative clergy could afford, politically, to deal with the land problem except by openly siding with the landlords and forcibly stopping the peasants. Thus, each faction, when controlling the government, proposed and enacted land bills that in every case had for their main purposes stopping the revolutionary movements of the peasantry, stabilizing the rural situation, extending control of the new government over the countryside, and appearing to offer genuine land reform to appease the peasantry. The first of these actions came in the early months after the revolution, when the religious, liberal-minded group formed the provisional government. The minister of agriculture of the provisional government, Dr. Izadi, issued several rules and regulations in order to stem land expropriation by the peasants. A few months later, on 25/6/1358 (September 1979), the Ministry of Agriculture issued a land distribution bill that affected only barren lands, which were not registered by anyone. As for eligible recipients, priority was given to such groups as educated people in the fields of agriculture, veterinarian medicine, and animal husbandry, and to retired government employees. It was not surprising that landless peasants were not included.[20] The policy of the religious, liberal, pragmatic government was clear. Land would be given to the capable investors. The Revolutionary Council followed the same policy after resignation of Bazergan in Sept. 1979, adding a limitation so that the investors were now allowed to own 10 to 150 hectares of land, depending upon the region. Apparently, after seventeen years of struggle and conflict over the confiscated land and official termination of the land reform, this was the policy that the Islamic Republic of Iran (IRI) finally adopted.

Dr. Izadi justified his bill by saying that in the shah's land reform "during the first stage, the landlords who owned more than one village lost all but one; the rest were bought by the government, which then distributed them among the peasants."[21] This seemed to assert that land distribution had already taken place and that Izadi needed only to make slight adjustments in the land holdings.

In addition, Izadi added that it is to be understood that there is a difference between a communist revolution and an Islamic one, in that the latter respects private ownership.[22] He continued,

> We say that the right of ownership belongs to those who revive the land; this is the Imam's position concerning the bill of ownership. When the Revolutionary Council attempted to introduce a section which would have specified the ownership limitation, the Imam Khomeini rejected it and said that there is no limitation to ownership in Islam; as long as one works, does not harm anyone, and earns his capital legitimately, then it is his own. We must first recognize the

difference between the Islamic economic system, which respects the right to private ownership, and socialism, which respects public ownership.[23]

He explained that this law also prevented expropriation of land by "aggressors" and "coveters."[24]

The law was based on such general policies by the "revolutionary government" as asking the peasants to pay delinquent debts incurred during the shah's land reform. In this connection, Mr. Qyumi-Nia, General Director of the Bank of Agriculture in Kerman province, announced that "those peasants who have not paid their obligations from the land reform are exempted from payment of delinquent interest, but they must pay the principal of their loans. Those peasants who, due to bad weather, are not able to pay their debts, can get extensions or make payment in installments."[25]

Although, the liberal faction of the revolutionary government dictated this policy, the other faction (the conservative clerics) also supported it, even as the radical Islamists opposed this alternative. The radicals' opposition to the peasants' continuing struggle for land was linked to clerical attempts to take control of such agricultural lands as the Pahlavi Foundation's lands, which had been registered to no owner since confiscation. Hence, the clerics were competing with the liberals. Relying on the religious beliefs of the people, the clergy eventually succeeded in gaining control over the newly established foundation of *Bonyad-i Mostaz'afien* (The Foundation for Dispossessed). This foundation, which had come into existence through direct order of the Ayatollah Khomeini, owned not only all such "non-possessor" agro-businesses, including much valuable and modernized agricultural land, but also many other properties such as hotels, cinemas, large buildings, industries, companies, and expensive private homes—all connected to fled or executed individuals who had been dependent upon the former regime. According to estimates, this foundation now controls one-third of Iran's economy.[26]

Revolutionary Council Land Reform Bill

The first period after the shah's fall ended with the events at the American Embassy and resignation of the provisional government. Up to that point, the provisional government, led by the liberal faction and the conservative clerics, opposed any type of real solution to the land problem. Then, on the eve of the occupation of the American Embassy, the balance of power within the government was changed in favor of the radical clerical faction. The liberal government of Bazergan was forced to resign, and the radical clerics imposed their dominance on the government.[27] Led by the clergy, the new government was formed from within the Revolutionary Council, which had been created after the revolution. The Revolutionary Council became, for the most part, the government.

Shortly before this event, the clerics had organized themselves into a new party, the Islamic Republic Party (IRP). Due to its clerical leadership, to its religious nature, and importantly to the indirect support of the Ayatollah Khomeini, it succeeded in receiving mass support throughout the country. While "the clerical bourgeoisie"[28] has controlled the leadership its body contained mostly the masses of the traditional petty bourgeoisie (traditional middle class), wholly dominated by Islamic culture.

IRP leadership tried to monopolize political power while simultaneously controlling all confiscated and "non-possessor" wealth. The lower and middle strata of the petty bourgeoisie (shopkeepers, for instance), as the mass base of the party, still expected to acquire something for which they had struggled vigorously during the revolution. In contrast to the desires of the leadership, they favored continuing the revolution to meet their demands. They played the major role in the events surrounding the American Embassy takeover—an anti-American move based on mass emotion, but also a synthesis of the contradiction between the leadership's will and the peoples' demands. Thereafter, they temporarily became more active and influential within the ruling circle.[29]

In this period, two opposing land policies were in operation: from one side, there were statements proposing confiscation of large-scale land holdings; from the other, death sentences were given to those who occupied land illegally.[30] It was in such a situation that the Revolutionary Council offered a Land Reform Bill.

The experiences of the new deputy minister of agriculture, Reza Esfahani, show clearly the conflicts within the government. He took the peasants' side and proceeded with the land distribution. Esfahani declared, "The most land is in the hands of feudals. In Naqadeh (Kurdistan) there are individuals who possess thousands of hectares of land. The society needs a just land reform." He continued:

> The lands of big landowners will be confiscated; the land will be distributed to peasants justly; the interest of agricultural loans will be omitted in coming weeks; at first, distribution will be done in Gonbad and Kurdistan, two regions where conflict between peasants and government had intensified.... We have decided to do a genuine land reform.[31]

In an interview, he was asked if his land reform program would start with confiscation of large-scale landholdings. He replied, "Yes."

Despite the objections of such landlords, Esfahani continued his program, proclaiming, "the deeds of 200,000 hectares of land have already been signed for distribution."[32] That was just the beginning of the end of his reform. His plans never materialized. According to Schirazi, his radical restrictions on private land ownership "met with stiff opposition and created a political atmosphere that pushed the formulation of a program for the rest of agriculture into the background."[33] The real power in Iran, with direct support of Khomeini, was in the hands of the middle bourgeoisie, both clerics and liberals, and in contrast to the petty bourgeoisie's demands they were naturally opposed to such a plan. They asked for Khomeini's aid, and a few months later the daily newspaper *Etela'at* headlined: "The Order of Imam Khomeini for an Islamic Land Reform Throughout the Country." In its lead article, the newspaper wrote, "Ayatollah Meshkini, Ayatollah Montazeri, and Ayatollah Dr. Beheshti were sent on duty to study Islamic land reform plans as designed by the Ministry of Agriculture."[34] When they revealed their decision, it became clear that the meaning of the phrase "study of Islamic land reform" was that the men were sent to prevent any real distribution of land at all.

In an interview in March 1980, Ayatollah Meshkini was asked if, in the Islamic land reform, landless and small-holding peasants had been considered. He replied, "All people will be given land. We do not have peasant and non-peasant. Anyone who can work on land and revive it should be given land." As to owner limitation, he said, "No limitation has been considered in this design."[35]

Since the Ayatollah Khomeini himself, along with other powerful ayatollahs, was behind the plan for Islamic land reform, Esfahani's more progressive proposals met difficulties. Eventually he retreated, criticizing himself: "I was too optimistic about the government when I began my work in the Ministry of Agriculture. I thought that the words that were promised to me would actually happen"[36] He explained, for instance, that "the banks did not cooperate with us as required. Capitalists were granted big loans while small loans—between six and ten thousand toman [about $1,000] were faced with many difficulties."[37]

There was a great distance between slogans and actions, he continued: "I was too optimistic about the revolutionary courts; I thought that they considered the rights of the people, but many of these revolutionary courts have issued orders in favor of the feudals. Those lands that we [the Ministry of Agriculture] gave the peasants have been returned to the feudals. I have to criticize myself; I feel guilty.... I submitted the disputed cases to the courts that ruled against the people and the revolution."[38] Realizing that he could do nothing, he chose to resign. In spite of his efforts, therefore, this period ended without any significant changes.

The period was followed by the election of Abolhasan Bani-Sadr as president and his appointment as the head of the Revolutionary Council. Bani-Sadr, a moderate Islamist who sided with neither faction of the government, received Khomeini's support even though he was not a cleric.[39] However, in the parliamentary election, the IRP—the radical and conservative clerics—seized the majority of seats in the Majlis (parliament) and became the leading force in the ruling circles. This duality became the beginning of a new political battle between the president and the Majlis. Finding an agrarian solution, however, was not a major part of this political battle. The clerics aimed to have absolute, monopolistic ideological control over all social, political, economic, and cultural aspects of society. This group was not concerned with development, but with power. Khomeini eventually sided with clerics, and in a hostile situation Bani-Sadr was left with no choice but to flee into exile.

Now it was the turn of both the president and the parliament to get involved with the land question. All the while, constant clashes between peasants and landlord/government forces had continued in Kurdistan, with sporadic clashes in other regions. The land dispute in Turkman-Sahra ended after a death squad associated with the hardliners of the government murdered four influential leaders and candidates for the Majlis in the region.

In an early speech on the land problem, Bani-Sadr proclaimed that "Land is abundant in Iran. Everyone can receive land. Those who own large holdings need not worry; if they wish, they will receive the value of their lands, and if they want land, the state will give them land."[40] Bani-Sadr intended to reduce the hostile tensions existing between landlords and peasants. He tried to keep both satisfied, calling himself the key for solving the prevailing social, economic, and political crises, but his attempt to sit on both sides of the fence did not work. The clashes continued. In the weeks following his coming into office, a particularly bloody clash happened in Turkman-Sahra between the Peasants' Councils and the government forces. In this instance, government forces had been involved in terrorizing four leaders of the Peasants' Councils in that area. Responding to this situation and trying to prevent further conflict, Bani-Sadr announced in a televised debate that earlier land reform efforts would be continued. It was, however, apparent that there would be stiff resistance to his plans. Bani-Sadr knew that in any case of real land reform, the first to lose would be the clerical faction—the group that now controlled the most modern agrarian sectors of the economy through its control of the Mostaz'afien Foundation.

Immediately after Bani-Sadr's television appearance, some of the powerful ayatollahs, such as the Ayatollahs Qomi and Ruhani, voiced their strong dissent to his "progressive plan" on land reform, and in a telegram they ordered him to stop. Since it is excellent background for the clergy's view on land reform, the entire text of the telegram is reproduced here:

Thursday, March 14, 1980
Etela'at (Daily Newspaper) #16098, p. 3.
In a telegram to the President, Ayatollah Rohani disagreed with the implementation of the Land Reform Bill.
From: City of Qom. Ayatollah Rohani sent the following telegram yesterday to the President of Iran:
To: Tehran. Mr. Bani-Sadr, the President. With best wishes. Parts of the Bill of Land Reform, which recently has been implemented, are against the holy religion and on the other hand it is also against the Constitution for the following reasons:
First, the Revolutionary Council does not have the right to approve it. Second, the Revolutionary Council has not approved it. Third, the Guardian Council has not reviewed it; the Leader of the Revolution has not confirmed it, and the Mojtaheds[41] have declared it against the religion. It is regrettable that in one of your television debates you stated that the Bill is under implementation. It is necessary that this major mistake be immediately corrected and that the implementation of the Bill be stopped so that in these historic moments the Muslims be relieved. Let the people with their unique religious sentiments and optimistic feelings toward the Islamic Republic participate in the election.
If you would like to be informed of the worries of the Muslim people, please send a representative to Qom to observe letters, petitions, and telegrams that have been sent to me by the people.
    Mohammad Sadiq Ruhani

Not surprisingly, because of the power of his opponents, Bani-Sadr had to forget his plan after this telegram. But the peasants did not forget, and they continued their struggle for agrarian reform.

After Bani-Sadr's failure, the clerical factions had to provide some alternative so that it could halt the revolutionary movement in the countryside and bring order to the villages. Thus, a Ceding of Land Bill was made into law. The Revolutionary Council had once ratified the original rendition of this bill, but it had then remained only on paper after it was criticized for being a non-Islamic plan. The Ceding of Land Bill that eventually emerged was the last bill to be ratified by the Revolutionary Council on land reform, and it has superseded all previous bills. To implement the plan, the Committee for Ceding of Land was formed. There were many similarities between the newly ratified bill and that of the provisional government. For example, study of the villages' conditions and even the shah's land reform law has shown us that poor and landless peasants truly needed land. But in the bill eventually made law, instead of the words "peasant" or "landless peasant (*Khwush-neshin*)," the phrase "real or legal individuals" was used. The bill determined the priority for receiving land as follows:

1. The local residents who have been residing in the locality for at least three years
2. The volunteers who obligate to reside in the locality
3. Educated individuals in the field of agriculture, veterinary medicine, and animal husbandry, who must not be employed by the government
4. Government employees who have decided to leave their jobs, to retire, or to be bought out.[42]

However, the term "legal individual" also referred to corporations. Notice that in all of this, once again, the emphasis was not on those who most needed the land.

As for the types of land affected by the bill, their descriptions were:

1. Dead land (lands that did not have a history of cultivation and exploitation). Included in this type are the lands not claimed and registered by anyone. Clearly, dead land requires substantial capital investment over a considerable period of time if it is to be converted into active land.
2. Waste and pasture land (land with a history of cultivation, but not during five consecutive years). This land is included in the distribution, if the owners are not known.
3. Active land (land that has been continuously cultivated and exploited. This type is the best land for exploitation.
4. Land developed by individuals or corporations, but ordered by an Islamic Court to be returned to the government.

The law explained that types 1 and 2 were to be possessed by the Islamic government, it being the government's duty to transfer them to eligible individuals or companies based on their needs and abilities and the interests of the entire society.[43] Again, there was no use of the word "peasants." Eligible subjects could be individuals, but the fact that companies also qualified provided a clue as to the real purpose of this reform. Also, the concepts "interests of society," and "abilities of individuals" were too ambiguous to be understood in practice. There were no clear criteria given for either concept. This quite possibly implied that, in many cases, while a peasant might not be eligible, a company might.

The amount of waste and pasture lands (type 2) were not great, nor were they ready for cultivation at the time of transference. Peasants usually do not have the "abilities" to revive such lands. Thus, it seems that eligible recipients for type 2 were mostly companies or wealthy individuals.

The last two types of land were actively cultivated land that could have been transferred to the peasants operating the landholdings. According to the law, owners themselves could hold land up to three times the average size of local holdings if they were directly involved in agriculture and twice the local average size if they were not so directly involved, the landlords receiving compensation for their transferred lands after any government dues had been paid.

However, Ayatollah Khomeini ordered that these last two types of land be exempted from the land reform legislation that was eventually passed into law. He apparently decided that their inclusion would not suit the current political climate and would not correspond to Islamic law. Hujat-Al Islam[44] Fazel Harandi, head of the Committee for Ceding of Land, announced in January 1981 that "The leader of the revolution, due to the prevailing political atmosphere in society and with regard to the exclusive current situation, at the present time, ordered a stop to articles (3) and (4) of this bill, and, following the statement of Imam Khomeini, we told the Committee to avoid even continuation of any investigation in this matter."[45] Furthermore, in an interview, when he was asked about the permitted size of agricultural land in the plan finally passed into law, he replied, "Someone may own just one hectare of land, but not lawfully, and someone may possess several hectares of land, but lawfully."[46] Thus, this reform bill was revised and re-revised so that in the end those who most needed land, the peasantry, again would receive the least.

This major shift in the policy needed a mechanism for uprooting the peasants' movement in the countryside. Village Councils were revived to achieve the goal. Village Councils had been established during the shah's Land Reform Program, but the Islamic Republic of Iran revived them for different purposes. By June 1982, there were over 25,000 Village Councils, and the figure reached 35,000 by February

1986 and 40,000 by December 1987.[47] As Asghar Schirazi writes, the Village Councils had political tasks.[48] Article 6 of the law's administrative regulations read: "The holy key task of the Village Councils lies in the preservation of the achievements of the Islamic Revolution, in the efforts that are to be made for enforcing the line of the Imam, and in the fight against all the groups that are active against Islam and the Islamic people."[49]Schirazi added: "In a speech to the president at a meeting of the Village Councils in November 1982, a representative of the councils reported on such activities, saying that they had spared no effort to uproot the counter-revolution and had also organized considerable help for the front in the war."[50]

Another trend connected to the final land reform bill was the move to revive the traditional *muzara'eh* system of landholding—a system almost abolished during the shah's regime. While radical individuals like Reza Esfahani, the deputy minister of agriculture in the first year after the revolution, rejected it as an outdated system, conservative clerics endorsed it as an Islamic method of cultivation. For example, Ayatollah Qomi, one of the high-ranking ayatollahs, referred to the *muzara'eh* system as a religious solution for land problems.[51] Fazel-Harandi, in his interview, had also revealed that "the Committee for Ceding of Land, in regard to those lands that the owners are not able to cultivate for any acceptable reason, will give those lands to peasants under the *muzara'eh* or tenancy."[52] As a result, some *vaqf* (endowment) lands, such as the Holly Foundation of Imam Reza in Khorasan, entered into *muzara'eh* (sharecropping) contracts with peasants.

This study has shown that both the liberal faction of the government and the conservative clergy had the same basic concern even though they suggested different policies toward land reform and were motivated by different economic goals. Both groups wanted to put an end to the growing revolutionary movement in the countryside. Consequently, both enacted at least the shell of a land reform program to satisfy peasant aspirations. Yet, because of the interests of both liberals and the clergy, land reform efforts were so watered down that their effects in reducing inequities were negligible or, if genuinely progressive (like Esfahani's), they ran into insurmountable obstacles. In all of this, the net effect for the peasants was not noticeably different than with the shah's land reform. Any gains made by the peasantry have been through autonomous and sometimes spontaneous mass action, or by lower-ranking individuals in the Committee for Ceding of Land, without the approval of the ruling government.

Because of an unclear land policy, agricultural production declined sharply in spite of encouragement by the government and the Ayatollah

Khomeini himself.[53] Two years after the revolution, the minister of health in the provisional government, Kazem Sami, later a member of the parliament, said that dependency on agricultural imports had increased.[54] Still later, Sami, a physician, was brutally stabbed to death in his office. He was the first victim of a series of political murders. An Iranian agricultural expert, discussing cotton production, wrote that it showed a 50% decline (from 132,000 tons to 60,000 tons) from the previous year—i.e., 1358 (1979).[55] The deputy minister of agriculture announced that imports of dry food for livestock (provender), in comparison with the past three years, had doubled.[56] According to a report published in the daily newspaper *Enqelab Islami*, "during 1980–81, wheat production decreased 920,000 tons or 53%."[57] Another report showed that the supply of wheat purchased externally with 40% inflation was imposed on consumers, whereas the increase in the price at which the government purchased wheat from peasants increased only about 11%.[58]

In October 1986, a new law declared the end of land reform in Iran. Following that law, the government assured private investors of secure land ownership. As a result, several thousand hectares of state and nationalized land were assigned for lease or sale to private investors. Despite the announcement, private investors remained hesitant to participate because most of the private agro-businesses, established during the shah's land reform, had been either squatted on, sequestered, or confiscated by the revolutionary institutions.[59] Less than a year later, in 1987, a new law was passed indicating that all confiscated lands would be transferred to peasants under joint ownership *(mosha')*. The result was that by December 1990 about 1,005,000 hectares of state and squatted lands were transferred to some 220,000 peasant families[60] and that by 1994, 12,399 *mosha'* cooperatives had been established.[61] This seems to be the final outcome of two decades of disputes, conflicts, and battles over land reform and land ownership in Iran.

[1] For a comprehensive study of the land question after the revolution, see Asghar Schirazi, *Islamic Development Policy: The Agrarian Question in Iran* (London: Lynne Rienner Publishers, 1993); Ali Shakoori, *The State and Rural Development in Post-Revolutionary Iran* (New York: Praeger, 2001); and Bahram, Tehrani, *A Research in the Economy of Iran (1354–1364),* vol. 2 (Paris: Khavaran, 1986).

[2] Mohammad Mosaddeq began initial attempts at reform of the land tenure system in Iran in 1951.

[3] According to Hernando De Sato, in his book *The Mystery of Capital: Why Capitalism Triumphs in the West and Fails Everywhere Else* (New York: Basic Books, 2000), the real problem in underdeveloped countries is the unclear and undetermined legal status of ownership. Throughout this book, I have tried to analyze this problem from a different angle—i.e., the lack of private ownership of the land throughout the history of these countries. The Land Reform Program of the Shah could not resolve the problem, so the job devolved to the revolutionary Islamic government to finalize the matter. What De Soto discussed in his book is what I initially referred to in my earlier book *why Iran Lagged Behind and the West Moved Forward?* (Tehran: Nashr-e Towse'a, 2000).

[4] For details, see A. Schirazi, op cit., 1993.

[5] Khomeini's interview with Lucien George, *LeMonde's* special envoy, (Paris: LeMonde, May 6, 1978).

[6] Marry Hoogland, "One Village in Revolution," *MERIP Report No. 87* (May 1980): 7–14.

[7] The Organization of the Iranian People's Fedaii Guerrillas (OIPFG), *Kar,* no. 94, 22 January 1981. For English text, see *Kar International, The Monthly Selected Works of the OPIFG,* no. 3, April 1981.

[8] Shahrzad Azad, "Workers' and Peasants' Councils in Iran," *Monthly Review,* 32, no. 5 (October 1980): 14–29.

[9] Ibid., 16. Concerning the objectives of the constitution of the Peasants' Councils, in a massive meeting (with more than 15,000 peasants participating) in Turkman-Sahra in the early days after the February victory, a five-point declaration was released mandating (1) recovery of the land confiscated by the former regime, (2) real and democratic land reform, (3) reduction in importation of agricultural products in order to protect local agriculture, (4) formation of rural and fishery councils, and (5) protection of the fishermen and carpet-weavers of the region. *Kar,* no. 1, 8 March 1979, cited in Azad, p. 25.

[10] The Turkman People's Political-Cultural Center, Headquarters of Turkman Peasants' Councils, *Life and Struggle of the People of Turkman* (Bahman 1358 (March 1980)): 151.

[11] Here, "liberal bourgeoisie" refers to those religious groups and individuals who believed in a free market economy and private ownership in contrast to the

revolutionary leftists who advocated socialism or the religious conservatives who sought a traditional society.

[12] For a comprehensive analysis of the formation of the new government, see OIPFG, "Nabard-e Khalq (People's Struggle)," *New Period*, no. 1 (1980).

[13] Asghar Schirazi., 1993, 64.

[14] Cited in *MERIP Report No. 87* (May 1980): 12.

[15] Cited in "Special Issue on Turkman-Sahra," *Kar*, 3, no. 40 (Monday, 29 Bahman, 1359 (February 1980)).

[16] Ayatollah Montazeri was named as the successor to the Ayatollah Khomeini before a dispute over massive executions of political prisoners caused a break between the two leaders. This dispute led not only to dismissal of Montazeri but also to his house arrest. For details, see the Khaterat-e Ayatollah Hosein Ali Montazeri, *Memoirs of Ayatollah Ali Montazeri* Qom, n.p., 15/2/1379 (April 2001).

[17] Ibid., 4.

[18] *Kar*, no. 36 (26 November 1979).

[19] Asghar Schirazi, 1993, 177.

[20] *Etela'at*, Daily Newspaper, Azar 4, 1358 (November 1979).

[21] *Islamic Republic* (daily Newspaper) (19 Mehr 1358), cited in *Kar*, no. 36 (26 November 1979).

[22] Ibid.

[23] Ibid.

[24] *Islamic Republic* (19 Mehr 1358), cited in *Kar*, no. 36.

[25] *Enqelab Islami* (daily newspaper), no. 128 (1958).

[26] Bahram Tehrani, *A Research*, vol. 2, (Paris: Khavaran, 1986): 475. In an interview, the head of this foundation said that the organization owns more than 300 large factories, 150 large buildings such as palaces and hotels, more than 70 per cent of the theaters, 50 mines, more than 120 construction companies, more than 300 trade and commercial companies, and thousands hectares of agro-business land. See *Kayhan* (daily newspaper) 20 Mordad, 1362, p. 22, cited in Bahram Tehrani, p. 457. Also see *Kar*, no. 99, 7 Esfand 1359 (March 1981).

[27] Mr. Bazergan, the resigned premier, and a few of his cabinet ministers were members of the Revolutionary Council.

[28] In Iran, the clerical bourgeoisie represents the traditional sectors of the commercial bourgeoisie and agriculture.

[29] For an analysis of the events involving the American Embassy, see *People's Struggle*, (Tehran: O.I.P.F.G., 1980).

[30] Ibid.

[31] *Etela'at* (daily newspaper), 10 Azar 1358 (November 1979). Gonbad and Kurdistan are two regions where the battles between peasants and government forces (both Army and Revolutionary Guards)/landlords have been especially bloody and still continue.

[32] O.I.P.F.G., *People's Struggle*, 105.

[33] Asghar Schirazi, op cit., 1993, 109.

[34] *Etela'at*, 9th Esfand, 1358 (March 1980).

[35] Ibid.

[36] *Enqelab-i Islami* (daily newspaper), no. 278, 24 Khordad 1359 (June 1980), cited in *Kar*, no. 65, 10 Teer 1359 (July 1980).

[37] Ibid.

[38] Ibid.

[39] Bani-Sadr's election resulted from tactical mistakes by the IRP during the presidential election. The IRP candidate, Jalalledien Farsi, was revealed to be of Afghan origin and ejected from the race on constitutional grounds just before the election. This unanticipated event resulted in conflict among party leadership, and some leaders did not endorse the new party candidate, Hasan Habibi. The liberals (the Bazergan faction) had their own candidate for president, Ahmad Madani, but Bani-Sadr, occupying a position between the two factions, was able to win the election with more than 70% of the vote.

[40] *Kayhan* (daily newspaper), 13 Esfand 1358 (March 1980).

[41] Mojtaheds, the highest-ranking ayatollahs, are permitted to issue opinions on matters of faith.

[42] Cited in *Kar* (weekly newspaper), no. 98, 30 Bahman 1359 (March 1981). For English text, see *Kar International*, no. 3, April 1981.

[43] *Kar*, no. 99, 7 Esfand 1359 (March 1981).

[44] "Hujat-Al Slam" is a religious title lower than "Ayatollah."

[45] Enqelab Islami, No. 440, 13th of Day, 1359 (January 1981).

[46] Ibid.

[47] Asghar Schirazi, op cit.

[48] Ibid.

[49] M. Wusuqi, *Jame'e Shenasi-ye Rustaei (Rural Sociology)* (Tehran, 1988). Cited in Asghar Schirazi, 268–69.

[50] Asghar Schirazi, 269. Original text from *Kayhan* (daily newspaper) 8 November 1982.

[51] *Kayhan*, 20 Esfand 1358 (March 1980).

[52] Ibid.

[53] *Enqelab Islami*, 15 Bahman, 1359 (February 1981).

[54] Ibid., 18 Bahman, 1359 (February 1981).

[55] Ibid., 23 1359 (January 1981).

[56] Ibid., 14 Bahman, 1359 (February 1981).

[57] Ibid., No. 499, 25 Esfand, 1359 (March 1981).

[58] Ibid., 16 Bahman, 1359 (February 1981).

[59] A. Schirazi, op cit.

[60] Ibid.

[61] A. Shakoori, op. cit.

Conclusion

My core view in this book is that the land tenure system in the East prevented these societies from developing capitalism, the engine of modern development in the West. The land tenure system was a legal system that originated from the appropriate traditions that made allowed societies to meet their needs. However, unlike in the West, this property system was integrated into religion and a despotic ruling system, which caused its structure to remain unchanged throughout the history of the region. I specifically traced the trends of the land tenure system under different dynasties in the history of Iran as a case study. I found that although there were some minor changes in some periods of time, the overall property system remained the same throughout Iran's history. This persistence can be primarily attributed to the geographical conditions, which formed the traditions and legal basis of the existing land tenure system. This legal system caused socioeconomic and political consequences in Iran that were different from those in the West. This shows that once a tradition is established it can be effective as an independent force to maintain the overall structure of a society for a long time. Therefore, removing or changing this tradition, which, again, was integrated into religion, would prove to be as difficult as changing its structural base. Specifically, we can refer to two conspicuous and prominent characteristics of these societies that continued to affect the land system in the East. These characteristics are (1) the claim of the king to be the "owner of all land", and (2) his word as "unquestionable law." In the case of religious traditions, once they are accepted as justifying an establishment or status quo and accepted as meeting the needs of a society, they are hard to be removed even when the original creators no longer exist. Because the king saw himself as "divine," he continued to keep up his claim as the representative of God on earth and continued to view his words as unquestionable edicts.

Feudalism was established in the West because of a natural setting different from that in the East. In short, farmers in the West won the ownership of uncultivated land when they could develop it. Once woods were cleared, individuals could cultivate the land for good. In the end, they could do the farming alone, because unlike in the East agriculture was not dependent upon artificial irrigation. In the East, clearing barren land was only the beginning of development. Peasants had to provide water resources if the cultivation was to continue. Providing water in a dry natural environment was not an easy task, and peasants could do it alone. Thus, they were dependent either upon the state for assistance or on some form of teamwork for irrigation, because irrigation required a major work effort that individual peasants were unable to provide. Land without water had no value in this region, as elsewhere. Therefore, the ownership of the cultivated land was often split between the peasants and the authorities who managed to control the water resources and the other factors of agriculture. Alternatively, due to the requirement for teamwork, collective ownership of undividable land (*mosha'a*) gradually developed instead of individual ownership. Westerners did not experience such difficulties. Therefore, land ownership developed along a different path. Capitalism, as a unique experience, emerged as the result of private ownership in the West, which brought about a drastic change in the history of that part of the world.

This study was undertaken not to show how capitalism operates but rather to explain how and why the West invented capitalism and why the East neither developed its own capitalism before or parallel with the West nor succeeded in adopting capitalism during the past three centuries that capitalism has been the dominant economic system. Eastern societies like Iran, in a close relationship with the West, began their capitalist path in the second half of the 20th century, but they are still far away from the Western type that was formed on a different legal and property system—private ownership of property. Societies in the East have yet to adopt and legitimize a permanent legal property system compatible with that of the West. Accumulation and circulation of capital as the beginning of capitalism needs a firm legal system of private ownership and security for capital investment.

The land tenure system in Third World countries will have to be changed in order to achieve political stability and economic productivity. Following the 1953 CIA coup d'etat in Iran, and preceding an economic crisis in the late 1950s, the United States government launched an abortive land reform program in Iran. The Iranian land reform program of this era was only one of the reformist measures led by the U.S. and supported by United Nations' experts during the 1950s and 1960s. Such programs were carried out after World War II, following the successful experiences of the Japanese land reform and because of threats of peasant revolts (which were due in part to the examples of communist-led land reform efforts in some of the "liberated" countries of Asia—Korea, Vietnam, and China, for example.

The proposed land reforms had two main purposes—one political, one economic. Many Third World countries suffered from very backward land tenure systems, and the landlord autocracies that dominated the social order were always threatened from below by the potential of an agrarian and political revolution. Reform was supposed to help prevent such revolutions. In addition, the old, traditional tenancy and sharecropping systems bonded and restricted the economies of these societies. Therefore, they had to be replaced by new and open capitalist relations of production, which might have integrated these countries into the world market.

In the Iranian case, unlike in many other countries, there was no large threat of peasant revolt against landlordism at that time. But economic changes were required. The land reform program of the late 1960s was dictated to the Iranian regime by the United States government because the Shah and other large landholders initially opposed any reform. But the Shah learned that he could not politically survive without the support of the U.S. and therefore agreed to implement the project. After being convinced that land reform could bring more stability to his regime, the Shah began the reform under his direct supervision.

England, as the traditional supporter of the Iranian landlords, opposed the plan. The British felt that it meant a strengthening of the capitalist faction of the regime that was mainly pro-American and a weakening of the landlord faction that was the British base in Iran. Rivalry between the U.S. and England, hinted at during the nationalization of the British-controlled petroleum industry in Iran in 1951, became more open at the time of the successful coup of 1953 and finally ended in favor of the U.S. and its land reform program. Still recovering from the damage of the World War II, England was not able to give Iran the financial aid she required, but American aid—cut earlier due to the opposition of the Iranian regime to the suggested land reform plan—resumed after the Shah agreed to the plan.

The general emphasis of the land reform project was to abolish the form of the old land tenure system. It aimed to do away with the outdated socioeconomic system of *muzara'eh*, which was a type of sharecropping based on the five agricultural elements—land, water, seed, draught animals, and labor. One share of ownership was allotted to each element and would go to whomever provided that element. Land reform was successful in this regard. The *muzara'eh* system was almost entirely replaced, for those who remained in rural areas, by a new form of tenancy and wage-labor relationship. The system that emerged was a modern, more advanced capitalist system that soon connected landlords to urban business. Manufactured and consumer goods flowed into remote areas of the countryside. The new land tenure led to the formation of new and different agricultural enterprises, such as agro-industrial companies and joint-stock agricultural companies, which expanded the mechanization of agriculture in many areas. A natural result of this was the release of more than five million rural workers from their bondage to the land. They migrated to urban areas, some not by choice, to sell their labor in the new markets.

Many of these released workers were to have been made landowners under the land reform program, but by execution of the law as finally written, half the landless village inhabitants were excluded in the first place. Among the remaining group who received land, many lost it due to the small amounts they received or because of an insufficient water supply. Consequently, only 10% of the peasants benefited from land distribution. So while the land reform project succeeded in eliminating various local authorities of the landlords and in creating a powerful central government, it did not improve either the peasants' living conditions or the country's agriculture.

The Shah's land reform replaced the traditional relations in rural areas with a "modern" mode of development. With the migration of about five million peasants to cities, the traditional culture was transferred to urban areas, where it strengthened the social position of religious institutions. In the past, landlords had influenced peasants politically, dictating to them with respect to how and for whom they should vote. After the implementation of the Shah's land reform and the migration of a great number of peasants to cities, the mosques influenced them. They found the mosque a place that gave them a sense of community and identity in the cities, where they felt alien. Peasants had economic conflict with the landlords before the land reform, and afterward they were faced directly with the government bureaucracies such as banks and the Ministry of Agriculture. Therefore, they found new allies in the religious community in the cities, and a new enemy—the government—in both the rural and urban areas. This change as the result of the land reform program, or the "white revolution," served the Islamic revolution and weakened the position of the Shah.

The second Iranian Revolution of the 20th century occurred in 1979, when the Shah was removed from the power. The new Islamic government confiscated thousands of privately owned properties, along with more than five hundred large, modern industrial, financial, agricultural, and commercial enterprises, most of which were owned by members of the Shah's regime. In 24 years of the Islamic Republic of Iran, conflict and tension have continued to exist between the supporters of the state economy and advocates of a free-market economy. The government still controls about 80% of the economy, and this empowers the state's domination over society that allows it to disregard the rights of citizens. This is the main obstacle to the economic and political development in Iran today. The state ownership of property not only allows the government to maintain a monopoly of power in society but also subordinates a great number of people by holding them dependent upon either its payroll or its financial aid and subsidies. This situation hinders democracy and the establishment of the organizations of civil society such as independent professional labor unions. And the question of property ownership has not yet been fully resolved, even after two revolutions in one century. The fear of confiscation of property by the rulers still persists. Although confiscation of property under a revolutionary government was expected, twenty-four years after the revolution investment is still not fully immune. Economic development is always heavily dependent upon a stable legal property system, which has yet to be achieved in Iran.

Government officials in the Middle East also continue to fear their own people, as a regime change might cause evaporation of their assets. Wealthy people in the Third World, including individuals in the Middle East, while their own countries are badly in need of loans and financial aid, deposit billions of dollars in Western financial institutions. The security of capital depends upon the dominant legal system and stability of the regime as the two most important factors in capitalist relations. While the removal of political leaders from office in the West has no significant effect on the economic stability of societies, political instability in Eastern societies can bring about great damage to nations' economic systems. Therefore, political change in the developing societies creates fear of economic instability and unpredictable economic loss. This factor alone holds back development in these countries.

When global capitalism became an unbeatable power in the world, both despotic authority and tribal relations began to disintegrate in the East. Because industrial capitalism has not fully developed in these societies, drastic changes such as revolution and consequent confiscation of land—as the Iranian case shows after the 1979 revolution—still is not over. This anxiety prevents full economic growth in these societies, in which the cost of capital is higher and its security lower than in the West. Therefore, in the age of globalization the flight of financial and intellectual capital to those societies with higher security and strong legal protection for private property becomes a norm. This further impedes development in the Middle East and keeps the balance in favor of the West. In a tough competition with Western production, the traditional sectors of society develop a hostile attitude toward modernity and its representative, the West.

Finally, if a less-developed status is undesirable, and if the Middle East is to find a way to alter this situation, then the only path to advancement is modernity with industrial capitalism is its core and replacement of traditional religious codes by secular law.

The United Nations Development Program (UNDP), in its 2003 report on the less-developed status of the Arab countries, wrote that the defective structures of the past and present—social, economic, and above all political—are responsible for the current situation in the Arab countries. Thus, the report proposes that these nations must remove or reform these structures in order to resolve the structural problems. The UNDP for Arab countries, the core part of the Middle East, suggests some fundamental and specific reforms, including freedom of expression, easy access to knowledge, and employment of women. These objectives, however, cannot be achieved unless the current governments in the region accept major political change. In this reform effort, peaceful and comprehensive support from the West is crucial. In Iran during the shah's regime, imposed economic reform, though defective, was achieved, but the monarch stubbornly resisted political reform. That resistance cost him his power and the West a close ally in a very strategic region of the world.

Glossary

abi	irrigated agriculture
amlak	*(pl. of melk)*, private landed estates; *amlak-i saltanati*, Crown landed estates
arbab	landlord, landowner; *arbab-ra'ayati*, landlord-peasant relations
a'ayan	trees and the fruit they hold, which grow in *a'ayan*
arseh	tangible property such as land which stands for *arseh* (trees and the fruit they hold)
ayish	fallow
band	simple hand-constructed dam
bigari	free labor services (corvee)
buneh	agricultural unit, peasant team work, a system of cumulative farming
dong	one sixth part of any piece of real estate
daymi	unirrigated agriculture, dry farming
dih	village; *dih-i intekhabi,* chosen village
gaavband	one who does not own agricultural land but possesses a yoke of oxen as one of the five agricultural elements (land, water, seed, oxen, and labor)
haq-i nasaq	cultivating right acquired in the soil by farming on specific agricultural land
Juft	yoke of oxen, plough land, or amount of land which could be ploughed by two oxen
kadkuda	village headman

khaleseh	state land and public domain
khurdeh-i maliki -	peasant's proprietorship
Khwushnishin -	inhabitant of a village who does not possess land, but who is involved in either agricultural work or village services
mazra'eh	hamlet, agricultural land without any dwelling houses, and cultivated by peasants from neighboring villages.
mubasher	bailiff
mujtahid	the highest-ranking ayatollahs who have right to issue opinions on matters of faith
mosha'a	jointly owned agricultural land
mutavalli	administrator of endowment
muzara'eh	a share-cropping contract between two parties, i.e., peasant and landlord, based on the agricultural elements (land, water, seed, plough animal, and labor)
qabz	*(pl. qubuz),* bill of exchange, official promissory paper
qanat	underground irrigation channel made artificially
roqabat	estates belonging to an endowment or to the state
rial	unit of currency roughly equal to 1/80 dollar
tuyul	assignment of state agricultural land or its revenue to someone who obliged himself to do a specific service for the government
tuyul-dar	*tuyul* holder
vaqf	*(pl. ougaf),* endowment (religious or charitable land; *vaqf-i khass*, private endowment
vaqf-i amm,	charitable endowment
zari'a	peasant who possesses one or more of the five agricultural elements

Bibliography

Abaadian, H. *Mabani-i Nazari-i Hokomat-i Mashruteh va Mashru 'e* (The Theoretical Base of   Constitutional and Shari'a Governments). Tehran: Ney, 1374.

Abrahamian, E. *Iran Between Two Revolutions.* Princeton, NJ: Princeton University Pres, 1982.

Adamiyat, F. *Endishe-hay-i Mirza Fatali Akhund Zadeh* (The Thoughts of Mirza Fatali Akhund Zadeh). Tehran: Kharazmi, 1349.

_____ *Fekr-i Azadi va Moqadimeh-i Nahzat-i Mashruteiyat-i Iran* (The Concept of Freedom and the Beginnings of the Constitutional Movement in Iran). Tehran: Sukhan, 1339 (1961).

_____ *Social Democracy Thought in the Constitutional Movement of Iran*, 1355 (1976).

_____ *Tarikh-i Fekre az Sumer ta Yonan va Rom* (The History of Thought from the Sumerians to the Greeks and Romans). Tehran: Roshangaran, 1374.

Afary, J. *The Iranian Constitutional Revolution, 1906–1911.* New York: Columbia University Press, 1996.

Akajdan et al. *The History of the Ancient World*, vol. 1, trans. Sadeq Ansari, Dr. Aliollah Hamedani, and Mohammad Baqer Momeni, 4th ed. Tehran: Andisheh, 1353.

Alamdari, K. "Globalization: Development in the Global Community, From the Perspective of Post-Developmentalism, *Farhang-e Towse'a*, nos. 37 and 38. Tehran.1377 (199).

_____ "Ta'adiel-e Eqtesadi and Masa'le-y Towse'a" ("Structural Adjustment Program and the Question of Development"), *Iran-e Farda*, no. 26, Tehran, 1374 (1996).

Algar, H. *Mirza Malkom Khan.* Berkeley: University of California Press, 1973.

Alvandi, M. "On the Distribution of the Harvest Based on the Five Factors of Production," in *The Question of Land and Peasants*, Tehran: Aagaah, Aagaah Book Collection, 1361.

Ambiorenson, R. "Asia in the Eyes and the Hearts of the Europeans: Analysis of European Theoreticians about Europe, From the Perspective of the History of Sciences and Ideas," trans. Seyyed Mohammad Fazl Hashemi, *Nameye Farhang: Research Quarterly on Cultural and Social Issues,* 6th year, no. 2, 22, Summer of 1375 (1997).

Amin, S. *Capitalism in the Age of Globalization: The Management of Contemporary Society.* London: Zed Books, 1997/1998.

Amir Arjomand, S. *The Political Dimensions of Religion.* New York: State University of New York Press, 1993.

_____ *The Shadow of God and the Hidden Imam: Religion, Political Order, and Social Change in Shiite Iran From the Beginning to 1890.* Chicago: University of Chicago Press, 1984.

Aqa Khan Kermani, M. *Letters From Exile,* contribution of Homa Nateq and Mohammad Firuz, Germany: Hafiz, 1365.

Aroonova M. R. and Ashrafian, K. Z. *The Government of Nader Shah, Afshar* tran. by Hamid Momeni. Tehran: Tehran University, 1352.

Aryanpour, A. H. *The Introduction to Sociology,* 7th ed. Tehran: Pocket Books, 1353.

Ashley, D. and Michael, D. Orenstein, *Sociological Theory: Classical Statements.* Boston: Allyn and Bacon, 1995.

Ashraf, A. "Historical Obstacles to the Development of Bourgeoisie in Iran." Journal of Iranian Studies II (2-3), USA: Spring-Summer 1969.

Ashraf, M. The Reconstruction of Religious Thought in Islam, (Lahore, 1965).

Ashtiani, A. "Jame'e Shenasi se doureh dar Tarikh-i Roshanfekri Iran-i Ma'aser" (The Sociology of Three Eras in the History of Intellectualism in Contemporary Iran)," *Kankash, No. 2, 3, Spring 1367 (1989).*

Atabai, B. *Barasi-i Tarikh-i Iran* (A Review of Iranian History), ed. Mahmood Goodarzi. Tehran: Donya-y Ketab, 1377 (1998).

Azad, S. "Workers' and Peasants' Councils in Iran." Monthly Review 32(5), October 1980, pp. 14-29.

Baran, A P. "A Morphology of Backwardness," in *Introduction to the "Developing Societies,"* eds. Hamza A. and Teodor S. New York: MR, 1982.

Barbee, L. et al. "Iranian Nationalism and the Great Powers: 1872-1954." *MERIP Report (Middle East Research and Information Project),* No. 37, 1975.

Barfield, T. "Turk, Persian, and Arab: Changing Relationships between Tribes and State in Iran and along Its Frontiers", in N. Keddie and R. Matthee eds. Iran and the Surrounding World. Seattle: University of Washington Press, 2002.

Bayat, M. *Iran's First Revolution, Shiism and the Constitutional Revolution of 1905-1909.* New York: Oxford University Press, 1991.

Bayes, J. & Tohidi, N., eds. *Globalization, Gender, and Religion: The Politics of Women's Rights in Catholic and Muslim Contexts.* New York: Palgrave, 2001.

Behnam, J. "Social Sciences, Intellectual Trends, and the Issue of Iran's Development Between 1337 and 1357, *Iran Nameh*, Year15, no. 2 (Spring 1376), 175-198.

Bella, R. *Religion and Progress in Modern Asia.* New York: Free Press, 1965.
_____ *Habits of Heart.* Berkeley: University of California Press, 1968.

Benab, Y. P. "Tabriz in Perspective: A Historical Analysis of the Current Struggle of Iranian Peoples." *RIPEH (The Review of Iranian Political Economy and History),* 11 (2), June 1978, pp. 1-42.

Bennett, G. H. "Land and Independence—America's Experience," *Land Reform,* edited by H. K. Parsons. The University of Wisconsin Press, 1956.

Berger, P. *The Sacred Canopy, Elements of a Sociological Theory of Religion.* New York: Doubleday and Company, Inc., 1967.

Bergmann, T. "Agrarian Reforms and Their Functions in the Development Process." *Land Reform, Land Settlement, and Cooperatives.* Food and Agriculture Organization of the United Nations (FAO-UN), N.U. No. 1, 1978.

Bernard, Lewis. "The Revolt of Islam: When the Conflict With the West Began, and How It Could End," *The New Yorker,* 5 January 2002.

Bernier, F. *Travels in the Mongul Empire A.D. 1656-1668.* Westminster, UK: Archibald Constable and Company, 1670.

Best, S. and Kellner D. *Postmodern Theory: Critical Interrogations.* New York: The Guilford Press, 1991.

Bill, A. J. *The Politics of Iran: Groups, Classes, and Modernization.* Columbus, OH: Charles E. Merrill Publishing Co., 1972.

Bloch, M. *Feudal Society.* Chicago: University of Chicago, 1961.

Borg, S. R. "New Patterns of Agrarian Reform in the Middle East and North Africa." *The Middle East Journal,* Spring 1977.

Bourdieu, P. *In Other Words: Essays Towards a Reflective Sociology.* Cambridge: Polity Press, 1990.

Brun, T., and Dumont, R. "Iran: Imperial Pretensions and Agricultural Dependence." *MERIP Report (Middle East Research and Information Project),* No. 71, 1978.

Cahoone, L. ed., *From Modernism to Postmodernism: An Anthology.* Cambridge, UK: Blackwell, 1996.

Cardoso, F. "Associated Dependent Development: Theoretical and Practical Implications," in *Authoritarian Brazil: Origins, Policies and Futures,* ed. Alfred Stepan. New Haven, CT: Yale University Press, 1973.

Chirot, D. *How Societies Change.* Thousand Oaks: Pine Forge Press, 1994.

Christensen, A. *Iran in the Sasanian Era,* 8th ed., trans. Rashid Yasemi. Tehran: Donya-ye Ketab, 1375/1997.

Christodoulou, D. "Agrarian Reform in Retrospect: Contributions to Its Dynamics and Related Fundamental Issues." *Land Reform, Land Settlement, and Cooperatives.* Food and Agriculture Organization of the United Nations (FAO-UN), No. 2, 1977.

Cook, F. J. "The Mystery of One Billion Dollars." *The Nation,* 12 April 1965.

Cumings, B. "The Origins and Development of the Northeast Asian Political Economy: Industrial Sectors, Products Cycles, and Political Consequences," *International Organization* 38, no. 1: 1–4, 0–14, 22–29, 33–35, and 38–40. Reprinted in Stephen Sanderson, *Sociological Worlds: Comparative and Historical Readings on Society.* Los Angeles: Roxbury Publishing Company, 1995. 155-166.

Dadjoo, K. et al. *The Scientific Socialism and the Class Struggle,* No. 1. Tehran: Sa'di, 1358/1980.

De Soto, H. *The Mystery of Capital: Why Capitalism Triumphs in the West and Fails Everywhere Else.* New York: Basic Books, 2000.

Dehqani, J. "Behavior: The Main Factor in Development," *The Social Sciences Magazine,* 2, no. 3 (Winter 1376): 40-51.

Demin, A. I. "Basic Forms of Tenure" *The Economic History of Iran, 1800-1914,* edited by C. Issawi. Chicago: University of Chicago Press, 1971, pp. 44–50.

Department of State (U.S.A.) *Land Reform--A World Challenge.* 1952.

Diamond, J. *Guns, Germs, and Steel: The Facts of Human Societies.* New York: W.W. Norton and Company, 1997/1999.

Djilas, M. *The New Class: An Analysis of the Communist System.* New York: Fredrich A. Praeger, 1957.

Donn, S. P. *The Fall and the Rise of the Asiatic Mode of Production.* Great Britain: Routledge and Kegan Paul Ltd., 1982.

Doostdar, A. *Derakhsheshha-ye Tiereh* (The Tarnished Glows), 2nd ed. Paris: *Khavaran,* 1377 (1999).

Dore, R. P. *Land Reform in Japan.* London: Oxford University Press, 1959.

Dorner, P. –Problems and Policies of Agricultural Development: The United States Experience.– In *Rural Development in a Changing World,* edited by R. Weitz. Cambridge, MA: MIT Press, 1971.

Dunn, P. S. *The Fall and Rise of the Asiatic Mode of Production.* UK: Routledge and Kegan Paul Ltd., 1982. (Persian trans. by Abbas Mokhber, Tehran: Markaz Publications, 1368).

Durant, W. *Caesar and Christ: The Story of Civilization, part III.* New York: Simon and Schuster, 1991.

_____ *Our Oriental Heritage* (part I of *The Story of Civilization*). New York: Simon and Schuster, Inc., 1935.

_____ *The Reformation: Part VI of the Story of Civilization.* New York: Simon and Schuster, Inc., 1957.

Duss, P. *Feudalism in Japan: Studies in World Civilizations,* 2nd ed. New York: Alfred Knopf, 1976.

Echo of Iran. *Iran Almanac. A Book of Facts,* published by the Echo of Iran. Years: 1963–1969, 1970, 1971, 1975, and 1976.

Engels, F. *Anti-Duhring: Herr Eugen Duhring's Revolution in Science.* New York: International Publishers, 1939.

_____ "The Force Theory," in *Guerrilla Warfare & Marxism,* William J. Pomeroy, ed. New York: International Publishers, 1968.

_____ *Socialism: Utopian and Scientific*, Introduction to English Edition, (1892), *Collected Works of Marx and Engels*. New York, International Publishers, 1968.

_____ *The Origin of the Family, Private Property and the State*. New York: International Publishers, 1975.

_____ *The Peasant War in Germany*. Moscow: Foreign Languages Publishing House, 1965.

Evans, P. *Dependent Development: The Alliance of Multinational, State, and Local Capitalism in Brazil*. Princeton, NJ: Princeton University Press, 1979.

Fazlollah, R. *The History of the Iranian Mongols (Historie des Mongols de la Perse)*, vol.1. Paris: M. Catermer, 1836.

Fereydoon Adamiyat. *The Thoughts of Mirza Aqa Khan Kermani*. Reprinted in Germany, 1992.

Feshahi, M. R. *Gozaresh-i Kotahi az Tahavolat-i Fekri va Ejtemai dar Jame'e Feodali-i Iran* (A Short Report on the Intellectual and Social Developments in Feudal Society of Iran). Tehran: Gutenberg, 1354 (1976).

Fischer, M. "Cultural Survival, Khuzistan." Unpublished research, second draft, August 1979.

Ghirshman, R. *Iran: From the Earliest Times to the Islamic Conquest*. New York: Penguin Books, 1954.

Giddens, A. "Post-Modernity or Radical Modernity? A Phenomenology of Modernity," in *Social Theory: The Multicultural and Classic Readings*, Charles Lemert, ed. Boulder, CO: Westview Press, 1993), 531–537.

_____ *The Consequences of Modernity*. Cambridge: Polity Press, 1990.

Goldthorpe, E. *The Sociology of Post-Colonial Societies: Economic Disparity, Cultural Diversity, and Development*. New York: Cambridge University Press, 1996.

Goruh-e Azadi-i Kar. *One Year Record of Islamic Republic of Iran, The Peasants' Problem*. No 1, 1358 (1979). In Persian.

Guerrero, A. *Philippine Society and Revolution*. Hong Kong: Ta Kung Pao, 1971.

Gunder Frank, A. *Sociology of Development and Underdevelopment of Sociology, or Underdevelopment or Revolution*. New York: MRP, 1969.

_____ *The Myth of Feudalism in Capitalism and Underdevelopment in Latin America*. New York: Monthly Review Press, 1967.

Hagen, E. *On the Theory of Social Change*. Homewood, IL: Dorsey Press, 1962.

Hajjarian, S. "The Development Planning and the Three-Dimensional Alliance Perspective," in *Ettela'at-e Siyasi and Eqtesadi*, (Political and Economic Journal): 10, nos. 103-104 (April-May 1996) (Tehran: Ordibehesht, 1974).

Hall, D. "Modern China and the Postmodern West" in *Culture and Modernity: East-West Philosophic Perspectives*, Eliot Deutsch, ed. Honolulu, HI: University of Hawaii, 1991.

Harris, M. *Cannibals and Kings: The Origins of Cultures.* New York: Random House, 1977.

Henslin, M. James. *Essentials of Sociology: A Down-to-Earth Approach,* 3rd ed. Boston: Allyn and Bacon, 2000.

Hewlett, R., and Markie, J. "Cooperative Farming as an Instrument of Rural Development: Examples from China, Vietnam, Tanzania, and India." *Land Reform, Land Settlement, and Cooperatives.* Food and Agriculture Organization of the United Nations (FAO-UN), No. 2, 1976.

Hitti, K. P. *The History of the Arabs,* 10th ed. New York: St. Martin's Press, 1970.

Holliday, F. "Iran: The Economic Contradictions." *MERIP Report (Middle East Research and Information Project),* No. 69, 1978, pp. 9-18.

_____ *Iran: Dictatorship and Development.* London: Penguin Books, 1979.

Homayoon, D. "Land Reform in Iran." *Tahqiqat-e Eqtesadi.* (Quarterly Journal of Economic Research.) Institute for Economic Research, University of Tehran, Nos. 3, 4, 1963.

Hoogland, E. J. "The Khwashnishin Population of Iran." *Iranian Studies, Journal of the Society for Iranian Studies* VI (4), Autumn 1973, pp. 229–245.

_____ "Rural Participation in the Revolution." *MERIP Report (Middle East Research and Information Protect),* No. 87, 1980.

_____ *The Effects of the Land Reform Program on Rural Iran, 1962–72.* Ph.D. dissertation, The Johns Hopkins University, 1975.

Hooglund, M. "One Village in Revolution." *MERIP Report (Middle East Research and Information Project),* No. 87, May 1980, pp. 7–14.

Hoselitz, B. F. *The Progress of Underdeveloped Areas.* Chicago: University of Chicago Press, 1952.

Hovar, C. *Iran and the Iranian Civilization,* trans. Hasan Anoosheh. Tehran: Amir Kabier, 1375 (1996).

Huntington, P. S. *The Clash of Civilizations and the Remaking of World Order.* New York: A Touchstone Book, 1977.

_____ "The Change to Change: Modernization, Development, and Politics," in Cyril E. Black, *Comparative Modernization.* New York: Free Press, 1976.

Ibn Khaldun, Abdulrahman. *The Muqaddimah: An Introduction to History,* trans. Franz Rosenthal, edited and abridged N. J. Dawood. Princeton, NJ: Princeton University Press, 1970.

Inkeles A. and Smith, D.H. *Becoming Modern.* Cambridge, MA: Harvard University Press, 1976.

_____ "A Model of the Modern, Theoretical and Methodological Issues," in *Comparative Modernization,* Cyril E. Black, ed. New York: Free Press, 1974, 320-348.

Institute for Economic Research (Tahqiqat-e Eqtesadi). The Quarterly Journal of Economic Research. Institute for Economic Research, Faculty of Economics, University of Tehran. No. 9–10, Aban 1943 (September 1965) and No. 11–12, Shahrivar 1344 (August/September 1966). No. 7, 8, April–September 1968; No. 15, 16, February 1968; No. 17, 18, April–September 1969. Tehran: University of Tehran.

Iran and Utah State University. *Half a Century of Friendship and A Decade of Contracts: Point 4.* Logan, UT: Utah State University, 1963.

Islami Naddooshan, M. A. "Parsi: The Basin of the First Empire in the World," quoted from Ettela'at Daily, *Azar,* 1375, copied from the Iranians' News Peyk, no. 75, 7th Year, April 1999 (Farvardin Mubed Shahrzady, R. *The Zoroastrian Worldview.* Tehran: The Organization of Foruhar Publications, 1367 (1989).

Islamic Republic, daily newspaper. Mehr 19, 1358 (1980).

Issawi, Ch. (ed.), *The Economic History of Iran, (1800–1914.)* Chicago: University of Chicago Press, 1971.

Ivanov, M. *The Constitutional Revolution of Iran,* Tehran, 1975.

Jacobs, N. "The Condition of Patrimonial Theory in Explaining the Roots of and Guiding Asian Development in the Twenty-First Century: A Theoretical Introduction," *Asian Perspective,* vol. 13, 2, Fall-Winter 1989.

_____ *Modernization Without Development: Thailand As An Asian Case Study.* New York: Praeger Publications, 1971.

_____*The Korean Road to Modernization and Development.* Chicago: University of Illinois Press, 1986.

_____ *The Sociology of Development: Iran as an Asian Case Study,* Praeger Special Studies in International Economics and Development. New York: Fredrick A. Praeger, 1966.

Jaami. *Gozashteh Cheragh-i Rah-i Ayandeh* (The Past as a Guiding Light For the Future). Published by the Liberation Front of Iranian People, Tehran: Farvardin, 1355 (1977).

Javanshire, F. M. *Eqtesad-i Siyasi: Shiveh Tulid-i Sarmayehdari* (Political Economy: Capitalist Mode of Production). Published by The Tudeh Party, n.d.

Jazani, B. *The History of the Past,* and the selected articles of in "19th of Bahman Teoric". Tehran, 1353.

_____ *Capitalism and Revolution in Iran.* (London: Zed Press, 1980).

_____ *Tarikh-i See Saleh-i Iran* (Three Decades History of Iran) Published by: The 19th Bahman Teoric, 1353 (1974).

Jones, R. *An Essay on the Distribution of Wealth and the Sources of Taxation.* New York: A.M. Kelley, 1964.

Kaminski, ed. *The History of the Middle Ages,* trans. Sadeq Ansari and Mohammad Baqer Momeni, vol. 4, 4th ed. Tehran: Andisheh, 1353.

Kasravi, A. "A Nationalist Defending a Unified Iran," trans. Asghar Azari, *Kankash,* nos. 2 and 3, 1367, pp. 177–217.

_____ *Some Articles, Shiism, Sufism and Bahaism. Germany, 1374 (1996),* San Jose, CA: Tooka, 1992.

_____ *The Constitutional Revolution of Iran.* Tehran: Amir Kabier, 1973.

_____ *Thoughts,* Collected by Alizadeh. Tehran: Toos, 1378.

Katouzian, M. A. "Land Reform in Iran, A Case Study in the Political Economy of Social Engineering." *The Journal of Peasant Studies* 1(2), 1974.

_____ *The Political Economy of Iran from the Constitutional Revolution to the End of the Pahlavi Dynasty*, trans. Mohammad Reza Nafisi and Kambiz Azizi. Tehran: Nashre Markaz, 1372 (1994).

Kayhan, M. "Iranian Rural Community On the Eve of the Land Reform." *Donya,* Political and Theoretical Organ of the Central Committee of the Tudeh Party of Iran, No. 12, March 1977, pp. 42–52.

Keddie, N. "The Iranian Village Before and After Land Reform." *Journal of Contemporary History*, 1968, 3(3), pp. 69–91.

_____ "Material Culture, Technology, and Geography: Toward a Holistic Comparative Study of Middle East," in *Comparative Muslim Societies and State in a World Civilization*, Juan Cole, ed. Ann Arbor, MI: University of Michigan Press, 1992. 31–62.

_____ *Historical Obstacles to Agrarian Change in Iran.* Berkeley: University of California Press, 1960.

_____ *Religion and Rebellion in Iran: The Tobacco Protest of 1891-1892.* London: Frank Cass, 1966.

_____ *The Roots of Revolution: Religion and Politics in Iran.* New Haven, CT: Yale University Press, 1981.

Khamsi, F. "Land Reform in Iran." *Monthly Review* 24(2), 1969.

Khatami, S. M. *Fear of the Wave: Selected Articles.* Tehran: Ministry of Culture and Islamic Guidance, 1372 (1994).

Khonji M. A. About the Asian mode of production in the *Monthly of Political and Economic Information*, 9th and 10th years, 1374–1375 (1996–1997).

_____ *An Essay on the Analysis of the History of the Medes and the Origin of D'iakonov's Theory.* Tehran: Tahoori Library, 1358 (1980).

Khosravi, K. *The Peasant Society in Iran.* Tehran: Payam, 1357 (1979).

_____ "Irrigation and Rural Community in Iran." *Journal of the Social Sciences* 3(1), February 1970, pp. 48-57.

_____ *The Land Cultivating Systems in Iran (From the Sasanian Era to the Seljuk Period).* Tehran: Payam, 1352 (1973).

_____ *The Peasant Society in Iran.* Tehran: Payam, 1357 (1979).

Khosravi, K. *The Rural Society in Iran*, 2nd ed. Tehran: Tehran University Press, 2535 (1977).

_____ *Jame'ah Shinasi-i rustaei-i Iran* (Rural Sociology of Iran). University of Tehran Press, 1978. In Persian

Kunert, H. "Criteria for the Evaluation of Agrarian Reform and Rural Development Programs." *Land Reform, Land Settlement, and Cooperatives.* Food and Agriculture Organization of the United Nations (FAO-UN), No. 1, 1976, pp. 89–95.

Lahiji Shahla and Kar, Mehrangiz. *Discovering Iranian Women's Identity in the Prehistoric Era and the Historical Era.* Tehran: Roshangaran, 1371 (1992).

Lambton, A.K.S. *Islamic Society in Persia.* London: University of London, 1954.

_____ *Landlord and Peasant in Persia: A Study of Land Tenure and Land Revenue Administration* Oxford, UK: Oxford University Press, 1953.

_____ *Qajar Persia: Eleven Studies.* Austin, TX: University of Texas Press, 1987.

_____ The Persian Land Reform, 1962–66. Oxford: Clarendon Press, 1969.

Landtman, G. *The Origin of the Inequality of Social Classes.* New York: Greenwood Press, 1968.

Langford, J. and Galileo, O. P. *Science and the Church.* New York: Desclee Company, 1966.

Lannoy, R. *The Speaking Tree: A Study of Indian Culture and Society.* Oxford, UK: Oxford University Press, 1975.

Lenin, V.I. *Collected Works*, vol. 20, 21. Moscow: Progress Publishers, 1971.

_____ *Imperialism as the Latest Phase of Capitalism.* Peking: Foreign Languages, 1371.

Levy, J. M. *Modernization, and the Structure of Societies.* Princeton, NJ: Princeton University Press, 1966.

Macionis, J. *Society: The Basis,* 3rd ed. New York: Prentice Hall, 1991.

Magdoff, H. *Imperialism: From the Colonial Age to the Present.* New York: Monthly Review Press, 1978.

Mandel, E. *The Formation of the Economic Thought of Karl Marx.* New York: Monthly Review Press, 1971.

_____ "The Future Results of British Rule in India," in *The Marx-Engels Reader*, ed. Robert Tucker. New York: Norton and Company, 1972.

_____*Correspondence Between Marx and Engels on Historical Materialism, the Organization of Communist Unity*, 1358 (1980).

_____ *The Capital*, vol. 1, chapters, 5, 10, 14, and 16. New York: International Publishers, 1967.

_____ *The Capital*, vol. 3. New York: International Publishers, 1894. pp. 325–331.

_____ *The Grundrisse*, ed. and trans. David Mclellan. New York: Harper Torchbooks, 1971.

Marx, K. and Engels, F. *On Colonialism: Article from the New York Tribune and other Writings.* New York: International Publishers, 1972.

_____ *The German Ideology*, ed. C.J. Arthur. London: Lawrence and Wishart, 1974.

_____ *The Communist Manifesto.* London: Elec Book, 1998.

_____ *Selected Correspondence.* Moscow: Foreign Languages Publishing House, 1953.

_____ Karl Marx and Friedrich. *On Colonialism.* New York: International Publishers, 1972.

Maslow, A. "Psychological Data and Value Theory," in *New Knowledge in Human Values*, Abraham Maslow, ed. New York: Harper & Row, 1959.

Mazdak. (Ed.). *Karnameh-i Mosaddeq va Hezb-i Tudeh* (The Record of Mosaddeq and the Tudeh Party). An Analysis of the Policies of Dr. M. Mosaddeq and the Tudeh Party. Published by Mazdak, 1352 (1973).

McClelland, C. D. *The Achieving Society.* New York: Free Press, 1961.

Medina, J. 0., Jr. "The Philippine Experience with Land Reform Since 1972: An Overview." *Land Reform, Land Settlement, and Cooperatives.* Food and Agriculture Organization of the United States FAO-UN), No. 1, 1976, pp. 1–17.

Mengisteab, K. and Logan, I. eds. *Beyond Economic Liberalization in Africa: Structural Adjustment and Alternatives.* London: Zed Books, 1995.

Michael, T. M. and Kandal, T. eds., *Studies of Development and Change in the Modern World.* New York: Oxford University Press, 1989.

Michels, R. *Political Parties.* New York: Dover Publications, 1959.

Milani, A. *Tajadod va Tajadod Setizi dar Iran (Modernity and Opposition to Modernity in Iran).* Tehran: Atiyah, 1378 (1999).

Mill, J. *History of British India.* Chicago: University of Chicago, 1975.

Mir Fetrus, A. *Some Considerations in the History of Iran, Islam and the True Islam,* (Canada/France). Tehran: Farhang, 1988.

_____ *Hallaj,* 5th edtion. Tehran, 1357 (1979).

Mirhaydar, H. Az Tuyul ta Enqelab-e Arzi, *Tuyul System to Agrarian Revolution.* Tehran: Amir Kabier, 2535 (1975).

Mirzaie, Q. *Farda Asir-i Dirooz* (Tomorrow a Captive of Yesterday): *The History of Iran and the Analysis of the Elements that Construct the Cultural and Governmental Structure.* Los Angeles: Mazda Publishers, 1976.

Mokyr, J. *The Lever of Riches: Technological Creativity and Economic Progress.* Cambridge, UK: Oxford University Press, 1990.

Momeni, B. "Iran on the Eve of the Constitutional Revolution," trans. Azad, S. *RIPEH (The Review of Iran Political Economy of History)* 1(2), June 1977. 80-92

Moore, B. Jr., *Social Origins of Dictatorship and Democracy: Lord and Peasant in the Making of the Modern World.* Boston: Beacon Press, 1966.

Mowqan, Y. "The History of Oriental Despotism," *Negah-e-nou,* No. 23, Azar-Bahman, 1973.

Mubarezien-i Rah-i Aarman-i Tabaqeh-i Kargar. *An Analysis of the Situation of the Rural Community in Iran.* Tehran, 1978.

Muhammadi, M. *On the Agrarian Policy of Iranian Government and For a Democratic Solution of Agrarian Problems.* Tudeh Publishing Center, 1973.

Munoz, G. M. *Islam, Modernization, and the West.* New York: I.B. Tauris Publishers, 1999.

Myrdal, G. *Asian Drama: An Inquiry into Poverty of Nations,* 3 vols. New York: Twentieth Century Fund/Random House, Penguin, 1968.

Navid, S. "In Search of Cultural Renaissance," *Nazm-e Novin,* no. 8, 1987, pp. 133–177.

Nehchiri, A. "Ahmad Kasravi: Aasy, ya Mosleh?" (Kasravi: A Rebel or A Reformer?) *Negah-e Nou,* no. 26, Aabaan 1374 (1976), pp. 52–79.

Niek-Aein, A. "A Study About Some of the Causes of the Rural Migration." *Donya,* Political and Theoretical Organ of the Central Committee of Tudeh Party of Iran, 11, February 1978, pp. 36–45.

Nirumand, B. *The New Imperialism in Action* (New York: Monthly Review Press, 1949).

Nomani, F. "Origin and Development of Feudalism in Iran: 300–1600 A.D." Dissertation, University of Illinois, 1972.

Nowshirvani, V. F., and Bildner, R. "Direct Foreign Investment in the Non-oil sectors of Iranian Economy." *Journal of Iranian Studies,* VI, Spring-Summer 1973. 66-110.

O.I.P.F.G (Organization of Iranian People Fedaii Guerrilla) *Research of the Economic Structure of Rural Fars,* Rural Area Research Series No. 3. Published by Confederation of Iranian Students-National Union (CISUN), 1974.

_____ *A Study About the Aryamehr Joint-Stock Agricultural Company.* Re-Published by Confederation of Iranian Students–National Union (CISUN), 1974.

_____ "On the Remains of Feudalism in Iran: Politics and Revolution." A Theoretical Journal, No. 1, pp. 19–47. Published by Eugene Iran Committee, August 1977.

_____ *Land Reform and its Direct Effects in Iran.* London: The Iran Committee, 1976.

_____ *Nabard-i Khan (People's Struggle),* New Period, No. 1, 1980.

_____ *Research of the Economic Structure of Rural Kerman,* Rural Area Research Series No. 4, 1975.

_____ *Study of Joint-Stock Agricultural Companies.* Published by the Organization of Iranian National Front Abroad, Middle East Section, 1953 (1974).

O.M.P.I. (Organization of Mojahedeen of People of Iran). *Rousta va Enqelab-e Sefeed (Villages and the White Revolution),* Tehran, 1974.

Pahlavi, M. R. Shah. Answer to History. New York: Stein and Day, 1980.

_____ *Mission for My Country.* New York: McGraw-Hill, 1960.

_____ The White Revolution. 2nd ed. Tehran: Kayhan Press, 1967.

_____ *Toward the Great Civilization.* Published by Offset Company, 1978. In Persian.

Parham, B. "Ibn Khaldun and the Power Theory," *Thinking Together and Uniformly, Selected Articles.* Tehran: Aagaah, 1378. 217-231.

Parham, S. *The Question of Land and Peasants, Aagaah Book: A Collection of Articles.* Tehran: Aagaah, 1361 (1983).

Parsa, B. "Arzyabi-i Eslahat-i Arzi va Nazariyat-i Ejtemaii-i Gunagun." *Andisheh,* No. 1, Farvardeen 1958 (1980).

Parson, H. K. (Ed.). *Land Tenure. Proceedings of the International Conference on Land Tenure and Related Problems in World Agriculture,* (Madison: The University of Wisconsin Press, 1956).

Paymaan, H. "On the Iranian Despotism," in Javad Mousavi Khorasani, *Book of Towse'a,* no. 10, 1974.

Pigolo N.V. and Sekaya et al., *The History of Iran from the Ancient Era to the End of the Eighteenth Century,* 5th ed., trans. Karim Keshavarz. Tehran: Payam, 1363.

Piran, P. "Se Sat-h-e Tahlil-e Vaqa'yi" (The Three Levels of Analyzing an Event)," in Abdolali Rezaie / Abbas Abdi, *New Choice: Sociological*

Analysis of the Events of the Khordad the Second. Tehran: Tarh-e-no, 1377.

Plan and Budget Organization. Fourth National Development Plan (1968–1972). Tehran: The Imperial Government of Iran, 1968.

Plekhanov, G. *Fundamental Problems of Marxism.* New York: New World, 1975.

_____ *The Evolution of the Monistic Theory of History,* trans. Jalal Alavinia and Saa'dollah Alizadeh, no publisher, no publication date.

_____ *Fundamental Problems of Marxism: The Materialism in Conception of History, The Role of Individual in History.* New York: International Publishers, 1975.

Pooriya, P. "Obstacles to the Development in Iran: Historical Factors (4)," *Politico-Economic Information,* May–June, 1371.

Raffia, B. *Perspectives, An Interview With Ali Mir Fetrus,* 2nd ed. Germany: Nashr-e Nima, 1997.

Razi, G. H. "Genesis of Party in Iran: A Case Study of the Interaction Between the Political System and Political Parties." *Iranian Studies, Journal of the Society for Iranian Studies* 111(2), Spring 1970.

Reza Qoli, A. *Jamea' Shenasi-e Noukhbeh Koshi (The Sociology of Elite Killing): Qaem Maqam, Amir Kabier, and Mossadeq,* 8th ed. Tehran: Nay, 1377 (1999).

Richards, H. "America's Shah Shahanshah's Iran." *MERIP Reports (Middle East Research and Information Project)* No. 40, December 1975.

_____ "Land Reform and Agribusiness in Iran." *MERIP Reports (Middle East. Research and Information Project)* No. 43, December 1975.

Robertson, R. *Globalization: Social Theory and Global Cultures.* London: Roland Sage Publications, 1996.

Rodes, I. R. (ed.), *Imperialism, and Underdevelopment: A Reader.* New York: Monthly Review Press, 1970.

Rostow, W. W. The *Stages of Economic Growth: A Non-Communist Manifesto.* London: Cambridge University Press, 1960.

_____ *The Process of Economic Growth.* 1st ed. New York: Norton, 1952.

Russell, B. *A History of Western Philosophy.* New York: Simon and Schuster, 1945/1972.

Sadeeq, J. *Meliyat and Enqelab dar Iran* (Nationality and Revolution in Iran). No publisher indicated, 1973.

Saeedi Sirjani A. A. *Vaqa-yi Ittefaqiyeh (Current Affairs),* ed. Tehran: 1361 (1983).

Safa, Z. *The History of Rational Sciences in Iran until Early Mid-Fifth Century,* vol. 1, 4th ed. Tehran: Amir Kabier Press, 2536 (Monarchy Calendar).

_____ *The History of Rational Sciences in the Islamic Civilization* (Tehran: Amir Kabier, 2536) (Monarchy Calendar).

Safari, H. *The Present Situation of Iranian Economy.* No publisher indicated, 1977.

Safi-Nejad, J. *Boneh: Nezaam ha-y Twolid Zeraei Jamei Qabl va Ba'ad az Aslahaat Arzi, (The Systems of Cumulative Farming Before and After the Land Reform),* 3rd ed. Tehran: Tous, 2535 (Monarchy Calendar) (1975).

Schirazi, A. *Islamic Development Policy: The Agrarian Question in Iran*, trans. P.J. Ziess-Lawrence. Boulder, CO and London: Lynne Rienner Publishers, 1993.

Schumpeter, J. A. *Imperialism and Social Classes*. New York: Kelly, 1951.

_____ (ed.), *Beyond the Impasse: New Directions in Development Theory*. London: Zed Books, 1993.

Selsam, H. et al., eds., *Dynamics of Social Change: A Reader in Marxist Social Science*. New York: International Publishers, 1975.

Seyf, A. Despotism, the Question of Property, and Capital Accumulation in Iran. Tehran: Resaanesh, 1380 (2001).

Shanin, T. "Defining Peasants: Conceptualization and De-conceptualization Old and New in a Marxist Debate," *Peasant Studies*, 8, no. 4, 1979.

Sidney, H. *The Hero in History*. Boston: Beacon Press, 1955.

Smith, A. *An Inquiry into the Nature and the Cause of the Wealth of Nations*, abridged, with commentary and notes by Laurence Dickey. Oxford: Cambridge, 1993.

Smith, D. A. *The Concept of Social Change: A Critique of the Functionalist Theory of Social Change*. Boston: Routledge and Kegan Paul, 1973.

Sohrab. *Okhtapous-i Sad Pa*. No publisher indicated, 1978.

Soudagar, M. R. A *Study of the Iranian Land Reform (1961–66). Tehran:* the Institute for Social and Economic Research, 1979.

Spuler, B. *The History of Iran During the First Centuries of Islam*, vol. 2, trans. Maryam Mir Ahmadi. Tehran: The Scientific and Cultural Publications, Inc., 1369 (1991).

_____ *The History of Iran in the First Centuries of Islam*, vol. 1, trans. Javad Falatoori. Tehran: The Scientific and Cultural Publications, Inc., 1349 (1971).

Stalin, J. "Dialectic Materialism and the Historical Materialism," in *Three Essays by Stalin*, The Marxist-Leninist Organization of Tufan, no. 8, Azar 1348.

Statistical Yearbook of Iran. Tehran, June 1976.

Stavenhagen, R. *Social Classes in Agrarian Societies*, trans. Judy Adler Hellman. New York: Anchor Books, 1975.

Stephenson, C. *Mediaeval Feudalism*. New York: Great Seal Books, 1942.

Sztompka, P. *The Sociology of Social Change*. Oxford, UK: Blackwell, 1994.

Tabari, E. *Some Analyses on Worldviews and Social Movements in Iran*, from the publications of the Tudeh Party of Iran, 1358 (1980).

_____ *The Disintegration of the Traditional System and the Birth of Capitalism in Iran*, from the publications of the Tudeh Party of Iran, 1354 (1976).

_____ *The Iranian Society During the Absolute Reign of Reza Shah._Tudeh Publishing Center, 1977.

Tabatabaei, S. J. *The Concept of Jurisprudence in the Political Thought of the Middle Ages*. Tehran: Pegah, 1980 (2002).

_____ *The Decline of Political Thinking in Iran*. Tehran: Kavir, 1373 (1995).

Talibov Tabrizi, A. *Ketab Ahmad: Constitutional Literature*. Tehran: Shabgir, 2536 (1977).

The Ministry of Agriculture. *Land Reform in Iran*. Tehran: Ministry of Agriculture, 1963.

The Statistical Center of Iran. The 1970 Results of Data Collected on Household Expenditures in Rural Areas, 1349. Tehran, 1970–71. In Persian.

The Turkman People's Political-Cultural Center, Headquarters of Turkman Peasants' Council. Life and *Struggle of the People of Turkman*. Bahman 1358 (March 1980). In Persian.

Tilly, Ch. "Flows of Capital and Forms of Industry in Europe, 1500–1900," *Theory and Society* 12 (1983): 102–113.

Tiva, M. "The Confrontations of the East and the West and the Views of Iranian Intellectuals," *Kankash*, nos. 2 and 3 (1367), 11–47.

Toynbee, A. *A Study of History*, D.C. Somerville, ed. (New York: Oxford University Press, 1974).

Tully, A. *The Inside Story About Our Government's Most Secret Organization*—The Central Intelligence Agency. New York: A Crest Book, 1962.

Turner, B. "Citizenship Studies: A General Theory," *Journal of Citizenship Studies*, vol. 1, 1, Feb. 1997.

Turner, J., Beeghly, L. and Power, C. *The Emergence of Sociological Theory*. 4th edition, New York: Wadsworth, 1998.

_____ *Religion and Social Theory*, 2nd ed. London: Sage Publications, 1997.

Ulyanovsky, R. A. (ed.), *The Comintern and the East*. Moscow: Progress Publishers, 1979.

Union of Democratic Filipinos. *People's War in the Philippines*. Published by the Katipunan ng mgo Demokratikong Pilipino (KDP), 1975.

United Nations. *Progress in Land Reform*. Third Report, 1962; Fourth Report, 1966; Fifth Report, 1970; Sixth Report, 1976. New York: Department of Economic and Social Affairs.

Vali, A. Pre-Capitalist Iran: A Theoretical History, London: I.B. Tauris, 1993.

Vardaasbi, A. *Iran Dar Pouyeh Tariekh (Iran in the Dynamics of History)*. Tehran: Qalam, 1357 (1979).

Wallerstein, I. "The Rise and Future Demise of the World Capitalist System: Concepts for Comparative Analysis, Comparative Studies," *Society and History* 16: 387–394 and 397–415.

_____ *Culture as the Ideological Battleground of the Modern World-System, in Global Culture: Nationalism, Globalization, and Modernity*, ed. Mike Featherstone. London: Sage, 1990. 31–55.

_____ *The Capitalist World Economy*. Oxford, UK: Cambridge University Press, 1979.

_____ *The Modern World System: Capitalism, Agriculture, and the Origins of the European World-Economy in the Sixteenth Century*. New York: Academic Press, 1994.

Warriner, D. *Land Reform in Principle and Practice*. Oxford: Clarendon Press, 1969.

Weber M. *The Theory of Social and Economic Organization*, New York: Free Press, 1947.

_____ *General Economic History*, trans. Frank H. Knight, New York: Collier Books, 1961.

_____ *Protestant Ethic and the Spirit of Capitalism*, Los Angels: Roxbury Publishing Company, 1995.

_____ *The Agrarian Sociology of Ancient Civilization*, trans. R. I. Frank, London: NLB, 1976, orig. 1909.

_____ *The Religion of India*, trans. and ed. Hans H. Gertis and Don Martindale Glencoe, IL: The Free Press, 1958.

_____ *The Sociology of Religion*, trans. Ephraim Fischoff, Boston: Bacon Press, 1964.

Weinbaum, G. M. "Agricultural Policy and Development Politics in Iran." The Middle East Journal 31(4), Fall 1977.

Wiarda, H. Political Development in Emerging Nations: Is There Still a Third World? USA: Wadsworth, 2003.

Wittfogel, K. A. *Oriental Despotism: A Comparative Study of Power*, New Haven, CT: Yale University Press, 1957.

Wolf, R. E. "Europe and the People Without History," Regents of the University of California (1983): 267-278 and 290-302.

_____ "The Emergence and Expansion of Industrial Capitalism," in op. cit., ed. Stephen K. Sanderson.

Yearly Statistics of Iran. Years 1966–1976. Published by Plan and Budget Organization, Statistical Center of Iran.

Yosefi Eshkevari, H. ed. *Religious Modernism: A Talk Between Hasan Yosefi Eshkevari and Bazergan*, Tehran: Qasideh, 1377 h.

Zabih, S. The Communist Movement in Iran, Berkeley, and Los Angeles: University of California Press, 1966.

Zarrinkub, A. H. *History of Persia in the Islamic Period (Early Islamic Centuries)*, Tehran: Kharazmi, 1990.

_____ *The History of the Iranian People (2) From the End of the Sasanian Era to the End of the Buyid Era*, Tehran: Amir Kabier, 1368 (1990).

_____ *The History of Iran After Islam*, Tehran: Amir Kabier, 1368 (1990).

_____ *Two Centuries of Silence: The Description of Events and Historical Situations of Iran During the First Two Centuries of Islam From the Arab Attack to the Emergence of Taherid's State*, Tehran: No publisher, 1330 (1952).

Zeitlin, M. I. *Ideology and the Development of Sociological Theory*, 6th ed., New Jersey: Prentice Hall, 1977.

Ziba Kalam, S. *How We Became We: Finding the Roots of Underdevelopment in Iran*, 4th ed., Tehran: Rozaneh, 1377.

Zonis, M. The Political Elite of Iran, Princeton: Princeton University Press, 1971.

No author indicated, *Religion and Rebellion in Iran: The Iranian Tobacco Protest of 1891–1892*. London: Frank Cass and Co., Ltd., 1966.

No author. *Mas'aleh-i dihqani va Mas'aleh-i Arzi dar Iran* (Peasants' Questions and Land Questions in Iran). No publisher indicated, 1980.

No author. *The Historical Roots and the Development of the Tobacco Movement* (collection of historical research in the recent era), no. 1, Tehran: no date.

Papers

Enqelab Islami, daily newspaper. No. 128, 1358; No. 278, Khurdad 24, 1359 June 1980); No. 440, Day 13, 1359 (January 1981); Day 23, 1359 (February 1981); Bahman 14, 1359 (February 1981); Bahman 15, 1359 (February 1981); Bahman 16, 1359 (February 1981); Bahman 18, 1359 (February 1981); Esfand 25, 1359 (March 1981).

Etela'at, daily newspaper. Aban 23, 1343 (October 1964); Ordibehesht 9, 1346 (April 1967); Azar 4, 1358 (November 1979); Azar 10, 1358 (November 1979); Esfand 9, 1358 (March 1980); No. 16098, p. 3.

Kar (weekly), No. 1, Esfand 1359 (8 March 1979). Special Issue About Turkman-Sahra 3(4), Bahman 29, 1359 (February 1980); No. 36, 26 November 1979; No. 65, Teer 10, 1359 (July 1980); No. 94, Bahman 2, 1359 (January 1981); No. 98, Bahman 30, 1359 (March 1981); No. 99, Esfand 7, 1359 (March 1981).

Kayhan, daily newspaper. Ordibehesht 1, 1349 (May 1970); Esfand 13, 1358 (March 1980); Esfand 20, 1358 (March 1980).

Le Monde (Paris). 4, 5 March 1972; May 1978.

Le Monde Diplomatic (Paris). May 1975.

Newsweek. No. 16, June 1975.

Reference Bureau. *The 1979 World Population Data Sheet of Population.* Washington, D.C.: Reference Bureau, Inc., 1979.

The Herald Tribune, 4 March 1978.

The New York Times. 24 April, 1948; 3 August, 1961; 23, 25, 30 May, 1961; 4 March, 1976.

Index